W9-AFT-410

NEW
TESTAMENT
GREEK

FOR BEGINNERS

J. Gresham Machen was professor of New Testament at Westminster Theological Seminary and the author of several books, including *The Origin of Paul's Religion*. **Dan G. McCartney** is professor of New Testament at Westminster and the coauthor of *Let the Reader Understand*.

NEW TESTAMENT GREEK

FOR BEGINNERS

Second Edition

J. Gresham Machen
Professor of New Testament,
Westminster Theological Seminary

Revised by Dan G. McCartney
Professor of New Testament,
Westminster Theological Seminary

Frequency List by Bruce M. Metzger
Foreword by Moisés Silva

Upper Saddle River, New Jersey 07458

Library of Congress Cataloging-in-Publication Data

Machen, J. Gresham (John Gresham), 1881–1937.
   New Testament Greek for beginners / J. Gresham
Machen ; revised by Dan G. McCartney ; frequency list by
Bruce M. Metzger ; foreword by Moisés Silva. — 2nd ed.
      p.   cm.
   Includes index.
   ISBN 0-13-184234-X
   1. Greek language, Biblical—Grammar Problems,
exercises, etc. 2. Bible. N.T.—Language, style Problems,
exercises, etc. I. McCartney, Dan. II. Title.
PA817.M3   2004
487'.4—dc21   99-21889

Editorial Director: Charlyce Jones-Owen
Senior Acquisitions Editor: Ross Miller
Assistant Editor: Wendy Yurash
Editorial Assistant: Carla Worner
Senior Media Editor: Deborah O'Connell
Director of Marketing: Beth Mejia
Marketing Assistant: Kimberly Daum
Production Editor: Kathy Sleys
Manufacturing Buyer: Christina Helder
Cover Designer: Bruce Kenselaar
Cover Printer: Lehigh Press, Inc.
Binder: RR Donnelley & Sons

The LaserGreek font used to print this work is available from Linguist's Software, Inc.,
PO Box 580, Edmonds, WA 98020-0580 USA tel (425) 775-1130 www.linguistsoftware.com

Credits and acknowledgments borrowed from other sources and reproduced, with
permission, in this textbook appear on appropriate page within text.

Pearson Education LTD.
Pearson Education Australia PTY, Limited
Pearson Education Singapore, Pte. Ltd
Pearson Education North Asia Ltd

Pearson Education, Canada, Ltd
Pearson Educación de Mexico, S.A. de C.V.
Pearson Education–Japan
Pearson Education Malaysia, Pte. Ltd

PEARSON
Prentice
Hall

10 9 8 7 6 5 4 3 2 1
ISBN 0-13-184234-X

Contents

Contents

Lesson

7

Contents

Lesson

Foreword

About one hundred years ago, J. Gresham Machen attended Johns Hopkins University, where he received a thorough education in the classics. His mentor, Basil Gildersleeve, was arguably the greatest American classical scholar of the nineteenth century. Gildersleeve used to entertain himself at church—on those occasions when the preacher was less than scintillating—by mentally translating the sermon into Greek as it was being preached.

Machen himself developed a love for the Greek language that was evident throughout his life. Even after he had pursued a theological degree at Princeton Theological Seminary, the possibility of a career in classical scholarship allured him for several years. One clear sign of his devotion to the field was his personal library, which can still be partially reconstructed by browsing the stacks of the Montgomery Library at Westminster Theological Seminary. I have often had opportunity to search there for important works of Greek scholarship published in the late nineteenth or early twentieth century, and more often than not I have found the book in question, beautifully bound and preserved, with Machen's signature.

Machen's reputation as a premier New Testament scholar during the 1920s and 1930s cannot be severed from his mastery of the Greek language. That fact might easily be overlooked by students familiar with his well-known books *The Origin of Paul's Religion* (1925) and *The Virgin Birth of Christ*

(1930). These works, which the mainstream biblical scholarship of his day regarded as brilliant contributions to the field, are not characterized by detailed Greek exegesis, and some readers might draw the conclusion that they could have been written by someone with only a modest knowledge of the language.

Nothing could be further from the truth. It is unimaginable that Machen would have been able to demonstrate the weaknesses of theories concerning Paul's religious thought, for example, if he had not immersed himself in the relevant Greek literature. F. F. Bruce, who himself began his career as a classicist, was fond of suggesting that twenty years of Greek study should be a prerequisite for anyone planning to write a New Testament theology. Indeed, it makes little sense to pretend that one can make a scholarly contribution to the understanding of a piece of ancient literature apart from a close familiarity with ancient literature as a whole in its original linguistic form. How seriously would we take an analysis of, say, Milton's *Paradise Lost*, if it were offered by a non-English speaker who had not read—and in fact *could not* read—widely in English literature?

The kind of competence in view here does not necessarily lead to a display of linguistic fireworks. In fact, such knowledge often does not even rise to the surface, but that does not mean it has been unproductive. Language students, to be sure, typically feel cheated if as a result of their hard work they cannot come up with exegetical razzle-dazzle. Teachers, therefore, afraid that their students will lose motivation, try hard to find interpretive "golden nuggets" that prove there is a rich payoff to language study. If used with much care, this approach can be helpful. But there is always the danger of feeding the common mind-set that says, "Something is valuable only if I can see its immediate relevance."

It is not the primary purpose of language study to provide the means for reaching astounding exegetical conclusions, although sound linguistic training can at least *prevent* students from adopting inadmissible interpretations. The true goal of learning New Testament Greek is rather to build a much broader base of knowledge and understanding than the student would otherwise have. Occasionally, this knowledge may indeed supply fairly direct answers to exegetical questions. But what matters most is the newly acquired ability to interpret texts *responsibly* on the basis of comprehensive rather than fragmented (and therefore distorted) information.

Of course, most people who take up the study of New Testament Greek do not intend to write technical and original works of scholarship. They want skills that will allow them to use commentaries and other reference works effectively. They also hope to do serious exegetical work on their own. But the principles and benefits of language learning remain fundamentally the same. An effective, reliable biblical exposition need not rely on complex discussions of the meanings of Greek words or on the supposed subtleties of the aorist tense, but it certainly should arise out of genuine firsthand familiarity with the original text.

Machen's *New Testament Greek for Beginners* is ideally suited to provide a solid foundation on which students can build just that kind of familiarity with the biblical text. When he took up a teaching post at Princeton Seminary in 1906, Machen's pedagogical gifts were nowhere more evident than in his elementary Greek classes. His erudition did not get in the way of presenting, in clear fashion, what was essential to acquire a reading knowledge of the language. Similarly, his textbook avoids technical explanations that are unnecessary at the early stages of language learning. (Because technical explanations are typically historical in nature, they can derail the efforts to understand a language as it functions at a particular stage in time.

To use the now fashionable terms, Machen's approach is *synchronic* rather than *diachronic*.)

Nevertheless, although the book has no gratuitous displays of erudition, only a master could have written it. Few people have the knack for explaining a difficult subject in brief and simple terms. Even fewer manage to do that without making subtly misleading statements. Machen's remarkable analytical powers, as well as his intensive and extensive exposure to the Greek language, made possible such a concise and reliable presentation of the grammar.

From time to time, one hears complaints that Machen's textbook is too difficult for today's students. Part of the reason is that in his day Machen could assume better knowledge of English grammar than we can today (the present revised edition minimizes that problem). In addition, however, it is important to appreciate that the textbook was intended as a tool not for self-teaching but for classroom use. No doubt Machen assumed that a capable teacher would provide the necessary guidance. It is no surprise that several generations of teachers have especially appreciated that Machen did not attempt to do their work for them. *New Testament Greek for Beginners* lays out all the essential facts and explanations in a straightforward and succinct fashion, thus allowing teachers to use their classroom time as they see fit.

Machen chose to illustrate grammatical points with simple forms, even if they do not appear as such in the Greek of the New Testament. Some have argued that "made-up" Greek of this type is artificial and that it is better to expose students to real Greek sentences from the beginning. This proposal sounds very good in theory, but so-called inductive approaches to New Testament Greek have not been a great success. Machen's rationale, as expressed in the preface, is sound, and the wisdom of his decision has been demonstrated many times over.

Dr. McCartney and the publisher are to be congratulated for reissuing this beginning grammar in a new dress. The revisions, without changing the character of the original, are consistently on target and will ensure its continued use well into the twenty-first century.

Moisés Silva

Preface to the Revised Edition

It has been more than eighty years since Dr. Machen produced his classic textbook on New Testament Greek. And yet, as this revision is being prepared, the original edition is still in print. As an unrevised textbook this surely has set some kind of record. A number of reasons might be adduced for this longevity: its clarity of organization, its pedagogical simplicity, its conciseness of presentation and description, its success in dividing and arranging the material, and no doubt its familiarity to three or four generations of New Testament Greek instructors. Yet much has changed since 1923. For one thing, our knowledge of many aspects of New Testament Greek has been considerably refined. Perhaps more important, the educational preparation of students is quite different at the end of the twentieth century than it was at the beginning. Very few students now arrive in class with a solid working knowledge of Latin, and many students do not even have good grounding in English grammar. Rudiments of language that Dr. Machen assumed all students would know can no longer be taken for granted.

Many instructors have argued that these are good reasons for preparing another grammar entirely and giving Machen's grammar an honored place in a museum, where it may be forgotten. And indeed, criticism of Machen, regarding both content and pedagogical effectiveness, has not been lacking. But surely an alternative is to revise Machen's grammar in light of our present situation, and thus make the effectiveness of this classic available to a new generation.

This revision is fairly conservative. Since one main advantage of the original is its familiarity, the reviser has tried to retain as much of its character and organization as possible. The following is an outline of the main differences from the original.

1. Although the lessons and section divisions remain essentially the same, there is a noticeable change in organization in the division of lesson 18 into two parts. Since—as Dr. Machen himself repeatedly stressed—the participle is crucial to understanding New Testament Greek, and since this lesson is usually the most difficult for students, it seemed wise to expand the explanations and illustrations in this lesson. But since lesson 18 was already inordinately long, it seemed best to divide it. In order to keep the lesson numbers in line with the original, the resulting lessons are numbered 18A and 18B.

2. Similarly, since the final three lessons cover not only the μι verbs but also a number of syntactical matters that often lead students to feel somewhat overwhelmed, I have removed some of the syntactical matters of lessons 31–33, along with δείκνυμι, ἀπόλλυμι, and οἶδα, to an additional lesson, numbered 34. This addition, of course, does not alter the numbering of earlier lessons.

3. The section numbers are not so easily retained as are the lesson numbers. Some new sections have been added, either to clarify some grammatical matters or to add some material that the original edition overlooked; several sections have been modified to a greater or lesser degree; and occasionally the order of sections has been altered. It was thus impracticable to keep section numbers the same, but for ease of reference the original sec-

tion numbers (where they correspond) have been included throughout in square brackets [ ]. Thus it should be possible for a student to use an old edition of Machen in a class where this new edition is the text, and longtime instructors who have memorized many of the original section numbers will not find it difficult to locate the section they have in mind.

4. Since many students may not know the terms of English grammar and syntax, a glossary has been added that defines basic grammatical and linguistic terms.

5. A few paradigms and charts have been added both in the text and in the back matter, in particular a list of prepositions and a chart of vowel contractions.

6. In the vocabulary section at the end of the book, some unusual verbal principal parts have been cross-referenced to their lexical forms to help students find the correct verb. To supplement the 400 or so vocabulary words introduced in the grammar, most of which appear about 50 times or more in the Greek New Testament, a 250-word list provided by Dr. Bruce M. Metzger has been added for words appearing 25–50 times.[1]

7. Accents are a frequent bone of contention among Greek instructors. It is the editor's conviction that students ought to learn the accents because they become useful in such matters as marking the contracting verbs and distinguishing progressive from second aorist participles even when the vocabulary item is not known. Furthermore, scholarly literature generally expects accenting to be done

1. Students who wish to advance further should consult Metzger's *Lexical Aids for Students of New Testament Greek,* now available through Baker Book House. In addition to listing all the words occurring ten times or more in the Greek New Testament, his book provides the English derivatives of many Greek words as an aid to memorization, identifies Greek word clusters related to the same root, and summarizes the range of meanings for Greek prepositions compounded with verbs.

properly. But the editor also acknowledges that accents make the difficult task of learning Greek more difficult, with little immediate payoff in ability to read the New Testament. Therefore, although the material on accents has been retained throughout, it is now set off from the main material, except for instances where the accents have some semantic importance.

8. Readers familiar with the original edition will note that the term "present" when referring to Greek tense has been changed throughout to "progressive," except when referring to the indicative mood. The reasons for this are explained in a footnote in lesson 18A.

9. Few students today have cut their teeth on the King James Bible and Shakespeare, and hence few know how to use correctly the antiquated second person. This edition therefore substitutes, for example, "you (s.)" for each "thee" and "thou" found in Machen's original.

10. The only other change worth mentioning here is the move of the vocative case from lesson 4 to lesson 28. Since the vocative is relatively rare and often unpredictable of form when it differs from the nominative, it seemed advisable to treat the vocative as a special case and introduce it with the imperative mood, thus reducing the memorization load in the earlier lessons.

Machen was successful in avoiding some of the linguistic faux pas of his day, and thus, although many other changes have been introduced relating to either pedagogical or linguistic concerns, they do not radically alter the character of Machen's original.

Many thanks are in order, of course. First, thanks go to my colleagues and mentors at Westminster Seminary. I should also like to thank two of our Ph.D. students, Messrs. John Makujina and Adam Brice, for their suggestions. Further, hearty thanks are expressed to Dr. Bruce M. Metzger for permitting the use of his supplemental word list. Special gratitude is due Mr. Wells Turner for his critical help in various stages of this venture. Finally, I am still, after thirty years, thankful to Mr. Ed Nelson, who first taught me Greek at Gordon-Conwell Seminary, using (of course) Machen's *New Testament Greek for Beginners*.

Though it may be doubted whether this grammar can be kept going for another eighty years, it is the reviser's hope that Dr. Machen's wonderful pedagogical accomplishment will minister to at least one more generation of students desirous of reading God's Word in the original languages.

Dan G. McCartney

Preface to the Original Edition

This textbook is intended primarily for students who are beginning the study of the Greek Testament either without any previous acquaintance with the Greek language or with an acquaintance so imperfect that a renewed course of elementary instruction is needed. Owing to the exigencies of the present educational situation, many who desire to use the Greek Testament are unable to approach the subject through a study of classical Attic prose. The situation is undoubtedly to be regretted, but its existence should not be ignored. It is unfortunate that so many students of the New Testament have no acquaintance with classical Greek, but it would be still more unfortunate if such students, on account of their lack of acquaintance with classical Greek, should be discouraged from making themselves acquainted at least with the easier language of the New Testament.

The New Testament usage will here be presented without any reference to Attic prose. But a previous acquaintance with Attic prose, even though it be only a smattering, will prove to be an immense assistance in the mastery of the course. By students who possess such acquaintance the lessons can be covered much more rapidly than by mere beginners.

The book is an instruction book, and not a descriptive grammar. Since it is an instruction book, everything in it is made subservient to the imparting of a reading acquaintance with the language. In a descriptive grammar, for example, the rules may be formulated with a lapidary succinctness which would here be out of place. The effort is made here to enter upon those explanations which the fifteen years' experience of the author in teaching New Testament Greek has shown to be essential. In a descriptive grammar, moreover, the illustrations would have to be limited to what can actually be found in the New Testament, but in the present book they are reduced so far as possible to an ideally simple form, which does not always appear in the New Testament books. In this way the vocabulary at every point can be confined to what the student has actually studied, and confusing footnotes can be avoided. It is highly important that only one grammatical point should be considered at a time. An introduction of illustrations taken from the New Testament would often so overlay the explanation with new words and with subsidiary usages unfamiliar to the student that the specific grammatical point under discussion would be altogether obscured. Of course, however, the effort has been made not to introduce into the illustrations any usages except those which are common in the New Testament idiom.

The character of the book as an instruction book has also determined the choice and order of the material. The treatment has been limited to a few essential points, and no attempt has been made to exhibit the real richness and flexibility of the New Testament language, which can be discovered only through reading. This limitation may in places give rise to criticism, as for example in connection with the treatment of participles. The author is well aware of the fundamentally non-temporal character of the tenses in the participle, and also of the great variety in the shades of thought which the participle can express. But after all it is highly important for the beginner to understand clearly the distinction between the present and the aorist participle, and that distinction can be made clear at the beginning only through the proper use of our temporal mode of thought. Only when what is simple and usual has been firmly impressed upon the student's mind by patient repetition can the finer and more difficult points be safely touched. The treatment of the participle, moreover, has been thrust as far forward as possible in the book, in order that ample time may be allowed for practising the usages which it involves. Experience shows that in learning to read New Testament Greek, the participle is almost the crux of the whole matter.

Special attention has been given to the exercises. Until the very last few lessons (and then only in the Greek-English exercises) the sentences have not for the most part been taken from the New Testament, since the book is intended as an instruction book in Greek and not as a stimulus to memory of the English Bible. At a later stage in the study of New Testament Greek, the student's memory of the English Bible is not an unmixed evil, for repeated reading of already familiar passages will often fix the meaning of a word in the mind far better than it could ever be fixed by the mere learning of a vocabulary. But in the early stages, such assistance will do far more harm than good. In the exercises, the effort has been made to exhibit definitely the forms and grammatical usages which have just been discussed in the same lesson, and also to keep constantly before the mind, in ever new relationships, the most important usages that have been discussed before.

The vocabularies have been limited to words which are very common in the New Testament or which require special explanation. Everywhere the effort has been made to introduce the words in the illustrations and exercises. The learning of lists of words, unless the words so learned are actually used, is a waste of time.

The author desires to express appreciation of the pioneer work which has been done in this country by Professor John Homer Huddilston, Ph.D., in his *Essentials of New Testament Greek*, First Edition, 1895, and also of the larger English book of Rev. H. P. V. Nunn, M.A., entitled *The Elements of New Testament Greek*, First Edition, 1913. The two books by John Williams White, *The Beginner's Greek Book*, 1895, and *The First Greek Book*, 1896, have also been consulted with profit, especially as regards the form of presentation. Among reference works, the new grammar of J. H. Moulton, *A Grammar of New Testament Greek*, edited by Wilbert Francis Howard, especially Part ii of Vol. II, on *Accidence*, 1920, and the work by E. D. Burton on *Moods and Tenses in New Testament Greek*, 1906, have been found particularly useful. Acknowledgment is also to be made to Blass-Debrunner, *Grammatik des neutestamentlichen Griechisch*, 1913, and to the convenient summary of classical usage in Goodwin's *Greek Grammar*. And both the *Greek-English Lexicon of the New Testament* of Grimm-Thayer and Moulton and Geden's *Concordance to the Greek Testament* have been found absolutely indispensable throughout. The advanced student will find much useful material in the large work of A. T. Robertson, *A Grammar of the Greek New Testament in the Light of Historical Research*, 1914.

The author is deeply grateful to Professor Edward Capps, Ph.D., LL.D., of Princeton University, who, in the most gracious possible way, has examined the proof of the book throughout, and (of course without becoming at all responsible for any faults or errors) has rendered invaluable assistance at many points. Much encouragement and help have also been received from the wise counsel and unfailing kindness of the Rev. Professor William Park Armstrong, D.D., of Princeton Theological Seminary.

J. Gresham Machen

Introduction

During the classical period, the Greek language was divided into a number of dialects, of which there were three great families—the Doric, the Aeolic, and the Ionic. In the fifth century before Christ, one branch of the Ionic family, the Attic, attained the supremacy, especially as the language of prose literature. The Attic dialect was the language of Athens in its glory—the language of Thucydides, of Plato, of Demosthenes, and of most of the other great prose writers of Greece.

Various causes contributed to make the Attic dialect dominant in the Greek-speaking world. First and foremost must be put the genius of the Athenian writers. But the political and commercial importance of Athens was also not without its effect. Hosts of strangers came into contact with Athens through government, war, and trade, and the Athenian colonies also extended the influence of the mother city. The Athenian empire, indeed, soon fell to pieces. Athens was conquered first by Sparta in the Peloponnesian war, and then, in the middle of the fourth century before Christ, along with the other Greek cities, came under the domination of the king of Macedonia, Philip. But the influence of the Attic dialect survived the loss of political power; the language of Athens became also the language of its conquerors.

24

Macedonia was not originally a Greek kingdom, but it adopted the dominant civilization of the day, which was the civilization of Athens. The tutor of Philip's son, Alexander the Great, was Aristotle, the Greek philosopher; and that fact is only one indication of the conditions of the time. With astonishing rapidity Alexander made himself master of the whole eastern world, and the triumphs of the Macedonian army were also triumphs of the Greek language in its Attic form. The empire of Alexander, indeed, at once fell to pieces after his death in 323 B.C.; but the kingdoms into which it was divided were, at least so far as the court and the governing classes were concerned, Greek kingdoms. Thus the Macedonian conquest meant nothing less than the Hellenization of the East, or at any rate it meant an enormous acceleration of the Hellenizing process that had already begun.

When the Romans, in the last two centuries before Christ, conquered the eastern part of the Mediterranean world, they made no attempt to suppress the Greek language. On the contrary, the conquerors to a very considerable extent were conquered by those whom they conquered. Rome itself had already come under Greek influence, and now it made use of the Greek language in administering at least the eastern part of its vast empire. The language of the Roman Empire was not so much Latin as it was Greek.

Thus in the first century after Christ, Greek had become a world language. The ancient languages of the various countries did indeed continue to exist, and many districts were bilingual—the original local languages existing side by side with the Greek. But at least in the great cities throughout the empire—certainly in the East—the Greek language was everywhere understood. Even in Rome itself there was a large Greek-speaking population. It is not surprising that Paul's letter to the Roman church is written not in Latin but in Greek.

But the Greek language had to pay a price for this enormous extension of its influence. In its career of conquest, it experienced important changes. The ancient Greek dialects other than Attic, although they disappeared almost completely before the beginning of the Christian era, may have exerted considerable influence upon the Greek of the new unified world. Less important, no doubt, than the influence of the Greek dialects, and far less important than might have been expected, was the influence of foreign languages. But influences of a more subtle and less tangible kind were mightily at work. Language is a reflection of the intellectual and spiritual habits of the people who use it. Attic prose, for example, reflects the spiritual life of a small city-state, which was unified by an intense patriotism and a glorious literary tradition. But after the time of Alexander, the Attic speech was no longer the language of a small group of citizens living in the closest spiritual association; on the contrary it had become the medium of exchange for peoples of the most diverse character. It is not surprising, then, that the language of the new cosmopolitan age was very different from the original Attic dialect upon which it was founded.

This new world language that prevailed after Alexander has been called, not inappropriately, "the Koiné." The word *koiné* means "common"; it is not a bad designation, therefore, for a language that was a common medium of exchange for diverse peoples. The Koiné, then, is the Greek world language that prevailed from about 300 B.C. to the close of ancient history at about A.D. 500.

The New Testament was written within this Koiné period. Linguistically considered, it is united in a very close way with the Greek translation of the Old Testament called the Septuagint, which was made at Alexandria in the centuries just preceding the Christian era, and with certain Christian writings of the early part of the second century after Christ, which are ordinarily associated under the name Apostolic Fathers. Though there are significant differences among these, so far as the bare instrument of expression is concerned the writings of the group belong together. Where, then, within the development of the Koiné is this whole group to be placed?

It has always been observed that the language of the New Testament differs strikingly from the great Attic prose writers such as Thucydides or Plato or Demosthenes. That fact is not surprising. It can easily be explained by the lapse of centuries and by the important changes that the creation of the new cosmopolitanism involved. But another fact is more surprising. It is discovered, namely, that the language of the New Testament differs not merely from that of the Attic prose writers of four centuries before, but also from that of the Greek writers of the very period within which the New Testament was written. The Greek of the New Testament is very different, for example, from the Greek of Plutarch.

This difference sometimes used to be explained by the hypothesis that the New Testament was written in a Jewish-Greek dialect—a form of Greek very strongly influenced by the Semitic languages, Hebrew and Aramaic. But since the beginning of the twentieth century another explanation has become increasingly accepted. This other explanation was first given an important impetus by the discovery, in Egypt, of the "nonliterary papyri." For the most part the Koiné had until recently been known to scholars almost exclusively through literature. But the dry air of Egypt has preserved even the fragile writing material of antiquity, and great numbers of documents such as wills, receipts, petitions, and private letters have been found. These documents are not "literature." Many of them were intended merely to be read once and then thrown away. They exhibit, therefore, not the polished language of books but the actual spoken language of everyday life. And on account of their important divergence from the language of such writers as Plutarch, they have revealed with new clearness the interesting fact that in the Koiné period there was a wide gap between the language of literature and the language of every day. The literary authors of the period imitated the great Attic models with more or less exactitude; they maintained an artificial literary tradition. The obscure writers of the nonliterary papyri, on the other hand, imitated nothing, but simply expressed themselves, without affectation, in the language of the street.

Now the language of the New Testament, at various points where it differs from the literature even of the Koiné period, often agrees with the nonliterary papyri. That discovery has suggested a new hypothesis to account for the apparent peculiarity of the language of the New Testament. It is now supposed that the impression of peculiarity that has been made upon the minds of modern readers by New Testament Greek is due merely to the fact that until recently our knowledge of the spoken as distinguished from the literary language of the Koiné period has been so limited. In reality, it is said, the New Testament is written simply in the popular form of the Koiné that was spoken in the cities throughout the whole of the Greek-speaking world.

This hypothesis undoubtedly contains a large element of truth. Undoubtedly the language of the New Testament is no artificial language of books and no Jewish-Greek jargon, but the natural, living language of the period. But the Semitic influence should not be underestimated. The New Testament writers were nearly all Jews, and all of them were strongly influenced by the Old Testament. In particular, they were influenced, so far as language is concerned, by the Greek translation of the Old Testament (the Septuagint), and the Septuagint was influenced, as most ancient translations were, by the language of the original. The Septuagint had gone far toward producing a Greek vocabulary to express the deepest things of the religion of Israel, and this vocabulary was profoundly influential in the New Testament. Moreover, the originality of the New Testament writers should not be ignored. They had come under the influence of new convictions of a transforming kind, and those new convictions had their effect in the sphere of language. Common words had to be given new and loftier meanings, and common people were lifted to a higher realm by a new and glorious experience. It is not surprising, then, that despite linguistic similarities in detail, the New Testament books, even in form, are vastly different from the letters that have been discovered in Egypt. The New Testament writers have used the common, living language of the day. But they have used it in the expression of uncommon thoughts, and the language itself, in the process, has been to some extent transformed. The Epistle to the Hebrews shows that even conscious art could be made the instrument of profound sincerity; and the letters of Paul, even the shortest and simplest of them, are no mere private jottings intended to be thrown away, like the letters that have been discovered upon the rubbish heaps of Egypt, but letters addressed by an apostle to the church of God. The cosmopolitan popular language of the Greco-Roman world served its purpose in history well. It broke down racial and linguistic barriers. And at one point in its life it became sublime.

Abbreviations

acc.	accusative	neut.	neuter
act.	active	nom.	nominative
adj.	adjective	opt.	optative
adv.	adverb	p., pass.	passive
aor.	aorist	p., pl., plur.	plural
conj.	conjunction	part.	participle
dat.	dative	perf.	perfect
dep.	deponent	pers.	person
fem.	feminine	plup.	pluperfect
fut.	future	prep.	preposition
gen.	genitive	pres.	present
imperf.	imperfect	prog.	progressive
impv.	imperative	pron.	pronoun
indic.	indicative	s., sg., sing.	singular
infin.	infinitive	subj.	subjunctive
m., mid.	middle	voc.	vocative
masc.	masculine		

Lesson I

The Alphabet

1. [1] The Greek alphabet is as follows:

Capital	Lower-case	Hand-written	Name	Pronun-ciation[1]
A	α	*α*	Alpha	a as in *father*
B	β	*β*	Beta	b
Γ	γ	*γ*	Gamma	g as in *got*[2]
Δ	δ	*δ*	Delta	d
E	ε	*ε*	Epsilon	e as in *get*
Z	ζ	*ζ*	Zeta	dz
H	η	*η*	Eta	a as in *late*
Θ	θ	*θ*	Theta	th
I	ι	*ι*	Iota	i as in *pizza* (if long), i as in *pit* (if short)

1. These equivalents correspond to the Erasmian pronunciation system most frequently used in New Testament scholarship. Though there is no consensus as to exactly how ancient Greek was pronounced, most scholars agree that it probably sounded much more like modern Greek than like this system. But the Erasmian system has the advantage of more clearly differentiating the vowels and diphthongs and therefore is pedagogically preferable.

2. Before κ, χ, ξ, or another γ, γ is pronounced like *ng,* as in *sing.*

31

Capital	Lower-case	Hand-written	Name	Pronun-ciation
K	κ	͘κ	Kappa	k
Λ	λ	λ͘·	Lambda	l
M	μ	μ	Mu	m
N	ν	͘·ν	Nu	n
Ξ	ξ	͘ξ	Xi	x (ks)
O	o	͘o	Omicron	o as in *por-ridge*
Π	π	·π͘	Pi	p
P	ρ	ρ	Rho	r
Σ	σ (ς)[1]	͘σ (S')	Sigma	s
T	τ	·τ͘	Tau	t
Υ	υ	·υ	Upsilon	French u or German ü (oo as in *boot* is acceptable)
Φ	φ	φ͘	Phi	ph (f)
X	χ	χ͘	Chi	German ch as in *Bach*
Ψ	ψ	·ψ͘	Psi	ps
Ω	ω	ω͘	Omega	o as in *note*

2. [2] The student is advised to learn the small letters thoroughly in connection with the first lesson, leaving the capital letters to be picked up later as they occur. Note that sentences are begun with lowercase letters, not with capitals. The dots in the "handwritten" column indicate where to start the letter. Note that only κ, λ, π, τ, χ, and ψ require more than one stroke. Before the formation of the letters is practiced, guidance should be obtained from the teacher.

1. ς is written at the end of a word; elsewhere σ.

The student should be careful not to confuse certain Greek letters with English look-alikes:

η is pronounced not like English *n* but like the long *a* sound.

ν is pronounced not like English *v* but like an *n*.

ρ is pronounced not like English *p* but like an *r*.

ω is pronounced not like English *w* but like a long *o*.

γ is pronounced not like English *y* but like a hard *g*.

χ is pronounced not like English *x* but like a breathy *k* or *ch* as in *Bach*.

3. [3] The Greek vowels are as follows:

Short	**Long**
α	α
ε	η
ο	ω
ι	ι
υ	υ

Note that α, ι, and υ can be either long or short. The long α and υ are pronounced very much like the corresponding short letters, except that the sound is held longer; the short ι is pronounced like *i* in *pit* and the long ι like *i* in *pizza*.

ε is always short, and η is the long of it; ο is always short, and ω is the long of it.

ι and υ are called *close* vowels; and the others *open* vowels.

4. [4] A *diphthong* is a combination of two vowels in a single syllable. The second letter of a diphthong is always a close vowel. The first letter is always an open vowel except in the case of υι. The common diphthongs are as follows:

αι, pronounced like *ai* in *aisle*

ει, pronounced like *ā* in *fate* (thus ει and η are pronounced alike) οι, pronounced like *oi* in *oil*

αυ, pronounced like *ow* in *cow*

ευ, pronounced like *eu* in *feud*

ου, pronounced like *oo* in *food*

υι, pronounced like *uee* in *queen*

Since ο, α, and ε are not close vowels, several combinations that would seem to correspond to diphthongs in English are not diphthongs in Greek (e.g., οο, εα, ιε). When such combinations are encountered, note that they are two separate syllables.

The diphthong ηυ (pronounced like "hey you" spoken rapidly without the initial *h* and *y*) is rare. When ι unites with long α, η, or ω to form one sound, the ι is written under the other letter instead of after it, and is called *iota subscript*. Thus ᾳ, ῃ, ῳ. This iota subscript has no effect whatever upon the pronunciation—ᾳ being pronounced like long α, ῃ like η, ῳ like ω—but the subscript does affect the meaning and must not be ignored.

5. [5] A vowel, a diphthong, or the letter ρ at the beginning of a word always has a *breathing*. The breathing stands over the letter; and in the case of a diphthong it stands over the second of the two component vowels.

The *rough* breathing (ʽ) indicates that an *h* sound is to be pronounced before the initial vowel or diphthong; the *smooth* breathing (ʼ) indicates that no such *h* sound is to be pronounced. Thus ἐν is to be pronounced *en*, and ἑν is to be pronounced *hen*; οὐ is to be pronounced *oo*, and οὑ is to be pronounced *hoo*.

The letter ρ at the beginning of a word always has a rough breathing mark. This results in an *hr* sound not found in English. Students unable to pronounce this combination may use the simple *r* sound.

6. [6] There are three *accents:* the *acute* (´), the *circumflex* (ˆ), and the *grave* (`). These accents stand over a vowel, and, in the case of a diphthong, over the second of the two component vowels. When a breathing and an accent stand over the same vowel, the breathing comes first, except in the case of the circumflex accent, which stands *over* the breathing. Thus οἴκου, οἶκος. The use of the accents will be studied in lesson 2. Here, simply observe that the stress in pronunciation is to be placed on the syllable that has any one of the accents.

7. [7] Punctuation

There are four marks of punctuation: the comma (,) and the period (.), both written on the line and corresponding to the comma and the period in English; the colon, which is a dot above the line (·) and takes the place of the English colon and semicolon; and the question mark (;), which looks like an English semicolon.

8. [8] Exercise

After learning to write the small letters of the alphabet and give the names of the letters in order, the student should practice pronouncing Greek words and sentences found anywhere in the book, beginning with the excerpt below. Throughout the entire study, great care should be devoted to pronunciation, and the Greek sentences should always be read aloud both in the preparation of the lessons and in the work of the classroom. In this way the language will be learned not only by the eye, but also by the ear, and will be fixed much more firmly in the memory.

The following is an excerpt from the prologue to the Gospel of John.

Ἐν ἀρχῇ ἦν ὁ λόγος, καὶ ὁ λόγος ἦν πρὸς τὸν θεόν, καὶ θεὸς ἦν ὁ λόγος. οὗτος ἦν ἐν ἀρχῇ πρὸς τὸν θεόν. πάντα δι᾽ αὐτοῦ ἐγένετο, καὶ χωρὶς αὐτοῦ ἐγένετο οὐδὲ ἕν. ὃ γέγονεν ἐν αὐτῷ ζωὴ ἦν, καὶ ἡ ζωὴ ἦν τὸ φῶς τῶν ἀνθρώπων· καὶ τὸ φῶς ἐν τῇ σκοτίᾳ φαίνει, καὶ ἡ σκοτία αὐτὸ οὐ κατέλαβεν.

Lesson 2

Accent

9. [9] Accents only occasionally differentiate words or have crucial semantic significance, but they often help in identifying forms. Therefore, although many beginning Greek grammars skip learning accents, it is recommended that they be observed and learned from the start.[1]

The Greek accents indicated in ancient times not stress (what we call accent), but musical pitch. But since it is impossible for us to reproduce the original pronunciation, the best we can do is to place the stress of the voice upon the syllable where the accent occurs, and give up any distinction in pronunciation between the acute, the circumflex, and the grave. Having adopted this method of pronunciation, we should adhere to it rigidly; for unless some one method is adhered to, the language can never be fixed in the memory.

10. [10] Preliminary Definitions

Every word is composed of one or more syllables. A syllable is an utterance unit with one, and only one, vowel or diphthong at its center. The vowel or diphthong may be preceded

---

1. It is much easier to learn accents along the way than to pick them up later, and thus they are retained in this revision. But many Greek instructors prefer to bypass accents until a later stage. If so, this lesson may be skipped. In subsequent chapters, material on accents that is not crucial for identifying words will be set off from the main text, placed at the end of the lesson, and set in smaller type.

and/or followed by a consonant or consonant cluster. For accentuation, the only thing that needs to be remembered is that each vowel or diphthong is the center of its own syllable.

The last syllable of a word is called the *ultima;* the one before that, the *penult;* and the one before that, the *antepenult.*

Thus, in the word λαμβάνομεν, the ultima is -μεν, the penult is -νο-, and the antepenult is -βα-.

Syllables containing a long vowel or a diphthong are long. But final αι and οι (that is, αι and οι coming at the very end of a word) are considered short so far as accent is concerned.

Thus the last syllable of ἀνθρώπους is long because it contains the diphthong ου; the last syllable of ἄνθρωποι is short because the οι is here final οι; the last syllable of ἀνθρώποις is long because here the οι has a letter after it and so, not being final οι, is long like any other diphthong.

Remember that ε and ο are always short, and η and ω always long. The quantity (long or short) of α, ι, and υ, must be learned by observation in the individual cases.

11. [11] General Rules of Accent

1. *The acute (´) can stand only on one of the last three syllables of a word; the circumflex (ˆ) only on one of the last two; and the grave (`) only on the last.*

Examples: This rule would be violated by ἄποστολος, for here the accent would stand on the fourth syllable from the end. It would also be violated by πιστεῦομεν, for here the circumflex would stand on the third syllable from the end.

2. *The circumflex accent cannot stand on a short syllable.*

3. *If the ultima is long,*

   a. *the antepenult cannot be accented,*

   b. *the penult, if it is accented at all, must have the acute.*

Examples: Rule 3a would be violated by ἀπόστολῳ or ἀπόστολου, because in these cases the ultima is long; but it is not violated by ἀπόστολε or ἀπόστολοι, because here the ultima is short. Rule 3b would be violated by δούλου or δούλων, but is not violated by δοῦλος or δοῦλοι.

4. *If the ultima is short, a long penult, if it is accented at all, must have the circumflex.*

Examples: This rule would be violated by δούλε or δούλοι; but it is not violated by δούλου, because here the ultima is not short, or by υἱός, because here, although a long penult comes before a short ultima, the penult is not accented at all. The rule does not say that a long penult before a short ultima must have the circumflex, but only that if it is accented at all it must have the circumflex rather than some other kind of accent.

5. *A long ultima can have either the acute or the circumflex.*

Examples: ἀδελφοῦ and ἀδελφού both conform to the general rules of accent. Further observation, based on other considerations, is necessary in order to tell which is right.

6. *An acute accent on the last syllable of a word, regardless of the length of its vowel, is changed to the grave when followed, without intervening mark of punctuation, by other words in a sentence.*

Examples: ἀδελφός is right where ἀδελφός stands alone; but ἀδελφός ἀποστόλου violates the rule—it should be ἀδελφὸς ἀποστόλου.

12. [12] These general rules of accent do not tell what the accenting of any individual word is to be; they only tell what it cannot be. In other words, they merely fix certain limits within which the accenting of Greek words must remain. What the accent actually is, within these limits, can be determined in part by special rules that will be introduced from time to time, but in very many cases must be learned by observation of the individual words. Thus if we have a form λυομενου to accent, the general rules would permit λυομενού or λυομενοῦ or λυομένου; any other way of accenting would violate the general rules. Or if we have a form προσωπον to accent, the gen-

39

eral rules would permit πρόσωπον, προσῶπον or προσωπόν. But which possibilities are actually to be chosen is a matter for further observation.

13. [15] Exercises

In all written exercises, the breathings and accents should be put in immediately after each word has been written, just as the *i* is dotted and the *t* crossed in English. It is just as wrong to wait until the end of a whole paradigm or a whole sentence to add the breathings and accents as it would be to wait similarly in English before crossing the *t*.

A. For the following words, list all the ways each word could be accented according to the general rules.

1. διηνοιγεν 2. καιομενη 3. καταλιθηναι 4. λαλουντων 5. γυναικες 6. ἀνοητοι 7. ἐγενετο 8. τουτοις 9. ἐκκλησια 10. ἐκκλησιαι 11. ἐκκλησιαις 12. ἐμπροσθεν 13. ἠν 14. δωρον 15. το

B. Are the following words accented correctly, so far as the general rules of accent are concerned? If not, tell in each case what rule (or rules) has been violated. Then accent each of the words in all the ways that the general rules of accent would permit.

1. ἔδιδομεν, ὥραι, πρόφηταις. 2. δόξῃ, ἐρῆμου, οὐρανον. 3. ἔρημος, βουλαί, λὺε.

[Note: The student should apply the principles of accent in the study of all subsequent lessons, observing how the rules are followed.]

Lesson 3

Present Active Indicative

14. [16] Vocabulary

The vocabularies should be learned after the paradigms and explanatory parts of the lessons, but before the exercises.

βλέπω, *I see*
γινώσκω, *I know*
γράφω, *I write*
διδάσκω, *I teach*

ἔχω, *I have*
λαμβάνω, *I take, I receive*
λέγω, *I say*
λύω, *I loose, I destroy*

15. [17] The Greek verb has *tense, voice,* and *mood,* like the verb in other languages.[1] The *present* tense (in the indicative) refers to present time; the *active* voice represents the subject as acting instead of being acted upon; the *indicative* mood makes an assertion, in distinction, for example, from a command or a wish.

16. [18] The present active indicative of the verb λύω, *I loose,* is as follows:

---

1. Students unfamiliar with grammatical terms may refer to the glossary in the back of the book.

	Sing.		**Plur.**	
1.	λύω	*I loose*	λύομεν	*we loose*
		or *am loosing*		or *are loosing*
2.	λύεις	*you* (s.) *loose*	λύετε	*you* (p.) *loose*
		or *are loosing*		or *are loosing*
3.	λύει	*he (she, it) looses*	λύουσι	*they loose*
		or *is loosing*		or *are loosing*

17. [19] The distinctions between *first person* (person speaking), *second person* (person spoken to), *third person* (person spoken of), and between *singular* and *plural numbers,* which in English are indicated for the most part by subject-pronouns, are indicated in Greek by the endings. Thus no pronoun is necessary to translate *we loose* into Greek; the *we* is sufficiently indicated by the ending -ομεν.

18. [20] The part of the verb that remains constant throughout the conjugation and has the various endings added to it is called the *stem.* Thus the present stem of λύω is λυ-. The present stem of a verb can be obtained by removing the final ω from the form given in the vocabulary. Thus the present stem of λέγω, *I say,* is λεγ-. The conjugation of the present active indicative of any verb in the vocabulary can be obtained by substituting the present stem of that verb for λυ- and then adding the endings -ω, -εις, -ει, -ομεν, -ετε, -ουσι, as they are given above.[1]

19. [21] The present tense is part of the *progressive* tense system, but it does double duty as both a progressive present and a simple present. Thus λύω could be translated either *I am loosing* or *I loose.*

20. [22] The second person, *you loose* or *you are loosing,* may of course be either singular or plural in English and may

---

1. These are the primary personal endings, which stand in the tenses called primary tenses, namely, the present, the future, and the perfect. (The secondary tenses, which in the indicative mood are associated with past time, are the imperfect, the aorist, and the pluperfect.)

be translated by the student either by λύεις or by λύετε except where the context makes plain which is meant. Where it is desired in the exercises to indicate whether singular or plural is meant, "you (s.)" or "you (p.)" will be used.

21. Parsing

To *parse* is to identify a particular verb according to its form. All the verbs in this chapter would be parsed as *present active indicative,* but to be fully parsed they must also be identified by *person* and *number* along with their *lexical form.*[1] Thus διδάσκετε is parsed as a *present active indicative second-person plural* of διδάσκω. Students should make it a practice to parse every verb when it is encountered, until recognition of a form is automatic.

Accent Matters

22. [13] *Rule of Verb Accent*

Verbs have recessive accent.

Explanation: The rule means that, in verbs, the accent goes back as far from the end of the word as the general rules of accent will permit. This rule definitely fixes the accent of any verb form; it is not necessary to know what verb the form is derived from or to have any other information whatever. Knowing that it is a verb form, one needs only to look at the ultima. If the ultima is short, an acute must be placed on the antepenult (supposing the word to have as many as three syllables); if the ultima is long, an acute must be placed on the penult.

Examples: Suppose a verb form ἐγινωσκου is to be accented. In accordance with the rule of verb accent, the

---

1. The lexical form is the form used as the entry word in a dictionary. Verbs in English use the infinitive as the lexical form, but in Greek the first-person singular of the present active indicative is used.

accent is trying to get as far back from the end of the word as the general rules of accent will permit. But ἔγινωσκου would violate rule 1 of the general rules noted in the previous lesson; and, since the ultima is long, ἐγίνωσκου would violate rule 3a. Therefore the penult must be accented. But ἐγινῶσκου would violate rule 3b. Therefore ἐγινώσκου is correct. On the other hand, if a verb form ἐγινωσκε is to be accented, although ἔγινωσκε is forbidden by rule 1, ἐγίνωσκε is permitted; and since verbs have recessive accent, that accenting, ἐγίνωσκε, is correct, and ἐγινῶσκε or ἐγινωσκέ would be wrong. If the verb has only two syllables, rule 4 often comes into play. Thus if the verb form σωζε is to be accented, the rule of recessive verb accent decrees that the syllable farthest from the end shall be accented. But rule 4 decrees that the accent shall be not σώζε but σῶζε.

23. [23] Exercises

Translate. All English-Greek exercises should be written.

A. 1. βλέπεις, γινώσκεις, λαμβάνεις. 2. γράφει, ἔχει, λέγει. 3. λύει, διδάσκει, βλέπει. 4. λαμβάνομεν, ἔχομεν, γινώσκομεν. 5. βλέπετε, λέγετε, γράφετε. 6. διδάσκουσι, λαμβάνουσι, λύουσι. 7. γινώσκετε, γινώσκεις, γινώσκομεν. 8. βλέπομεν, διδάσκουσι, λέγει. 9. ἔχεις, βλέπουσι, λαμβάνομεν.

B. 1. We are knowing, we see, we are seeing. 2. They are loosing, they loose, he looses. 3. He is loosing, you (p.) have, you (s.) know. 4. I am taking, we know, they say. 5. She has, we are writing, they see. 6. It says, he writes, she receives.

[The teacher should continue such drill orally, until the student can recognize the Greek words rapidly both by sight and by sound and translate the English sentences rapidly into Greek.]

Lesson 4

The Second Declension • Order of Words
• Movable ν

24. [24] Vocabulary

ἀδελφός, ὁ, *a brother*

ἄνθρωπος, ὁ, *a man, a person,*
a human being; plur. *men,*
people

ἀπόστολος, ὁ, *an apostle*

δοῦλος, ὁ, *a slave, a servant*

δῶρον, τό, *a gift*

θάνατος, ὁ, *a death*

ἱερόν, τό, *a temple*

καί, conj., *and*

λόγος, ὁ, *a word*

νόμος, ὁ, *a law*

οἶκος, ὁ, *a house*

υἱός, ὁ, *a son*

Each noun given in the vocabularies will always be accompanied by its appropriate article.

25. [25] There are three *declensions* in Greek. The second declension is given before the first for purposes of convenience, since it is easier and has a larger number of common nouns.

26. [26] There is no indefinite article in Greek, and so ἀδελφός means either *brother* or *a brother* (usually the latter). Greek has, however, a definite article, and where the Greek article does not appear, the definite article should not be inserted in the English translation. Thus ἀδελφός does not mean *the brother*. In the plural, English, like Greek, has no

45

indefinite article. δοῦλοι, therefore, means simply *servants*. But it does not mean *the servants*.

27. [27] The noun in Greek has *gender, number,* and *case*.

28. [28] **Gender.** There are three genders: *masculine, feminine,* and *neuter*. Although most nouns that refer to females are feminine, and most nouns that refer to males are masculine, grammatical gender is not the same as sex. Most feminine and masculine nouns are not identifiably female or male, and in fact refer to things. On the other hand, a few neuter nouns refer to people; for example κοράσιον, τό, *a young girl*.

Almost all nouns of the second declension ending in -ος are masculine; and all nouns of the second declension ending in -ον are neuter. But the gender of nouns must often be learned by observation of the individual nouns. The vocabularies will always list nouns with their articles. The masculine article, ὁ, indicates masculine gender; the feminine article, ἡ, feminine gender; and the neuter article, τό, neuter gender.

29. [29] **Number.** There are two numbers: *singular* and *plural*. Verbs agree with their subject in number.

30. [30] **Case.** There are four cases: *nominative, genitive, dative,* and *accusative*.[1]

31. [31] The declension of λόγος, ὁ, *a word*, is as follows:

	Sing.		**Plur.**	
Nom.	λόγος	*a word*	λόγοι	*words*
Gen.	λόγου	*of a word*	λόγων	*of words*
Dat.	λόγῳ	*to or for a word*	λόγοις	*to or for words*
Acc.	λόγον	*a word*	λόγους	*words*

---

1. [37] A fifth case, the vocative, is used for direct address. Since the vocative is little used and is usually identical to the nominative, it need not be memorized separately. It does have a few unique forms, which will be discussed in lesson 28.

32. [33] The *stem* of a noun is that part of the noun that remains constant when the various endings are added. The stem of λόγος is λογο-, and all other second-declension nouns, like λόγος, have stems ending in o. The second declension, therefore, is sometimes called the o-declension. But this final o of the stem becomes so much disguised when the endings enter into combination with it, that it is more convenient to regard λογ- as the stem and -ος, -ου, etc., as the endings. At any rate observe, however, that o (with the long of it, ω) is the characteristic vowel in the last syllable of second-declension nouns.

33. [34a] The *nominative* case is the case of the subject of a sentence. In the sentence ἀπόστολος γινώσκει, *an apostle knows*, the nominative case of the noun ἀπόστολος specifies it as the subject. Therefore, a pronoun *(he, she, it)* is not needed. We should not translate the sentence as *an apostle, he knows* but simply as *an apostle knows*.

34. [34b] The *accusative* case is the case of the direct object of a verb. Thus βλέπω λόγον means *I see a word*.

35. [35] The *genitive* case expresses various kinds of relationships, such as possession, source, and separation. The genitive can usually be translated by using the word *of*. Thus λόγοι ἀποστόλου means *words of an apostle* or *an apostle's words*. The genitive's other important uses will be learned later as they are encountered.

36. [36] The *dative* case also expresses various relationships, such as instrumentality, location, or reception. It is the case of the indirect object of a verb. Thus λέγω λόγον ἀποστόλοις means *I say a word to apostles*. The dative's other important uses will be learned later.

37. [41] The declension of δῶρον, τό, *a gift*, is as follows:

47

	Sing.	**Plur.**
Nom.	δῶρον	δῶρα
Gen.	δώρου	δώρων
Dat.	δώρῳ	δώροις
Acc.	δῶρον	δῶρα

38. [42] Note that δῶρον is a neuter noun. In all neuter nouns, of all declensions, the accusative of both numbers is like the nominative, and in the first and second declensions the nominative and accusative plural always end in short α.

39. [43] Order of Words

The normal order of the sentence in Greek is like that in English—subject, verb, object. There is no special tendency, as in Latin, to put the verb at the end. But Greek can vary the order for purposes of emphasis or euphony much more freely than English. Thus the sentence *an apostle says a word* is in Greek normally ἀπόστολος λέγει λόγον. But λέγει ἀπόστολος λόγον and λόγον λέγει ἀπόστολος are also translated *an apostle says a word*. The English translation must be determined by observing the *endings,* not by observing the order.

40. [44] Movable ν

The -ουσι of the third-person plural of the verb often has a ν, called *movable* ν, added to it. This most often happens at the end of a sentence or where the following word begins with a vowel or the letter τ. Thus βλέπουσιν ἀποστόλους. But it can occur anywhere. Thus either λύουσι δούλους or λύουσιν δούλους is correct.

It should not be supposed that this movable ν occurs at the end of every verb form ending in a vowel when the next word begins with a vowel. On the contrary, it occurs only in a very few forms, which must be learned as they appear.

Accent Matters

41. [14] *Rule of Noun Accent*

In nouns, the accent remains on the same syllable as in the nominative singular, so nearly as the general rules of accent will permit.

Explanation: This rule differs from the rule of verb accent in that it does not of itself fix the accent of noun forms. The accent on the nominative singular (the form given in the vocabularies) must be learned by observation for every noun separately, just as the spelling of the word must be learned. So much is merely a part of the learning of the vocabularies. But once the accent on the nominative singular is known, the accents on the other forms of the noun may be discovered by applying the rule. Examples:

1. If there be a noun λογος, neither the general rules of accent in §11 (lesson 2) nor the rule of noun accent will determine whether the accent is λόγος or λογός. But once it has been determined that the accent is λόγος, then the accent on the other forms of the noun can be determined. The other forms, without the accent, are λογου, λογῳ, λογον, λογοι, λογων, λογοις, λογους. On every one of these forms the acute will stand on the penult since (a) the rule of noun accent decrees that the accent remains there if the general rules of accent permit, and since (b) the general rules of accent never forbid the accent to be placed on a penult, and since (c) rule 2 of the general rules decrees that only an acute accent can stand on a short syllable.

2. In the case of a noun οἶκος, its various forms being after the analogy of λόγος above, (a) and (b) of the considerations mentioned above with regard to λόγος still hold.

But (c) does not hold, since here the penult is not short but long. In this case, rules 3b and 4 will determine when the accent is acute and when it is circumflex. When the ultima is long, the accent (on the penult) will be acute, and when the ultima is short, the accent (on the penult) will be circumflex. Thus οἶκος, οἴκου, οἴκῳ, οἶκον, οἶκοι, οἴκων, οἴκοις, οἴκους.

3. In the case of the noun ἄνθρωπος, ὁ, *a human being*, the accent is trying in every other form to get back to the antepenult, in accordance with the rule of noun accent, since it is the antepenult that is accented in the nominative singular. But where the ultima is long, the accent cannot get back to the antepenult, since that would violate rule 3a. The nearest syllable to the antepenult that it can reach in these cases is the penult. The rule of noun accent decrees that that nearest syllable is the one upon which the accent must stand. But since the ultima is long in these cases, rule 3b decrees that the accent (upon the penult) shall be an acute not a circumflex. Thus ἄνθρωπος, ἀνθρώπου, ἀνθρώπῳ, ἄνθρωπον, ἄνθρωποι, ἀνθρώπων, ἀνθρώποις, ἀνθρώπους.

42. [38] The declension of δοῦλος, ὁ, *a servant*, along with that of ἄνθρωπος, ὁ, is given in §598. Note that these nouns differ from λόγος only in that the accent is different in the nominative singular and therefore the application of the general rules of accent works out differently.

43. [39] This is also true of υἱός, ὁ, *a son*, but the accent on the ultima calls for special comment. Its declension is as follows:

	Sing.	**Plur.**
Nom.	υἱός	υἱοί
Gen.	υἱοῦ	υἱῶν
Dat.	υἱῷ	υἱοῖς
Acc.	υἱόν	υἱούς

44. [40] Here the rule of noun accent decrees that the accent must be on the ultima in all cases, because it was there in the nominative singular. But which accent shall it be? The general rules of accent answer this question where the ultima is short; for of course only an acute, not a circumflex, can stand on a short syllable. But where the ultima is long, the general rules of accent will permit either an acute or a circumflex. A special rule is therefore necessary. It is as follows:

In the second declension, when the ultima is accented at all, it has the circumflex in the genitive and dative of both numbers, elsewhere the acute.

Explanation: The "elsewhere" really refers only to the accusative plural, because in the nominative and vocative singular and plural and in the accusative singular the general rules of accent would forbid the circumflex, the ultima being short in these cases.

45. [45] Exercises

Translate. Parse all verb forms.

A. 1. ἀδελφὸς βλέπει ἄνθρωπον. 2. δοῦλος γράφει λόγους. 3. ἀπόστολοι διδάσκουσιν ἄνθρωπον. 4. ἀπόστολοι λύουσι δούλους. 5. δοῦλος λαμβάνει δῶρα. 6. λαμβάνουσιν υἱοὶ οἴκους. 7. δούλους καὶ οἴκους λαμβάνουσιν ἀδελφοί. 8. βλέπομεν ἱερὰ καὶ ἀποστόλους. 9. δούλους βλέπετε καὶ ἀδελφούς. 10. γράφεις λόγον ἀποστόλῳ. 11. διδάσκει ἄνθρωπον. 12. ἀδελφὸς λέγει λόγον ἀποστόλῳ. 13. ἀδελφὸς ἀποστόλων γινώσκει νόμον. 14. δοῦλοι γινώσκουσι νόμον καὶ λαμβάνουσι δῶρα. 15. γινώσκουσιν ἄνθρωποι θάνατον. 16. λαμβάνομεν δῶρα καὶ ἔχομεν ἀδελφούς. 17. ἀποστόλοις καὶ δούλοις λέγομεν λόγους θανάτου. 18. ἀδελφοὶ καὶ δοῦλοι γινώσκουσιν καὶ βλέπουσιν ἱερὰ καὶ δῶρα. 19. γράφει ἀπόστολος νόμον καὶ λέγει λόγους υἱοῖς δούλου. 20. υἱοὶ ἀποστόλων λέγουσι λόγους καὶ λύουσι δούλους.

B. 1. A servant is writing a law. 2. A son sees words. 3. Brothers are loosing servants. 4. Sons take gifts. 5. An apostle sees a servant and a gift. 6. Servants and sons are saying a word to a brother. 7. We see gifts and servants. 8. Men see words and gifts of a brother and houses of apostles and sons. 9. Words and laws we write to brothers; a word of death we say to a servant. 10. A son is seeing temples and houses. 11. Humans know death. 12. You (s.) receive an apostle's gift (= a gift of an apostle). 13. You (p.) are writing a brother's word to a servant. 14. I loose servants and say words to sons and brothers. 15. A son sees death. 16. They know laws and teach servants of an apostle.

Lesson 5

The First Declension

46. [46] Vocabulary

ἀλήθεια, ἡ, *truth*

βασιλεία, ἡ, *a kingdom*

γραφή, ἡ, *a writing, a Scripture*

δόξα, ἡ, *glory*

εἰρήνη, ἡ, *peace*

ἐκκλησία, ἡ, *a church*

ἐντολή, ἡ, *a commandment*

ζωή, ἡ, *life*

ἡμέρα, ἡ, *a day*

καρδία, ἡ, *a heart*

παραβολή, ἡ, *a parable*

φωνή, ἡ, *a voice*

ψυχή, ἡ, *a soul, a life*

ὥρα, ἡ, *an hour*

47. [47] All nouns of the first declension ending in α or η are feminine, and conversely all feminine nouns of the first declension end in α or η.

48. There are three types of feminine first-declension nouns: (1) those that have α in their endings throughout the singular, (2) those with η throughout the singular, and (3) those that have α in the nominative and accusative singular and η in the genitive and dative singular. (The plural endings are the same for all three types.)

49. [48] The declension of ὥρα, ἡ, *an hour*, is as follows:

	Sing.	**Plur.**
Nom.	ὥρα	ὧραι
Gen.	ὥρας	ὡρῶν
Dat.	ὥρᾳ	ὥραις
Acc.	ὥραν	ὥρας

50. [49] The stem of ὥρα is ὡρα-, and the first declension is sometimes called the α-declension, because its stems end in α. Since, however, the final vowel of the stem enters into various combinations with the endings, it is more convenient for the beginner to regard ὡρ- as the stem and -α, -ας, etc., as the endings. Notice that α is characteristic of this declension as ο is of the second declension.

51. Note that ὥρας, the genitive of ὥρα, is the *same case* as the λόγου of λόγος. Though the *form* of the ending is different, the *function* is the same. Thus ὥρας means *of an hour,* just as λόγου means *of a word.*

52. [54] The declension of δόξα, ἡ, *glory,* is of the type that mixes α and η in the singular endings:

	Sing.	**Plur.**
Nom.	δόξα	δόξαι
Gen.	δόξης	δοξῶν
Dat.	δόξῃ	δόξαις
Acc.	δόξαν	δόξας

53. [55] The change to η in the genitive and dative singular occurs in all first-declension nouns except when the letter before the α is ε, ι, or ρ.

54. [56] Some first-declension nouns have η throughout the singular. The declension of γραφή, ἡ, *a writing, a Scripture,* is as follows:

	Sing.	**Plur.**
Nom.	γραφή	γραφαί
Gen.	γραφῆς	γραφῶν
Dat.	γραφῇ	γραφαῖς
Acc.	γραφήν	γραφάς

55. [57] When a first-declension noun ends in η in the nominative singular, the η is retained throughout the singular. But the plurals of all first-declension nouns are alike.

Accent Matters

56. [51] The genitive plural of all first-declension nouns shows an exception to the rule of noun accent. The rule of noun accent would require the accent to remain on the same syllable as in the nominative singular. But nouns of the first declension have a circumflex on the ultima in the genitive plural no matter where the accent was in the nominative singular.

57. [50] Observe that in the ultimas of ὥρα and βασιλεία the α is long in the nominative, genitive, and accusative singular and in the accusative plural. Thus, except for the genitive plural, an acute lies on the penult throughout.

58. [53] The declension of ἀλήθεια, ἡ, *truth*, which has a short α in the ultima of the nominative singular, is as follows:

	Sing.	**Plur.**
Nom.	ἀλήθεια	ἀλήθειαι
Gen.	ἀληθείας	ἀληθειῶν
Dat.	ἀληθείᾳ	ἀληθείαις
Acc.	ἀλήθειαν	ἀληθείας

When in the first declension the α in the ultima is short in the nominative singular, it is also short in the accusative

55

singular. In the accusative plural the α is long in all first-declension nouns. The accent follows the noun rule everywhere except in the genitive plural (see §56).

59. [58] In the first declension (exactly as in the second, see §44), when the ultima is accented at all, it has the circumflex in the genitives and datives of both numbers, elsewhere the acute.

60. [59] Exercises

A. 1. ψυχὴ βλέπει ζωήν. 2. βασιλεία γινώσκει ἀλήθειαν. 3. ἄνθρωπος γράφει ἐντολὰς καὶ νόμους. 4. ἀπόστολοι λαμβάνουσι δούλους καὶ δῶρα καὶ ἐκκλησίας. 5. ἀπόστολοι καὶ ἐκκλησίαι βλέπουσι ζωὴν καὶ θάνατον. 6. υἱὸς δούλου λέγει παραβολὴν ἐκκλησίᾳ. 7. παραβολὴν λέγομεν καὶ ἐντολὴν καὶ νόμον. 8. βασιλείας γινώσκετε καὶ ἐκκλησίας. 9. ἐκκλησίαν διδάσκει ἀπόστολος καὶ βασιλείαν δοῦλος. 10. νόμον καὶ παραβολὴν γράφει ἄνθρωπος ἐκκλησίᾳ. 11. καρδίαι ἀνθρώπων ἔχουσι ζωὴν καὶ εἰρήνην. 12. φωνὴ ἀποστόλων διδάσκει ψυχὰς δούλων. 13. ὥρα ἔχει δόξαν. 14. φωναὶ ἐκκλησιῶν διδάσκουσι βασιλείας καὶ ἀνθρώπους. 15. βλέπεις δῶρα καὶ δόξαν. 16. γράφει ἐκκλησίᾳ λόγον ζωῆς. 17. λέγει καρδίαις ἀνθρώπων παραβολὴν καὶ νόμον. 18. γράφει ἐκκλησίᾳ υἱὸς ἀποστόλου.

B. 1. A kingdom receives glory. 2. Churches are saying parables to hearts of men. 3. A heart of a man is teaching an apostle, and a voice of an apostle is teaching a servant. 4. We have writings of apostles. 5. Churches have peace and glory. 6. A day sees life and death. 7. Apostles receive temples and kingdoms. 8. We see houses and temples and churches. 9. A servant says a parable to hearts of men. 10. We know voices of churches and words of truth. 11. A voice of an apostle says a parable to souls of men.

Lesson 6

Adjectives of the First and Second Declension
• The Article • Agreement • Use of the Article
• Attributive and Predicate Positions
of Adjectives • Substantive Use of Adjectives

61. [60] Vocabulary

ἀγαθός, -ή, -όν, adj., *good*

ἄλλος, -η, -ο, adj., *other*

δίκαιος, -α, -ον, adj., *righteous*

ἐγείρω, *I raise up*

ἔρημος, ἡ, *a desert*

ἔσχατος, -η, -ον, adj., *last*

κακός, -ή, -όν, adj., *bad*

καλός, -ή, -όν, adj., *good, beautiful*

κύριος, ὁ, *a lord, the Lord*

μικρός, -ά, -όν, adj., *small, little*

νεκρός, -ά, -όν, adj., *dead*

ὁ, ἡ, τό, art., *the*

ὁδός, ἡ, *a road, a way*

πιστός, -ή, -όν, adj., *faithful*

πρῶτος, -η, -ον, adj., *first*

Note that ἔρημος and ὁδός are feminine, though nearly all nouns of the second declension ending in -ος are masculine.

62. [61] The declension of the adjective ἀγαθός, *good,* is as follows:

	Sing.			Plur.		
	Masc.	**Fem.**	**Neut.**	**Masc.**	**Fem.**	**Neut.**
Nom.	ἀγαθός	ἀγαθή	ἀγαθόν	ἀγαθοί	ἀγαθαί	ἀγαθά
Gen.	ἀγαθοῦ	ἀγαθῆς	ἀγαθοῦ	ἀγαθῶν	ἀγαθῶν	ἀγαθῶν
Dat.	ἀγαθῷ	ἀγαθῇ	ἀγαθῷ	ἀγαθοῖς	ἀγαθαῖς	ἀγαθοῖς
Acc.	ἀγαθόν	ἀγαθήν	ἀγαθόν	ἀγαθούς	ἀγαθάς	ἀγαθά

This declension, like all declensions of adjectives, and of the article, etc., is to be learned across and not in vertical columns—that is, the nominative singular is to be given in all three genders before the genitive is given, and the genitive singular is to be given in all three genders before the dative is given, and so on.

Note that the masculine of the adjective ἀγαθός is declined exactly like a masculine noun of the second declension, the feminine exactly like a feminine noun in η of the first declension, and the neuter exactly like a neuter noun of the second declension.

63. [62a] The declension of μικρός, *small,* is as follows:

	Sing.			Plur.		
	Masc.	**Fem.**	**Neut.**	**Masc.**	**Fem.**	**Neut.**
Nom.	μικρός	μικρά	μικρόν	μικροί	μικραί	μικρά
Gen.	μικροῦ	μικρᾶς	μικροῦ	μικρῶν	μικρῶν	μικρῶν
Dat.	μικρῷ	μικρᾷ	μικρῷ	μικροῖς	μικραῖς	μικροῖς
Acc.	μικρόν	μικράν	μικρόν	μικρούς	μικράς	μικρά

Note that long α not η stands in the feminine of these adjectives when the preceding letter is ρ or a vowel (compare §53).

64. [63] The declension of the article is as follows:

	Sing.			Plur.		
	Masc.	**Fem.**	**Neut.**	**Masc.**	**Fem.**	**Neut.**
Nom.	ὁ	ἡ	τό	οἱ	αἱ	τά
Gen.	τοῦ	τῆς	τοῦ	τῶν	τῶν	τῶν
Dat.	τῷ	τῇ	τῷ	τοῖς	ταῖς	τοῖς
Acc.	τόν	τήν	τό	τούς	τάς	τά

65. [64] The forms ὁ, ἡ, οἱ, αἱ are *proclitics*. A proclitic is a word that goes so closely with the following word as to have no accent of its own.

66. [65] Note that except for (1) these irregular proclitic forms and (2) the form τό in the nominative and accusative singular (instead of τόν), the article is declined like the adjective ἀγαθός.

67. [66] Agreement

Adjectives, including the article, agree with the nouns that they modify, in gender, number, and case, but *not necessarily* in the form of the endings. For example, if a second-declension (o-declension) noun is feminine, its endings will usually differ from those of its adjective, but the actual gender, number, and case will still agree.

Examples: (1) ὁ λόγος, τοῦ λόγου, τῷ λόγῳ, βλέπω τὸν λόγον, οἱ λόγοι, τῶν λόγων, τοῖς λόγοις, βλέπω τοὺς λόγους. (2) τὸ δῶρον, τοῦ δώρου, etc. (3) ἡ ὥρα, τῆς ὥρας, τῇ ὥρᾳ, βλέπω τὴν ὥραν, αἱ ὧραι, etc. (4) ἡ ὁδός (note that ὁδός is feminine), τῆς ὁδοῦ, τῇ ὁδῷ, βλέπω τὴν ὁδόν, αἱ ὁδοί, τῶν ὁδῶν, ταῖς ὁδοῖς, βλέπω τὰς ὁδούς. (5) καλὸς λόγος, etc., καλὴ ὥρα, καλὴ ὁδός, etc.

68. [67] Use of the Article

The use of the article in Greek corresponds roughly to the use of the definite article in English. Thus λόγος means *a word;* ὁ λόγος means *the word;* λόγοι means *words;* οἱ λόγοι means *the words.* The differences between the Greek and the English use of the article must be learned by observation as they occur. For now, the presence or absence of the Greek article should always be carefully indicated in the English translation.

Lesson 6

Attributive and Predicate Positions of Adjectives

69. [68] Adjectives are used in two distinct ways: (1) attributively, (2) predicatively.

In the phrase *the good word*, the adjective *good* is an *attributive* adjective; it identifies the particular word or kind of word we are mentioning. We are not mentioning all words, or any word, or a word generally, but only the *good* word.

In the sentence *the word is good*, the adjective *good* is a *predicate* adjective; with the verb *is* it makes an assertion about the subject, *the word*.

70. [69] In Greek, the distinction between the attributive and the predicate adjective is of vastly more importance than in English; indeed, as will be observed later, some of the most important and characteristic parts of Greek grammar are based upon this distinction.

71. [70] *The good word* is an attributive phrase. It can be expressed in two common ways in Greek—either by ὁ ἀγαθὸς λόγος or by ὁ λόγος ὁ ἀγαθός. What is characteristic of the *attributive position* of the Greek adjective is that the adjective has an article immediately in front of it. The first of the two alternatives, ὁ ἀγαθὸς λόγος, is just like English; it has the order (1) article, (2) attributive adjective, (3) noun, and is a literal translation of *the good word*. The second alternative, which puts the noun first and then the adjective, must repeat the article in order to keep an article immediately before the adjective: ὁ λόγος ὁ ἀγαθός, which means literally *the word—(namely) the good one.* But this latter Greek form is much more common than the cumbersome English equivalent, and like ὁ ἀγαθὸς λόγος it should be translated simply *the good word.*

72. [71] *The word is good*, which is a sentence containing a predicate, can also be expressed in two ways in Greek—depending on whether the noun or adjective comes first—

60

either by ὁ λόγος ἀγαθός or by ἀγαθὸς ὁ λόγος (the simple copula, meaning *is*, can be omitted in Greek). The *predicate position* of the adjective in Greek is marked by the fact that the
adjective is *not* preceded immediately by an article.

73. [72] The matter can be summarized as follows:

Attributive Position of the Adjective	ὁ ἀγαθὸς λόγος or ὁ λόγος ὁ ἀγαθός	= *the good word*
Predicate Position of the Adjective	ὁ λόγος ἀγαθός or ἀγαθὸς ὁ λόγος	= *the word is good*

74. [73] The student should fix this distinction in the mind
by thoughtful reading aloud of the above and similar phrases,
until ἀγαθὸς ὁ λόγος, for example, is automatically recognized
as meaning *good (is) the word,* and comes to be dissociated
entirely from the idea *the good word.* If this advice be heeded,
a solid foundation will have been laid for the mastery of a large
part of Greek syntax.

75. [74] This distinction between the attributive and the
predicate position of the adjective can be made in Greek only
when the noun has the article. Thus ἀγαθὸς λόγος or λόγος
ἀγαθός (the noun here not having the article) may mean either
a good word (attributive) or *a word is good* (predicate). Context is the only guide to which is correct.

76. [75] Substantive Use of Adjectives

An adjective, especially one with the article, that does not
accompany a noun with which it agrees, can be used as though
it were a noun. The adjective can thus function as the equivalent of a noun. This is sometimes done in English with the

plural; for example, "blessed are *the meek*" means "blessed are the meek *people*," even though *people* is not expressed. But in Greek this idiom is much more frequent, and occurs in the singular as well as the plural, and of course with the added distinctions of masculine, feminine, and neuter.

Examples: ὁ ἀγαθός means *the good man;* ἡ ἀγαθή, *the good woman;* τὸ ἀγαθόν, *the good thing;* οἱ ἀγαθοί, *the good men* (or *the good people*); αἱ ἀγαθαί, *the good women;* τὰ ἀγαθά, *the good things.*

Accent Matters

77. [62b] The accent in the genitive plural feminine of all adjectives of the second and first declension follows the regular noun rule and not the special rule for nouns of the first declension (§56).

78. [76] Exercises

A. 1. ἀγαθή ἡ ἐκκλησία καὶ ἡ βασιλεία κακή. 2. ἡ κακὴ καρδία τῶν ἀνθρώπων γινώσκει θάνατον. 3. οἱ ἀπόστολοι βλέπουσι τοὺς μικροὺς οἴκους καὶ τὰς κακὰς ὁδούς. 4. οἱ δοῦλοι οἱ κακοὶ λύουσι[1] τὸν οἶκον τοῦ ἀποστόλου. 5. οἱ κακοὶ λύουσι τὸ ἱερόν. 6. ὁ κύριος τῆς ζωῆς[2] ἐγείρει τοὺς νεκρούς. 7. οἱ λόγοι τῆς ἀληθείας διδά-σκουσι τοὺς ἄλλους ἀποστόλους. 8. οἱ δίκαιοι λαμβάνουσι τὰ δῶρα τοῦ κυρίου τὰ καλά. 9. ὁ κακὸς βλέπει τὴν ἔρημον καὶ τοὺς ἐσχάτους οἴκους. 10. πρῶτοι οἱ δοῦλοι· ἔσχατοι οἱ κύριοι. 11. τῇ ἐκκλησίᾳ τῇ μικρᾷ γράφει ὁ κύριος λόγον ἀγαθόν. 12. τοὺς πι-στοὺς βλέπει ὁ πιστός. 13. ἔσχατοι οἱ δοῦλοι οἱ κακοί· πρῶτοι οἱ υἱοὶ οἱ ἀγαθοί. 14. ὁ υἱὸς τοῦ ἐσχάτου ἀδελφοῦ βλέπει τὰς καλὰς ἐκκλησίας τοῦ κυρίου. 15. ἄλλην παραβολὴν λέγομεν τῇ κακῇ

1. λύω sometimes means *I destroy.*

2. Abstract nouns, and nouns such as ζωή, often have the article where it is omitted in English.

βασιλείᾳ. 16. πρώτη ἡ ἐκκλησία· ἐσχάτη ἡ ἄλλη βασιλεία. 17. ταῖς πισταῖς λέγει ὁ κύριος παραβολὴν καλὴν καὶ τοῖς πιστοῖς. 18. ὁ ἀγαθὸς γράφει ἀγαθά· ὁ κακὸς κακά. 19. ἀγαθὸς ὁ δοῦλος καὶ λέγει καλά. 20. ἡ ἀλήθεια πιστὴ καὶ ἡ ὥρα κακή.

B. 1. To the first church the Lord writes the first parable. 2. The good woman sees the ways of the desert. 3. The good things are first, and the bad things (are) last.[1] 4. Death is bad, and life is good. 5. The Lord of the kingdom raises up the faithful men and the faithful women. 6. The good know the bad, and the bad (know) the good. 7. The good words we say to the church, and the bad words we write to the brothers. 8. You (s.) see the good days of the Lord of life. 9. The roads are good, and the men bad. 10. The first gift is last, and the last (gift) first. 11. The good servants know the truth and the glory of the Lord. 12. The last day takes the bad servants. 13. The men are destroying the beautiful temples and the small houses. 14. The righteous have another house. 15. The church is receiving the other people. 16. I know the other ways. 17. The Lord is saying the other parable to the first church.

1. As in English, the verb (or other shared element) of a compound sentence can be "understood" in the second half.

Lesson 7

Masculine Nouns of the First Declension
• Prepositions

79. [77] Vocabulary

ἄγγελος, ὁ, *an angel, a mes-*
senger
ἄγω, *I lead*
ἀπό, prep. with gen., *from*
βάλλω, *I throw, I cast, I put*
διά, prep. with gen.,
through; with acc., *on*
account of
εἰς, prep. with acc., *into*
ἐκ (ἐξ before vowels), prep.
with gen., *out of*
ἐν, prep. with dat., *in*
θεός, ὁ, *a god, God* (When it
means *God,* θεός may
have the article.)

κόσμος, ὁ, *a world*
λίθος, ὁ, *a stone*
μαθητής, ὁ, *a disciple*
μένω, *I remain*
μετά, prep. with gen., *with;*
with acc., *after*
οὐρανός, ὁ, *heaven*
πέμπω, *I send*
πρός, prep. with acc., *to,*
toward, in the presence of
προφήτης, ὁ, *a prophet*
τέκνον, τό, *a child*
τόπος, ὁ, *a place*
φέρω, *I bear, I bring*

80. [78] Nouns of the first declension ending in -ης are masculine. Almost all words of this type refer to a person of a particular occupation.

81. [79] The declension of προφήτης, ὁ, *a prophet,* is as follows:

	Sing.	**Plur.**
Nom.	προφήτης	προφῆται
Gen.	προφήτου	προφητῶν
Dat.	προφήτῃ	προφήταις
Acc.	προφήτην	προφήτας

Although προφήτης is masculine, it is a true first-declension noun, being just like a feminine noun of the first declension except in the nominative and genitive singular.

μαθητής is declined like προφήτης, except for the accent.

Prepositions

82. [80] Prepositions express relationship. Thus in the sentence *the book is in the desk,* the preposition *in* expresses a certain relationship between the book and the desk. In the sentence *the book is on the desk,* a different relationship is expressed (by the preposition *on*).

In English, nouns standing after prepositions are always in the same case (the "objective" case). But in Greek, the case, not the preposition, is primary, and the preposition serves to clarify the nature of the relationship indicated in a general way by the case. Therefore different prepositions go with different cases.

83. [81a] The dative case indicates *location, instrumentality, accompaniment,* or *reception.* The preposition ἐν is always coupled with the dative case to mean *in* a particular location. Thus *in the house,* when it indicates where someone or something *is staying*, is expressed by ἐν τῷ οἴκῳ; *in the truth* by ἐν τῇ ἀληθείᾳ, etc.

84. [81b] The accusative case indicates *direction* or *focus*. The preposition εἰς is always coupled with the accusative case to mean *into*. Thus *into the house* is expressed by εἰς τὸν οἶκον. Note that motion *into the house* could also be expressed with *in the house*, but *in the house* could also be used to convey quite a different notion, namely, location. In the sentence, *I am going in the house*, the word *in* indicates direction, and thus is translated using εἰς with the accusative case. In the sentence, *I am staying in the house*, the word *in* indicates location, and thus is ἐν with the dative.

85. [81c] The genitive case indicates *source, possession,* or *separation*. Thus the preposition ἀπό is coupled with the genitive to mean *from*. Thus *from the house* is expressed by ἀπὸ τοῦ οἴκου.

86. [82–83] In general, therefore, relationships of location, instrumentality, or accompaniment will be indicated by prepositions with the dative; relationships of direction or focus by prepositions with the accusative; and relationships of source, possession, or separation by prepositions with the genitive. But a very great number of usages of prepositions cannot be reduced to any general rule. It is not always easy to see, for example, how the ideas of source, separation, or possession are related to some of the prepositions that go with the genitive case. So, for example, μετά with the genitive means *with*, even though one would expect *with* to be expressed by a preposition with the dative.

87. [85] ἐν, εἰς, ἐκ, and ἀπό each go with only one case, and πρός is not commonly used with any case except the accusative. But many other prepositions can go with more than one case. From the preceding discussion it should be evident that a preposition coupled with one case will have quite a different meaning when coupled with a different case. Thus διά with the genitive means *through;* διά with the accusative, *on account of;* μετά with the genitive means *with;* μετά with the accusative, *after.*

88. [86] In studying the vocabularies, therefore, it is quite insufficient to learn how the prepositions are to be translated; it is also necessary to learn with what case they are construed in any particular meaning. Thus it is insufficient to say that ἐν means *in.* Rather, one should say that "ἐν-with-the-dative" means *in.* The phrase "ἐν-with-the-dative" should form in the student's mind one absolutely indivisible idea; ἐν should never be thought of apart from its case. In the same way, but still more obviously, it is insufficient to say that μετά means *with* or *after.* Rather, one should say that "μετά-with-the-genitive" means *with,* and that "μετά-with-the-accusative" means *after.* This same method of study should be applied to all prepositions.

89. [87] Prepositions are among the most difficult problems in any attempt to learn a new language. Most languages have only a small number of prepositions that must do service for hundreds of possible relations between nouns or other substantives, and each language apportions these relationships among its few prepositions differently. So the various relationships expressed in Greek by "ἐν-with-the-dative" will sometimes correspond to English *in,* sometimes to *by,* or *within,* or *with,* or even *at.* Students should strive to gain an intuitive understanding of the semantic range of each preposition-with-case, and then the context will indicate what English phrase is best suited. However, at this stage it is more important to maintain *precision* in learning the prepositions themselves. Thus one should learn the common English meaning and stick with it consistently in the exercises. Once this common meaning is firmly grasped, then one can proceed to nuance one's understanding of the preposition-with-case. But a reversal of this method will lead to hopeless confusion. Let the student, therefore, so far as prepositions are concerned, adhere for the present rigidly to the translations given in the vocabularies.

90. [88] Few things are more necessary for a correct understanding of the New Testament than a precise acquaintance with the common prepositions. The prepositions therefore should always be singled out from the vocabularies for special attention, and when new prepositions are learned the old ones should be reviewed.

Accent Matters

91. [84] It should be observed that ἐν, εἰς, and ἐκ are all proclitics (see §65) and thus have no accents.

92. [89] Exercises

A. 1. οἱ μαθηταὶ τῶν προφητῶν μένουσιν ἐν τῷ κόσμῳ. 2. οἱ κακοὶ βάλλουσιν λίθους εἰς τὸν οἶκον τῶν μαθητῶν. 3. ὁ θεὸς πέμπει τοὺς ἀγγέλους εἰς τὸν κόσμον. 4. ὁ προφήτης πέμπει τοὺς μαθητὰς τοῦ κυρίου ἐκ τῶν οἴκων εἰς τὴν ἐκκλησίαν. 5. ὁ θεὸς ἐγείρει τοὺς νεκροὺς ἐκ θανάτου. 6. λαμβάνετε τὰ καλὰ δῶρα ἀπὸ τῶν τέκνων. 7. ἄγομεν τὰ τέκνα ἐκ τῶν οἴκων. 8. μετὰ τοὺς ἀγγέλους πέμπει ὁ θεὸς τὸν υἱόν. 9. μετὰ τῶν ἀγγέλων ἄγει ὁ κύριος τοὺς δικαίους εἰς τὸν οὐρανόν. 10. διὰ τῶν ὁδῶν τῆς ἐρήμου φέρουσιν οἱ δοῦλοι τὰ δῶρα εἰς ἄλλον τόπον. 11. διὰ τῶν γραφῶν τῶν προφητῶν γινώσκομεν τὸν κύριον. 12. διὰ τὴν δόξαν τοῦ θεοῦ ἐγείρει ὁ κύριος τοὺς νεκρούς. 13. φέρουσιν τοὺς νεκροὺς εἰς τὴν ἔρημον. 14. οἱ μαθηταὶ διδάσκουσι τὰ ἀγαθὰ τέκνα ἐν τῇ ἐκκλησίᾳ. 15. ὁ κύριος λέγει παραβολὴν τοῖς μαθηταῖς ἐν τῷ ἱερῷ. 16. διὰ τὴν ἀλήθειαν βλέπουσιν οἱ προφῆται τὸν θάνατον. 17. ἀπὸ τῆς ἐρήμου ἄγουσιν οἱ μαθηταὶ τοὺς ἀγαθοὺς δούλους καὶ τοὺς υἱοὺς τῶν προφητῶν πρὸς τοὺς μικροὺς οἴκους τῶν μαθητῶν. 18. διὰ τὴν βασιλείαν τοῦ θεοῦ φέρομεν τὰ κακά. 19. διὰ τὰς ψυχὰς τῶν ἀδελφῶν βλέπει κακά. 20. καλὸς ὁ οὐρανός· κακὸς ὁ κόσμος. B. 1. In the world we have death, and in the church life. 2. The prophets lead the righteous disciples of the Lord into the way of the desert. 3. The child is throwing a stone into the little house. 4. The man is saying a good word to the disciples and is leading the disciples to the Lord.[1] 5. The disciples are remaining in the church and are saying a parable to the other prophets. 6. Through the voice of the prophet the Lord is teaching the disciples. 7. On account of the church the disciples and the apostles write good words to the brothers. 8. On account of the children the prophet is sending the evil men into the desert. 9. After the Lord the apostle sees the disciple. 10. The prophets are teaching the disciples with the children. 11. They are bringing the disciples to the Lord. 12. The Lord is remaining with the prophet in another place. 13. The righteous are leading the disciples through the desert to the Lord. 14. We see the days of the Son of God in the evil world. 15. Evil are the days; good are the churches. 16. Through the word of the Lord, God raises the dead.

---

1. Care should be taken to distinguish the two ways in which the English word *to* is used in this sentence.

Lesson 8

Personal Pronouns • Present Indicative
of εἰμί • Enclitics

93. [90] Vocabulary

αὐτός, -ή, -ό, pron., *he, she, it*   ἡμεῖς, pron., *we*
δέ, conj., *but, and*   σύ, pron., *you* (s.)
ἐγώ, pron., *I*   ὑμεῖς, pron., *you* (p.)
εἰμί, *I am*

94. [91] The conjunction δέ is *postpositive*—that is, it cannot stand first in its clause. Ordinarily it stands second.

Example: ὁ δοῦλος γινώσκει τὸν ἀπόστολον, ὁ δὲ ἀπόστολος βλέπει τὸν κύριον, *the servant knows the apostle and the apostle sees the Lord.*

Personal Pronouns

95. [94] The declension of the personal pronoun of the first person is as follows:

	Sing.		**Plur.**	
Nom.	ἐγώ	*I*	ἡμεῖς	*we*
Gen.	ἐμοῦ or μου	*of me, my*	ἡμῶν	*of us, our*
Dat.	ἐμοί or μοι	*to* or *for me*	ἡμῖν	*to* or *for us*
Acc.	ἐμέ or με	*me*	ἡμᾶς	*us*

The forms ἐμοῦ, ἐμοί, ἐμέ are the forms used when emphasis is desired. The unemphatic forms, μου, μοι, με, have no accent (see §101).

96. [95] The declension of the personal pronoun of the second person is as follows:

	Sing.		**Plur.**	
Nom.	σύ	*you* (s.)	ὑμεῖς	*you* (p.)
Gen.	σοῦ	*of you, your* (s.)	ὑμῶν	*of you, your* (p.)
Dat.	σοί	*to* or *for you* (s.)	ὑμῖν	*to* or *for you* (p.)
Acc.	σέ	*you* (s.)	ὑμᾶς	*you* (p.)

The forms σου, σοι, and σε are unaccented except when they are emphatic. When they are emphatic, they have the accents given in the paradigm.

97. [96] The declension of the personal pronoun of the third person is as follows:

Sing.

	Masc.		**Fem.**		**Neut.**	
Nom.	αὐτός	*he*	αὐτή	*she*	αὐτό	*it*
Gen.	αὐτοῦ	*of him, his*	αὐτῆς	*of her, hers*	αὐτοῦ	*of it, its*
Dat.	αὐτῷ	*to* or *for him*	αὐτῇ	*to* or *for her*	αὐτῷ	*to* or *for it*
Acc.	αὐτόν	*him*	αὐτήν	*her*	αὐτό	*it*

Plur.

	Masc.		**Fem.**		**Neut.**	
Nom.	αὐτοί	*they*	αὐταί	*they*	αὐτά	*they*
Gen.	αὐτῶν	*of them, their*	αὐτῶν	*of them, their*	αὐτῶν	*of them, their*
Dat.	αὐτοῖς	*to* or *for them*	αὐταῖς	*to* or *for them*	αὐτοῖς	*to* or *for them*
Acc.	αὐτούς	*them*	αὐτάς	*them*	αὐτά	*them*

Note that the declension of αὐτός is like that of ἀγαθός, except for the form αὐτό in the nominative and accusative singular neuter.

98. [97] The Use of Pronouns

1. A pronoun is a word that stands instead of a noun. Example: The sentence *I see the disciple and teach him* means the same thing as *I see the disciple and teach the disciple*. The pronoun *him* stands instead of the second occurrence of the noun *disciple*.

2. The noun for which a pronoun stands is called its *antecedent*.

Thus in the sentence *I see the disciple and teach him*, the antecedent of *him* is *disciple*.

3. A pronoun agrees with its antecedent in gender[1] and number, but the case of a pronoun is determined by its function in the sentence.

Examples:

a. βλέπω τὸν μαθητὴν καὶ διδάσκω αὐτόν, *I see the disciple and teach him.* Here μαθητήν is the antecedent of αὐτόν, and since μαθητήν is of masculine gender and singular number, αὐτόν also is masculine singular. αὐτόν is accusative, however, not because μαθητήν is accusative but because it is the direct object of διδάσκω.

b. μένω ἐν τῷ οἴκῳ καὶ γινώσκω αὐτόν, *I remain in the house and know it.* Here οἴκῳ is the antecedent of αὐτόν, and since οἴκῳ is of masculine gender and singular number, αὐτόν also is masculine singular. In English the neuter pronoun *it* is used, because the noun *house*, like all nouns denoting inanimate objects, is neuter in English. But in Greek the word for house is masculine, and therefore the masculine pronoun is used in referring to it. Hence the translations, *he, she*, etc., given in the paradigm above for the masculine and feminine of the Greek pronoun of the third person are correct only when

1. Note that first- and second-person pronouns in Greek do not have different forms for gender; the same form serves for both masculine and feminine.

the antecedents are nouns denoting persons. In other cases, the pronouns will be neuter in English even when they are masculine or feminine in Greek. Observe further that the pronoun does not agree with its antecedent in case, but only in gender and number. In the sentence just given the antecedent οἴκῳ is dative after the preposition ἐν, whereas αὐτόν has its own construction, being the object of the verb γινώσκω.

c. ἡ ἐκκλησία διδάσκει ἐμέ, καὶ ἐγὼ διδάσκω αὐτήν, *the church teaches me and I teach it.* αὐτήν agrees in gender and number, but not in case, with ἐκκλησία.

d. βλέπω τοὺς μαθητὰς καὶ διδάσκω αὐτούς, *I see the disciples and teach them.*

e. βλέπω τὰ τέκνα καὶ διδάσκω αὐτά, *I see the children and teach them.* In English in the plural the personal pronoun is the same in form for all three genders, whereas in Greek it varies.

4. The personal pronouns are not used in the nominative case unless there is emphasis upon them.

a. The reason for this rule is that the ending of the verb indicates sufficiently whether the subject is first, second, or third person. Thus λέγω means *I say.* The ἐγώ, therefore, is not put in unless there is emphasis upon it.

b. Emphasis is usually caused by contrast. Thus in the sentence ἐγὼ λέγω, σὺ δὲ γράφεις, *I say, but you write,* ἐγώ and σύ are emphatic because they are contrasted with each other. And in the sentence ἐγὼ λέγω, "*I say,*" the natural inference is that someone else does *not* say. The insertion of the emphatic ἐγώ naturally suggests an implied (though here not an expressed) contrast.

c. αὐτός is almost never used as a personal pronoun in the nominative case. The place of it, in the nominative, is taken usually by certain other words, and it itself has in the nominative case a use distinct from its use as a personal pronoun. These matters will be reserved for future study.

5. To express possession, the unemphatic forms of the personal pronouns should be used, and the English phrases *my word* and the like should be turned around into the form *the word of me* before they are translated into Greek.

Examples: *my word*, ὁ λόγος μου; *your* (s.) *word*, ὁ λόγος σου; *his word*, ὁ λόγος αὐτοῦ; *her word*, ὁ λόγος αὐτῆς; *its word*, ὁ λόγος αὐτοῦ; *their word*, ὁ λόγος αὐτῶν.

6. After prepositions, the emphatic forms of the personal pronouns are ordinarily used.

Examples: ἐξ ἐμοῦ, not ἔκ μου; ἀπ᾽ ἐμοῦ,[1] not ἀπό μου; δι᾽ ἐμοῦ, not διά μου; ἐν ἐμοί, not ἔν μοι. But πρός με is common.

Present Indicative of εἰμί

99. [98] The present indicative of the verb εἰμί, *I am*, is as follows:

Sing.			**Plur.**	
1.	εἰμί	*I am*	ἐσμέν	*we are*
2.	εἶ	*you* (s.) *are*	ἐστέ	*you* (p.) *are*
3.	ἐστί(ν)	*he (she, it) is*	εἰσί(ν)	*they are*

All these forms except εἶ ordinarily occur without an accent (see below on *enclitics*). The accents given in the paradigm occur only when required by the rules given below in §101. Note, however, that εἶ should always be written with a circumflex accent to distinguish it from an entirely different word, εἰ, which means *if*.

ἐστί(ν) and εἰσί(ν) have the movable ν (see §40).

100. [99] The verb εἰμί links the subject to another word or phrase to define or describe the subject, and thus takes a predicate nominative, not an accusative, to complete its meaning.

---

1. The final vowel of prepositions is frequently elided (dropped) before words that begin with a vowel. The elision is marked by an apostrophe.

Examples: ὁ ἀπόστολος ἄνθρωπός ἐστιν, *the apostle is a man;* ὁ ἀπόστολός ἐστιν ἀγαθός, *the apostle is good.*

In the sentence *the apostle says the word,* it is asserted that the apostle does something to the word; *the word* is therefore the object of the action denoted by the verb, and stands in the accusative case. But in the sentence *the apostle is a man,* it is not asserted that the apostle does anything to a man. *A man,* therefore, stands here not in the accusative case but in the predicate nominative.

Accent Matters

Enclitics

101. [92] The unemphatic forms of first- and second-person singular pronouns (μου, μοι, με, σου, σοι, σε), and all the forms of the present indicative of εἰμί (except the second singular) are *enclitic.* An enclitic is a word that goes so closely with the preceding word as to have normally no accent of its own.

Enclitics are thus to be distinguished from *proclitics,* which go so closely with the *following* words as to have no accent of their own (see §65). Proclitics give rise to no special rules of accent; they simply have no accent and produce no changes in the accenting of preceding or following words. But the case is very different with enclitics, which give rise to the following rules:

A. Accenting of the word before an enclitic:

1. The word before an enclitic does not change an acute on the last syllable to a grave.

Example: ἀδελφὸς μου is incorrect; ἀδελφός μου is correct.

2. If the word before an enclitic has an acute on the antepenult, or a circumflex on the penult, it takes an additional accent (an acute) on the ultima.

Examples: ἄνθρωπός μου, δῶρόν σου, ἄνθρωπός ἐστιν, δῶρόν ἐστιν.

75

3. If the word before an enclitic is itself a proclitic or an enclitic, it has an acute on the ultima.

Examples: εἴς με, ἄνθρωπός μού ἐστιν.

B. Cases in which an enclitic has an accent of its own:

1. An enclitic of two syllables retains its own accent when it follows a word that has an acute on the penult.

Example: ὥρα ἐστίν is correct because ἐστίν is an enclitic of two syllables. ὥρα μου, on the other hand, is correct because μου is an enclitic of only one syllable.

2. An enclitic retains its accent when there is emphasis on the enclitic or when the enclitic begins a clause.

102. [93] It may help to fix these rules in the memory, if the enclitic in every case be regarded as forming one word with the word that precedes it and then the general rules of accent be applied. These enclitic rules may then be regarded as attempts to avoid violations of the general rules. Thus if ἄνθρωποσεστιν or ἄνθρωποσμου or ἄνθρωποσμε be regarded as one word, the accenting of that word violates the general rule that the accent cannot get further back from the end than the antepenult; and δῶρονμου violates the general rule that the circumflex cannot get further back from the end than the penult. Something, therefore, needs to be done. And what is actually done is to put in an additional accent to break up the long series of unaccented syllables. Following out a similar principle, the accent of ὥραεστιν would become ὥράεστιν. But two acutes were not desired in immediate juxtaposition in a single word. Therefore in this case an alternative way out of the difficulty was adopted, and the enclitic was made to retain its own accent.

This way of considering the matter, however, will not quite work out in all cases. ὥραμου, for example, would violate the general rule that the accent cannot stand on the antepenult if the ultima is long.

103. [100] Exercises

A. 1. οἱ μαθηταί σου γινώσκουσι τὴν βασιλείαν καὶ ἄγουσι τοὺς ἀδελφοὺς αὐτῶν εἰς αὐτήν. 2. διδάσκω τοὺς ἀδελφούς μου καὶ λέγω αὐτοῖς παραβολήν. 3. λέγει αὐτῷ, ἐγώ εἰμι ἡ ὁδὸς καὶ ἡ ἀλήθεια καὶ ἡ ζωή. 4. δι᾽ ἐμὲ βλέπεις συ τὸν θάνατον, σοὶ δὲ ἐγὼ λέγω λόγους κακούς. 5. διὰ σοῦ ἄγει ὁ θεὸς τοὺς πιστοὺς εἰς τὴν βασιλείαν αὐτοῦ καὶ δι᾽ αὐτῶν τοὺς ἄλλους. 6. δι᾽ ἡμᾶς μένει ὁ κύριος ἐν τῷ κόσμῳ. 7. ἐγώ εἰμι δοῦλος, σὺ δὲ ἀπόστολος. 8. ἀγαθός ἐστιν ὁ κύριος καὶ ἀγαθοί ἐστε ὑμεῖς. 9. μαθηταί ἐστε τοῦ κυρίου καὶ ἀδελφοὶ τῶν ἀποστόλων αὐτοῦ. 10. ὁ ἀπόστολος πιστός ἐστιν, οἱ δὲ δοῦλοι αὐτοῦ κακοί. 11. ἡ ἐκκλησία πιστή ἐστιν, ἡμεῖς δὲ βλέπομεν αὐτήν. 12. βλέπομέν σε καὶ λέγομέν σοι παραβολήν. 13. δοῦλοι ἐσμέν, δούλους δὲ διδάσκομεν. 14. οἱ δοῦλοι ἡμῶν βλέπουσιν ἡμᾶς, ἡμεῖς δὲ διδάσκομεν αὐτούς. 15. ἀφ᾽ ὑμῶν[1] λαμβάνει ὁ ἀδελφός μου δῶρα καλά, καὶ πέμπει αὐτὰ πρός με διὰ τῶν δούλων αὐτοῦ. 16. γινώσκομεν τὴν ὁδόν, καὶ δι᾽ αὐτῆς ἄγομέν σε εἰς τὸν οἶκον ἡμῶν. 17. μετὰ τῶν ἀδελφῶν ἡμῶν βλέπομεν τοὺς μαθητὰς τοῦ κυρίου ἡμῶν. 18. μετὰ τὰς ἡμέρας τὰς κακὰς βλέπομεν τὴν βασιλείαν τοῦ κυρίου ἡμῶν. 19. μεθ᾽ ἡμῶν[2] βλέπεις αὐτόν. 20. μεθ᾽ ὑμῶν ἐσμεν ἐν τοῖς οἴκοις ὑμῶν.

B. 1. Your (p.) servants are in the house of the Lord. 2. My house is in the desert. 3. The prophet knows his disciples and brings them into his houses. 4. Through my word you (p.) have glory. 5. On account of our children you (p.) see evil days. 6. In our days the world is evil. 7. God knows our souls and brings them out of death. 8. You (p.) are our sons, and we are your disciples. 9. We are in the kingdom of God with your (s.) faithful disciples. 10. We say a parable to you (s.), but you are saying another word to us. 11. The way is

1. Before the rough breathing, the π of ἀπ᾽ becomes φ.
2. Before the rough breathing, τ of μετ᾽ becomes θ.

bad, but we lead the children in it. 12. My brother takes gifts from you (p.), but you write an evil word to him. 13. My house is bad, but your (p.) disciples bring the children out of it. 14. My disciples are leading their brothers to me. 15. I see and know my sons and lead them to my Lord. 16. God knows his church and leads it out of death into his kingdom. 17. Your (s.) commandments are good and righteous, and lead us into life. 18. Our Lord is sending his apostles to me. 19. We are sending our servants into your (p.) house, but you are taking our gifts from us. 20. You (p.) are good, but your disciples are evil.

Lesson 9

*Adverbs • The Demonstrative Pronouns οὗτος
and ἐκεῖνος • Further Uses of αὐτός*

104. [101] Vocabulary

ἀγάπη, ἡ, *love*
ἁμαρτία, ἡ, *a sin, sin*
βαπτίζω, *I baptize*
διδάσκαλος, ὁ, *a teacher*
ἐκεῖνος, -η, -ο, pron., *that*
ἐπαγγελία, ἡ, *a promise*
εὐαγγέλιον, τό, *a gospel*
κρίνω, *I judge*

νῦν, adv., *now*
οὗτος, αὕτη, τοῦτο, pron., *this*
οὕτως, adv., *thus, so*
πονηρός, -ά, -όν, adj., *evil*
πρόσωπον, τό, *a face*
χαρά, ἡ, *joy*

105. Adverbs modify a verb, an adjective, or another adverb. They indicate the manner, time, or circumstances of an action or attribute. Adverbs are not declined—they always have the same form.

106. [102] Demonstrative pronouns are pronouns that point. The "near" demonstrative pronoun οὗτος, *this,* which points to something close at hand, is declined as follows:

| | **Sing.** | | | **Plur.** | | |
	Masc.	**Fem.**	**Neut.**	**Masc.**	**Fem.**	**Neut.**
Nom.	οὗτος	αὕτη	τοῦτο	οὗτοι	αὗται	ταῦτα
Gen.	τούτου	ταύτης	τούτου	τούτων	τούτων	τούτων
Dat.	τούτῳ	ταύτῃ	τούτῳ	τούτοις	ταύταις	τούτοις
Acc.	τοῦτον	ταύτην	τοῦτο	τούτους	ταύτας	ταῦτα

The puzzling variations between ου and αυ in the first syllable of this word may be more easily remembered if it be observed that an o-vowel (in the diphthong ου) stands in the first syllable where an o-vowel (o or the long of it, ω) stands in the second syllable, and an α-vowel (in the diphthong αυ) stands in the first syllable where an α-vowel (α or the closely related vowel η) stands in the second syllable.

107. [103] The declension of the "far" demonstrative pronoun ἐκεῖνος, *that,* is like the declension of adjectives in -ος, -η, -ον, except that ἐκεῖνο stands instead of ἐκεῖνον in the nominative and accusative singular neuter.

108. [104] Use of the Demonstrative Pronouns οὗτος **and** ἐκεῖνος

1. οὗτος and ἐκεῖνος are frequently used with nouns. When they are so used, the noun with which they are used has the article, and they themselves stand in the predicate, not in the attributive, position (see §§69–75), whether they are used as a predicate or not.

Examples: *This word,* οὗτος ὁ λόγος or ὁ λόγος οὗτος; *that word,* ἐκεῖνος ὁ λόγος or ὁ λόγος ἐκεῖνος; *I see this church,* βλέπω ταύτην τὴν ἐκκλησίαν (or τὴν ἐκκλησίαν ταύτην); *these words,* οὗτοι οἱ λόγοι or οἱ λόγοι οὗτοι; *those words,* ἐκεῖνοι οἱ λόγοι or οἱ λόγοι ἐκεῖνοι; *this good word,* οὗτος ὁ καλὸς λόγος or ὁ καλὸς λόγος οὗτος.

2. οὗτος and ἐκεῖνος are frequently used by themselves, without nouns, in the same way as substantive adjectives (see §76), though demonstratives have no article, of course.

Examples: οὗτος, *this man* (or *this person*); αὕτη, *this woman;* τοῦτο, *this thing;* οὗτοι, *these men;* αὗται, *these women;* ταῦτα, *these things.*

3. The English word *that* represents several notions corresponding to different words in Greek. In the sentence *that word is true,* the word *that* is a demonstrative pronoun, for which Greek uses ἐκεῖνος. But *that* can also introduce a relative clause, as in the sentence *the words that Moses spoke are true.* Here a quite different word, or perhaps a different syntactical construction entirely, would be used in Greek. The word *that* can also introduce indirect discourse, as in *Moses said that his words were true.* The student must be careful to differentiate between the various uses of *that.*

109. [105] Further Uses of αὐτός

In addition to its use as a personal pronoun of the third person, αὐτός is also used adjectivally, modifying a noun that appears in the sentence, rather than standing in the place of a noun. When used adjectivally, αὐτός may be in either the attributive or predicate position, agreeing in gender, number, and case with the noun it modifies.

1. In the attributive position (preceded by an article), αὐτός means *same.* In this case it functions just like any other attributive adjective.

Examples: ὁ αὐτὸς ἀπόστολος or ὁ ἀπόστολος ὁ αὐτός, *the same apostle;* ἡ αὐτὴ ἐκκλησία or ἡ ἐκκλησία ἡ αὐτή, *the same church;* τοῖς αὐτοῖς δούλοις or τοῖς δούλοις τοῖς αὐτοῖς, *to or for the same servants.*

81

2. As with other attributive adjectives, αὐτός can be used substantively.
Examples: ὁ αὐτός, *the same man*; ἡ αὐτή, *the same woman;* τὸ αὐτό, *the same thing.*
3. In the predicate position, αὐτός intensifies the noun it modifies. In English we translate the intensifier with a -self word, such as *himself, herself, itself, themselves, yourselves,* etc.
Examples: αὐτὸς ὁ ἀπόστολος or ὁ ἀπόστολος αὐτός, *the apostle himself;* αὐτὴ ἡ ἐκκλησία or ἡ ἐκκλησία αὐτή, *the church itself;* αὐτοῖς τοῖς δούλοις or τοῖς δούλοις αὐτοῖς, *to or for the servants themselves.*
4. In its intensive use, αὐτός often goes with pronouns, or with the unexpressed subject of a verb.
Examples: αὐτὸς ἐγὼ λέγω or αὐτὸς λέγω, *I myself say;* αὐτὸς σὺ λέγεις or αὐτὸς λέγεις, *you* (s.) *yourself say;* αὐτὸς λέγει, *he himself says;* αὐτὴ λέγει, *she herself says;* αὐτοὶ ἡμεῖς λέγομεν or αὐτοὶ λέγομεν, *we ourselves say.*
Notice that αὐτός is used to intensify not just third-person subjects, but also those of the first and second person.
5. Both the attributive and intensive uses of αὐτός may occur in any case.
Examples: τοῖς ἀνθρώποις αὐτοῖς, *to the men themselves;* τῆς αὐτῆς ὥρας, *of the same hour.*
Therefore context will sometimes be the only indication whether, for example, τοῦ λόγου αὐτοῦ means *of his word* or *of the word itself.*
The student should be careful not to confuse the feminine intensive αὐτή with the feminine demonstrative pronoun αὕτη. Both occur in the predicate position, but note that the breathing mark of the demonstrative is rough, and its accent is on the first syllable.
110. [106] The principal uses of adjectives and of the pronouns studied thus far may be reviewed as follows:

The good word =	ὁ καλὸς λόγος or ὁ λόγος ὁ καλός	Attributive position
The word is good =	καλὸς ὁ λόγος or ὁ λόγος καλός	Predicate position
This word =	οὗτος ὁ λόγος or ὁ λόγος οὗτος	Predicate position
That word =	ἐκεῖνος ὁ λόγος or ὁ λόγος ἐκεῖνος	Predicate position
The word itself =	αὐτὸς ὁ λόγος or ὁ λόγος αὐτός	Predicate position
The same word =	ὁ αὐτὸς λόγος or ὁ λόγος ὁ αὐτός	Attributive position

My word =	ὁ λόγος μου
His word =	ὁ λόγος αὐτοῦ
I see him =	βλέπω αὐτόν
I see this man =	βλέπω τοῦτον
I see these things =	βλέπω ταῦτα

111. [107] Exercises

A. 1. οὗτοι οἱ διδάσκαλοι κρίνουσιν αὐτὸν τὸν ἀπόστολον.
2. ὁ δὲ αὐτὸς διδάσκαλος ἔχει τὴν αὐτὴν χαρὰν ἐν τῇ καρδίᾳ

83

αὐτοῦ. 3. νῦν λαμβάνω αὐτὸς τὸ αὐτὸ εὐαγγέλιον ἀπὸ τοῦ κυρίου μου. 4. οὗτος βλέπει ἐκεῖνον καὶ κρίνει αὐτόν. 5. μετὰ ταῦτα ἔχετε αὐτοὶ τὴν ἀγάπην τοῦ κυρίου ἐν ταῖς καρδίαις ὑμῶν. 6. οὗτοι ἔχουσι χαράν, ἐκεῖνοι δὲ ἔχουσιν ἁμαρτίαν. 7. αὕτη δέ ἐστιν ἡ φωνὴ τοῦ κυρίου αὐτοῦ. 8. οὕτως γινώσκομεν τοῦτον καὶ βλέπομεν τὸ πρόσωπον αὐτοῦ. 9. λαμβάνομεν ταῦτα τὰ δῶρα ἀπὸ τοῦ αὐτοῦ καὶ βλέπομεν αὐτόν. 10. αὐτὸς βαπτίζεις ἐκεῖνον καὶ εἰ ἀδελφὸς αὐτοῦ. 11. εἰς τὴν αὐτὴν ἐκκλησίαν ἄγομεν τού-τους τοὺς διδασκάλους ἡμῶν τοὺς ἀγαθούς. 12. αὐτὸς ἐγὼ ἔχω ταύτην τὴν ἐπαγγελίαν τοῦ κυρίου μου. 13. αὕτη βλέπει τὸ πρόσωπον τοῦ κυρίου αὐτῆς. 14. αὐτὴ γινώσκει αὐτὴν τὴν ἀλή-θειαν. 15. ἀγαθή ἐστιν ἡ ἐπαγγελία σου καὶ ἀγαθὴ εἶ αὐτή. 16. ἐκεῖνοί εἰσιν μαθηταὶ τοῦ αὐτοῦ διδασκάλου. 17. οὗτός ἐστιν διδάσκαλος ἐκείνου, ἐκεῖνος δὲ τούτου. 18. οὗτος διδάσκει τοὺς ἀγαθοὺς καὶ αὐτός ἐστιν ἀγαθός. 19. μετὰ τὰς ἡμέρας ἐκείνας διδάσκαλοί ἐσμεν τούτων τῶν δούλων. 20. μετὰ τῶν πιστῶν ἔχομεν ἐπαγγελίας ἀγαθάς, οἱ δὲ πονηροὶ βλέπουσιν ἡμέρας κακάς.

B. 1. These churches know the Lord himself. 2. The same disciples know him and see his face. 3. Those teachers judge the same churches and lead them into the same joy. 4. We ourselves have this sin in our hearts. 5. This is the love of our God. 6. These are the faithful churches of our Lord. 7. The apostle himself baptizes his brothers and leads them to you (s.). 8. Through this gospel we have life. 9. On account of these teachers we see death. 10. He himself knows us, and from him we receive this promise. 11. On account of the same gospel we ourselves send these apostles to you (p.). 12. Into this world he sends the Lord himself. 13. I see this man, and the broth-ers see him. 14. Now we are baptizing those disciples of our Lord and are sending the same disciples into the desert. 15. My disciples know my voice and bring these things to me. 16. Through these things we bring the same gospel into the same world. 17. We are disciples of the Lord, but you are disciples of the evil one. 18. This sin leads our children into death. 19. The sins of these churches are leading other men into the same sins. 20. His disciples have this sin in their hearts and are teaching men so. 21. I know the sins of the disciples and the disciples themselves.

Lesson 10

Present Passive and Middle Indicative • Deponent Verbs • ὑπό with the Genitive • The Dative of Means • Compound Verbs • The Position of οὐ • Various Cases with Verbs

112. [108] Vocabulary

ἀκούω, *I hear* (may take the genitive, but also takes the accusative)

ἀλλά, conj., *but* (stronger adversative than δέ)[1]

ἁμαρτωλός, ὁ, *a sinner*

ἀποκρίνομαι, dep., *I answer* (takes the dative)

ἄρχω, *I rule* (takes the genitive); middle, *I begin*

γίνομαι, dep., *I become* (takes a predicate nominative, not an accusative)

διέρχομαι, dep., *I go through*

εἰσέρχομαι, dep., *I go in, I enter*

ἐξέρχομαι, dep., *I go out*

ἔρχομαι, dep., *I come, I go*

ὅτι, conj., *that, because*

οὐ (οὐκ before vowels, οὐχ before the rough breathing), proclitic, *not*

πορεύομαι, dep., *I go*

σώζω, *I save*

ὑπό, prep. with gen., *by* (expressing agent); with accusative, *under*

---

1. The conjunction ἀλλά, *but* (accent on the ultima), should be distinguished from the neuter plural adjective ἄλλα (from ἄλλος), which means *other things*.

113. [109a] There are three voices in Greek: active, middle, and passive.

The *active* and the *passive* voices are used as in English. In active voice the subject is performing the action. In passive voice the subject is being acted upon.

114. [112] The present passive indicative of λύω is as follows:

Sing.		**Plur.**	
1. λύομαι	*I am being loosed*	λυόμεθα	*we are being loosed*
2. λύῃ	*you (s.) are being loosed*	λύεσθε	*you (p.) are being loosed*
3. λύεται	*he (she, it) is being loosed*	λύονται	*they are being loosed*

115. [111] The personal endings in the passive (and the middle as well; see below) of the so-called *primary tenses* are -μαι, -σαι, -ται, -μεθα, -σθε, -νται. These we will sometimes refer to as the "primary B" endings. Between the stem and the personal endings is placed a connecting vowel, called the *theme vowel*. In the progressive system, which includes the present and imperfect tenses, the theme vowel varies between o and ε (o standing before μ and ν; ε before other letters). The second-person singular, λύῃ (note well the iota subscript under the η), is a shortened form for λύεσαι. Thus the present passive indicative of λύομαι is conjugated by adding to the stem λυ- the endings -ομαι, -ῃ, -εται, -ομεθα, -εσθε, -ονται.[1]

116. [113] The present active indicative, λύω, remember, may be translated either *I loose* or *I am loosing*. The passive

1. The variable o/ε theme vowel also appears in the present active indicative (see §18), preceding the "primary A" endings (-ω, -ις, -ι, -μεν, -τε, -ουσι), but in the present active the theme vowel is sometimes obscured by absorption into the ending.

of *I loose,* in English, is *I am loosed;* the passive of *I am loosing* is *I am being loosed.* Both *I am loosed* and *I am being loosed* might, therefore, have been given in the translation of λύομαι (passive). But *I am loosed* could mean *I am now in a loosed condition,* in which case it indicates a present state resultant upon a past action and would be translated into Greek, not by the present tense, but by the perfect tense. Therefore, since *I am loosed* is ambiguous, the student is advised, at least in the earlier lessons, always to adopt the translations *I am being loosed, you are being loosed,* etc., for the present passive.

Example: σώζομαι means *I am being saved.* It represents the action as taking place at the present time. It could also be translated *I am saved* in such a sentence as *every day I am saved from some new trouble.* Here *I am saved* is present because it indicates customary action. But in the majority of cases *I am saved* means *I am in a saved condition resultant upon an action that took place in the past,* which would correspond to the Greek perfect tense, not to the Greek present tense. It will be seen, therefore, that the translation *I am loosed* for λύομαι, though it is not wrong (since λύομαι may sometimes be translated in this way), could be misleading.

117. [109b] The *middle* voice represents the subject as acting in some way that concerns itself, or as acting upon something that belongs to itself. For example, ἐνδύω means *I dress (someone else),* whereas ἐνδύομαι means *I get dressed.* Unlike the passive, however, the meaning of the middle is usually quite unpredictable, and in the case of some verbs it is easiest to learn the middle voice as though it were a different word. Thus ἄρχω means *I rule,* but ἄρχομαι (middle) does not mean *I rule myself;* it means *I begin.*

118. [109c] The middle of λύω does not occur in the New Testament. But it is very important to learn it, since it will enable the student to recognize the middle of other verbs. The translations given in the paradigms for the middle of λύω serve to indicate, in a rough sort of way, the general function of the middle voice rather than the actual meaning of the middle voice of this particular verb.[1]

119. [110] The middle voice in the present is conjugated exactly like the passive. The present middle indicative of λύω is as follows:

Sing.		**Plur.**	
1. λύομαι	*I loose* or *am loosing for myself*	λυόμεθα	*we loose* or *are loosing for ourselves*
2. λύῃ	*you* (s.) *loose* or *are loosing for yourself*	λύεσθε	*you* (p.) *loose* or *are loosing for yourselves*
3. λύεται	*he (she, it) looses* or *is loosing for him- (her-, it-)self*	λύονται	*they loose* or *are loosing for themselves*

120. [109d] The same endings that were used to form the passive are here affixed to form the middle voice. In certain other tenses they are entirely distinct. This may seem like it could lead to confusion; in the exercises for the lessons in this grammar, if a form could be either middle or passive, it should be translated as a passive.

121. [116] Deponent Verbs

Several verbs occur not in the active voice in the New Testament but only in the middle or passive voice, with an essentially active meaning. These are called *deponent* verbs. In fact, there are very few middle-voice verbs in the New Testament

---

1. For the curious, the middle λύομαι in Greek literature meant *I redeem* (from slavery), but the New Testament uses an entirely different word for *redeem*.

that occur in the active voice as well, and thus almost all of the middle-voice verbs we will encounter are deponent.[1] These deponent verbs, whether middle or passive, are ordinarily translated by an English word in the active voice. For example, πορεύομαι (middle) means *I go*, not *I am going for myself* or *I am being gone* or the like.

122. [114] ὑπό with the Genitive

The preposition ὑπό with the genitive expresses the *agent* by which an action is performed. This usage occurs principally with the passive voice.

Example: ὁ ἀπόστολος λύει τὸν δοῦλον means *the apostle looses the servant.* If the same thought be expressed by the passive voice, the object of the active verb becomes the subject of the passive, and the subject of the active verb becomes the genitive object of ὑπό. Thus ὁ δοῦλος λύεται ὑπὸ τοῦ ἀποστόλου means *the servant is being loosed by the apostle.*

123. [115] The Dative of Means

The simple dative without any preposition sometimes expresses *means* or *instrument.*
Examples:
1. ἐγείρονται τῷ λόγῳ τοῦ κυρίου, *they are being raised up by* (by means of) *the word of the Lord.* Compare ἐγείρονται ὑπὸ τοῦ κυρίου, *they are being raised up by the Lord.* The comparison will serve to distinguish ὑπό with the genitive (expressing the active personal agent) from the dative expressing means. Generally, an agent (ὑπό with genitive) is a person; a means (dative) is a thing or action.

---

1. Therefore, rarely is there any uncertainty as to whether a word is passive in meaning or a middle.

2. ἄγομεν τοὺς δούλους μετὰ τῶν υἱῶν αὐτῶν λόγοις καλοῖς, *we are leading the servants with their sons with good words.* This example will serve to distinguish the dative expressing means from μετά with the genitive expressing accompaniment. The two ideas, though they are logically quite distinct, happen often to be expressed by the same preposition, *with,* in English. μετά with the genitive means *with* in the sense of *in company with;* the dative means *with* in the sense of *by means of.*

Sometimes the dative of means occurs with the preposition ἐν. Thus ἐν λόγῳ can mean *by means of* (or *with*) *a word.*

124. [117] Compound Verbs

Prepositions are frequently prefixed to verbs. The meaning of the verb is modified by the preposition in a way that is sometimes easily understood from the common meaning of the preposition. But the matter is not always so simple; frequently the meaning of the compound verb cannot easily be determined from the separate meanings of its two component parts.

Example: ἐκ means *out of,* and πορεύομαι means *I go.* Hence ἐκπορεύομαι means *I go out.* But the meaning of ἀποκρίνομαι, *I answer,* is not easily derived from the meanings of its component parts (ἀπο = *from;* κρίνομαι = *I am being judged*).

125. [118] The Position of οὐ

The negative, οὐ, precedes the word that it negates. And since in the great majority of cases the negative in a sentence negates the verb, the normal place of οὐ is immediately before the verb.

Examples: οὐ λύω, *I do not loose,* or *I am not loosing;* οὐ λύομαι, *I am not being loosed.*

Lesson 10

126. [119] Various Cases with Verbs

Many verbs take the genitive case and many the dative case
to complete their meaning, where the corresponding verbs in
English take a direct object.

Examples: ἀκούω τῆς φωνῆς, *I hear the voice* (but ἀκούω
may also take the accusative); ἀποκρίνομαι τῷ ἀποστόλῳ, *I
answer the apostle.*

127. [120] Exercises

A. 1. λύονται οὗτοι οἱ δοῦλοι ὑπὸ τοῦ κυρίου. 2. τῷ λόγῳ τοῦ
κυρίου ἀγόμεθα εἰς τὴν ἐκκλησίαν τοῦ θεοῦ. 3. οὐκ ἀκούετε τῆς
φωνῆς τοῦ προφήτου, ἀλλ᾿¹ ἐξέρχεσθε ἐκ τοῦ οἴκου αὐτοῦ. 4. τῷ
λόγῳ αὐτοῦ τοῦ κυρίου γίνεσθε μαθηταὶ αὐτοῦ. 5. ἐκεῖνοι οἱ
ἀγαθοὶ διδάσκαλοι οὐκ εἰσέρχονται εἰς τοὺς οἴκους τῶν
ἁμαρτωλῶν. 6. οὐ βαπτίζονται οἱ ἁμαρτωλοὶ ὑπὸ τῶν ἀποστόλων, ἀλλ᾿ ἐξέρχονται ἐκ τούτων τῶν οἴκων πρὸς ἄλλους
διδασκάλους. 7. λέγετε ἐκείνοις τοῖς ἁμαρτωλοῖς ὅτι σώζεσθε
ὑπὸ τοῦ θεοῦ ἀπὸ τῶν ἁμαρτιῶν ὑμῶν. 8. ἄρχει αὐτὸς ὁ θεὸς τῆς
βασιλείας αὐτοῦ. 9. εἰρήνην ἔχει ἡ ἐκκλησία, ὅτι σώζεται ὑπό
τοῦ κυρίου αὐτῆς. 10. οὐκ ἀποκρινόμεθα τῷ ἀποστόλῳ ὅτι οὐ
γινώσκομεν αὐτόν. 11. οὐχ ὑπὸ τῶν μαθητῶν σώζῃ ἀπὸ τῶν
ἁμαρτιῶν σου, ἀλλ᾿ ὑπ᾿ αὐτοῦ τοῦ θεοῦ. 12. οὐ πορεύῃ ἐν τῇ ὁδῷ
τῇ κακῇ, ἀλλὰ σώζῃ ἀπὸ τῶν ἁμαρτιῶν σου καὶ οἱ ἀδελφοί σου
ἀκούουσι τῆς φωνῆς τοῦ κυρίου. 13. μετὰ τῶν ἀδελφῶν αὐτοῦ
ἄγεται εἰς τὴν βασιλείαν τοῦ θεοῦ τῇ φωνῇ τῶν ἀποστόλων.
14. οὐ γίνῃ μαθητὴς τοῦ κυρίου, ὅτι οὐκ εἰσέρχῃ εἰς τὴν ἐκκλησίαν αὐτοῦ. 15. ὁ ἀδελφός μου ἐν λόγῳ σώζεται ὑπὸ τοῦ κυρίου
τοῦ αὐτοῦ. 16. δοῦλοι οὐκ ἐστε, ἀλλὰ υἱοί.

---

1. The final vowel of ἀλλά is often elided before a word that begins
with a vowel. The elision is marked by an apostrophe.

B. 1. These churches are being saved by God from death.
2. I am being saved by him and am being taught by his word.
3. We are becoming disciples of the good apostle, but you (p.)
are not hearing his voice. 4. I am a sinner, but am being taught
by the apostles of the Lord. 5. I am an evil servant, but you
are becoming a teacher of this church. 6. The evil men say to
those churches that our brothers do not see the face of the
Lord. 7. The world is being destroyed by the word of our God.
8. We know the Lord because we receive good gifts from him
and are being taught by him in parables. 9. You (s.) are writing these things to your brothers and are being saved from
your sin. 10. He is teaching others and is himself being taught
by this apostle. 11. That disciple is not answering this prophet,
because he does not know his words. 12. You are saying to
this church that you are a bad servant. 13. You are abiding in
that temple, because you are not servants of the Lord. 14. We
do not see the faces of our Lord's disciples,[1] because we are
not in their houses. 15. In our Lord's house are joy and peace.
16. God rules this world by his word. 17. These sinners are
not entering into the Lord's house, but are going out into the
desert. 18. These words are being written by God to his faithful churches.

1. The phrase should be turned around into the form *the disciples of
our Lord* before it is translated into Greek. A similar transposition should
be made in other similar phrases.

Lesson 11

*Imperfect Active Indicative • Augment
of Compound Verbs • Imperfect Indicative of εἰμί*

128. [121] Vocabulary

αἴρω, *I take up, I take away*

ἀναβαίνω, *I go up* (ἀνα-
means *up.*)

ἀποθνήσκω, *I die*

ἀποκτείνω, *I kill*

ἀποστέλλω, *I send* (πέμπω is
the general word for *send,*
while ἀποστέλλω means *I
send with a commission.*)

ἄρτος, ὁ, *a piece of bread, a
loaf, bread*

βαίνω, *I go* (The simple verb
does not occur in the
New Testament, but the
compounds with various

prepositions are exceed-
ingly common.)

ἐσθίω, *I eat*

κατά, prep. with gen., *against;*
with acc., *according to*
(κατά, of which the original meaning was *down,*
has many meanings in the
New Testament.)

καταβαίνω, *I go down*

μέν . . . δέ, *on the one hand . . .
on the other* (Used in contrasts, the μέν often is best
left untranslated and the
δέ then best translated
by *but.*)

οὐκέτι, adv., *no longer*
παρά, prep. with gen., *from;* with dat., *beside, in the presence of;* with acc., *alongside of*
παραλαμβάνω, *I receive, I take along*

σύν, prep. with dat., *with* (a close synonym of μετά with gen.)
συνάγω, *I gather together*
τότε, adv., *then*

129. [122] The *imperfect* tense is the past form of the progressive system, just as the present tense is the present form of the progressive system.[1] But while the present tense in Greek may mean either simple present action or continuous action in the present, Greek sharply distinguishes simple past action from continuous or repeated action in the past.

Greek imperfect can sometimes be translated with an English simple past, because English simple past can sometimes mean a continuous or repeated action (e.g., *last year I walked a mile every day*). But it is better at this point for the student always to translate the Greek imperfect with the English imperfect. Thus ἐλύομεν means *we were loosing*. The simple past *we loosed* is better reserved for the *aorist* tense, which will be introduced in lesson 14.

130. [123] The imperfect active indicative of λύω is as follows:

Sing.		**Plur.**	
1.	ἔλυον	*I was loosing*	ἐλύομεν	*we were loosing*
2.	ἔλυες	*you (s.) were loosing*	ἐλύετε	*you (p.) were loosing*
3.	ἔλυε(ν)	*he (she, it) was loosing*	ἔλυον	*they were loosing*

1. The imperfect tense would therefore be better named the *past progressive*, but the term *imperfect* is so common in grammars that it is retained here as well.

95

131. [124] The imperfect indicative, like the indicative of the other *secondary* (past time) tenses (see §18 footnote), places an *augment* at the beginning of the stem of the verb.

132. [125] In verbs that begin with a consonant, the augment consists of an ἐ- prefixed to the stem.

Examples: ἔλυον, *I was loosing;* ἐγίνωσκον, *I was knowing.*

133. [126] In verbs that begin with a vowel, the augment consists in the lengthening of that vowel. But α lengthens not to long α but to η.

Examples: The imperfect of ἐγείρω is ἤγειρον; of ἀκούω, ἤκουον; of αἴρω, ἦρον (note that the ι becomes a subscript).

134. [127] The personal endings in the active of the *secondary tenses* (the "secondary A" endings) are as follows:

	Sing.	**Plur.**
1.	-ν	-μεν
2.	-ς	-τε
3.	none	-ν (or -σαν)

135. [128] The theme vowel (the variable vowel placed between the stem and the personal endings) is, in the imperfect as in the present, ο before μ and ν, and ε before other letters. Thus the imperfect active endings, added on to the augmented stem, are -ον, -ες, -ε, -ομεν, -ετε, -ον.

136. [130] Observe that the first-person singular and the third-person plural are alike in form. Only the context can determine whether ἔλυον means *I was loosing* or *they were loosing.*

137. [129] The third-person singular, ἔλυε(ν), has the movable ν (under the conditions mentioned in §40).

Augment of Compound Verbs

138. [131] In compound verbs (see §124), the augment comes after the preposition and before the stem. This addition may then change the prepositional prefix. If the preposition ends with a vowel, that vowel is usually dropped both before a verb that begins with a vowel and before the augment. The prefix ἐκ is changed to ἐξ before the augment.

Examples: The imperfect of ἐκβάλλω is ἐξέβαλλον; of ἀποκτείνω, ἀπέκτεινον; of καταβαίνω, κατέβαινον; of συνάγω, συνῆγον.

139. [133] Imperfect Indicative of εἰμί

The imperfect indicative of εἰμί is as follows:

	Sing.		**Plur.**	
1.	ἤμην	*I was*	ἦμεν	*we were*
2.	ἦς	*you* (s.) *were*	ἦτε	*you* (p.) *were*
3.	ἦν	*he (she, it) was*	ἦσαν	*they were*

Though the resemblance to the regular imperfect is noticeable, the differences are significant enough that the student should memorize this paradigm separately. Especially notice that the ν of the third-person singular ἦν is *not* movable.

Accent Matters

140. [134] *Accent of* ἔστι(ν)

After οὐκ and certain other words the third-person singular present indicative of εἰμί is accented on the first syllable. This does not apply to the other forms of εἰμί. Thus οὐκ ἔστιν, but οὐκ ἐσμεν, etc.

141. [132] Notice that in compound verbs the accent does not go back of the augment. Thus συνῆγον is correct, not σύνηγον.

142. [135] Exercises

A. 1. ἠκούομεν τῆς φωνῆς αὐτοῦ ἐν ἐκείναις ταῖς ἡμέραις, νῦν δὲ οὐκέτι ἀκούομεν αὐτῆς. 2. ὁ δὲ μαθητὴς τοῦ κυρίου ἔλεγε παραβολὴν τοῖς ἀδελφοῖς αὐτοῦ. 3. ἀπέκτεινον οἱ δοῦλοι τὰ τέκνα σὺν τοῖς μαθηταῖς. 4. τότε μὲν κατέβαινον εἰς τὸν οἶκον, νῦν δὲ οὐκέτι καταβαίνω. 5. παρελαμβάνετε τὸν ἄρτον παρὰ τῶν δούλων καὶ ἠσθίετε αὐτόν. 6. διὰ τὴν ἀλήθειαν ἀπέθνησκον οἱ μαθηταὶ ἐν ταῖς ἡμέραις ἐκείναις. 7. συνῆγεν οὗτος ὁ ἀπόστολος εἰς τὴν ἐκκλησίαν τοὺς μαθητὰς τοῦ κυρίου ἡμῶν. 8. νῦν μὲν διδασκόμεθα ὑπὸ τῶν ἀποστόλων, τότε δὲ ἐδιδάσκομεν ἡμεῖς τὴν ἐκκλησίαν. 9. ὁ κύριος ἡμῶν ἦρε τὰς ἁμαρτίας ἡμῶν. 10. τότε μὲν ἀνέβαινον εἰς τὸ ἱερόν, νῦν δὲ οὐκέτι ἀναβαίνουσιν. 11. πονηροὶ ἦτε, ἀγαθοὶ δὲ ἐστέ. 12. ὑμεῖς μέν ἐστε ἀγαθοί, ἡμεῖς δέ ἐσμεν πονηροί. 13. τότε ἤμην ἐν τῷ ἱερῷ καὶ ἐδίδασκέ με ὁ κύριος. 14. λέγομεν ὑμῖν ὅτι ἐν τῷ οἴκῳ ὑμῶν ἦμεν. 15. ἐξέβαλλες αὐτοὺς ἐκ τοῦ ἱεροῦ. 16. ἀπέστελλον οἱ ἄνθρωποι τοὺς δούλους αὐτῶν πρός με. 17. ὁ κύριος ἀπέστελλεν ἀγγέλους πρὸς ἡμᾶς. 18. ἐν τῷ κόσμῳ ἦν καὶ ὁ κόσμος οὐκ ἔβλεπεν αὐτόν. 19. δοῦλος ἦς τοῦ πονηροῦ, ἀλλὰ νῦν οὐκέτι εἶ δοῦλος. 20. τοῦτό ἐστι τὸ δῶρον τοῦ ἀνθρώπου, καλὸν δὲ οὐκ ἔστιν. 21. ἐν ἀρχῃ[1] ἦν ὁ λόγος, καὶ ὁ λόγος ἦν πρὸς τὸν θεόν, καὶ θεὸς ἦν ὁ λόγος.

B. 1. The servant was saying these words against them. 2. According to the word of the apostle, they were going up into the temple. 3. The Lord was in his temple. 4. They were killing our children. 5. You (p.) were dying in those days on account of the kingdom of God. 6. You (s.) were taking away the sins of your disciples. 7. The prophet was sending the same servants into the small house. 8. We are no longer sinners, because we are being saved by the Lord from the sin of our hearts. 9. I was receiving this bread from the apostle's servants. 10. Then he was writing these things to his brothers.

1. ἀρχή, ἡ, *a beginning*.

11. In that hour we were in the desert with the Lord. 12. They are good, but they were evil. 13. You (s.) were good, but we were sinners. 14. Then I was a servant, but now I am a son. 15. The sons of the prophets were gathering these things together into the temple. 16. Now I am being sent by the Lord to the children of the disciples, but then I was sending the righteous men into the desert.

Lesson 12

Imperfect Middle and Passive Indicative
• *Singular Verb with Neuter Plural Subject*
• *Uses of καί and οὐδέ* • *Summary*
of Progressive Indicatives

143. [136] Vocabulary

ἀπέρχομαι, dep., *I go away*
βιβλίον, τό, *a book*
δαιμόνιον, τό, *a demon*
δέχομαι, dep., *I receive*
ἐκπορεύομαι, dep., *I go out*
ἔργον, τό, *a work*
ἔτι, adv., *still, yet*
θάλασσα, ἡ, *a lake, a sea*
καί, conj., *and, also, even;*
    καί . . . καί, *both . . . and*
κατέρχομαι, dep., *I go down*

οὐδέ, conj., *and not, nor, not*
    even; οὐδέ . . . οὐδέ, *nei-*
    ther . . . nor
οὔπω, adv., *not yet*
περί, prep. with gen., *con-*
    cerning, about; with acc.,
    around
πλοῖον, τό, *a boat*
συνέρχομαι, dep., *I come*
    together
ὑπέρ, prep. with gen., *in*
    behalf of; with acc., *above*

144. [137] As in the present tense, so also in the imperfect, the middle and passive voices are alike in form.

145. [138] The imperfect middle indicative of λύω is as follows:

	Sing.		**Plur.**	
1.	ἐλυόμην	*I was loosing for myself*	ἐλυόμεθα	*we were loosing for ourselves*
2.	ἐλύου	*you (s.) were loosing for yourself*	ἐλύεσθε	*you (p.) were loosing for yourselves*
3.	ἐλύετο	*he (she, it) was loosing for him-(her-, it-)self*	ἐλύοντο	*they were loosing for themselves*

146. [139, 141] The personal endings in the middle of the secondary tenses (the "secondary B" endings) are -μην, -σο, -το, -μεθα, -σθε, -ντο. In New Testament Greek, the original form of the second person (-εσο) is shortened to -ου (e.g., ἐλύεσο becomes ἐλύου).

147. [140] The variable theme vowel, as in the active of the imperfect, and in all three voices of the present, is o before μ and ν, and ε before other letters.

148. [142] Great care should be taken to pronounce clearly both the long vowel in the ultima of the form ἐλυόμην and the accent on the penult, to distinguish it from the first-person plural active form ἐλύομεν.

149. [143] The imperfect passive indicative of λύω is as follows:

	Sing.		**Plur.**	
1.	ἐλυόμην	*I was being loosed*	ἐλυόμεθα	*we were being loosed*
2.	ἐλύου	*you (s.) were being loosed*	ἐλύεσθε	*you (p.) were being loosed*
3.	ἐλύετο	*he (she, it) was being loosed*	ἐλύοντο	*they were being loosed*

101

150. [144] Verbs that are deponent in the present are also deponent in the imperfect.

Example: The imperfect indicative of ἔρχομαι, *I come,* is ἠρχόμην, *I was coming.*

151. [145] Singular Verb with Neuter Plural Subject

A neuter plural subject may have its verb in the singular.

Examples: τὰ δαιμόνια ἐξήρχετο, *the demons were going out;* ταῦτά ἐστι τὰ καλὰ δῶρα, *these are the good gifts.*

This strange idiom, however, is by no means invariable in New Testament Greek; the neuter plural subject often has its verb in the plural like any other plural verb.

Example: τὰ τέκνα σώζονται, *the children are being saved.*

Uses of καί and οὐδέ

152. [146] The simple connective use of καί, where it means *and,* has already been studied. But καί has other uses. Frequently it means *also* or *even.* When it is thus used, it stands before the word with which it is logically connected. In the case of *also,* the English order is the reverse of the Greek order; in the case of *even,* it is the same as the Greek order.

Examples: τοῦτο δὲ καὶ ἐγὼ λέγω, *but this I also say;* γινώσκουσι καὶ τὰ τέκνα τὸν νόμον, *even the children know the law.*

153. [147] οὐδέ, like καί, is often simply connective and means *and not* or *nor.* But like καί it has other uses. It often means *not even.*

Examples: τοῦτο δὲ οὐ λέγω ἐγὼ οὐδὲ λέγουσιν αὐτὸ οἱ ἄλλοι, *but this I do not say, nor do the others say it* (simple connective use of οὐδέ); τὴν δόξαν τοῦ θεοῦ βλέπουσιν οὐδὲ οἱ μαθηταί, *not even the disciples see the glory of God.*

154. [148] Finally, καί . . . καί and οὐδέ . . . οὐδέ are used correlatively, and mean, respectively, *both . . . and,* and *neither . . . nor.*

Examples: (1) τοῦτο λέγουσιν καὶ οἱ ἀπόστολοι καὶ οἱ δοῦλοι, *both the apostles and the servants say this;* (2) τοῦτο λέγουσιν οὐδὲ οἱ ἀπόστολοι οὐδὲ οἱ δοῦλοι, *neither the apostles nor the servants say this.*

155. Summary of Progressive Indicatives

The word formation of the entire progressive indicative system, which includes the present and the imperfect, may now be summarized as follows:

		Sing.	Plur.
Present Active			
stem + o/ε +	**1.**	λύ-(ο)-ω	λύ-ο-μεν
primary A endings =	**2.**	λύ-ε-ις	λύ-ε-τε
	3.	λύ-ε-ι	λύ-(ο)-ουσι
Present Middle			
stem + o/ε +	**1.**	λύ-ο-μαι	λυ-ό-μεθα
primary B endings =	**2.**	λύ-ῃ (= ε-σαι)	λύ-ε-σθε
	3.	λύ-ε-ται	λύ-ο-νται
Present Passive			
stem + o/ε +	**1.**	λύ-ο-μαι	λυ-ό-μεθα
primary B endings =	**2.**	λύ-ῃ (= ε-σαι)	λύ-ε-σθε
	3.	λύ-ε-ται	λύ-ο-νται
Imperfect Active			
augment + stem + o/ε +	**1.**	ἔ-λυ-ον	ἐ-λύ-ο-μεν
secondary A endings =	**2.**	ἔ-λυ-ες	ἐ-λύ-ε-τε
	3.	ἔ-λυ-ε	ἔ-λυ-ο-ν
Imperfect Middle			
augment + stem + o/ε +	**1.**	ἐ-λυ-ό-μην	ἐ-λυ-ό-μεθα
secondary B endings =	**2.**	ἐ-λύ-ου (= ε-σο)	ἐ-λύ-ε-σθε
	3.	ἐ-λύ-ε-το	ἐ-λύ-ο-ντο
Imperfect Passive			
augment + stem + o/ε +	**1.**	ἐ-λυ-ό-μην	ἐ-λυ-ό-μεθα
secondary B endings =	**2.**	ἐ-λύ-ου (= ε-σο)	ἐ-λύ-ε-σθε
	3.	ἐ-λύ-ε-το	ἐ-λύ-ο-ντο

Lesson 12

All the sets of endings used in the indicative mood have now been introduced. A verb formation chart can be found at §649 that shows how each of the tenses is regularly formed using these endings.

156. [149] Exercises

A. 1. ἐγράφοντο οὗτοι οἱ λόγοι ἐν βιβλίῳ. 2. ἐδιδασκόμην ὑπ' αὐτοῦ ἐκ τῶν βιβλίων τῶν προφητῶν. 3. ἐν ἐκείναις ταῖς ἡμέραις καὶ ἐδιδασκόμεθα ὑπ' αὐτοῦ καὶ ἐδιδάσκομεν τοὺς ἄλλους, ἀλλὰ νῦν οὐδὲ διδασκόμεθα οὐδὲ διδάσκομεν. 4. ἀπήρχοντο οἱ ἁμαρτωλοὶ πρὸς τὴν θάλασσαν. 5. ἐξεπορεύετο πρὸς αὐτὸν ἡ ἐκκλησία, ἀλλὰ νῦν οὐκέτι ἐκπορεύεται. 6. οὔπω βλέπομεν τὸν κύριον ἐν τῇ δόξῃ αὐτοῦ, ἀλλὰ ἐδιδασκόμεθα ὑπ' αὐτοῦ καὶ ἐν ταῖς ἡμέραις ταῖς κακαῖς. 7. ἐλέγετο ἐν τῷ ἱερῷ καλὸς λόγος περὶ τούτου τοῦ ἀποστόλου. 8. περὶ αὐτὸν ἐβλέπετο ἡ δόξα αὐτοῦ. 9. ἐφέρετο τὰ δῶρα καὶ πρὸς τοὺς πονηρούς. 10. ἐδέχου τὰ βιβλία ἀπὸ τῶν προφητῶν. 11. συνήρχοντο οἱ μαθηταὶ πρὸς τοῦτον. 12. τὰ ἔργα τοῦ πονηροῦ πονηρά ἐστιν. 13. οὐδὲ αὐτὸς πονηρὸς οὐδὲ τὰ ἔργα πονηρά. 14. ὑπὲρ τῆς ἐκκλησίας αὐτοῦ ἀπέθνῃσκεν ὁ κύριος. 15. οὐκ ἔστιν μαθητὴς ὑπὲρ τὸν διδάσκαλον αὐτοῦ οὐδὲ δοῦλος ὑπὲρ τὸν κύριον αὐτοῦ. 16. ἐν τῷ πλοίῳ ἦγου πρὸς τὸν κύριον διὰ τῆς θαλάσσης. 17. ἐξήρχεσθε ἐκ τῶν οἴκων ὑμῶν. 18. ταῦτα τὰ δαιμόνια ἐξήρχετο διὰ τοῦ λόγου αὐτοῦ. 19. ἠκούοντο καὶ ἤκουον· ἀκούονται καὶ ἀκούουσιν. 20. ἠρχόμην πρὸς τὸν κύριον, ἦγον δὲ καὶ τοὺς ἄλλους.

B. 1. Those words were being heard by the same apostle, but now they are no longer being heard. 2. These books were being written by him in behalf of his servants. 3. I was not yet being taught by this man, but I was leading the others to him. 4. You (p.) are not above me nor am I above you. 5. You (s.) were sending others to him and were being sent by him to others. 6. The demons were going out of the children. 7. You (p.) were coming in and going out in the church. 8. We were not yet going away to the sinners, but were still hearing the voice of the apostle and were being taught concerning the Lord out of the books of the prophets. 9. They were going down to the sea and were going through it in boats. 10. Neither the evil nor the good were answering the Lord. 11. We were both seeing and hearing these disciples. 12. You (s.) were being saved by the word of the Lord. 13. Not by your (p.) works but by the Lord were you being saved from your sins. 14. Not even the good are saved by works. 15. Through the word of the Lord we were becoming good disciples. 16. You (s.) were not dying in behalf of him, but he was dying in behalf of you.

Lesson 13

Future Active and Middle Indicative

157. [150] Vocabulary

ἀναβλέπω, fut. ἀναβλέψω, I look up, I receive my sight

βήσομαι, I will go, dep. fut. of βαίνω

γενήσομαι, I will become, dep. fut. of γίνομαι

γνώσομαι, I will know, dep. fut. of γινώσκω

διδάξω, I will teach, fut. of διδάσκω

διώκω, fut. διώξω, I pursue, I persecute

δοξάζω, fut. δοξάσω, I glorify

ἐλεύσομαι, I will come, I will go, dep. fut. of ἔρχομαι

ἕξω, I will have, fut. of ἔχω (note the rough breathing mark)

κηρύσσω, fut. κηρύξω, I proclaim, I preach

λήμψομαι, I will take, I will receive, dep. fut. of λαμβάνω

προσεύχομαι, dep., fut. προσεύξομαι, I pray

τυφλός, ὁ, a blind man

158. [151] The present and imperfect tenses, in all three voices, are formed on the progressive stem, to which the personal endings, being joined to the stem by the variable theme vowel ο/ε, are added. But the future active and middle are

106

formed on the *future stem*, which is ordinarily formed by adding the tense suffix σ to the stem of the verb. Thus, while λυ- is the stem of the verb (which in the case of λύω is also the progressive stem), λυσ- is the future stem.

159. [152] The future, being a primary tense, has primary personal endings like the present tense. The variable theme vowel is also the same. Therefore the future active and middle indicative are conjugated exactly like the present active and middle, except that the future has λυσ- at the beginning instead of λυ-.

160. [154] The future active indicative of λύω is as follows:[1]

	Sing.		**Plur.**	
1.	λύσω	*I will loose*	λύσομεν	*we will loose*
2.	λύσεις	*you* (s.) *will loose*	λύσετε	*you* (p.) *will loose*
3.	λύσει	*he (she, it) will loose*	λύσουσι(ν)	*they will loose*

161. [155] The future middle indicative of λύω is as follows:

	Sing.		**Plur.**	
1.	λύσομαι	*I will loose for myself*	λυσόμεθα	*we will loose for ourselves*
2.	λύση	*you* (s.) *will loose for yourself*	λύσεσθε	*you* (p.) *will loose for yourselves*
3.	λύσεται	*he (she, it) will loose for him-(her-, it-)self*	λύσονται	*they will loose for themselves*

---

1. Until a few decades ago, the non-emphatic future in English was expressed using "shall" for first person and "will" for second and third, but since modern speech employs "will" for all three persons (reserving "shall" for the emphatic future) this revision uses "will" throughout the paradigm.

162. [153] It will be remembered that in the present and imperfect tenses the middle and passive are alike in form. But in the future the passive is quite different from the middle and will be reserved for a subsequent lesson. λύσομαι, therefore, means *I will loose for myself,* but it does not mean *I will be loosed.*

163. [156] Future Active and Middle of Stems Ending in a Consonant

When the stem of a verb ends in a consonant, the addition of the tense suffix σ brings two consonants together. The following results then occur:

1. π, β, φ (called *labials* because they are pronounced by means of the lips) form with the following σ the compound sibilant ψ (ps).[1]
Examples: The future of πέμπω is πέμψω, and of γράφω, γράψω.

2. κ, γ, χ (called *velars* because they are pronounced by touching the velum with the back of the tongue) form with the following σ the compound sibilant ξ (ks).
Examples: The future of ἄγω is ἄξω, and of ἄρχω, ἄρξω.

3. τ, δ, θ, ζ (called *dentals* because they are formed by touching the teeth with the tongue) drop out before the σ.
Examples: The future of πείθω is πείσω, and of δοξάζω, δοξάσω.

Formation of the Future Stem and Other Tense Stems of Various Verbs

164. [157] In the case of many verbs, however, the verb stem is quite different from the stem used in the present and imperfect tenses (the progressive stem).

---

1. For more on consonant classification and the meaning of these terms, see chart 4 (§652) and the glossary in the back of the book.

Example: The verb stem of κηρύσσω is not κηρυσσ- but κηρυκ-. From κηρυκ- the future κηρύξω is formed by the rule given in §163.

165. [158] In general, the future of a Greek verb cannot certainly be formed by any rules; it must be looked up in the lexicon for every individual verb, so numerous are the irregularities.

166. [159] The Greek verb is for the most part exceedingly regular in deriving the individual forms indicating voice, mood, person, and number from the basal tense stems. But the formation of those basal tense stems from the stem of the verb (and still more from the progressive stem) is often exceedingly irregular. The basal tense stems, from which all the rest of the verb is formed, are six in number. These six, given with the personal ending for the first-person singular indicative, are called the *principal parts*. So far, only two of the six principal parts of λύω have been learned. From the first of the principal parts, λύω, all of the present and imperfect in all three voices is formed; from the second, λύσω, all of the future active and middle. The present and imperfect together form the *progressive system;* the future active and middle form the *future system.*

167. [160] The regularity of the Greek verb in making the individual forms within each tense system from the first form of the tense system, and the great irregularity in making the first forms themselves, may be illustrated by the very irregular verb ἔρχομαι. We would certainly never have expected that the future of ἔρχομαι would be ἐλεύσομαι; but once we have learned from the lexicon that ἐλεύσομαι is the first-person singular of the future, then the third-person plural, ἐλεύσονται, for example, can be derived from it exactly as λύσονται is derived from λύσομαι, which in turn is derived from λύσω.

Lesson 13

Deponent Future of Certain Verbs

168. [164] Some verbs are deponent in one tense but not in another.

Examples: βαίνω has a future of the middle form, βήσομαι. It is thus deponent in the future but not in the present.

169. [161] From this point on, it will be assumed that the student will use the general vocabularies and paradigms at the back of the book. The method of using them may be illustrated as follows:

1. Suppose we wish to translate *they will eat* into Greek. The first step is to look up the word *eat* in the English-Greek vocabulary. It says there that *eat* is expressed by the word ἐσθίω. The next step is to look up the word ἐσθίω in the Greek-English vocabulary. With it, in the Greek-English vocabulary, the principal parts are given. The second of the principal parts is the future φάγομαι, a deponent middle. It is the future that we want, because *they will eat* is future. Since φάγομαι is a deponent future middle, we are looking for the future middle indicative (third-person plural). That can be derived from φάγομαι after the analogy of λύω. If we consult the paradigm of λύω, we discover that the future middle indicative third-person plural is formed from the second of the principal parts by retaining the λυσ- of λύσω and putting on -ονται instead of -ω. Treating φάγομαι in the same way, we keep φαγ- and add -ονται to it. Thus φάγονται is the desired form.

2. If the form σώσει is found in the Greek-English exercises, we will naturally guess that the second σ is the sign of the future just as the σ is in λύσει. We will therefore look up verbs beginning with σω-. Without difficulty σώζω will be found, and its future (the second of the principal parts) is discovered to be σώσω, of which, of course, σώσει is simply the third-person singular.

3. Similarly, if we see a form ἄξω, we should at once surmise that the σ concealed in the double consonant ξ is the σ

110

of the future. The present, therefore, will naturally be ἄκω or ἄγω or ἄχω. It may be necessary to try all three of these in the vocabulary until it be discovered that ἄγω is correct. Of course these processes will soon become second nature and will be performed without thought of the individual steps. **170.** [162] The more difficult forms will be listed separately in the vocabularies, with references to the verbs from which they come. **171.** [163] But the forms of compound verbs will not be thus listed. For example, the student who sees ἀπελεύσεσθε in the exercises should observe that ἀπ- is evidently the preposition ἀπό with its final vowel elided. The simple verb form, then, with the preposition removed, is ἐλεύσεσθε. The first-person singular would be ἐλεύσομαι. This form will be found in the Greek-English vocabulary and will be designated as the future of ἔρχομαι. Therefore, since ἐλεύσεσθε comes from ἔρχομαι, ἀπελεύσεσθε will come from ἀπέρχομαι, and that is the verb that the student must finally look up.

172. [165] Exercises

A. 1. ἄξει ὁ κύριος τοὺς μαθητὰς αὐτοῦ εἰς τὴν βασιλείαν. 2. γνωσόμεθα καὶ τοὺς ἀγαθοὺς καὶ τοὺς πονηρούς. 3. λήμψεσθε τὰ πλοῖα ἐκ τῆς θαλάσσης. 4. λύσεις τοὺς δούλους. 5. ἔξουσιν οἱ πονηροὶ οὐδὲ χαρὰν οὐδὲ εἰρήνην. 6. ἐν ἐκείνῃ τῇ ὥρᾳ ἐλεύσεται ὁ υἱὸς τοῦ ἀνθρώπου[1] σὺν τοῖς ἀγγέλοις αὐτοῦ. 7. ἁμαρτωλοὶ ἐστέ, γενήσεσθε δὲ μαθηταὶ τοῦ κυρίου. 8. διώκουσιν οἱ πονηροὶ τοὺς προφήτας, ἀλλ᾽ ἐν ταῖς ἡμέραις τοῦ υἱοῦ τοῦ ἀνθρώπου οὐκέτι διώξουσιν αὐτούς. 9. προσεύξῃ τῷ θεῷ σου καὶ δοξάσεις αὐτόν. 10. τότε γνώσεσθε ὅτι αὐτός ἐστιν ὁ κύριος. 11. ταῦτα γνώσομαι οὐδὲ ἐγώ. 12. ἄλλους διδάξει ὁ δοῦλος, ἀλλ᾽ ἐμὲ διδάξει

---

1. ὁ υἱὸς τοῦ ἀνθρώπου, *the Son of Man*. This is the form in which the phrase occurs in the Gospels as a self-designation of Jesus.

ὁ διδάσκαλος ὁ πιστός. 13. ἐκεῖνα λήμψονται οἱ ἀπόστολοι, ταῦτα δὲ καὶ οἱ ἀδελφοί. 14. διὰ τοῦ λόγου τοῦ κυρίου ἀναβλέψουσιν οἱ τυφλοὶ οὗτοι. 15. ὁ προφήτης αὐτὸς γράψει ταῦτα ἐν ταῖς γραφαῖς. 16. ἐλεύσονται κακαὶ ἡμέραι. 17. ἀπελεύσῃ καὶ σὺ εἰς τὰς ὁδοὺς τῶν πονηρῶν καὶ διδάξεις οὕτως τοὺς ἀνθρώπους. 18. κηρύξουσιν καὶ αὐτοὶ τὸ εὐαγγέλιον ἐν τούτῳ τῷ κόσμῳ τῷ κακῷ. 19. ἐλεύσεται καὶ αὕτη πρὸς αὐτόν, καὶ αὐτὸς διδάξει αὐτήν. 20. ἐκηρύσσετο τὸ εὐαγγέλιον ἐν ταῖς ἡμέραις ταῖς κακαῖς, κηρύσσεται δὲ καὶ νῦν, ἀλλ᾽ ἐν ἐκείνῃ τῇ ἡμέρᾳ ἐλεύσεται ὁ κύριος αὐτός. 21. κηρύσσομεν Χριστὸν κύριον, ἡμεῖς δὲ δοῦλοι ὑμῶν διὰ τὸν κύριον.

B. 1. The church will send servants to me. 2. These women will become good. 3. These words I will write in a book. 4. These things will come into the world in those days. 5. Now he is not yet teaching me, but in that hour he will both teach me and know me. 6. They were pursuing these women in the evil days, and they will pursue them even into the other places. 7. Then will blind men pray to the Lord, but evil men will not pray. 8. The gifts were being taken by us from the children, but we will take them no longer. 9. We will pray for (in behalf of) the same children in the church. 10. In this world we have death, but in the kingdom of God we will have both love and glory. 11. Then we were being taught by the apostles, but in that day we also will teach. 12. In those days I was persecuting you (p.), but now you will persecute me. 13. You (s.) will not go down to the sea, but will pursue these women with their children into the desert. 14. They were preaching this gospel, but now they will no longer preach it. 15. These things are evil, but you (p.) will have good things in that day. 16. The Lord will come to his church in glory.

Lesson 14

First Aorist Active and Middle Indicative
• *Constructions with* πιστεύω

173. [166] Vocabulary

ἀπολύω, ἀπολύσω, ἀπέλυσα,
 I release (ἀπό + λύω)
ἐκήρυξα, *I preached, I pro-*
 claimed, aor. of κηρύσσω
ἐπιστρέφω, ἐπιστρέψω,
 ἐπέστρεψα, *I turn, I return*
 (ἐπί + στρέφω)
ἑτοιμάζω, ἑτοιμάσω, ἡτοί-
 μασα, *I prepare*
ἤδη, adv., *already*
θαυμάζω, θαυμάσω, ἐθαύ-

μασα, *I wonder, I marvel,*
 I wonder at
θεραπεύω, θεραπεύσω, ἐθε-
 ράπευσα, *I heal*
πείθω, πείσω, ἔπεισα, *I per-*
 suade
πιστεύω, πιστεύσω, ἐπί-
 στευσα, *I believe*
ὑποστρέφω, ὑποστρέψω,
 ὑπέστρεψα, *I return* (ὑπό
 + στρέφω)

174. [167] The Greek *aorist* tense is formed in two distinct
ways, depending on which verb is being used. The *first aorist*
(or "weak" aorist) is not, however, a different tense from the
second ("strong") *aorist,* which will be studied in the next les-

113

son—the first and second aorists are simply two different ways of forming the same tense. In English, the past tense of *bake* is *baked*. But the past tense of *take* is *took*. Whereas the past of *bake* simply adds a *d*, the past of *take* changes the vowels. But *baked* is not a different tense from *took;* the verb *bake* and the verb *take* form the *preterit* (simple past) in two different ways.

175. [168] The aorist is like the imperfect in that in the indicative mood it refers to past time. But the imperfect refers to continuous or repeated (progressive) action in past time, while the aorist indicative is the simple past tense. Thus the imperfect ἔλυον means *I was loosing,* while the aorist ἔλυσα means *I loosed.* It will be remembered that in present tense this distinction between the simple assertion of the act and the assertion of continued (or repeated) action is not made in Greek (λύω, therefore, means either *I loose* or *I am loosing*). But the Greek language makes a much sharper distinction between simple past and progressive past than does English. Aorist and imperfect are entirely different.

176. The distinction between the aorist and imperfect illustrates that tense functions differently in Greek than in English. Where English tense is primarily indicative of the *time* of the action, Greek tense primarily indicates not time but *aspect*— that is, whether the action is looked at as a whole, a process, or a state. Verbs within the *progressive* tense system, namely the present and imperfect, are regarded as ongoing, repeated, continuous, or customary actions. Verbs within the *perfect* tense system (which will be studied in lesson 29) are regarded as indicating a state of affairs resulting from a completed action. But verbs within the *aorist* tense system have no such kind of action in view. In fact, the word *aorist* is from the Greek word ἀόριστος, which means *undefined, indefinite.* Thus when a speaker wishes simply to say that something happened and does not wish to indicate that it was a progressive (or a perfective) action, the aorist is used.

177. [169] This explains why the aorist tense will often be translated by the English perfect. English speakers frequently use the perfect to refer to a simple past action when they are unconcerned about the specific time of a past action or about events intervening between the action of the perfect verb and the time of speaking. The Greek aorist indicative is used to refer to a simple past action whether or not a specific time or intervening events are in view.

Example: ἠκούσατε τὴν φωνήν μου could be translated either *you heard my voice* or *you have heard my voice*. Both sentences merely assert that the action has taken place at some unspecified time in the past. But if a *then* were added, it would specify the time of the action, and the English would use the simple past. Thus τότε ἠκούσατε τὴν φωνήν μου would be translated *then you heard my voice* not *then you have heard my voice*.

178. [170] The context will usually determine whether a Greek aorist is to be translated in English by the simple past tense (e.g., *I loosed*) or by the perfect tense (e.g., *I have loosed*). The former translation should be adopted in the exercises unless the context clearly calls for an English perfect. What the student needs to understand first is that the aorist is the *simple* tense, where neither resultant state nor progression is in view.

179. [171] The first aorist active indicative of λύω is as follows:

Sing.		**Plur.**	
1. ἔλυσα	*I loosed*	ἐλύσαμεν	*we loosed*
2. ἔλυσας	*you* (s.) *loosed*	ἐλύσατε	*you* (p.) *loosed*
3. ἔλυσε(ν)	*he* (*she, it*) *loosed*	ἔλυσαν	*they loosed*

115

180. [172] The aorist, being a secondary tense (like the imperfect), has the augment. The augment is the same for the aorist as it is for the imperfect (see §§131–33).

181. [173] The aorist, like the imperfect, has the secondary endings. It will be remembered (see §134) that these, in the active voice, are as follows:

	Sing.	**Plur.**
1.	-v	-μεν
2.	-ς	-τε
3.	none	-v (or -σαν)

182. [174] Notice that in the first aorist the v is dropped in the first-person singular.

183. [175] Before these personal endings, there is added in the first aorist the tense suffix σ, as in the future, but with α as the connecting theme vowel rather than the variable theme vowel ο/ε. Thus where the future has σο or σε, the aorist has σα.[1]

184. [176] In the third-person singular this σα is changed to σε. ἔλυσε(ν) may have the movable v, like the ἔλυε(ν) of the imperfect.

185. [177] The form ἐλύσαμεν—to take it as an example—may be divided as follows: ἐ/λύ/σ/α/μεν. ἐ is the augment, λυ is the stem of the verb, σ is the tense formant for the first aorist, α is the theme vowel for the first aorist, and μεν is the secondary personal ending in the first-person plural active.

186. [178] The first aorist middle indicative of λύω is as follows:

1. Actually, this α as the theme vowel is the most distinctive marker of the first aorist, since some first aorists have different stems rather than an added σ.

Sing.		**Plur.**	
1. ἐλυσάμην	*I loosed for myself*	ἐλυσάμεθα	*we loosed for ourselves*
2. ἐλύσω	*you (s.) loosed for yourself*	ἐλύσασθε	*you (p.) loosed for yourselves*
3. ἐλύσατο	*he (she, it) loosed for, him-(her- it-)self*	ἐλύσαντο	*they loosed for themselves*

187. [179] As in the future tense, so in the aorist tense, the passive voice is entirely distinct in form from the middle. ἐλυσάμην, therefore, means *I loosed for myself*, but it does not mean *I was loosed*. Most aorist middle forms in the New Testament are those of deponent verbs.

188. [180] Like the aorist active, the aorist middle has the secondary personal endings. It will be remembered (see §146) that in the middle these secondary personal endings are as follows:

	Sing.	**Plur.**
1.	-μην	-μεθα
2.	-σο	-σθε
3.	-το	-ντο

189. [181] These endings are preceded, as in the active, by the tense suffix σα. No changes occur except in the second-person singular, where ἐλύσω is a shortened form of an original ἐλύσασο.

190. [182] The form ἐλυσάμεθα—to take it as an example—is made up as follows: ἐ/λυ/σ/ά/μεθα. ἐ is the augment, λυ is the stem of the verb, σ is the first aorist tense formant, α is the first aorist theme vowel, and μεθα is the secondary personal ending in the first-person plural middle.

117

191. [183] The changes caused by the joining of the σα of the first aorist tense suffix to the stems of various verbs are like those caused by the σο and σε of the future. As in the case of the future, however, it cannot be predicted with certainty what the aorist of a Greek verb will be. Every verb must be looked up in the lexicon separately. For this purpose the student should use the general vocabulary at the end of the book in the manner described in §§169–71; except that, for the aorist active and middle, we will be interested in the third of the principal parts, not in the second.

192. [184] Constructions with πιστεύω

The verb πιστεύω takes a dative object, not an accusative. Thus πιστεύω τῷ ἀνθρώπῳ means *I believe the man*, i.e., *I think he is telling me the truth*. But the New Testament also has the stronger notion of believing *in* someone, or entrusting oneself to someone, which is expressed by the verb πιστεύω followed by εἰς with the accusative. This is to be translated by *I believe in* or *on*. Thus πιστεύω εἰς τὸν κύριον means *I believe in the Lord* or *I believe on the Lord*, meaning *I put my confidence in the Lord*. It must not be supposed, however, that the preposition εἰς with the accusative here really means *in* like ἐν with the dative. Rather, the Greek language merely expresses the act of believing in a different way from the English; Greek speaks of putting one's faith *into* or *toward* someone.

193. [185] Exercises

A. 1. ἀπέλυσεν ὁ κύριος τὸν δοῦλον αὐτοῦ, ὁ δὲ δοῦλος οὐκ ἀπέλυσε τὸν ἄλλον. 2. ἤδη ἐπέστρεψαν οὗτοι πρὸς τὸν κύριον, ἐκεῖνοι δὲ ἐπιστρέψουσιν ἐν ταῖς ἡμέραις ταῖς κακαῖς. 3. ἐπιστεύσαμεν εἰς τὸν κύριον καὶ σώσει ἡμᾶς. 4. καὶ ἐπίστευσας εἰς αὐτὸν καὶ πιστεύσεις. 5. ὑπέστρεψας πρὸς τὸν κύριον καὶ ἐδέξατό σε εἰς τὴν ἐκκλησίαν αὐτοῦ. 6. ἐν ἐκείναις ταῖς ἡμέραις ἐπορεύεσθε ἐν ταῖς ὁδοῖς ταῖς κακαῖς. 7. ἐπεστρέψατε πρὸς τὸν κύριον καὶ ἐθεράπευσεν ὑμᾶς. 8. ἐκεῖνοι πονηροί, ἀλλ᾽ ἡμεῖς ἐπείσαμεν αὐτούς. 9. ἡτοίμασα ὑμῖν τόπον ἐν τῷ οὐρανῷ. 10. ἐδεξάμην σε εἰς τὸν οἶκόν μου, ἀλλ᾽ οὗτοι οἱ πονηροὶ οὐκ ἐδέξαντο. 11. ἀνέβλεψαν οἱ τυφλοί. 12. ἔσωσα ὑμᾶς ἐγώ, ὑμεῖς δὲ ἐμὲ οὐκ ἐδέξασθε εἰς τοὺς οἴκους ὑμῶν. 13. πονηροὶ ἦσαν αὐτοί, πονηροὺς δὲ ἔπεμψαν εἰς τὴν ἐκκλησίαν. 14. ἐδίδαξάς με ἐν τῷ ἱερῷ. 15. τότε ἠκούσαμεν ταύτας τὰς ἐντολάς, ἄλλας δὲ ἀκούσομεν ἐν τῇ ἐκκλησίᾳ. 16. ἐν ἐκείνῃ τῇ ὥρᾳ ἐξελεύσονται ἐκ τοῦ κόσμου, τότε δὲ ἐδέξαντο ἡμᾶς. 17. ἤκουσαν αὐτοῦ καὶ ἐθαύμασαν. 18. ἐδέξω σὺ τὸ εὐαγγέλιον, οὗτοι δὲ οὐ δέξονται αὐτό. 19. οὐδὲ ἠκούσαμεν τὸν κύριον οὐδὲ ἐπιστεύσαμεν εἰς αὐτόν.

B. 1. We did not receive the gospel, because we did not hear the voice of the apostle. 2. In those days we were not believing in the Lord, but this disciple persuaded us. 3. The sinner turned to the Lord and already is being taught by him. 4. The servants have prepared houses for you (p.). 5. This blind man believed in the Lord. 6. The children wondered, and the disciples believed. 7. You (s.) did not pray to the Lord, and on account of this he did not heal you. 8. Those evil men pursued these women into the desert. 9. I have preached the gospel to them. 10. You (p.) persecuted me, but I did not persecute you. 11. These blind men glorified the Lord because he had healed[1] them. 12. Through his disciples he proclaimed his gospel to the world. 13. The promises are good, and we received them. 14. You (p.) have received the same promises and believed on the same Lord. 15. He has not preached the gospel, nor does he preach it now. 16. That woman has neither glorified the Lord nor received the children.

---

1. The English pluperfect is often to be translated by the Greek aorist.

Lesson 15

Second Aorist Active and Middle Indicative

194. [186] Vocabulary

γάρ, conj., postpositive (see §94), *for*

ἔβαλον, *I threw, I cast,* 2nd aor. of βάλλω

ἐγενόμην, *I became,* dep. 2nd aor. of γίνομαι

εἶδον,[1] *I saw,* 2nd aor. of βλέπω (may also be regarded as 2nd aor. of ὁράω)

εἶπον, *I said,* 2nd aor. of λέγω

ἔλαβον, *I took,* 2nd aor. of λαμβάνω

ἤγαγον, *I led,* 2nd aor. of ἄγω

ἦλθον, *I came, I went,* 2nd aor. of ἔρχομαι

ἤνεγκα, *I bore, I brought,* 1st aor. of φέρω (conjugated like the 1st aor. of λύω, but with -κα instead of -σα)

1. In the New Testament, εἶδον has, in the indicative, almost exclusively first aorist endings instead of second aorist endings, and in other verbs also first aorist endings are often placed on second aorist stems. See J. H. Moulton, *A Grammar of New Testament Greek,* vol. 2, *Accidence and Word-Formation,* edited by W. F. Howard (Edinburgh: Clark, 1929), 208f. n. 1. It is therefore rather a concession to weakness when εἶδον and others are here treated as second aorists throughout. But this procedure will probably be better until the nature of the second aorist becomes thoroughly familiar to the student. The first aorist endings can afterwards be easily recognized when they occur (compare §544).

λείπω, *I leave* (2nd aor.
   ἔλιπον, *I left*)
ὄψομαι, *I will see*, dep. fut.
   of βλέπω (may also be
   regarded as future of
   ὁράω)
πίπτω, *I fall* (2nd aor. ἔπεσον,
   I fell)

προσφέρω, *I bring to* (takes
the accusative of the
thing that is brought and
the dative of the person
to whom it is brought.
Example: προσφέρω τὰ
τέκνα τῷ κυρίῳ, *I bring
the children to the Lord*)

195. [187] It has already been observed that the second aorist is not a different tense from the first aorist, but only a different way of forming the same tense. Very few verbs, therefore, have both a first aorist and a second aorist, just as very few verbs in English form their preterit (simple past) both by adding *-ed* and by making changes within the body of the word.

Thus the preterit of *like* is *liked*, and the preterit of *strike* is *struck*, but *like* has no preterit *luck*, nor has *strike* a preterit *striked*. The uses of the tense *liked* are exactly the same as the uses of the tense *struck*. So also in Greek the uses of the second aorist are exactly the same as the uses of the first aorist.

196. [188] It cannot be determined beforehand whether a verb is going to have a first aorist or a second aorist, nor, if it has a second aorist, what the form of that second aorist will be. These matters can be settled only by an examination of the lexicon for each individual verb.

197. [189] Second aorist differs formally from first aorist in two ways: (1) second aorist uses o/ε rather than α as the theme vowel connecting the stem to the endings, and (2) instead of adding a tense-formant σ, second aorist uses a different, often simpler, verbal stem from that used in the progressive system.

121

Examples: (1) λαμβάνω has a second aorist ἔλαβον, λαβ-
being the second aorist stem and λαμβαν- the progressive
stem. (2) βάλλω has a second aorist ἔβαλον, βαλ- being the
second aorist stem and βαλλ- the progressive stem.

198. [190] Upon the second aorist stem are formed the second aorist active and middle. The aorist passive of all verbs is
different from the aorist middle, whether the aorist middle is
first aorist or second aorist. ἐλιπόμην, therefore, which in form
is the aorist middle of λείπω, does not mean *I was left.* In order
to translate *I was left,* an entirely different form, the aorist
passive, would be used.

199. [191] The second aorist, being a secondary tense, has
an augment, which is just like the augment of the imperfect.
Thus a second aorist stem like λιπ- (of λείπω), which begins
with a consonant, prefixes ἐ to make the augment (the stem
λιπ- thus making ἔλιπον), while a second aorist stem like ἐλθ-,
which begins with a vowel, lengthens that vowel (the stem
ἐλθ- thus making ἦλθον).

200. [192] The second aorist, being a secondary tense, has
secondary personal endings. But instead of an α as in the first
aorist, the variable connecting vowel (the theme vowel) is ο/ε,
exactly as in the present and imperfect. The second aorist
indicative, therefore, is conjugated exactly like the imperfect,
except that the imperfect is formed on the progressive stem,
while the second aorist indicative is formed on the second
aorist stem. Thus ἐλείπομεν means *we were leaving* (imperfect),
whereas ἐλίπομεν means *we left* (second aorist). Sometimes a
single letter serves to distinguish imperfect from second aorist.
ἐβάλλομεν, for example, means *we were throwing* (imperfect),
whereas ἐβάλομεν means *we threw* (second aorist).

201. [193] Since the aorist of λύω is a first aorist, we must
use a different word for the second aorist paradigms. The second aorist active indicative of λείπω, *I leave,* is as follows:

Sing.		**Plur.**	
1. ἔλιπον	*I left*	ἐλίπομεν	*we left*
2. ἔλιπες	*you (s.) left*	ἐλίπετε	*you (p.) left*
3. ἔλιπε(ν)	*he (she, it) left*	ἔλιπον	*they left*

202. [194] The second aorist middle indicative of λείπω is as follows:

Sing.	**Plur.**
1. ἐλιπόμην	ἐλιπόμεθα
2. ἐλίπου	ἐλίπεσθε
3. ἐλίπετο	ἐλίποντο

Again, these are middle forms only, not passive, and will mostly be used with deponent verbs.

203. [195] Exercises

A. 1. καὶ εἴδομεν τὸν κύριον καὶ ἠκούσαμεν τοὺς λόγους αὐτοῦ. 2. οὐδὲ γὰρ εἰσῆλθες εἰς τοὺς οἴκους αὐτῶν οὐδὲ εἶπες αὐτοῖς παραβολήν. 3. ἐν ἐκείνῃ τῇ ὥρᾳ ἐγένοντο μαθηταὶ τοῦ κυρίου. 4. οὗτοι μὲν ἐγένοντο μαθηταὶ ἀγαθοί, ἐκεῖνοι δὲ ἔτι ἦσαν πονηροί. 5. προσέφερον αὐτῷ τοὺς τυφλούς. 6. ἔπεσον ἐκ τοῦ οὐρανοῦ οἱ ἄγγελοι οἱ πονηροί. 7. τὰ μὲν δαιμόνια ἐξεβάλετε, τὰ δὲ τέκνα ἐθεραπεύσατε. 8. τοὺς μὲν πονηροὺς συνηγάγετε ὑμεῖς εἰς τοὺς οἴκους ὑμῶν, τοὺς δὲ ἀγαθοὺς ἡμεῖς. 9. οὐκ ἐκήρυξας τὸ εὐαγγέλιον ἐν τῇ ἐκκλησίᾳ, οὐδὲ γὰρ ἐγένου μαθητής. 10. νῦν μὲν λέγετε λόγους ἀγαθούς, εἶπον δὲ οὗτοι τοὺς αὐτοὺς λόγους καὶ ἐν ταῖς ἡμέραις ἐκείναις. 11. ἐπιστεύσαμεν εἰς τὸν κύριον, οἱ γὰρ μαθηταὶ ἤγαγον ἡμᾶς πρὸς αὐτόν. 12. ταῦτα μὲν εἶπον ὑμῖν ἐν τῷ ἱερῷ, ἐκεῖνα δὲ οὔπω λέγω. 13. τότε μὲν εἰσήλθετε εἰς τὴν ἐκκλησίαν, ἐν ἐκείνῃ δὲ τῇ ἡμέρᾳ εἰσελεύσεσθε εἰς τὸν οὐρανόν. 14. τότε ὀψόμεθα τὸν κύριον ἐν τῇ δόξῃ αὐτοῦ· ἐπιστεύσαμεν γὰρ εἰς αὐτόν. 15. ὁ μὲν κύριος ἐξ-ἦλθε τότε ἐκ τοῦ κόσμου, οἱ δὲ μαθηταὶ αὐτοῦ ἔτι μένουσιν ἐν αὐτῷ. 16. ταύτας τὰς ἐντολὰς ἔλαβον ἀπὸ τοῦ κυρίου, ἤμην γὰρ μαθητὴς αὐτοῦ. 17. τότε μὲν παρελάβετε τὴν ἐπαγγελίαν παρὰ τοῦ κυρίου, νῦν δὲ καὶ κηρύσσετε αὐτὴν ἐν τῷ κόσμῳ. 18. ἤλθετε πρὸς τὸν κύριον καὶ παρελάβετε παρ' αὐτοῦ ταῦτα. 19. συνήγαγεν ἡμᾶς αὐτὸς εἰς τὴν ἐκκλησίαν αὐτοῦ. 20. εἶδον οἱ ἄνθρωποι τὸν υἱὸν τοῦ θεοῦ· ἐγένετο γὰρ αὐτὸς ἄνθρωπος καὶ ἔμενεν ἐν τούτῳ τῷ κόσμῳ.

B. 1. We did not see him, for we were not yet disciples of him. 2. The apostle brought the sinners to him. 3. You (p.) did not hear me, but you came to my disciples. 4. You (p.) entered into this house, but the others went out of it. 5. The sinners were going into their houses, but the apostles saw the Lord. 6. In those days we will see the Lord, but in the evil days we did not see him. 7. Your (s.) brothers were taking gifts from the children, but the apostles took the children from them. 8. You became a servant of the apostle, but the apostle became to you even a brother. 9. You (p.) have become a church of God, for you have believed on his Son. 10. He has gathered together his disciples into his kingdom. 11. The faithful teacher said that the Lord is good. 12. They believed in the Lord and brought others also to him. 13. They heard the children and came to them. 14. We received joy and peace from God, because we were already entering into his kingdom. 15. The disciples say that the apostles saw the Lord and received this from him. 16. You (p.) went out into the desert, but the apostle said these things to his brothers.

Lesson 16

Aorist Passive Indicative • *Future Passive Indicative*

204. [196] Vocabulary

ἀναλαμβάνω, *I take up*

ἐβλήθην, *I was thrown, I was cast,* aor. pass. of βάλλω

ἐγενήθην, *I became,* aor., pass. in form, of γίνομαι

ἐγνώσθην, *I was known,* aor. pass. of γινώσκω

ἐδιδάχθην, *I was taught,* aor. pass. of διδάσκω

ἐκηρύχθην, *I was preached, I was proclaimed,* aor. pass. of κηρύσσω

ἐλήμφθην, *I was taken, I was received,* aor. pass. of λαμβάνω

ἐπορεύθην, *I went,* aor., passive in form, of πορεύομαι

ἠγέρθην, *I was raised,* aor. pass. of ἐγείρω

ἠκούσθην, *I was heard,* aor. pass. of ἀκούω

ἠνέχθην, *I was borne, I was brought,* aor. pass. of φέρω

ἤχθην, *I was led,* aor. pass. of ἄγω

ὤφθην, *I was seen,* aor. pass. of βλέπω (may also be regarded as aor. pass. of ὁράω)

125

205. [197] The aorist passive indicative and the future passive indicative are formed on the aorist passive stem, which appears in the *sixth* place among the principal parts. The fourth and fifth of the principal parts will be studied in a subsequent lesson.

206. [198] The aorist passive stem is ordinarily formed by adding θε to the verb stem. In the indicative mood, this θε is lengthened to θη. Thus the aorist passive stem of λύω appears as λυθη-.

207. [199] The aorist being a secondary tense, the augment, formed exactly as in the case of the imperfect (see §§131–33), is prefixed to the tense stem, and the secondary personal endings are added. The personal endings of the aorist passive are, surprisingly, the secondary A endings that are elsewhere associated with the *active* form (see §134), and are like those that are used in the imperfect active indicative except that in the third-person plural the alternative ending -σαν is chosen instead of -ν. In the aorist passive indicative, the personal endings are added directly to the final η of the tense stem, and the η does not vary.

208. [201] The aorist passive indicative of λύω is as follows:

	Sing.		**Plur.**	
1.	ἐλύθην	*I was loosed*	ἐλύθημεν	*we were loosed*
2.	ἐλύθης	*you (s.) were loosed*	ἐλύθητε	*you (p.) were loosed*
3.	ἐλύθη	*he (she, it) was loosed*	ἐλύθησαν	*they were loosed*

209. [200] The future passive indicative is formed by adding -σο/ε to the aorist passive stem (with its θε lengthened to θη), which, however, since the future is a primary not a secondary tense, has in the future no augment. To this future passive stem, λυθησο/ε, the middle primary endings are added, and the future passive is conjugated exactly like the present passive, except that the stem is λυθησο/ε instead of just λυο/ε.

210. Thus, for example, if we wish to write the Greek for *he will be seen*, we must first look for the sixth principal part (aorist passive) of *I see* (ὁράω or βλέπω). After discovering that the aorist passive is ὤφθην, we must then (1) remove the augment and the secondary ending, so that ὠφθην becomes ὀφθη-, and (2) add a sigma (σ) followed by the appropriate theme vowel (ο or ε) and the third-person primary B ending (-ται), forming ὀφθήσεται, *he will be seen*. Similarly, *we will be brought* is based on the sixth principal part of φέρω, which is ἠνέχθην. Dropping the augment and the secondary ending yields the stem ἐνεχθη- to which is added the σο/ε and the first-person plural primary B ending (-μεθα), resulting in ἐνεχθησόμεθα.

211. [202] The future passive indicative of λύω is as follows:

Sing.		**Plur.**	
1. λυθήσομαι	*I will be loosed*	λυθησόμεθα	*we will be loosed*
2. λυθήσῃ	*you* (s.) *will be loosed*	λυθήσεσθε	*you* (p.) *will be loosed*
3. λυθήσεται	*he (she, it) will be loosed*	λυθήσονται	*they will be loosed*

212. [203] The uses of the parts of the verb that have been studied so far may be summarized as follows:

Tense	Voice	Example (1st pers. sg.)	Meaning	Principal Part
Present Indicative	Active	λύω	*I loose, I am loosing*	First
	Middle	λύομαι	*I loose for myself, I am loosing for myself*	
	Passive	λύομαι	*I am being loosed*	
Imperfect Indicative	Active	ἔλυον	*I was loosing*	
	Middle	ἐλυόμην	*I was loosing for myself*	
	Passive	ἐλυόμην	*I was being loosed*	
Future Indicative	Active	λύσω	*I will loose*	Second
	Middle	λύσομαι	*I will loose for myself*	
	Passive	λυθήσομαι	*I will be loosed*	Sixth
Aorist Indicative	Active	1st aor. ἔλυσα	*I loosed*	Third
		2nd aor. ἔλιπον	*I left*	
	Middle	1st aor. ἐλυσάμην	*I loosed for myself*	
		2nd aor. ἐλιπόμην	*I left for myself*	
	Passive	ἐλύθην	*I was loosed*	Sixth

Formation of Aorist Passive Stems of Verbs Whose Verb Stems End in a Consonant

213. [204] Before the θ of the aorist passive tense-suffix, a final π or β of the verb stem is changed to φ, a final κ or γ is changed to χ, and a final τ, δ, ζ, or θ is changed to σ. The changes in the case of π, β, κ, γ can be remembered if it be observed that θ is equivalent to *th* and that what the changes amount to is adding on an *h* to the preceding letters so as to make them conform to the *th*. Thus before *th, p* or *b* becomes *ph*, and *k* or *g* becomes *ch*.

Examples: The aorist passive of πέμπω is ἐπέμφθην, of ἄγω, ἤχθην, of πείθω, ἐπείσθην.

214. [205] Like the other principal parts, however, the aorist passive of a Greek verb cannot be formed with any certainty on the basis of general rules, but must be noted for each verb separately.

215. [206] Irregular Aorist Passive and Future Passive

Some verbs have an aorist and future passive form that does not have the customary θ in the tense stem. However, they are conjugated exactly like the regular aorist and future passives, with the *e* theme vowel (η) before the secondary A endings (for the aorist passive indicative) or before σ and the primary B endings (for the future passive indicative).

Example: The aorist passive indicative of γράφω is ἐγράφην, ἐγράφης, ἐγράφη, ἐγράφημεν, ἐγράφητε, ἐγράφησαν. Commensurately, the future passive is γραφήσομαι, etc.

Since all aorist and future passive endings have this *e* vowel throughout the conjugation, it is this *e* vowel rather than the θ that most reliably marks aorist and future passives.

Aorist and Future of Deponent Verbs

216. [207] Some deponent verbs have passive, not middle, forms.

Example: The aorist of ἀποκρίνομαι, *I answer*, is ἀπεκρίθην, *I answered.*[1]

---

1. But occasionally ἀποκρίνομαι has middle forms.

Lesson 16

217. [208] Some deponent verbs have both middle and passive forms. Example: The aorist of γίνομαι, *I become*, is either ἐγενόμην, *I became*, or ἐγενήθην, *I became*. ἐγενόμην and ἐγενήθην mean exactly the same thing, both the middle and the passive forms having active meaning. Likewise, the future of πορεύομαι may be either πορεύσομαι (middle) or πορευθήσομαι (passive). Both forms mean *I will go*.

218. [209] Exercises

A. 1. ἐπιστεύσαμεν εἰς τὸν κύριον καὶ ἐγνώσθημεν ὑπ᾽ αὐτοῦ. 2. ταῦτα ἐγράφη ἐν τοῖς βιβλίοις. 3. ἐδιδάξατε τὰ τέκνα, ἐδιδάχθητε δὲ καὶ αὐτοὶ ὑπὸ τοῦ κυρίου. 4. ἐλήμφθησαν οἱ πιστοὶ εἰς τὸν οὐρανόν, ἐξεβλήθησαν δὲ ἐξ αὐτοῦ οἱ ἄγγελοι οἱ πονηροί. 5. ἐγερθήσονται οἱ νεκροὶ τῷ λόγῳ τοῦ κυρίου. 6. οὗτοι οἱ τυφλοὶ συνήχθησαν εἰς τὴν ἐκκλησίαν. 7. ἐξεβλήθη τὰ δαιμόνια· ὁ γὰρ κύριος ἐξέβαλεν αὐτά. 8. πέμπονται μὲν καὶ νῦν οἱ μαθηταί, ἐπέμφθησαν δὲ τότε οἱ ἀπόστολοι καὶ πεμφθήσονται ἐν ἐκείνῃ τῇ ἡμέρᾳ καὶ οἱ ἄγγελοι. 9. εἰσῆλθες εἰς τὴν ἐκκλησίαν καὶ ἐβαπτίσθης. 10. ἐπιστεύθη ἐν κόσμῳ,[1] ἀνελήμφθη ἐν δόξῃ. 11. οἱ ἁμαρτωλοὶ ἐσώθησαν ἐν ἐκείνῃ τῇ ὥρᾳ καὶ ἐγενήθησαν μαθηταὶ τοῦ κυρίου. 12. ἐπορεύθημεν εἰς ἕτερον τόπον· οὐ γὰρ δέξονται ἡμᾶς οὗτοι. 13. ἐδοξάσθη ὁ υἱὸς τοῦ ἀνθρώπου, καὶ ὁ θεὸς δοξασθήσεται ἐν αὐτῷ. 14. τὸ εὐαγγέλιον ἐκηρύχθη ἐν ταῖς ἡμέραις ἐκείναις, κηρυχθήσεται δὲ καὶ νῦν. 15. ἑτοιμασθήσεται ἡμῖν τόπος ἐν οὐρανῷ κατὰ τὴν ἐπαγγελίαν τοῦ κυρίου. 16. τὰ τέκνα προσηνέχθησαν τῷ κυρίῳ. 17. εἶδον οὗτοι τὸ πρόσωπον τοῦ κυρίου καὶ ἤκουσαν τῆς φωνῆς αὐτοῦ. 18. ἐν τῷ μικρῷ οἴκῳ ἀκουσθήσεται ἡ φωνὴ τοῦ ἀποστόλου. 19. πρῶτός εἰμι τῶν ἁμαρτωλῶν, ἐσώθην δὲ καὶ ἐγώ. 20. ὀψόμεθα μὲν τοὺς ἀγγέλους, ὀφθησόμεθα δὲ καὶ ὑπ᾽ αὐτῶν.

1. The article is often omitted with κόσμος (see §335).

B. 1. This is the church of God, but the sinners were brought into it. 2. This man was cast out on account of the gospel. 3. I was sent to the sinners, but you (p.) were being sent to your brothers. 4. You (s.) did not receive the gospel, but the others received it and were saved. 5. These words have been written by the apostles. 6. The servants will come into the house, but the sons were baptized in that hour. 7. You (p.) will see the Lord in heaven, but the apostles were taught by him. 8. The disciples brought the blind men to the Lord, but the children were led by others. 9. The gifts were being received from the servants, but the law was proclaimed to the world. 10. A place was prepared for the brothers. 11. We went to the sea, but our sons will go into the temple. 12. After these things, they were taken up into glory. 13. The Son of Man was raised up from the dead[1] and was glorified. 14. The promises of God were heard in the world.

---

1. *From the dead,* ἐκ νεκρῶν.

Lesson 17

The Third Declension

219. [210] Vocabulary

ἅγιος, -α, -ον, adj., *holy;* οἱ
   ἅγιοι, *the saints*
αἷμα, αἵματος, τό, *blood*
αἰών, αἰῶνος, ὁ, *an age;* εἰς
   τὸν αἰῶνα, *for ever;* εἰς
   τοὺς αἰῶνας τῶν αἰώνων,
   for ever and ever
ἄρχων, ἄρχοντος, ὁ, *a ruler*
γράμμα, γράμματος, τό, *a
   letter*

ἐλπίς, ἐλπίδος, ἡ, *a hope*
θέλημα, θελήματος, τό, *a will*
νύξ, νυκτός, ἡ, *a night*
ὄνομα, ὀνόματος, τό, *a name*
πνεῦμα, πνεύματος, τό, *a
   spirit, the Spirit*
ῥῆμα, ῥήματος, τό, *a word*
σάρξ, σαρκός, ἡ, *flesh*
σῶμα, σώματος, τό, *a body*

220. [211] The declensions of (1) ἐλπίς, ἐλπίδος, ἡ, *a hope,*
(2) νύξ, νυκτός, ἡ, *a night,* and (3) ἄρχων, ἄρχοντος, ὁ, *a ruler,*
are as follows:

132

		ἐλπίς, ἡ, **stem** ἐλπιδ-	νύξ, ἡ, **stem** νυκτ-	ἄρχων, ὁ, **stem** ἀρχοντ-
Sing.	**Nom.**	ἐλπίς	νύξ	ἄρχων
	Gen.	ἐλπίδος	νυκτός	ἄρχοντος
	Dat.	ἐλπίδι	νυκτί	ἄρχοντι
	Acc.	ἐλπίδα	νύκτα	ἄρχοντα
Plur.	**Nom.**	ἐλπίδες	νύκτες	ἄρχοντες
	Gen.	ἐλπίδων	νυκτῶν	ἀρχόντων
	Dat.	ἐλπίσι(ν)	νυξί(ν)	ἄρχουσι(ν)
	Acc.	ἐλπίδας	νύκτας	ἄρχοντας

221. [212] The case endings in the third declension are as follows:

	Sing.	**Plur.**
Nom.	-ς or none	-ες
Gen.	-ος	-ων
Dat.	-ι	-σι
Acc.	-α	-ας

222. [213] These case endings are added to the stem, and the stem can be discovered, not from the nominative, as is possible in the first and second declensions, but only by dropping off the -ος of the genitive singular. Thus the genitive singular must be known before any third-declension noun can be declined.

223. [214b] The dative plural -σι(ν) may have the movable ν (see §40).

224. [215] The nominative is formed in various ways, which it will probably be most convenient not to try to classify.

225. [217] In the dative plural the combination of consonants formed by the -σι of the case ending coming after the final consonant of the stem causes various changes, which are in general the same as those set forth in §163. But where the

133

stem ends in ντ, the ντ is dropped before the following σ, and the preceding vowel is lengthened, ε to ει, α to long α, and ο to ου. Thus the dative plural of ἄρχων (gen. ἄρχοντος) is not ἄρχοντσι but ἄρχουσι.

226. [218] The gender of third-declension nouns, except in the case of certain special classes like the neuter nouns ending in -μα, -ματος (see §229), cannot easily be reduced to rules, and so must be learned for each noun separately.

227. [219] Thus if the student is asked what the word for *flesh* is, it is quite insufficient to say that it is σάρξ. What one must rather say is that it is σάρξ, σαρκός, ἡ. Without the genitive singular, it would be impossible to determine the stem; and unless the stem is known, of course the noun cannot be declined. And without knowing the gender, one could not use the word correctly. One could not tell, for example, whether ὁ σάρξ or ἡ σάρξ or τὸ σάρξ would be correct. Therefore, when memorizing vocabulary from this point on, the student should learn the nominative singular, genitive singular, and article for each noun.

228. [220] These extra requirements, coupled with the difficulty of the dative plural, make the third declension less easy than the first and second. Once the case endings have been thoroughly mastered and have been distinguished clearly from those of the other two declensions, however, the declension is not difficult.

229. [222] Nouns in -μα

An important class of nouns in -μα, with stems ending in -ματ, are declined like ὄνομα. These nouns are all neuter. The declension of ὄνομα, ὀνόματος, τό, *a name,* is as follows:

	Sing.	**Plur.**
Nom./Acc.	ὄνομα	ὀνόματα
Gen.	ὀνόματος	ὀνομάτων
Dat.	ὀνόματι	ὀνόμασι(ν)

Since ὄνομα is a neuter noun, its accusative of both numbers is like the nominative, and its nominative and accusative plural always end in α (see §38).

230. [223] The declensions of other third-declension nouns will be found in §§600–607 and can be referred to as they are needed.

Accent Matters

231. [214a] Note that in masculine and feminine third-declension nouns, the α is short both in the accusative singular ending and in the accusative plural ending.

232. [221] Monosyllables of the Third Declension

Monosyllabic nouns of the third declension have the accent on the ultima in the genitive and dative of both numbers. In the genitive plural it is the circumflex.

Example: σάρξ, σαρκός, σαρκῶν.

This rule is an exception to the rule of noun accent. In accordance with the rule of noun accent, the accent would remain on the same syllable as in the nominative singular so nearly as the general rules of accent would permit.

233. [224] Exercises

A. 1. ἐλπίδα οὐκ ἔχουσιν οὐδὲ τὸ πνεῦμα τὸ ἅγιον. 2. διὰ τὴν ἐλπίδα τὴν καλὴν ἤνεγκαν ταῦτα οἱ μαθηταὶ τοῦ κυρίου. 3. ταῦτά ἐστιν τὰ ῥήματα τοῦ ἁγίου πνεύματος. 4. ἐγράφη τὰ ὀνόματα ὑμῶν ὑπὸ τοῦ θεοῦ ἐν τῷ βιβλίῳ τῆς ζωῆς. 5. τῷ λόγῳ τοῦ κυρίου ἔσωσεν ἡμᾶς ὁ θεός. 6. οἱ ἄρχοντες οἱ πονηροὶ οὐκ ἐπίστευσαν εἰς τὸ ὄνομα τοῦ κυρίου. 7. ταῦτα εἶπον ἐκεῖνοι τοῖς ἄρχουσιν τούτου τοῦ αἰῶνος. 8. ὄψεσθε ὑμεῖς τὸ πρόσωπον τοῦ κυρίου εἰς τὸν αἰῶνα, ἀλλ᾽ οὐκ ὄψονται αὐτὸ οἱ πονηροί, ὅτι οὐκ ἐπίστευσαν εἰς τὸ ὄνομα αὐτοῦ. 9. οὐκέτι κατὰ σάρκα γινώσκομεν τὸν κύριον. 10. ἐν τῇ σαρκὶ ὑμῶν εἴδετε τὸν θάνατον, ἀλλὰ διὰ τοῦ ἁγίου πνεύματος ἔχετε ἐλπίδα καλήν. 11. τὸ μὲν γράμμα ἀπο-

κτείνει, ἐν τῷ δὲ πνεύματι ἔχετε ζωήν. 12. βλέπομεν τὸ πρόσωπον τοῦ κυρίου καὶ ἐν νυκτὶ¹ καὶ ἐν ἡμέρᾳ. 13. ἐδίδαξαν οἱ μαθηταὶ καὶ τοὺς ἄρχοντας καὶ τοὺς δούλους. 14. ἐν ἐκείνῃ τῇ νυκτὶ
εἴδετε τὸν ἄρχοντα τὸν πονηρόν. 15. μετὰ τῶν ἀρχόντων ἤμην
ἐν ἐκείνῳ τῷ οἴκῳ. 16. μετὰ δὲ ἐκείνην τὴν νύκτα ἦλθεν οὗτος
ἐν τῷ πνεύματι εἰς τὴν ἔρημον. 17. ταῦτά ἐστιν ῥήματα ἐλπίδος
καὶ ζωῆς. 18. ἤγαγεν αὐτὸν τὸ ἅγιον πνεῦμα εἰς τὸ ἱερόν.
19. ταῦτα τὰ ῥήματα ἐκηρύχθη ἐν ἐκείνῃ τῇ νυκτὶ τοῖς δούλοις
τοῦ ἄρχοντος. 20. ἠγέρθησαν τὰ σώματα τῶν ἁγίων.

B. 1. By the will of God we believed on the name of the
Lord. 2. The rulers did not receive this hope from the apostle,
because they did not believe in the Lord. 3. We shall know the
will of God for ever. 4. In this age we have death, but in that
age hope and life. 5. In our flesh we remain in this age, but
through the Spirit of God we have a good hope. 6. By the will
of God we were saved from our sins through the blood of the
Lord. 7. In those days you (p.) saw the rulers. 8. This age is
evil, but in it we have hope. 9. These words we wrote to the
rulers. 10. We came to the good ruler and to the apostle of the
Lord. 11. In our bodies we will see death, but we will be raised
up according to the word of God. 12. You (p.) were persecuted
by the ruler, but the blood of the Lord saves you from sin.
13. We wrote those good words to the evil ruler. 14. This night
became to them an hour of death, but they believed on the
name of the Lord. 15. The evil spirits were cast out by the word
of the Lord.

---

1. In phrases such as ἐν νυκτί and ἐν ἡμέρᾳ, the article is often omitted.

Lesson 18A

Progressive Participles • Use of Participles • Tense of Participles • The Negatives οὐ and μή

234. [225] Vocabulary

κεφαλή, ἡ, *a head*
κράζω, κράξω, ἔκραξα, *I cry out*
πίνω, πίομαι (very irregular future), ἔπιον, *I drink*

προσέρχομαι, dep., *I come to, I go to,* with dative
ὤν, οὖσα, ὄν, *being,* progressive participle of εἰμί

235. [226] The declension of λύων, λύουσα, λῦον, *loosing,* the progressive active participle of λύω, is as follows:[1]

---

1. In keeping with the terminology of the grammarians of his time, Machen used the term "present participle" in his original text. This, however, can be confusing, in that it suggests a present time value to these participles, and most modern grammars, including this revision, prefer the term "progressive" to refer to this tense system.

	Sing. Masc.	Fem.	Neut.
Nom.	λύων	λύουσα	λῦον
Gen.	λύοντος	λυούσης	λύοντος
Dat.	λύοντι	λυούσῃ	λύοντι
Acc.	λύοντα	λύουσαν	λῦον

	Plur. Masc.	Fem.	Neut.
Nom.	λύοντες	λύουσαι	λύοντα
Gen.	λυόντων	λυουσῶν	λυόντων
Dat.	λύουσι(ν)	λυούσαις	λύουσι(ν)
Acc.	λύοντας	λυούσας	λύοντα

236. [227] This declension, like the declension of other adjectives, should be learned across, and not down the columns (see §62).

237. [228a] Observe that the masculine and neuter are declined according to the third declension (the masculine exactly like ἄρχων) and the feminine according to the first declension (like δόξα).

238. The declension of the participle of εἰμί is just like the endings of the progressive active participle of λύω, but with accents and breathings:

	Sing. Masc.	Fem.	Neut.	Plur. Masc.	Fem.	Neut.
Nom.	ὤν	οὖσα	ὄν	ὄντες	οὖσαι	ὄντα
Gen.	ὄντος	οὔσης	ὄντος	ὄντων	οὐσῶν	ὄντων
Dat.	ὄντι	οὔσῃ	ὄντι	οὖσι(ν)	οὔσαις	οὖσι(ν)
Acc.	ὄντα	οὖσαν	ὄν	ὄντας	οὔσας	ὄντα

239. [230] The declension of λυόμενος, -η, -ον, *loosing for him-(her-, it-)self,* the progressive middle participle, and of

138

λυόμενος, -η, -ον, *being loosed,* the progressive passive participle of λύω, is as follows:

	Sing.		
	Masc.	**Fem.**	**Neut.**
Nom.	λυόμενος	λυομένη	λυόμενον
Gen.	λυομένου	λυομένης	λυομένου
Dat.	λυομένῳ	λυομένῃ	λυομένῳ
Acc.	λυόμενον	λυομένην	λυόμενον
	Plur.		
	Masc.	**Fem.**	**Neut.**
Nom.	λυόμενοι	λυόμεναι	λυόμενα
Gen.	λυομένων	λυομένων	λυομένων
Dat.	λυομένοις	λυομέναις	λυομένοις
Acc.	λυομένους	λυομένας	λυόμενα

Notice that this declension is like that of adjectives of the second and first declension.

240. [231] The progressive participles are formed on the progressive (present) stem of the verb (see §158). The progressive participles of any regular verb can be made by adding -ων, -ουσα, -ον for active, and -όμενος, -ομένη, -όμενον for middle and passive, to the progressive stem of that verb.

241. [232] Use of Participles

Participles are verbal adjectives. English present participles are the verb forms with -*ing* on the end: doing, having, saying, etc. Greek participles are far more complex. Being adjectives, they have gender, number, and case; and like other adjectives, they agree in gender, number, and case with the nouns that they modify. On the other hand, since they partake of the nature of verbs, (a) they have tense and voice, (b) they receive, like other

parts of a verb, adverbial modifiers, and (c) if they are participles of a transitive verb, they can take a direct object.
Examples:

1. ὁ ἀπόστολος λέγων ταῦτα ἐν τῷ ἱερῷ βλέπει τὸν κύριον, *the apostle, saying these things in the temple, sees the Lord.* Here the participle λέγων, which means *saying*, goes with ἀπόστολος, which is in the nominative case and singular number, and is a masculine noun. The participle, therefore, must itself be nominative singular masculine in order to agree with ἀπόστολος. On the other hand, the participle is enough of a verb to have tense and voice. It is in the progressive tense because the action that it denotes is represented as in progress at the same time as the action of the leading verb βλέπει; it is in the active voice because it represents the apostle as doing something, not as having something done to him. And it has the adverbial modifier ἐν τῷ ἱερῷ and the direct object ταῦτα. However, it has no subject, as a finite verb (e.g., an indicative) would have; for the noun ἀπόστολος, which denotes the person represented as performing the action denoted by the participle, is not the subject of the participle, but is the noun with which the participle, like any other adjective, agrees.

2. βλέπομεν τὸν ἀπόστολον λέγοντα ταῦτα ἐν τῷ ἱερῷ, *we see the apostle saying these things in the temple.* Here the noun with which the participle agrees is accusative singular masculine. Therefore the participle must also be accusative singular masculine. But its direct object and its adverbial modifier are the same as in example 1.

3. προσερχόμεθα τῷ ἀποστόλῳ λέγοντι ταῦτα ἐν τῷ ἱερῷ, *we come to the apostle while he is saying these things in the temple.* Here the participle λέγοντι agrees with a masculine noun in the dative singular and must therefore itself be dative singular masculine. But in this example it is quite impossible to translate the participle literally. The translation, *we come to*

the apostle saying these things in the temple, would not do at all, for in that English sentence the participle *saying* would be understood as agreeing not with *the apostle* but with the subject of the sentence, *we.* It is necessary, therefore, to give up all attempts at translating the participle "literally." Instead, we must express the idea expressed by the Greek participle in an entirely different way—in this case by the use of a temporal clause. When such temporal clauses are used to translate a Greek *progressive* participle, they are usually introduced by *while.* Such a free translation would have been better than the literal translation even in example 1, although there the literal translation was not absolutely impossible. It would have been better to translate ὁ ἀπόστολος λέγων ταῦτα ἐν τῷ ἱερῷ βλέπει τὸν κύριον by *while the apostle is saying these things in the temple, he sees the Lord.*

4. διδασκομένῳ ὑπὸ τοῦ ἀποστόλου προσέρχονται αὐτῷ οἱ δοῦλοι, *while he is being taught by the apostle, the servants are coming to him.* Here διδασκομένῳ agrees with αὐτῷ, which, like τῷ ἀποστόλῳ in the preceding example, is dative with the verb προσέρχομαι. διδασκομένῳ is the present *passive* participle of διδάσκω.

242. [233] Tense of Participles

The tense of the participle *does not denote time.* Indeed, except in the indicative mood, tense in Greek only represents a certain way of looking at the action.[1] The progressive tense of a participle denotes an action as in progress, or continuing, or being repeated. The progressive participle, therefore, is used

---

1. Even in the indicative mood, time is really only a secondary feature of the tense; occasionally Greek present indicative is used in reference to past or future events, and a few times aorist indicative is used in reference to some present or future events. Only the future tense in Greek is really closely tied with a time.

if the action denoted by the participle is to be represented as an action in progress when the action denoted by the leading verb takes place, no matter whether the action denoted by that verb is past, present, or future. The time of a participle is thus relative to the time of the leading verb.

Examples:

1. διδασκομένῳ ὑπὸ τοῦ ἀποστόλου προσῆλθον αὐτῷ οἱ δοῦλοι, *while he was being taught by the apostle, the servants came to him.* Here the action denoted by the participle διδασκομένῳ, though it is past with reference to the time when the sentence is spoken or written, is in progress at the time of the leading verb—that is, the teaching was in progress at the time of the coming of the servants. Hence the *progressive* participle is used.

2. πορευομένῳ ἐν τῇ ὁδῷ προσέρχονται αὐτῷ οἱ μαθηταὶ αὐτοῦ, *while he is going in the way, his disciples are coming to him.* Since the main verb is present tense, the action of the participle is also taking place in the present. Notice also that the participles of a deponent verb (πορεύομαι in this case), like other parts of that verb, are active in meaning though passive in form.

3. πορευόμενος ἐν τῇ ὁδῷ εἶδεν τυφλόν, *while he was going in the way, he saw a blind man.* Note that the participle frequently agrees with the unexpressed subject of a verb. Similarly, λέγων ταῦτα εἶδεν τυφλόν means *while he was saying these things, he saw a blind man,* and λέγοντες ταῦτα εἴδετε τυφλόν means *while you were saying these things, you saw a blind man.*

4. ἐσθίοντας τὸν ἄρτον αὐτῶν διδάξει αὐτούς, *while (in the future) they are eating their bread, he will teach them.* Here the action of the main verb is future, so the participle's action is also future, though in English a relative clause that takes place in the future is most commonly expressed with a present tense verb. The translation could have read,

while they will be eating their bread, he will teach them, but this is not idiomatic English. The main thing to note again is that the action of the progressive participle is *in progress* at the time, whenever that is, that the leading verb takes place.

243. Since the action of the progressive participle is in progress when the leading verb takes place, clauses containing such participles often indicate the time during which the main verbal action occurs, and all of the examples above have been so translated. But participles also serve a variety of other purposes, such as cause ("since"), or means ("by"), which must be determined by their context. At this stage, however, the student is advised to translate progressive participles with the word "while," unless the context makes perfectly clear that another function is in view.

244. [256] The Negatives οὐ and μή

Generally speaking, οὐ is the negative of the indicative; μή is the negative of the other moods, including the infinitive and the participle. Exceptions will be noted as they are encountered.

Example: μὴ πιστεύων οὐ σώζεται, *while not believing, he is not being saved*, or *because he is not believing, he is not being saved*. Here μή negates the participle πιστεύων, and οὐ negates the indicative σώζεται.

245. [239] The importance of this lesson and the three following lessons can hardly be overestimated. Without understanding thoroughly the use of participles, it is impossible to master the later lessons or to read the Greek New Testament. The participle is quite the crucial matter in the study of Greek.

246. When parsing participles, the student should identify the tense, voice, mood (the fact that it is a participle), gender, number, case, and the lexical form.

Accent Matters

247. [228b] The accent in the genitive plural feminine of the progressive active participle follows the *noun* rule for the first declension, not the adjective rule (see §§56, 77).

248. [229] Remember that in the accusative plural the α in the ending is short in the third declension but long in the first declension. This will be helpful when working with progressive active participles, whose masculine and neuter are declined according to the third declension (the masculine exactly like ἄρχων) and whose feminine is declined according to the first declension (like δόξα).

249. Exercises

A. 1. διωκόμενοι ὑπὸ τοῦ ἄρχοντος προσευχόμεθα τῷ θεῷ. 2. ἐξερχομένοις ἐκ τῆς ἐκκλησίας λέγει ἡμῖν ταῦτα. 3. ἐξήλθομεν πρὸς αὐτοὺς ἄγοντες τὰ τέκνα. 4. ταῖς ἐκκλησίαις διωκομέναις ἐγράφετε λόγους ἐλπίδος. 5. ἐν τῇ νυκτὶ ἐλεύσεται ὁ κύριος τοῖς δούλοις ἐσθίουσι καὶ πίνουσι, καὶ ἀπολύσει τὸν οἶκον αὐτῶν. 6. καταβαίνων εἰς τὴν ὁδὸν οὔπω ὄψῃ τοὺς ἁγίους. 7. οἱ πονηροὶ ἄρχοντες ἔλυσαν τοὺς οἴκους τῶν πιστῶν κηρυσσόντων τὸ εὐαγγέλιον. 8. διδασκόμενα τὰ τέκνα ἐν τῷ ἱερῷ ἦχον τὴν χαράν. 9. μηδὲ[1] διδάσκοντας μηδὲ διδασκομένους οἱ πονηροὶ λήμψονται τοὺς μαθητάς. 10. σωζόμενα ἀπὸ τῆς ἁμαρτίας αὐτῶν τὰ τέκνα ἀκούει τῆς φωνῆς τοῦ κυρίου. 11. οἱ μαθηταὶ πορευόμενοι παρὰ τὴν θάλασσαν ἠνέχθησαν τῷ κυρίῳ. 12. οἱ μαθηταὶ πορευομένῳ παρὰ τὴν θάλασσαν ἠνέχθησαν τῷ κυρίῳ. 13. ἐκβαλλομένη ἐκ τοῦ οἴκου ὑμῶν ἔλεγεν καλὰ ῥήματα ὑμῖν. 14. ἐγράφη ἡμῖν ταῦτα τὰ ῥήματα προσφέρουσι τὰ δῶρα τῷ τυφλῷ. 15. ἤδη ἔπεμπε ὁ ἄρχων τοὺς κακοὺς κατὰ τῶν πρώτων μαθητῶν ἀκουόντων τῶν παραβαλῶν. 16. ἐσθίοντες και πίνοντες ἄνθρωποι ὄψονται τὸν υἱὸν τοῦ ἀνθρώπου ἐρχόμενον ἐν τῇ δόξῃ. 17. ἔκραξεν διδάσκων ἐν τῷ ἱερῷ ὁ κύριος καὶ λέγων· γι-

---

1. μηδέ... μηδέ means *neither... nor* (see §291 and compare with §154).

νώσκετέ με; 18. ὧν¹ κεφαλὴ τῆς ἐκκλησίας αὐτοῦ ὁ κύριος αὐτῇ ἐδίδασκεν ἐντολάς. 19. τὸν λόγον αὐτοῦ οὐκ ἔχετε ἐν ὑμῖν μένοντα.² 20. τῷ αὐτῷ ἔπεμψα τὸν ἄρτον μὴ ἔχοντι ἄρτον. B. 1. While I was praying in my house, the Lord sent me a gift. 2. While gathering in the temple, the disciples spoke true words. 3. The voice of the prophets, while it was being heard in the house, was believed. 4. While the faithful women remained in the temple, they were seeing the Lord's face. 5. The temple, as long as³ it remains, is a place for the faithful. 6. During the time that you (s.) are being saved, you are also teaching children. 7. We were writing to the disciples while they were being persecuted. 8. At the time that the disciples were getting into the boat, they were saying words of joy and hope. 9. While the glory of the Lord was being spoken by the angels, the people saw it. 10. Those children, while receiving gifts, were being gathered by the rulers. 11. When he was praying in the desert, he saw the face of an angel. 12. While the promises remain, my soul will be faithful. 13. We will bring the children to the Lord, persuading them that they have good promises. 14. Believing the promises, you (p.) will have peace. 15. While you were being persecuted, in joy you lifted up your heads, knowing that the Lord saved you. 16. Since you (s.) are not hearing the Scriptures, you do not know the truth.

1. This is one instance where the participle should be taken not in a temporal sense ("while") but in a causal sense ("since").
2. Again, this is not a temporal participle; it simply indicates in what way the verbal action takes place.
3. Phrases like "so long as" or "during the time that" are of course equivalent to "while," and may be expressed with a progressive participle.

Lesson 18B

*Attributive Participles • Substantive
Use of Participles*

250. Vocabulary

ἀσπάζομαι, dep., *I greet, I
salute*

γλῶσσα, ἡ, *a tongue, a language*

ἕκαστος, -η, -ον, adj., *each*

μυστήριον, τό, *a mystery, a
secret*

οἶνος, ὁ, *wine*

πρεσβύτερος, ὁ, *an old man,
an elder* (leader in the
church)

σημεῖον, τό, *a sign, a miracle*

σοφία, ἡ, *wisdom*

251. [234] Attributive Participles

The participle, like any other adjective, can stand in the *attributive* position.

Examples:

1. Recall (see §71) that ὁ ἀγαθὸς ἀπόστολος means *the good apostle*. In exactly the same way ὁ λέγων ταῦτα ἐν τῷ ἱερῷ ἀπόστολος means *the saying-these-things-in-the-temple apostle*. The participle (with its modifiers) is here an adjective in the attri-

butive position; it takes the exact place of the attributive adjective ἀγαθός in the phrase ὁ ἀγαθὸς ἀπόστολος. It is more usual, however, to place the attributive participle (with its modifiers) in the second of the two alternative positions in which the attributive adjective can stand. Thus the usual order would be ὁ ἀπόστολος ὁ λέγων ταῦτα ἐν τῷ ἱερῷ. Here the λέγων ταῦτα ἐν τῷ ἱερῷ takes the exact place of ἀγαθός in the phrase ὁ ἀπόστολος ὁ ἀγαθός, which is one of the two ways in which *the good apostle* can be expressed.

Of course the "literal" translation, *the saying-these-things-in-the-temple apostle*, is not good English. The idiomatic English way of expressing the same idea is *the apostle who is saying these things in the temple.*

The difference between this attributive use of the participle and the use that appears in example 1 in §241 should be noticed very carefully. In the sentence ὁ ἀπόστολος λέγων ταῦτα ἐν τῷ ἱερῷ βλέπει τὸν κύριον, the participle λέγων, being in the *predicate*, not in the attributive, position, goes only somewhat loosely with ὁ ἀπόστολος (though it agrees with it), and really modifies also the verb βλέπει—that is, it relates something as in progress when the action denoted by βλέπει took place. But the addition of the one little word ὁ before λέγων makes an enormous difference in the meaning. When that word is added we have the sentence ὁ ἀπόστολος ὁ λέγων ταῦτα ἐν τῷ ἱερῷ βλέπει τὸν κύριον, *the apostle who says these things in the temple sees the Lord.* Here λέγων stands in the attributive position and does not in any way modify the verb βλέπει; but it tells *what* apostle is being spoken of. Suppose someone asks us what apostle we are talking about. We could reply, "Not the good apostle or the bad apostle, or the great apostle or the small apostle, but *the saying-these-things-in-the-temple* apostle." It will be seen that the attributive participle identifies the particular apostle that we are talking about.

147

2. Compare εἶδον τοὺς ἀποστόλους λέγοντας ταῦτα, *I saw the apostles while they were saying these things* or *I saw the apostles saying these things*, with εἶδον τοὺς ἀποστόλους τοὺς λέγοντας ταῦτα, *I saw the apostles who were saying these things*. In the latter case the (attributive) participle tells *which* apostles we are talking about.

252. Distinguishing Predicate and Attributive Participles

The *attributive* participle is strictly an adjective, serving to modify a noun or other substantive. Therefore the attributive participle is in the attributive position. This means that the attributive participle will *usually* have an article in front of it, even if the substantive it modifies does not have an article. Since the attributive participle is functioning as an adjective, the participle and everything associated with the participle all give further information about the noun or substantive it agrees with and modifies.

Predicate participles, on the other hand, serve as adverbs; that is, they modify either a verb, an adjective, an adverb, or even another participle. In other words, predicate participles give the *circumstances* relating to the action of the verb on which it depends (such as *when* it took place, or *why*, or *how*). They are therefore sometimes called *circumstantial* participles. Predicate or circumstantial participles *never* have an article. Thus, it is by observing whether the participle has an article in front of it that one can tell if a participle is predicate (indicating circumstances) or attributive (indicating which substantive).

253. Progressive tense, in both predicate and attributive participles, indicates progressive action. As noted in §242, predicate participles derive a time from the fact that they indicate that the participial action is in progress when that of the leading verb occurs. With attributive participles this may often be the case, but is not necessarily so. Progressive tense in the case of an attributive participle indicates only that the action is regarded as continual, repeated, or habitual. This may be reflected in English translation by the use of either the present or imperfect, depending on the context.

Example: τὰ διδασκόμενα τέκνα ἦλθεν εἰς τὸ ἱερόν, *the children who were being taught went into the temple.* In this case *the children who were being taught* could also have been translated *the children who are being taught,* because the participle διδασκόμενα only indicates continual action of some sort, not its time. Only context will indicate which time ought to be assigned in order to translate it into English.

254. [235] Substantive Use of Participles

The participle, like any other adjective, can be used substantively with the article.

Remember that ὁ ἀγαθός means *the good man;* ἡ ἀγαθή, *the good woman;* τὸ ἀγαθόν, *the good thing;* οἱ ἀγαθοί, *the good men,* etc. In exactly the same way ὁ λέγων ταῦτα ἐν τῷ ἱερῷ means *the saying-these-things-in-the-temple man.* The participle (with its modifiers), just like the adjective, tells *which* man we are talking about. But how will the same idea be expressed in idiomatic English? There are various closely related ways— for example, *the man who is saying these things in the temple,* or *the one who is saying these things in the temple,* or *he who is saying these things in the temple.* Notice, however, that none of these English phrases is a literal translation of the Greek. The Greek ὁ does not mean *the man* or *the one* or *he.* It means *the,* and it is just as simple an article as the article in the phrase *the cat* or *the dog* or *the house.* But in English we do not often use the article with the substantive participle. Therefore we have to reproduce the idea of the Greek ὁ λέγων by a phrase of which the individual parts have little to do with the individual parts of the Greek phrase. It is only the total meaning of the English phrase that is the same as the total meaning of the Greek phrase.

The following examples should also be examined:

1. εἶδον τὸν λέγοντα ταῦτα ἐν τῷ ἱερῷ, *I saw the one who was saying these things in the temple.* Here the Greek uses the progressive participle because the time of the action denoted by the participle is concurrent with the action denoted by the leading verb, even though the action denoted by the leading verb here happens to be in past time.

2. εἶδον τοὺς λέγοντας ταῦτα, *I saw those who were saying these things.*

3. ὁ ἀδελφὸς τῆς λεγούσης ταῦτα δοῦλός ἐστιν, *the brother of the woman who is saying these things is a servant.*

4. ὁ πιστεύων εἰς τὸν ἐγείροντα τοὺς νεκροὺς σώζεται, *he who believes on the one who raises the dead is being saved.*

5. τὸ σῷζον τὸ θέλημα τοῦ θεοῦ ἐστιν, *the thing that saves* (or *that which saves*) *is the will of God.*

6. τὰ βλεπόμενα οὐ μένει εἰς τὸν αἰῶνα, *the things that are seen do not remain for ever.*

255. [236] The following summary of the substantive uses of the participle may be found useful:

Act.	ὁ λύων	*the loosing man*	= *the man who looses, the one who looses, he who looses*
Mid.	ὁ λυόμενος	*the loosing-for-himself man*	= *the man who looses for himself, the one who looses for himself, he who looses for himself*

Pass.	ὁ λυόμενος	the being-loosed man	= the man who is being loosed, the one who is being loosed, he who is being loosed
Act.	τὸ λῦον	the loosing thing	= the thing that looses, that which looses
Act.	οἱ λύοντες	the loosing men	= the men who loose, the ones who loose, those who loose

256. [237] Notice that the English word *he* in the phrase *he who looses* is not a real—certainly not an ordinary—personal pronoun, but merely the light antecedent of the relative pronoun *who*. *He* has no value of its own but goes in the closest possible way with *who*, so as to form the phrase *he who*. The Greek language, strangely as it may seem to us, possesses no such light antecedent of the relative. The ordinary Greek way, therefore, of expressing the idea *he who looses* is to use article with participle and say *the loosing man*, ὁ λύων. Similarly, the English word *that* in the phrase *that which looses*, and the English word *those* in the phrase *those who loose*, are not really demonstrative adjectives or pronouns; they do not really "point out" anything. They are very different, for example, from the demonstratives in the phrases *that house across the street* or *those trees over there on the campus*. The *that* and the *those* in these sentences could be accompanied by a pointing finger; they are real demonstratives. But the *that* and the *those* in the phrases *that which looses* or *those that loose* are simply light antecedents of the relative, and for them the Greek has no equivalent. Such phrases, therefore, must be cast into an entirely different mold before they can be translated into Greek.

257. [238] As already noted in lesson 9 (see §108), the English word *that* has a number of widely different uses. It is (1) a conjunction, (2) a demonstrative adjective or pronoun, (3) a light antecedent of the relative, and (4) a relative pronoun like *which*.

Example: *I know that that which saves the men that receive that gospel is the grace of God.* Here the first *that* is a conjunction; the second, the light antecedent of the relative; the third, a relative pronoun; the fourth, a real demonstrative. The Greek language has a different way of expressing each of these uses of *that*. The sentence in Greek would be as follows: γινώσκω ὅτι τὸ σῷζον τοὺς δεχομένους ἐκεῖνο τὸ εὐαγγέλιον ἡ χάρις τοῦ θεοῦ ἐστιν.

The two uses of the English word *those* may be illustrated by the sentence, *those who believe will receive those good men*, οἱ πιστεύοντες δέξονται ἐκείνους τοὺς ἀγαθούς.

258. Analyzing the Participle: A Summary

When the student encounters a participle, it is necessary to take careful note of the following:

1. The participle's position. If it has an article before it, it is an attributive participle.

2. The participle's agreement. If it is in attributive position and agrees with a noun or other substantive, it is identifying *which* substantive. If it is in the predicate position, the substantive it agrees with is the understood subject of the action of that participle. If it has an article but does not go with another substantive, it is itself a substantive, to be translated as *the one who*, or the like.

3. The participle's tense. The progressive participle indicates action *in progress*. For the predicate position participle, this means that the participial action is in progress at the time

when the action of the leading verb occurs. (The aorist participle will be discussed in the next lesson.)
4. The participle's voice. As with any verb, voice will indicate whether the understood subject of the participial action (the substantive it agrees with) is acting, being acted on, or acting with respect to itself.

259. [240] Exercises

A. 1. ὁ ἔχων τὸν υἱὸν ἔχει τὴν ζωήν. 2. ὁ σὲ δεχόμενος δέχεται καὶ τὸν κύριον. 3. ταῦτα τὰ μυστήρια λέγομεν τοῖς πορευομένοις εἰς τὸν οἶκον περὶ τοῦ ἐγείροντος τοὺς νεκρούς. 4. ὁ λόγος ὁ λεγόμενος διὰ τῶν προφητῶν ἐστιν σοφία. 5. αἱ ἐκκλησίαι αἱ διωκόμεναι ὑπὸ τῶν ἀρχόντων πιστεύουσιν εἰς τὸν κύριον. 6. οἱ πιστεύοντες εἰς τὸν κύριον σώζονται. 7. γινώσκει ὁ θεὸς τὰ γραφόμενα ἐν τῷ βιβλίῳ τῆς ζωῆς. 8. ἕκαστον τῶν τέκνων τῶν ἀκουόντων τὸν πρεσβύτερον λέγοντα τὸν λόγον τοῦ θεοῦ ἔλαβεν δῶρα. 9. εἴδομεν τοὺς λαμβάνοντας τὰ δῶρα ἀπὸ τῶν τέκνων. 10. οὗτός ἐστιν ὁ ἄρχων ὁ δεχόμενός με εἰς τὸν οἶκον αὐτοῦ. 11. ἅγιοί εἰσιν οἱ πιστεύοντες εἰς τὸν κύριον καὶ σωζόμενοι ὑπ᾽ αὐτοῦ. 12. τοῦτό ἐστι τὸ πνεῦμα τὸ σῶζον ἡμᾶς. 13. ἦσαν ἐν τῷ οἴκῳ τῷ λυομένῳ ὑπὸ τοῦ ἄρχοντος. 14. ἦσαν ἐν τῷ οἴκῳ λυομένῳ ὑπὸ τοῦ ἄρχοντος. 15. αὕτη ἐστὶν ἡ ἐκκλησία ἡ πιστεύουσα εἰς τὸν κύριον. 16. διδασκόμενοι ὑπὸ τοῦ κυρίου ἐπορεύεσθε ἐν τῇ ὁδῷ τῇ ἀναβαινούσῃ εἰς τὴν ἔρημον. 17. ἐκηρύχθη ὑπ᾽ αὐτῶν τὸ εὐαγγέλιον τὸ σῶζον τοὺς ἁμαρτωλούς. 18. τοῦτό ἐστιν τὸ εὐαγγέλιον τὸ κηρυσσόμενον ἐν τῷ κόσμῳ καὶ σῶζον τοὺς ἀνθρώπους. 19. αὐτοῖς ἐπέμφθη σημεῖον ἀπ᾽ οὐρανοῦ ἀσπαζομένοις με. 20. ἔτι ὄντα ἐν τῷ ἱερῷ εἴδομεν αὐτόν.

B. 1. While he was still in the[1] flesh, the Lord was saving those who were believing on him. 2. While we were being taught in the temple, we were being persecuted by the ruler.

1. In such phrases, the article is often omitted in Greek.

3. Those who are being saved by the Lord know him who saves them. 4. Those who were proclaiming these things received, themselves also, the things that were being proclaimed by them. 5. She who is receiving the Lord into her house sees the face of the one who saves her. 6. While he was still teaching in the temple, we saw him. 7. While we were teaching in the temple, we saw the one who saves us. 8. The hope that is seen is not hope. 9. The Lord said to those who were believing on him that God saves sinners. 10. The brothers of those who persecute the disciples do not have hope. 11. Those who say these things do not know the one who saves the church. 12. We were cast out by the ruler who persecutes the church. 13. This is the voice that is being heard by those who believe in the Lord. 14. While I was remaining in the house, I saw the women who were taking gifts from the disciples. 15. Being preached by those who believe in the Lord, the gospel will lead men into the church. 16. The faithful ones will see the Lord going up into heaven. 17. Not even the angels who see the face of God know the mystery of the coming kingdom. 18. Each one who has a tongue will cry out to God.

Lesson 19

Aorist Active and Middle Participles
• Use of the Aorist Participle

260. [241] Vocabulary

ἀγαγών, *having led,* 2nd aor.
  act. part. of ἄγω
ἀπέθανον, *I died,* 2nd aor. of
  ἀποθνήσκω
ἀπεκρίθην, *I answered,* aor.
  indic., pass. in form, of
  ἀποκρίνομαι
εἰπών, *having said,* 2nd aor.
  act. part. of λέγω
ἐλθών, *having come,* 2nd
  aor. act. part. of ἔρχομαι

ἐνεγκών, *having borne, hav-*
  ing brought, 2nd aor. act.
  part. of φέρω (the 1st
  aorist form of this verb,
  ἤνεγκα, is more common
  in the indicative)
ἰδών, *having seen,* 2nd aor.
  act. part. of βλέπω (or
  ὁράω)

261. [242] The declension of λύσας, λύσασα, λῦσαν, *hav-*
ing loosed, the aorist active participle of λύω, is as follows:

155

	Sing.		
	Masc.	**Fem.**	**Neut.**
Nom.	λύσας	λύσασα	λῦσαν
Gen.	λύσαντος	λυσάσης	λύσαντος
Dat.	λύσαντι	λυσάσῃ	λύσαντι
Acc.	λύσαντα	λύσασαν	λῦσαν

	Plur.		
	Masc.	**Fem.**	**Neut.**
Nom.	λύσαντες	λύσασαι	λύσαντα
Gen.	λυσάντων	λυσασῶν	λυσάντων
Dat.	λύσασι(ν)	λυσάσαις	λύσασι(ν)
Acc.	λύσαντας	λυσάσας	λύσαντα

262. [243] Like the progressive active participle, the aorist active participle is declined according to the third declension in the masculine and neuter, and according to the first declension in the feminine.

263. [244] The characteristic σα, which in first aorists is the sign of the aorist system, appears throughout. The student should remember that the actual aorist stem of any verb can only certainly be known by reference to its third principal part. But the aorist system of most first aorists typically adds a σ to the verb stem, and all first aorists use α as the theme vowel.

264. [245] The augment, however, does not appear on the participle; it is used only in the indicative mood. Thus, although the aorist active indicative of λύω is ἔλυσα, the aorist active participle is not ἐλύσας, but λύσας, and although the aorist active indicative of ἀκούω is ἤκουσα, the aorist active participle is not ἠκούσας but ἀκούσας. Therefore, to form the aorist participle, one must remove the augment from the third principal part of a verb before adding the appropriate participial ending.

265. [246] The declension of λυσάμενος, -η, -ον, *having loosed for him-(her-, it-)self,* the aorist middle participle of λύω, is as follows:

Sing.

	Masc.	Fem.	Neut.
Nom.	λυσάμενος	λυσαμένη	λυσάμενον
Gen.	λυσαμένου	λυσαμένης	λυσαμένου
Dat.	λυσαμένῳ	λυσαμένῃ	λυσαμένῳ
Acc.	λυσάμενον	λυσαμένην	λυσάμενον

Plur.

	Masc.	Fem.	Neut.
Nom.	λυσάμενοι	λυσάμεναι	λυσάμενα
Gen.	λυσαμένων	λυσαμένων	λυσαμένων
Dat.	λυσαμένοις	λυσαμέναις	λυσαμένοις
Acc.	λυσαμένους	λυσαμένας	λυσάμενα

266. [247] Like the progressive middle participle, the aorist middle participle is declined like an ordinary adjective of the second and first declensions. The aorist passive participle is quite different, and is reserved for the following lesson.

267. [248] Like the aorist active participle and the rest of the aorist system, the aorist middle participle is formed on the aorist stem. In the first aorist verbs, the characteristic σα appears throughout.

268. [249] Second aorist participles are formed differently. The declension of ἰδών, ἰδοῦσα, ἰδόν, *having seen*, the second aorist active participle of βλέπω (it may also be regarded as coming from ὁράω), is as follows:

Sing.

	Masc.	Fem.	Neut.
Nom.	ἰδών	ἰδοῦσα	ἰδόν
Gen.	ἰδόντος	ἰδούσης	ἰδόντος
Dat.	ἰδόντι	ἰδούσῃ	ἰδόντι
Acc.	ἰδόντα	ἰδοῦσαν	ἰδόν

157

	Plur.		
	Masc.	**Fem.**	**Neut.**
Nom.	ἰδόντες	ἰδοῦσαι	ἰδόντα
Gen.	ἰδόντων	ἰδουσῶν	ἰδόντων
Dat.	ἰδοῦσι(ν)	ἰδούσαις	ἰδοῦσι(ν)
Acc.	ἰδόντας	ἰδούσας	ἰδόντα

269. [250a] Note that the second aorist active participle is declined not like the first aorist but like the progressive active participle, except that its accent falls on the ending (see §277).

270. Any verb that has a second aorist in the indicative will have a second aorist rather than first aorist participle. The third principal part is determinative for all the forms of the aorist system of a verb.

271. [251] Remember that the augment appears only in the indicative mood, and must therefore be dropped from the third of the principal parts before the aorist participle can be formed. In irregular verbs like βλέπω (ὁράω) the dropping of the augment in the second aorist sometimes gives difficulty. The third of the principal parts of βλέπω (ὁράω) is εἶδον. Without the augment the second aorist stem is ἰδ-, for ι was here irregularly augmented to ει. On the other hand, the second aorist participle of λέγω is εἰπών (εἶπον being the second aorist indicative), because here εἰπ- was the second aorist stem and, being regarded as long enough already, was not changed at all for the augment.

272. [252] The aorist participles of a few other such verbs, where the dropping of the augment from the third of the principal parts in order to get the aorist stem might give difficulty, will be included in the vocabularies. Ordinarily, however, students are expected to perform the necessary processes for themselves. Thus if a form ἀποθανών is found in the exercises, the student is expected to see that this form is the participle of a second aorist of which the indicative (with the augment)

158

is ἀπέθανον. This form, since the verb is irregular, will be found in the general vocabulary.

273. [253] The second aorist middle participle is declined exactly like the progressive middle participle and differs from the progressive middle participle only in that it is formed on the second aorist stem instead of on the progressive stem. Thus λαβόμενος is the second aorist middle participle of λαμβάνω, ἔλαβον being the second aorist active indicative (third of the principal parts).

274. [254] Use of the Aorist Participle

As noted in §242, the tense of the participle indicates not time but perspective on the kind of action. Thus aorist participles do not indicate past time. As with progressive participles, the time of an action indicated by an aorist participle must be determined by reference to the action of its leading verb. But whereas progressive participles in the predicate position denote action in progress at the time of the leading verb, aorist participles have no such progressivity in view. Ordinarily, aorist participles in the predicate position refer to action *prior to* the action of the leading verb, whether the action denoted by that verb is past, present, or future.

Examples:

1. ὁ ἀπόστολος εἰπὼν ταῦτα ἐν τῷ ἱερῷ βλέπει τὸν κύριον, *the apostle, having said these things in the temple, is seeing the Lord.* Here εἰπών, the aorist participle, denotes action prior to the action denoted by βλέπει. Compare example 1 in §241.

2. εἰπὼν ταῦτα ἀπῆλθεν, *having said these things, he went away.* The literal translation of the participle is here perfectly possible. But it would be more idiomatic English to translate *after he had said these things, he went away.* Compare λέγων ταῦτα ἀπῆλθεν, *he went away saying these things* or *while he was saying these things, he went away.* Notice that when a

Greek progressive participle is translated by a temporal clause in English, the English word that best introduces the temporal clause is *while*, and when it is an aorist participle that is to be translated into English, the English word that best introduces the temporal clause is *after*.[1] In the case of the aorist participle, the verb in the resulting English temporal clause will often be perfect ("has seen," etc.) or pluperfect ("had seen," etc.)—perfect when the leading verb is present or future, and pluperfect when the leading verb is past.

3. εἰπὼν ταῦτα ἀπέρχεται, *having said these things, he goes away*, or *after he has said these things, he goes away*.

4. προσῆλθον αὐτῷ εἰπόντι ταῦτα, *they came to him after he had said these things*. Here the literal translation of the participle would be impossible in English, because in the English sentence *they came to him, having said these things*, the *having said* would agree not with *him* but with the subject of the sentence, *they*, and the sentence would be a translation not of προσῆλθον αὐτῷ εἰπόντι ταῦτα but of προσῆλθον αὐτῷ εἰπόντες ταῦτα. Compare with προσῆλθον αὐτῷ εἰπόντι ταῦτα the sentence προσῆλθον αὐτῷ λέγοντι ταῦτα, which means *they came to him* while *he was saying these things*.

5. ἐλθόντες πρὸς τὸν κύριον ὀψόμεθα αὐτόν, *having come to the Lord, we will see him*, or *after we have come to the Lord, we will see him*.

275. [255] The aorist participle can of course be used attributively or substantively with the article (see §§251, 254).

1. As was true of progressive participles, not all aorist participles in predicate position are concerned with the *temporal* circumstances of the verb modified by the participle. Manner or means (*how* something occurred), cause (*why* it occurred), and a number of other types of circumstances may be indicated. But at this point, *consistency* in translation, which reflects the student's awareness of the tense of the participle, is strongly advised, and always translating the aorist predicate participle with an "after" clause is the best way to ensure this consistency.

Examples:

1. ὁ μαθητὴς ὁ ἀκούσας ταῦτα ἐν τῷ ἱερῷ ἦλθεν εἰς τὸν οἶκον, *the having-heard-these-things-in-the-temple disciple went into the house,* or *the disciple who heard/had heard these things in the temple went into the house.* On the other hand, ὁ μαθητὴς ἀκούσας ταῦτα ἐν τῷ ἱερῷ ἦλθεν εἰς τὸν οἶκον would mean *the disciple, after he had heard these things in the temple, went into the house.*

2. ὁ ἀκούσας ταῦτα ἀπῆλθεν, *the having-heard-these-things man went away,* or *he/the one/the man who heard/had heard these things went away.* On the other hand ἀκούσας ταῦτα ἀπῆλθεν would mean *having heard these things, he went away* or *after he had heard these things, he went away.* In the former sentence ὁ ἀκούσας tells what man we are talking about, while ἀκούσας without the article merely adds a detail about a person who is designated in some other way or not designated at all.

3. εἶδον τὰς εἰπούσας ταῦτα, *I saw the having-said-these-things women,* or *I saw the women who had said these things.*

The student should compare with these examples the corresponding examples given for the progressive participle.

276. It is important to remember that the aorist tense of the participle does not itself indicate time; it only denotes that *no particular kind of action* is in view (see §176). In all the above examples, therefore, the use of English past tenses is simply a concession to the fact that English demands a temporal indication. The Greek participle itself does not provide that information, and the translator must derive time from the context, usually the leading verb.

Accent Matters

277. [250b] The accent on the nominative masculine and neuter forms of second aorist participles does not follow the verb rule of recessive accent, but is on the ultima. There-

161

after the noun rule is followed, the accent remaining on the same syllable throughout, except in the genitive plural feminine, where §56 comes into play. This is a case where accents help us out. If a participle is encountered having an -ων, -ουσα, -ον ending, it is very likely a participle, but unless we already know the verb and its principal parts, it is impossible to tell by its form whether it is a progressive or second aorist. But the accent on the ending, if by the general rules it could be placed earlier, is a good indication that the participle in question is second aorist.

278. [257] Exercises

A. 1. λαβόντες ταῦτα παρὰ τῶν πιστευόντων εἰς τὸν κύριον ἐξήλθομεν εἰς τὴν ἔρημον. 2. πισταί εἰσιν αἱ δεξάμεναι τοὺς διωκομένους ὑπὸ τοῦ ἄρχοντος. 3. εἴδομεν αὐτοὺς καὶ μένοντας ἐν τῷ οἴκῳ καὶ ἐξελθόντας ἐξ αὐτοῦ. 4. οἱ πιόντες τὸν οἶνον ἐκεῖνον ἦλθον πρὸς τοὺς ἀγαγόντας τὸν μαθητὴν ἐκ τοῦ ἱεροῦ. 5. ταῦτα εἴπομεν περὶ τοῦ σώσαντος ἡμᾶς. 6. οὗτοί εἰσιν οἱ κηρύξαντες τὸ εὐαγγέλιον, ἀλλ᾽ ἐκεῖνοί εἰσιν οἱ διώξαντες τοὺς πιστεύοντας. 7. προσενεγκόντες τῷ κυρίῳ τὸν διωκόμενον ὑπὸ τοῦ ἄρχοντος τοῦ πονηροῦ ἀπήλθετε εἰς ἄλλον τόπον. 8. προσῆλθον τῷ κυρίῳ ἐλθόντι εἰς τὸ ἱερόν. 9. ἐπίστευσας εἰς αὐτὸν εἰπόντα ταῦτα τὰ μυστήρια. 10. ταῦτα εἶπον ἐξελθὼν ἐκ τῆς ἐκκλησίας. 11. ὁ μὴ ἰδὼν τὸν κύριον οὐκ ἐπίστευσεν εἰς αὐτόν. 12. ταῦτα εἶπεν ὁ κύριος ἔτι ὢν ἐν τῇ ὁδῷ τοῖς ἐξελθοῦσιν ἐκ τοῦ οἴκου καὶ πορευομένοις μετ᾽ αὐτοῦ. 13. ἀκούσαντες τὰ λεγόμενα ὑπὸ τοῦ κυρίου ἐπίστευσαν εἰς αὐτόν. 14. εἴδομεν τοὺς γενομένους μαθητὰς τοῦ κυρίου καὶ ἔτι μένοντας ἐν τῇ ἐλπίδι αὐτῶν τῇ πρώτῃ. 15. τὰ τέκνα τὰ λαβόντα ταῦτα ἀπὸ τῶν ἀκουσάντων τοῦ κυρίου εἶδον αὐτὸν ἔτι ὄντα ἐν τῷ οἴκῳ. 16. ἰδοῦσαι αὗται τὸν κηρύξαντα τὸ εὐαγγέλιον ἐκεῖνο ἦλθον πρὸς αὐτὸν ἐρχόμενον εἰς τὸν οἶκον. 17. οἱ ἄγγελοι οἱ πεσόντες ἐκ τοῦ οὐρανοῦ πονηροὶ ἦσαν. 18. ὁ τὸν λόγον μου ἀκούων καὶ πιστεύων τῷ πέμψαντί με ἔχει ζωήν. 19. ταῦτα ἀπεκρίθη τοῖς προσ-

ενεγκοῦσιν αὐτῷ τὸν οἶνον. 20. ἀπήλθομεν μὴ ἰδόντες τὸν διδά-
ξαντα ἡμᾶς. 21. φαγόντες καὶ πιόντες τὸ σῶμα καὶ τὸ αἷμα τοῦ
κυρίου εἰσελεύσονται εἰς τὰ μυστήρια τῆς βασιλείας.

B. 1. Those who have not seen the apostle do not know him.
2. I did not see him who had believed on the Lord. 3. I saw
him after he had believed on the Lord, but you (p.) saw him
while he was still in the kingdom of the evil one. 4. Having
heard these things, we believed on him who had died in behalf
of us. 5. We came to those who were going in the way. 6. We
shall see the signs of the apostles after we have gone into this
house. 7. Those men said to those who had gone into the house
that the Lord is good. 8. While we were saying these things,
we were going into our house. 9. When they had received these
gifts from the ones who had brought them, they came together
into the church. 10. These are the women who received the
one who had taught them. 11. When these men had seen the
Lord, they were brought to the rulers. 12. The disciples who
had come into the church were baptized by the apostles who
had seen the Lord. 13. The blind man who had received this
man was with those who were persecuting him. 14. The
demons that were being cast out cried out against him who
was casting them out. 15. As we were going through the desert,
we taught those who were with us. 16. We saw the servant
when he had believed on the Lord and was still in the house.
17. Having eaten my bread and drunk my wine, you (s.) are
now persecuting me.

Lesson 20

*Aorist Passive Participle • Genitive Absolute
• Elliptical Constructions • Participial Phrases
with Verbs of Perception*

279. [258] Vocabulary

γραφείς, *having been written,*
  2nd aor. pass. part. of
  γράφω (declined like a 1st
  aor. pass. part.)
ἐκεῖ, adv., *there*
εὐθέως or εὐθύς, adv., *immediately, right away*
ἱμάτιον, τό, *a garment*

οἰκία, ἡ, *a house* (a synonym
  of οἶκος)
παιδίον, τό, *a little child*
στρατιώτης, ὁ, *a soldier*
συναγωγή, ἡ, *a synagogue*
φυλακή, ἡ, *a guard, a prison*

280. [259] The declension of λυθείς, λυθεῖσα, λυθέν, *having
been loosed,* the aorist passive participle of λύω, is as follows:

164

	Sing.		
	Masc.	**Fem.**	**Neut.**
Nom.	λυθείς	λυθεῖσα	λυθέν
Gen.	λυθέντος	λυθείσης	λυθέντος
Dat.	λυθέντι	λυθείσῃ	λυθέντι
Acc.	λυθέντα	λυθεῖσαν	λυθέν

	Plur.		
	Masc.	**Fem.**	**Neut.**
Nom.	λυθέντες	λυθεῖσαι	λυθέντα
Gen.	λυθέντων	λυθεισῶν	λυθέντων
Dat.	λυθεῖσι(ν)	λυθείσαις	λυθεῖσι(ν)
Acc.	λυθέντας	λυθείσας	λυθέντα

281. [260] Like the progressive active participle and the aorist active participle, the aorist passive participle is declined according to the third declension in the masculine and neuter, and according to the first declension in the feminine.

282. [261] The characteristic -θε, which it will be remembered is the sign of the aorist passive system (derived from the sixth of the principal parts), appears throughout. This -θε, as in the rest of the aorist passive system, is added to the verb stem.

283. [262] In the aorist passive participle, the theme vowel, that is, the ε of the -θε ending, is not lengthened to -η. Thus, to form the aorist passive participle from the sixth principal part, (a) the augment must be dropped, and (b) the -θη must be changed to -θε. In cases where the sixth principal part lacks the θ, so will the participle, but the connecting or theme vowel, the ε, will always be present. Then the appropriate ending found in §280 may be added to this theme vowel.

Example: To form the aorist passive participle for "having been taught," the student must discover from the vocabularies that the sixth principal part of διδάσκω, *I teach*, is ἐδιδά-

165

χθην. Dropping the augment and shortening the η to ε yields διδαχθε-, to which are added the endings: διδαχθείς, διδαχθεῖσα, διδαχθέν.

284. [264] Like the other aorist participles, the aorist passive participle indicates only the action itself, not its duration, and ordinarily refers to action prior to the time of the leading verb; and to it applies also all that has been said about the attributive and substantival uses of the participle.

Examples:

1. ἐκβληθέντα τὰ δαιμόνια ὑπὸ τοῦ κυρίου ἀπῆλθεν εἰς τὴν θάλασσαν, *the demons, having been cast out by the Lord, went away into the sea,* or *when/after the demons had been cast out by the Lord, they went away into the sea.*

2. ἐγερθέντι ἐκ νεκρῶν προσῆλθον αὐτῷ, *they came to him after he had been raised from the dead.*

3. οἱ διδαχθέντες ὑπὸ τοῦ ἀποστόλου ἦλθον εἰς τὸν οἶκον, *the having-been-taught-by-the-apostle men came into the house,* or *the men/the ones/those who had been taught by the apostle came into the house.*

285. [265] The following summary will serve for the review of what has been learned thus far about participles:

A. Participles

Pro-	Act.	λύων	= *loosing*
gressive	Mid.	λυόμενος	= *loosing for himself*
	Pass.	λυόμενος	= *being loosed*
Aorist	Act.	λύσας	= *having loosed*
	Mid.	λυσάμενος	= *having loosed for himself*
	Pass.	λυθείς	= *having been loosed*

B. Article with Participle

Pro-gressive	Act.	ὁ λύων, the loosing man	= the man who looses, the one who looses, he who looses
	Mid.	ὁ λυόμενος, the loosing-for-himself man	= the man who looses for himself, the one who looses for himself, he who looses for himself
	Pass.	ὁ λυόμενος, the being-loosed man	= the man who is being loosed, the one who is being loosed, he who is being loosed
Aorist	Act.	ὁ λύσας, the having-loosed man	= the man who (has) loosed, the one who (has) loosed, he who (has) loosed
	Mid.	ὁ λυσάμενος, the having-loosed-for-himself man	= the man who (has) loosed for himself, the one who (has) loosed for himself, he who (has) loosed for himself
	Pass.	ὁ λυθείς, the having-been-loosed man	= the man who (has been/was) loosed, the one who (has been/was) loosed, he who (has been/was) loosed

286. [266] Genitive Absolute

A genitive noun or pronoun with a genitive participle in the predicate position often stands out of connection with the rest of the sentence in the construction called the *genitive absolute*.

Lesson 20

Examples:

1. εἰπόντων ταῦτα τῶν ἀποστόλων οἱ μαθηταὶ ἀπῆλθον, *the apostles having said these things, the disciples went away.* Here εἰπόντων and τῶν ἀποστόλων stand in the genitive absolute. ἀποστόλων is not the subject of any verb, the subject of the only finite verb in the sentence being μαθηταί, nor has it any other connection with the framework of the sentence. It is therefore *absolute* (i.e., it is not dependent on any other word in the sentence). In the English translation, *the apostles having said* is in the absolute case, which in English grammar is called the nominative absolute. But this nominative absolute is much less common in English than the genitive absolute is in Greek. Usually, therefore, it is better to translate the Greek genitive absolute by a clause, thus giving up any attempt at a "literal" translation. For example, instead of the "literal" translation of the sentence just given, it would have been better to translate, *after the apostles had said these things, the disciples went away.* Of course, all that has already been said about the tense of the participle applies to the participle in the genitive absolute as well as in other constructions.

Notice that the genitive absolute is normally used only when the noun or pronoun going with the participle is different from the subject of the finite verb. Thus in the sentence εἰπόντες ταῦτα οἱ ἀπόστολοι ἀπῆλθον, *the apostles, having said these things, went away,* or *after the apostles had said these things, they went away,* the word ἀπόστολοι has a construction in the sentence; it is the subject of the leading verb ἀπῆλθον. Therefore it is not "absolute." But in the former example it is not the apostles but someone else that is represented as performing the action denoted by the leading verb. Hence, in that former example ἀποστόλων is not the subject of the sentence but genitive absolute.

168

2. λέγοντος αὐτοῦ ταῦτα οἱ μαθηταὶ ἀπῆλθον, *while he was saying these things, the disciples went away*. Compare λέγων ταῦτα ἀπῆλθεν, *while he was saying these things, he went away* or *he went away saying these things*.

3. τῶν μαθητῶν διδαχθέντων ὑπὸ τοῦ κυρίου ἐξῆλθον εἰς τὴν ἔρημον οἱ δοῦλοι, *after the disciples had been taught by the Lord, the servants went out into the desert*. Compare οἱ μαθηταὶ διδαχθέντες ὑπὸ τοῦ κυρίου ἐξῆλθον εἰς τὴν ἔρημον, *after the disciples had been taught by the Lord, they went out into the desert*.

All this can be confusing because we expect the genitive to mean *of*, but this use of the genitive case does not indicate possession or source or any of the other regular meanings of the genitive; it is used simply to distance the participle and its understood subject from any particular substantive in the main sentence. Genitive absolutes are therefore always in the *predicate* position. A genitive participle in the predicate position will most often be a genitive absolute.

287. Elliptical Constructions

As in English, when a conjunction joins two clauses that share one or more parts of the sentence (verb, subject, object), the shared element may be dropped from the second clause. This is ordinarily not strange to English speakers, but when this principle is applied to Greek participles, it can become confusing.

Example: τοῦ κυρίου διδάσκοντος τοὺς ἀποστόλους, καὶ ἀποστόλων τέκνα, οἱ πιστεύσαντες τῷ λόγῳ ἐσῴζοντο, *while the Lord was teaching the apostles, and (while) the apostles (were teaching) the children, those who believed the word were being saved*. Though the plural ἀποστόλων would require a plural participle, the context makes it obvious that the same lexical unit found in the first clause is to be supplied.

169

288. Participial Phrases with Verbs of Perception

Verbs involving perception or knowledge (for example, βλέπω, γινώσκω, εὑρίσκω, ἀκούω) may take participial phrases as their object. Example: εἶδον τὸν ἄνθρωπον διδάσκοντα ἐν τῷ ἱερῷ, *I saw the man teaching in the temple*. Of course, this could have been translated *I saw the man while he was teaching in the temple*. But since εἶδον is a verb of perception, the direct object is not just *the man* but *the fact that the man was teaching*.

Accent Matters

289. [263] The paradigm of §280 evinces that the aorist passive participle has an irregular accent, the accent being always on the theme vowel (the ε [or ει] of the θε ending), except in the feminine genitive plural, where the rules mentioned in §§56, 247 come into play.

290. [267] Exercises

A. 1. πορευθέντος τοῦ ἄρχοντος πρὸς τὸν κύριον οἱ δοῦλοι εἶπον ταῦτα τοῖς μαθηταῖς. 2. πορευθεὶς πρὸς αὐτοὺς ὁ ἄρχων ἐπίστευσεν εἰς τὸν κύριον. 3. πιστευσάντων ὑμῶν εἰς τὸν κύριον εὐθὺς ἐπίστευσε καὶ ὁ ἄρχων. 4. εἰσελθόντος εἰς τὴν οἰκίαν τοῦ ἐγερθέντος ὑπὸ τοῦ κυρίου οἱ μαθηταὶ ἐθαύμασαν. 5. ἐκβλη-θέντος αὐτοῦ ἐκ τῆς συναγωγῆς συνήχθησαν οἱ ἄρχοντες. 6. ἐκ-βληθέντα ἐκ τῆς συναγωγῆς ἐδίδαξεν αὐτὸν ὁ κύριος. 7. εἰπόν-τος ταῦτα τοῦ πνεύματος τοῦ ἁγίου οἱ μαθηταὶ ἐκήρυξαν τὸν λόγον τοῦ θεοῦ. 8. τοῖς θεραπευθεῖσιν ὑπ᾽ αὐτοῦ εἴπετε ῥήματα ἐλπίδος καὶ ζωῆς. 9. παραλημφθέντος τούτου τοῦ σημείου ἀπὸ τοῦ κυρίου εὐθέως εἴπομεν τοῖς ἄλλοις τὰ μυστήρια τὰ ἐν ταῖς γραφαῖς ὄντα. 10. ὄψονται τὸν υἱὸν τοῦ ἀνθρώπου ἐρχόμενον ἐν νεφέλαις.[1] 11. βληθέντες εἰς φυλακὴν διὰ τὸ εὐαγγέλιον τὸ

1. νεφέλη, ἡ, *a cloud*.

κηρυχθὲν αὐτοῖς ὑπὸ τοῦ ἀποστόλου ἔκραξαν ἐκεῖ τῷ σώσαντι αὐτούς. 12. ἀναλημφθέντος αὐτοῦ εἰς οὐρανὸν εἰσῆλθον οἱ μαθηταὶ εἰς τὴν οἰκίαν αὐτῶν. 13. ἐδέξασθε τοὺς ἐκβληθέντας ἐκ τῆς συναγωγῆς καὶ τὰς δεξαμένας αὐτοὺς εἰς τὰς οἰκίας αὐτῶν. 14. αὐταί εἰσιν αἱ διωχθεῖσαι καὶ ἔτι διωκόμεναι ὑπὸ τῶν πρεσβυτέρων. 15. αὕτη ἐστὶν ἡ σοφία τοῦ θεοῦ ἡ κηρυχθεῖσα ἐν τῷ κόσμῳ ὑπὸ τῶν ἰδόντων τὸν κύριον. 16. τῶν στρατιωτῶν διωξάντων ἡμᾶς εἰς τὴν οἰκίαν ἐδέξαντο ἡμᾶς οἱ ὄντες ἐκεῖ. 17. διωχθέντας ἡμᾶς ὑπὸ τῶν στρατιωτῶν ἐδέξαντο οἱ ὄντες ἐν τῇ οἰκίᾳ. 18. εἰσερχομένῳ σοι εἰς τὴν οἰκίαν προσῆλθον οἱ ἄρχοντες, εἰσελθόντα[1] δὲ ἐξέβαλον. 19. ταῦτα μὲν εἶπον αὐτοῖς προσφέρουσι τὰ παιδία τῷ κυρίῳ, ἐκεῖνα δὲ προσενεγκοῦσιν. 20. πορευομένου μὲν τοῦ κυρίου μετὰ τῶν μαθητῶν αὐτοῦ ἔλεγον οἱ ἀπόστολοι ταῦτα, ἐλθόντος δὲ εἰς τὴν οἰκίαν ἐκεῖνα. 21. ταῦτα εἶπον ὑμῖν ἔτι οὖσιν μετ᾽ ἐμοῦ. 22. ὑμῖν τοῖς πιοῦσι τὸν οἶνον τοῦ οὐρανοῦ ὁ κύριος λέγει μυστήρια.

B. 1. When the soldiers had taken the garments from the children, the disciples were cast out of the house. 2. When the disciples had been cast out of the synagogue, they came to us. 3. While we were coming into our house, the Lord said these things to the rulers. 4. The Lord said those things to you (p.), both while you were with him in the way and after you had come to the ruler. 5. Those who had heard the apostle saying these things saw the house that had been destroyed by the soldiers. 6. When the rulers had heard the things that were being said by the Lord, they persecuted the disciples. 7. While the disciples were being persecuted by the rulers, the apostles were going into another house. 8. Those who went into the house of the ruler were my brothers. 9. When our names have been written into the book of life, we will see the Lord. 10. Having been brought to the Lord by these disciples, we see him

---

1. What noun or pronoun is naturally to be supplied as that with which εἰσελθόντα agrees?

for ever. 11. These are the rulers who have become disciples of you (s.). 12. When the apostle had been cast into prison, the disciples who had heard these things went away into another place. 13. After those women had been cast into prison, we went away into the desert. 14. When those who had been cast into prison had seen the man who had been raised up, they marveled and believed on the Lord. 15. When the disciples had led to the Lord those who had been persecuted on account of him, those servants came to us bringing good gifts. 16. Those who have not received this hope from God will not enter into the kingdom of heaven.

Lesson 21

The Subjunctive Mood

291. [268] Vocabulary

ἁμαρτάνω, *I sin*

δικαιοσύνη, ἡ, *righteousness*

ἐάν, conditional particle, with subjunctive, *if*

εἰ, with indicative, *if*

εὐαγγελίζομαι, dep. with middle forms, *I preach the gospel, I preach the gospel to* (with acc. of the message preached and either acc. or dat. of the person to whom it is preached)

ἵνα, conj., with subjunctive, *in order that*

λαός, ὁ, *a people*

λοιπός, -ή, -όν, adj., *remaining;* οἱ λοιποί, *the rest* (= *the remaining persons*)

μακάριος, -α, -ον, adj., *blessed*

μαρτυρία, ἡ, *a witnessing, a testimony, a witness*

μηδέ, *and not, nor, not even* (with moods other than the indicative); μηδέ . . . μηδέ, *neither . . . nor*

μηκέτι, *no longer* (with moods other than the indicative)

ὄχλος, ὁ, *a crowd, a multitude*

292. [269] The subjunctive mood occurs only in the progressive and aorist tenses (except for very rare occurrences in the perfect). It has *primary* personal endings throughout, *even in the aorist.* The personal endings are preceded throughout by a long variable theme vowel ω/η instead of the short variable theme vowel ο/ε that occurs in the progressive (i.e., present) indicative. This lengthened theme vowel is the key to recognizing the subjunctive mood.

293. [270] The progressive active subjunctive of λύω is as follows:

	Sing.	**Plur.**
1.	λύω	λύωμεν
2.	λύῃς	λύητε
3.	λύῃ	λύωσι(ν)

294. [271] The progressive middle and passive subjunctive of λύω is as follows:

	Sing.	**Plur.**
1.	λύωμαι	λυώμεθα
2.	λύῃ	λύησθε
3.	λύηται	λύωνται

295. [272] Notice that these progressive subjunctive forms are like the progressive (present) indicative forms except that a long vowel comes immediately after the stem, while in the indicative there is a short vowel. Instead of the ο of the indicative, the subjunctive has ω, and instead of the ε of the indicative, the subjunctive has η (ι after η being subscripted). The only exceptions are (1) in the present active third-person plural, where ω in the subjunctive stands instead of ου in the indicative, and (2) in the present middle and passive second-person singular, where the indicative already has η (in λύῃ).[1]

296. [273] The -ωσι(ν) of the third-person plural active may have the movable ν.

1. The alert student will have observed that the form λύῃ could be either second-person singular present middle or passive indicative, second-person singular progressive middle or passive subjunctive, or third-person singular progressive active subjunctive. Context must determine which is correct. Similarly, the context must determine whether the first-person singular λύω is present active indicative or progressive active subjunctive;

297. [274] The aorist active subjunctive of λύω is as follows:

	Sing.	Plur.
1.	λύσω	λύσωμεν
2.	λύσῃς	λύσητε
3.	λύσῃ	λύσωσι(ν)

298. [275] The aorist middle (not passive) subjunctive of λύω is as follows:

	Sing.	Plur.
1.	λύσωμαι	λυσώμεθα
2.	λύσῃ	λύσησθε
3.	λύσηται	λύσωνται

299. [276] The endings (with lengthened theme vowel) are exactly the same in the aorist active and middle subjunctive as they are in the progressive active and middle subjunctive. But these endings (with theme vowel) are in the aorist added to the aorist stem, whereas in the progressive they are added to the progressive stem. The σ makes all the difference.

300. [277] There is in the aorist subjunctive, of course, no augment (see §264).

301. [278] The second aorist active and middle subjunctive is conjugated exactly like the first aorist subjunctive. Of course, instead of adding the first aorist tense formant (σ), the subjunctive endings are added directly to the second aorist stem. For example, the second aorist active subjunctive of λείπω is λίπω, λίπῃς, λίπῃ, etc.

---

whether first-person singular λύσω is future active indicative or aorist active subjunctive; and whether λύσῃ is second-person singular future middle indicative, third-person singular aorist active subjunctive, or second-person singular aorist middle subjunctive.

302. [279] The aorist passive subjunctive of λύω is as follows:

	Sing.	Plur.
1.	λυθῶ	λυθῶμεν
2.	λυθῇς	λυθῆτε
3.	λυθῇ	λυθῶσι(ν)

303. [280] The aorist passive subjunctive, like the aorist active subjunctive, has the primary A personal endings. The endings (with the lengthened theme vowel) are exactly like those in the progressive active subjunctive, but they are affixed to the (unaugmented) aorist passive stem. However, note that the customary θε of the aorist passive stem appears to be missing the ε. Actually the ε is there, but it has been contracted with the ω and η endings, which fact is marked by the presence of a circumflex accent.

304. [281] Thus, to form the aorist subjunctive of a verb, one must (1) identify the appropriate principal part (third or sixth), (2) remove the augment in the manner explained in §§271–72, and (3) affix the appropriate elongated theme vowel (ω or η) and the primary endings. In the case of the aorist passive subjunctive, there is the added step of dropping the ε and adding a circumflex accent to the η or ω.

305. [282] Subjunctive of εἰμί

The progressive subjunctive of εἰμί is the same as the bare elongated primary endings, with breathing marks and circumflex accents:

	Sing.	Plur.
1.	ὦ	ὦμεν
2.	ᾖς	ἦτε
3.	ᾖ	ὦσι(ν)

There is no aorist of εἰμί in any mood.

306. [283] The Tenses in the Subjunctive

In the subjunctive mood there is absolutely no distinction of time between the tenses; the aorist tense does not refer to past time and the progressive subjunctive does not necessarily refer to present time. The distinction between the progressive and the aorist concerns merely the way in which the action is regarded. The aorist subjunctive refers to the action without saying anything about its continuance or repetition, while the progressive subjunctive looks at the action as continuing or as being repeated. Thus ἵνα λύσω means simply *in order that I may loose*, while ἵνα λύω means *in order that I may be loosing*, or the like. But ordinarily it is quite difficult to bring out the difference in an English translation without many extra words. The progressive and the aorist subjunctive will usually have to be translated exactly alike. The student should use the aorist in the exercises unless there is some reason for using the progressive, since the aorist presents the action in a simpler way, without any added thought of its duration.

307. The meaning of the subjunctive in Greek is generally to indicate *potentiality*, as opposed to the indicative, which generally assumes a real situation. It is used in a variety of circumstances such as future (uncertain) conditions, clauses indicating purpose or intent, or exhortations.

308. [285] The Hortatory Subjunctive

The first-person plural of the subjunctive is used in exhortations.

Example: πιστεύσωμεν εἰς τὸν κύριον, *let us believe on the Lord.*

This is like an imperative addressed to a group in which the speaker includes him- or herself. In English we accomplish this by using the helping phrase "let us."

309. [286] The Subjunctive in Purpose Clauses

Purpose is expressed by ἵνα with the subjunctive. The subjunctive is used because intention or purpose is only a *desired result*, not necessarily an actual one.

Examples: (1) ἐρχόμεθα ἵνα ἴδωμεν αὐτόν, *we are coming in order that we may see him.* (2) ἤλθομεν ἵνα ἴδωμεν αὐτόν, *we came in order that we might see him.*

310. [287] ἵνα, *in order that,* with the subjunctive, must be distinguished sharply from ὅτι, *that,* with the indicative. The latter introduces indirect discourse.

Example: Compare λέγουσιν ὅτι γινώσκουσι τὸν κύριον, *they say that they know the Lord,* with τοῦτο λέγουσιν ἵνα ἀκούωσιν οἱ μαθηταί, *they say this (in order) that the disciples may hear.*

The Subjunctive in Future Conditions

311. [288] Future conditions are, of course, inherently uncertain and are expressed by ἐάν with the subjunctive; other conditions by εἰ with the indicative.[1]

Examples:

1. ἐὰν εἰσέλθωμεν εἰς τὴν οἰκίαν ὀψόμεθα τὸν κύριον, *if we go into the house, we will see the Lord.* Here ἐὰν εἰσέλθωμεν clearly refers to a possible future. Compare εἰ μαθηταί ἐσμεν τοῦ κυρίου σωθησόμεθα, *if we are disciples of the Lord, we will*

1. This simple rule does not cover all of the facts. For example, it takes no account of "present general" conditions, which are expressed, like future conditions, by ἐάν with the subjunctive. In the sentence *if a fish is taken out of water, it dies* (a present general condition), the contemplated possibility of a fish being removed from water is concerned not with anything currently happening but with the general consequences of certain (possible) events. It is perhaps unnecessary, however, to trouble the beginner with this additional category. In general, the simple rule given in the text will serve fairly well for New Testament Greek. The exceptions can be noted as they occur. Conditions contrary to fact are treated in §577.

be saved. Here the meaning is *if it is now a fact that we are disciples of the Lord, we shall be saved.* Hence εἰ . . . ἐσμεν refers to a present real condition. It is already either true or not true that we are disciples—it is not potential or uncertain.

2. ἐὰν διδάσκητε τοὺς ἀδελφοὺς πιστοί ἐστε διδάσκαλοι, *if you teach the brothers, you are faithful teachers.*[1] Here the meaning is *if at any time you might be engaged in teaching the brothers, you are faithful teachers.* ἐὰν διδάσκητε here refers to a possible but not certain future. Compare εἰ διδάσκετε τοὺς ἀδελφοὺς πιστοί ἐστε διδάσκαλοι, *if you are teaching the brothers, you are faithful teachers.* Here the meaning is *if it is a real fact that you are now engaged in teaching the brothers, you are faithful teachers.* Notice that in order to distinguish εἰ with the indicative from ἐάν with the subjunctive, it is often advisable in English to use a form of *is* with a present participle (an -*ing* word) to translate the present indicative after εἰ. Thus *if you are teaching* implies a present real condition, while *if you teach* is usually a future or uncertain condition.

312. [289] The preceding examples will show that the difference between the two kinds of conditions treated here concerns only the *protasis* (the if-clause). Various moods and tenses can stand in the *apodosis* (the conclusion) after either kind of protasis. A hortatory subjunctive, for example, can stand after a simple present condition. For example, εἰ μαθηταί ἐσμεν τοῦ κυρίου διδάσκωμεν τοὺς ἀδελφούς, *if we are disciples of the Lord* [i.e., *if that is now a fact*], *let us teach the brothers.*

313. [290] Notice also that one cannot always tell from the mere form of the English sentence whether a condition is present or future, real or potential. In modern colloquial English we often use the present indicative to express a future condi-

---

1. Note the use here of the progressive subjunctive. Why is the progressive appropriate in this example?

tion. For example, in the sentence *if it rains tomorrow, we will not go to the picnic*, the phrase *if it rains* clearly refers to the indefinite future and would be ἐάν with the subjunctive in Greek. It is the *meaning* of the English sentence, then, and not the mere form, that should be noticed in determining what the Greek will be.

314. [284] The negative of the subjunctive is μή, in accordance with the rule given in §244.

A negative future or possible condition is expressed by ἐάν μή with a subjunctive verb, and a negative real condition by εἰ μή with the indicative.[1] Both of these may be translated by the English *except* or *unless*.

Examples: (1) ἐὰν μὴ πιστεύῃ οὐκ εἰσελεύσεται εἰς τὴν βασιλείαν τοῦ θεοῦ, *unless he believes, he will not enter into the kingdom of God*. (2) οὐκ ἀπεστάλην εἰ μὴ εἰς τὴν οἰκίαν τῶν ἀδελφῶν μου, *I was not sent, except to the house of my brothers*.

Negative purpose clauses use the phrase ἵνα μή, literally, *in order that not*. This is sometimes expressed by the English word *lest*, but phrases such as *so that (someone) might not (do something)* are also serviceable.

Example: ταῦτα εἶπεν ἐν παραβολαῖς ἵνα μὴ ἀκούσωσιν οἱ πονηροὶ τὸν λόγον, *these things he said in parables so that the evil men might not hear the word*.

315. [291] Exercises

A. 1. ταῦτα λέγω ἵνα ὑμεῖς σωθῆτε. 2. ἐὰν μὴ δέξησθε τὴν μαρτυρίαν ἡμῶν, οὐ σωθήσεσθε. 3. ἐὰν μὴ ἴδῃ οὗτος τὸν κύριον, οὐ πιστεύσει εἰς αὐτόν. 4. εἰ κηρύσσεται ἡμῖν ὅτι ἀγαθός ἐστιν ὁ κύριος, ἀγαθοὶ ὦμεν καὶ ἡμεῖς, ἵνα διδάσκωμεν τοὺς λοιπούς. 5. εὐηγγελισάμην αὐτοὺς ἵνα σωθῶσιν καὶ ἔχωσιν ζωήν. 6. μηκέτι ἁμαρτάνωμεν, ἵνα γενώμεθα μαθηταὶ πιστοί. 7. μα-

---

1. This is an exception to the rule given in §244.

κάριοί εἰσιν οἱ ὄχλοι, ἐὰν ἀκούσωσιν τὰ ῥήματά μου. 8. ἐὰν εἰσέλθωσιν εἰς ἐκείνην τὴν οἰκίαν οἱ πιστεύοντες εἰς τὸν κύριον, εὐαγγελισόμεθα αὐτοὺς ἐκεῖ. 9. ἐκηρύξαμεν τούτῳ τῷ λαῷ τὰ ῥήματα τῆς ζωῆς, ἵνα δέξωνται τὴν ἀλήθειαν καὶ σωθῶσιν. 10. προσέλθωμεν τῷ ἰδόντι τὸν κύριον, ἵνα διδάξῃ ἡμᾶς περὶ αὐτοῦ. 11. ταῦτα εἰπόντων αὐτῶν ἐν τῷ ἱερῷ οἱ ἀκούσαντες ἐδέξαντο τὰ λεγόμενα, ἵνα κηρύξωσιν αὐτὰ καὶ τοῖς λοιποῖς. 12. πιστεύσωμεν εἰς τὸν ἀποθανόντα ὑπὲρ ἡμῶν, ἵνα γράψῃ τὰ ὀνόματα ἡμῶν εἰς τὸ βιβλίον τῆς ζωῆς. 13. ἐλεύσομαι πρὸς τὸν σώσαντά με, ἵνα μὴ λύω τὰς ἐντολὰς αὐτοῦ μηδὲ πορεύωμαι ἐν ταῖς ὁδοῖς τοῦ θανάτου. 14. ταῦτα εἶπον ἐν τῷ ἱερῷ, ἵνα οἱ ἀκούσαντες σωθῶσιν ἀπὸ τῶν ἁμαρτιῶν αὐτῶν καὶ ἔχωσιν τὴν δικαιοσύνην τοῦ θεοῦ. 15. εἰ εἴδετε ταῦτα ἐν ταῖς ἡμέραις ταῖς κακαῖς, ὄψεσθε τὰ αὐτὰ καὶ νῦν καὶ εἰς τὸν αἰῶνα. 16. ἐὰν μὴ διδαχθῇς ὑπὸ τοῦ κυρίου, οὐ γνώσῃ αὐτὸν εἰς τὸν αἰῶνα. 17. ὁ λύων τὰς ἐντολὰς τοῦ θεοῦ οὐκ ἔχει ἐλπίδα, ἐὰν μὴ ἐπιστρέψῃ πρὸς τὸν κύριον. 18. ταῦτα παρέλαβεν ἀπὸ τοῦ ἀποθανόντος ὑπὲρ αὐτοῦ, ἵνα παραλαβόντες αὐτὰ οἱ λοιποὶ σωθῶσιν καὶ αὐτοί. 19. συνελθόντες εἰς τὴν οἰκίαν δεξώμεθα τὴν μαρτυρίαν τοῦ εὐαγγελισαμένου ἡμᾶς. 20. διωξάντων τῶν στρατιωτῶν τοὺς ἁγίους ἵνα μὴ πιστεύσωσιν εἰς τὸν σώσαντα αὐτούς, συνῆλθον οὗτοι εἰς τὴν συναγωγήν.

B. 1. Let us receive the witness of these men, in order that we may be saved. 2. If we do not turn to the Lord, we will not know him. 3. If the Lord prepares a place for us, we will enter into heaven. 4. If we received this commandment from the Lord, let us preach the gospel to the multitudes. 5. If these men are disciples of the Lord, they will not persecute the saints. 6. If these rulers persecute those who believed on the Lord, they will not come to the Lord in order that they may be saved. 7. If he sees the woman who received the saints, he will take the little children from her. 8. When the disciples had said these things to the saints, they were taught by the Lord in order that they might sin no longer. 9. If the Son of Man came in order that he might save sinners, let us receive his witness. 10. If we know the Lord, let us not persecute his saints nor cast them out of the synagogue. 11. If the crowds who have heard the Lord see him in that synagogue, they will come to him in order that he may say to them words of hope. 12. Unless he says these things to the multitudes, they will not be saved. 13. If you (s.) see in that night the one who saved you, the ruler will persecute you, in order that you may not preach the gospel to the others. 14. The Lord came to us, in order that we might preach the gospel to you (p.). 15. The faithful servants came, in order that they might bring to us those garments.

Lesson 22

The Progressive and Aorist Infinitives
• The Articular Infinitive • Indirect Discourse
• Proper Names

316. [292] Vocabulary

δεῖ, impersonal verb, used
  only in third person, *it is*
  necessary

ἔξεστι(ν), impersonal verb,
  used only in third person,
  it is lawful

θέλω, *I wish*

Ἰησοῦς, Ἰησοῦ, ὁ, *Jesus*

Ἰουδαῖος, ὁ, *a Jew*

κελεύω, *I command*

κώμη, ἡ, *a village*

μέλλω, *I am about* (to do
  something), *I am going*
  (to do something)

ὀφείλω, *I owe, I ought*

πάσχω, *I suffer*

πρό, prep. with gen., *before*

σωτηρία, ἡ, *salvation*

Φαρισαῖος, ὁ, *a Pharisee*

Χριστός, ὁ, *Christ;* ὁ Χριστός,
  Christ, or *the Messiah*

317. [293] The progressive and aorist infinitives of λύω are
as follows:

	Progressive		**Aorist**	
Act.	λύειν	*to loose*	λῦσαι	*to loose*
Mid.	λύεσθαι	*to loose for*	λύσασθαι	*to loose for*
		one's self		*one's self*
Pass.	λύεσθαι	*to be loosed*	λυθῆναι	*to be loosed*

318. Since infinitives are indeclinable, to parse an infinitive involves only identifying the tense, the voice, and the fact that it is an infinitive.

319. [294] Notice that the progressive infinitives are formed upon the progressive stem, the aorist active and middle infinitives upon the aorist active stem (with the characteristic -σα in the first aorist), and the aorist passive infinitive upon the aorist passive stem (with the characteristic -θε lengthened to -θη).

320. [296] The second aorist active infinitive of λείπω is λιπεῖν, and the second aorist middle infinitive is λιπέσθαι. These are like the progressive infinitives in their endings except for the accent. They are formed, of course, upon the second aorist stem. The aorist passive infinitive of λείπω is λειφθῆναι.

321. [297] Since εἰμί has no aorist or perfect tense, it has only one infinitive form, εἶναι.

322. [298] The infinitive is a verbal noun. That is, the action of the verb becomes a *thing* that functions in a sentence the way any other noun can function (subject, direct object, etc.). In many cases the use of the Greek infinitive is so much like that of the infinitive in English as to call for no comment. Thus θέλω ἀκούειν τὸν λόγον means *I wish to hear the word*. Here the English is a literal translation of the Greek. ἀκούειν is the direct object of *I wish*.

323. [299] As with the subjunctive mood, the tense of the infinitive does not indicate time. The progressive infinitive views the action as continuing or repeating; the aorist infinitive refers to it in no such special way. It is usually impossible to bring out the distinction in an English translation.

324. [300] The negative of the infinitive is μή.

The Articular Infinitive

325. [301] The Greek infinitive, being a verbal noun, can have the article, like any other noun. It is treated as an indeclinable neuter noun, and so has the neuter article. Though the infinitive itself is not declined, the article is, and so the case of the infinitive can be determined by its article as well as by its use in the sentence.

326. [302] The infinitive with the article can stand in most of the constructions in which any other noun can stand. Thus καλόν ἐστι τὸ ἀποθανεῖν ὑπὲρ τῶν ἀδελφῶν means *the act of dying in behalf of the brothers is good*, or, less literally, *it is good to die in behalf of the brothers*. Here τὸ ἀποθανεῖν is a noun in the nominative case, being the subject of the verb ἐστι.

327. [303] Of particular importance is the use of the articular infinitive after prepositions.

Examples: μετὰ τὸ λῦσαι, *after the act of loosing;* ἐν τῷ λύειν, *in* or *during the process of loosing;* διὰ τὸ λυθῆναι, *on account of the fact of being loosed;* μετὰ τὸ λυθῆναι, *after the fact of being loosed;* πρὸ τοῦ λῦσαι, *before the act of loosing;* εἰς τὸ λῦσαι, *into the act of loosing*. This last preposition, εἰς, is frequently used with the articular infinitive to express purpose. If one act is done so as to get *into* another act, it is done for the purpose of that other act. Thus εἰς τὸ λῦσαι means *in order to loose*.

328. [304] So far, the infinitive has been viewed as a noun. But it is also partly a verb, and as partly a verb the infinitive can have not only, as the participle can, adverbial modifiers

185

and a direct object but also a subject. The subject of the infinitive is in the *accusative* case.[1]

Examples:

1. ἐν τῷ λέγειν αὐτοὺς ταῦτα, *in* (or *during*) *the circumstance that they were saying these things* = *while they were saying these things.* Here αὐτούς is the subject of the infinitive λέγειν, and ταῦτα is the direct object of it.

2. μετὰ τὸ ἀπολυθῆναι τὸν ὄχλον ἀπῆλθεν ὁ κύριος, *after the circumstance that the crowd was dismissed, the Lord went away,* or *after the crowd had been dismissed, the Lord went away.* The same thought might have been expressed by ἀπολυθέντος τοῦ ὄχλου ἀπῆλθεν ὁ κύριος.

3. διὰ δὲ τὸ λέγεσθαι τοῦτο ὑπὸ τῶν ὄχλων ἀπῆλθεν ὁ ἀπόστολος, *and on account of the circumstance that this was being said by the crowds, the apostle went away,* or *because this was being said by the crowds, the apostle went away.*

4. ταῦτα δὲ εἶπον ὑμῖν εἰς τὸ μὴ γενέσθαι ὑμᾶς δούλους τῆς ἁμαρτίας, *and these things I said to you, with the tendency toward the result that you should not become servants of sin,* or *and these things I said to you in order that you might not become servants of sin.*

329. [305] Note that the articular infinitive with prepositions is usually to be translated into English by a clause introduced by a conjunction. But it must not be supposed that the details of such translation have anything to do with the details of the Greek original. It is rather the total idea expressed by

---

1. Technically speaking, the accusative "subject" of an infinitive is a special accusative of reference (see §494), not a true subject. Occasionally we have something like this in English; for example, *I want him to leave.* In certain instances, it may appear that the understood subject of an infinitive is in the dative case: οὐκ ἔξεστίν σοι ἔχειν αὐτήν means *it is not lawful for you to have her.* But again, speaking technically, the σοι in this instance is really a dative of respect (see §493): *with respect to you, to have her is not lawful.*

the Greek phrase that is transferred into a totally different idiom.

Indirect Discourse

330. [306] Indirect discourse is sometimes expressed by the accusative and infinitive.

Example: ἔλεγον οἱ ὄχλοι αὐτὸν εἶναι τὸν προφήτην, *the crowds were saying that he was the prophet.*

331. [307] But usually, indirect discourse is expressed by ὅτι with the indicative. The usage is similar to that in English but with the following important difference:

332. [308] In indirect discourse in English we change tense and mood as well as person to reflect the perspective of the reporter. Thus the direct discourse *he said, "I will see the Lord"* is expressed in indirect discourse by *he said that he would see the Lord,* and *he said, "I teach children"* becomes *he said that he taught children.* In Greek, however, contrary to English usage, the same mood and tense are retained as those that stood in the direct discourse lying behind the indirect. Thus the difference between direct and indirect discourse in Greek is only that the person of the verb in the indirect discourse changes to the perspective of the reporter—that is, from first person to second or third. When translating, then, one must alter the tense and mood according to English usage.

Examples:

1. λέγει ὅτι βλέπει τὸν ἀπόστολον, *he says that he sees the apostle.* Here the direct discourse lying behind the indirect is *I see the apostle,* for such are the actual words of the speaker; such are the words that would have stood in the quotation if quotation marks had been used. In this sentence there is no difference between the Greek and the English usage.

2. εἶπεν ὅτι βλέπει τὸν ἀπόστολον, *he said that he saw the apostle.* Here βλέπει is in the present tense because the direct

discourse lying behind the indirect discourse is *I see the apostle*—those were the actual words of the speaker. The tense of the direct discourse, *I see*, is retained in the indirect discourse (though of course the person is changed). English, on the other hand, changes the tense in the indirect discourse when the leading verb is in past time. Thus, although a perfectly literal translation was possible in example 1, a literal translation would be misleading in example 2.

3. εἶπεν ὁ μαθητὴς ὅτι εἶδεν τὸν ἀπόστολον, *the disciple said that he had seen the apostle.* Here the direct discourse was *I saw the apostle,* or *I have seen the apostle.* English throws the tense in the indirect discourse a step further back (*had seen* instead of *saw* or *has seen*); Greek retains the same tense.

4. εἶπεν ὅτι ὄψεται τὸν ἀπόστολον, *he said that he would see the apostle.* The direct discourse was *I will see.* English changes *will* to *would*; Greek retains the same tense.

Proper Names

333. [309] Proper names in Greek (spelled with a capital letter) often have the article. Of course the article must be omitted in an English translation.

334. [310] The declension of Ἰησοῦς, ὁ, *Jesus,* is as follows:

Nom.	Ἰησοῦς
Gen.	Ἰησοῦ
Dat.	Ἰησοῦ
Acc.	Ἰησοῦν

335. [311] Certain nouns referring to persons or things that, instead of being only one of a class, are unique are treated as proper nouns, the article being either inserted or omitted. So θεός or ὁ θεός, *God;* πνεῦμα or τὸ πνεῦμα, *the Spirit;* κόσμος or ὁ κόσμος, *the world;* νόμος or ὁ νόμος, *the Law.*

336. Impersonal Verbs

The verbs ἔξεστι(ν), *it is lawful, it is permitted,* and δεῖ, *it is necessary,* are not conjugated (although δεῖ does have an imperfect form, ἔδει). They are almost always used with an infinitive as their subject. Thus διδάσκειν τὰ τέκνα ἔξεστιν means *to teach the children is lawful,* or, more idiomatically, *it is lawful to teach the children.*

The infinitive with δεῖ may, like other infinitives, have an accusative "subject," so that δεῖ + acc. + inf. means *it is necessary that* [acc. noun] [do the action of the infinitive], or [acc. noun] *must* [do the action of the infinitive]. An infinitive with ἔξεστι may appear with a dative "subject." Thus, ἔξεστι + dat. + inf. means *it is lawful for* [dat. noun] *to* [do the action of the infinitive], or [dat. noun] *is permitted to* [do the action of the infinitive].

Examples: δεῖ τὸν δοῦλον ἀκούειν τὸν κύριον αὐτοῦ, *it is necessary that the slave hear his lord,* or *the slave must hear his lord;* οὐκ ἔξεστιν τοῖς μὴ διδαχθεῖσιν διδάσκειν, *those who have not been taught are not permitted to teach.*

Accent Matters

337. [295] The first aorist active infinitive is accented upon the penult, even where this involves an exception to the rule of verb accent. Thus πιστεῦσαι, *to believe,* not πίστευσαι. The accent of the aorist passive infinitive is also irregular, being a circumflex placed on the η of the ending, as in λυθῆναι. Second aorist infinitives, like second aorist participles, are accented on the connecting vowel of the ending, as in λιπεῖν, λιπέσθαι.

338. [312] Exercises

A. 1. δεῖ τὸν υἱὸν τοῦ ἀνθρώπου πάσχειν. 2. κελεύσας δὲ τοὺς ὄχλους ἀπολυθῆναι ἐξῆλθεν εἰς τὴν ἔρημον. 3. οὐκ ἔστιν καλὸν λαβεῖν τὸν ἄρτον τῶν τέκνων καὶ ἐκβαλεῖν αὐτόν. 4. ἤρξατο δὲ ὁ Ἰησοῦς λέγειν τοῖς Ἰουδαίοις ὅτι δεῖ αὐτὸν ἀπελθεῖν. 5. μέλλει γὰρ ὁ υἱὸς τοῦ ἀνθρώπου ἔρχεσθαι ἐν δόξῃ μετὰ τῶν ἀγγέλων αὐτοῦ. 6. εἰ θέλει μετ᾽ ἐμοῦ ἐλθεῖν, δεῖ αὐτὸν ἀποθανεῖν. 7. καλόν σοί ἐστιν εἰς ζωὴν εἰσελθεῖν. 8. ἐν δὲ τῷ λέγειν με τοῦτο ἔπεσε τὸ πνεῦμα τὸ ἅγιον ἐπ᾽ αὐτούς.[1] 9. μετὰ δὲ τὸ ἐγερθῆναι τὸν κύριον ἐδίωξαν οἱ Ἰουδαῖοι τοὺς μαθητάς αὐτοῦ. 10. πρὸ δὲ τοῦ βληθῆναι εἰς φυλακὴν τὸν προφήτην ἐβάπτιζον οἱ μαθηταὶ τοῦ Ἰησοῦ τοὺς ἐρχομένους πρὸς αὐτούς. 11. διὰ δὲ τὸ εἶναι αὐτὸν ἐκεῖ συνῆλθον οἱ Ἰουδαῖοι. 12. θέλω γὰρ ἰδεῖν ὑμᾶς, ἵνα λάβητε δῶρον ἀγαθόν, εἰς τὸ γενέσθαι ὑμᾶς μαθητὰς πιστούς. 13. ἀπέθανεν ὑπὲρ αὐτῶν ὁ Ἰησοῦς εἰς τὸ σωθῆναι αὐτούς. 14. ἔπεμψεν ὁ θεὸς τὸν Ἰησοῦν, ἵνα ἀποθάνῃ ὑπὲρ ἡμῶν, εἰς τὸ δοξάζειν ἡμᾶς τὸν σώσαντα ἡμᾶς. 15. εἶπεν ὁ τυφλὸς ὅτι βλέπει τοὺς ἀνθρώπους. 16. εἶπεν ὁ Ἰησοῦς ὅτι ἐλεύσεται ἐν τῇ βασιλείᾳ αὐτοῦ. 17. ταῦτα ἔλεγεν ὁ ἀπόστολος ἔτι ὢν ἐν σαρκί, εἰς τὸ πιστεῦσαι εἰς τὸν Ἰησοῦν τοὺς ἀκούοντας. 18. κελεύσας ἡμᾶς ὁ Ἰησοῦς ἐλθεῖν εἰς τὴν κώμην εὐθὺς ἀπέλυσε τὸν ὄχλον. 19. σωθέντες ὑπὸ τοῦ Ἰησοῦ ὀφείλομεν καὶ πάσχειν διὰ τὸ ὄνομα αὐτοῦ. 20. ἐν τῷ πάσχειν ἡμᾶς ταῦτα ἔλεγον οἱ ἀδελφοὶ ὅτι βλέπουσι τὸν Ἰησοῦν.

B. 1. While Jesus was preaching the gospel to the people, the Pharisees were commanding the soldiers to bring him. 2. After Jesus had commanded the crowds to go away, his disciples came to him. 3. If we wish to see Jesus, let us go into this village. 4. They said that it was lawful for them to take these garments. 5. They saw that it was necessary for the Son of Man to suffer these things. 6. After Jesus had said these things to the Pharisees, the multitudes went away. 7. On account of our not being disciples of Jesus, the ruler will command us to go away. 8. After salvation had been proclaimed

---

1. The preposition ἐπί (shortened to ἐπ᾽ when the word following begins with a vowel) means "on, to, against" with the accusative case.

to the people, Jesus taught his disciples. 9. When we suffer these things we ought to pray to the one who has saved us. 10. We will be saved in that hour, because we have believed on the name of Jesus. 11. Those who had come into that village saw that Jesus was in the house. 12. Let us not sin, for God will not receive into his kingdom those who sin and do not turn to him. 13. While these men were praying to God, the soldiers were persecuting the church. 14. And when they had entered into this village, they said that they wished to see Jesus. 15. This woman came to see the works of the Christ. 16. The men were brought to Jesus Christ in order that he might heal them. 17. For the church to be saved, its head must die.

Lesson 23

Contracting Verbs

339. [313] Vocabulary

ἀγαπάω, *I love* (the most frequent word for *I love* in the New Testament)

ἀκολουθέω, *I follow* (takes the dative)

Γαλιλαία, ἡ, *Galilee*

δηλόω, *I show, I make clear*

εὐλογέω, *I bless*

εὐχαριστέω, *I give thanks*

ζητέω, *I seek*

θεωρέω, *I gaze at, I stare intently at*

καλέω, καλέσω, ἐκάλεσα, —, —, ἐκλήθην, *I call*

λαλέω, *I speak*

παρακαλέω, *I exhort, I comfort*

περιπατέω, *I walk*

ποιέω, *I do, I make*

προσκυνέω, *I worship* (usually takes the dative)

σταυρόω, *I crucify*

τηρέω, *I keep*

τιμάω, *I honor*

φιλέω, *I love* (occurs much less frequently in the New Testament than ἀγαπάω)

χώρα, ἡ, *a country, a region*

Rules of Contraction

340. [314] Two vowels or a vowel and a diphthong are often united into a single long vowel or diphthong. The process by which they are united is called *contraction*.

341. [315] It must not be supposed, however, that contraction *always* takes place when two vowels or a vowel and a diphthong (even in the combinations set forth in the following rules) come together within a word. But it consistently occurs in the progressive tenses when the stem of the verb ends in α, ε, or ο. These verbs are called *contracting* (or *contract*) verbs.

342. [316.A–B] The rules of contraction are as follows:[1]

A. *Vowel with Vowel*

1. An open and a close vowel, when the open vowel comes first, are united in the diphthong that is composed of the two vowels in question.

Example: ε-ι makes ει. Notice, however, that when the close vowel comes before the open vowel, a diphthong is never formed. Thus ι-ε (for example, in ἱερόν), is always two syllables, never a diphthong.

2. Two like vowels form the common long.

Examples: α-α makes long α; ε-η makes η; ο-ω makes ω.

3. But ε-ε makes ει, and ο-ο makes ου. This rule forms an exception to rule 2.

4. An ο- sound (ο or ω) overcomes α, ε, or η (whether the o-sound comes first or second), and forms ω.

Examples: α-ο makes ω; ε-ω makes ω.

5. But ε-ο and ο-ε make ου. This rule forms an exception to rule 4.

---

1. The following formulation of the rules of contraction is, in essentials, that which was given in John Williams White, *The Beginner's Greek Book* (Boston: Ginn & Co., 1895), 75f.

6. When α and ε or η come together, whichever one comes first overcomes the other and forms its own long.

Examples: α-ε and α-η make long α; ε-α makes η.

B. *Vowel with Diphthong*

1. A vowel disappears by absorption before a diphthong that begins with the same vowel.

Examples: ε-ει makes ει; o-ου makes ου.

2. When a vowel comes before a diphthong that does not begin with the same vowel, it is contracted with the diphthong's first vowel. The diphthong's second vowel disappears, unless it is ι, in which case it becomes subscript.

Examples: α-ει makes ᾳ (α is first contracted with ε in accordance with rule A6, and then the ι becomes subscript); α-ου makes ω (α is contracted with o by rule A4, and the υ disappears); ε-ου makes ου (ε is contracted with o by rule A5, and υ disappears).

3. But o-ει and o-η make οι.

343. The student may find it easier simply to memorize the contraction possibilities, represented in the following chart:

Final Vowel of Stem / First Vowel of Ending	α	ε	η	ει	η	o	ου	ω
α	α	α	α	ᾳ	ᾳ	ω	ω	ω
ε	η	ει	η	ει	η	ου	ου	ω
o	ω	ου	ω	οι	οι	ου	ου	ω

344. [318] There are two apparent exceptions to the general rules and the chart: (1) the progressive active infinitive of verbs in -αω is contracted from -άειν to -ᾶν instead of -ᾳν, and (2) the progressive active infinitive of verbs ending in -oω is contracted from -όειν to -οῦν instead of -οῖν. These are not real exceptions, however, because the -ειν ending of infinitives is itself a contraction of ε-εν.

Progressive System of Contracting Verbs

345. [317] The student should write out in the uncontracted forms the progressive system (present and imperfect tense in the indicative, along with all progressive forms of the other moods) of τιμάω, *I honor*, φιλέω, *I love*, and δηλόω, *I make clear*, and should then write the contracted form opposite to each uncontracted form, applying the rules of contraction. The results can be tested by the conjugations of these verbs that are given in §§632–34.

346. [319] Contraction is carried out in all the forms of the progressive participles.

347. [320] In general, the uncontracted forms of these verbs in -άω, -έω, and -όω do not occur in the New Testament. The reason why the uncontracted forms, and not the contracted forms, of the present active indicative first-person singular are given in the lexicons is that the uncontracted forms must be known before the verb can be conjugated, since it makes a great difference for the conjugation whether τιμῶ, for example, is contracted from τιμάω, τιμέω, or τιμόω.

Principal Parts of Verbs in -άω, -έω, and -όω

348. [321] Verbs whose stems end in a vowel regularly lengthen that vowel (α as well as ε being lengthened to η, and ο to ω) before the tense suffixes (e.g., the -σο/ε of the future system, the -σα of the first aorist system, and the -θε of the aorist passive system). Thus the principal parts of τιμάω, so far as we have learned them, are τιμάω, τιμήσω, ἐτίμησα, —, —, ἐτιμήθην (not τιμάω, τιμάσω, etc.); the principal parts of

φιλέω are φιλέω, φιλήσω, etc.; and the principal parts of δηλόω
are δηλόω, δηλώσω, etc.[1]

349. [322] It is very important that the student learn to
reverse the process involved in this rule. Thus, if a form φανερωθείς be found in the Greek-English exercises, the student
should first remember that the -θε in φανερωθείς is evidently
the sign of the aorist passive system. The verb stem without
the tense suffix would be φανερω-. But since the final vowel
of the verb stem is lengthened before the tense suffix -θε, the
verb stem was φανερο- and the verb was φανερόω.

Or if a form ἠρωτήθη be found, the student should first
remember that the -θη is evidently the ending of the aorist
passive indicative, third-person singular, like ἐλύθη. But the
aorist passive indicative has the augment, which if the verb
begins with a vowel, consists in the lengthening of that vowel.
Therefore, to get the verb, the η at the beginning of ἠρωτήθη
must be shortened. But η is the long of either α or ε. It cannot be determined, therefore, whether the verb began with α
or ε. Again, the η just before the -θη in ἠρωτήθη was the lengthened form of the verb stem. The verb stem therefore ended in
either α or ε. Accordingly, there are four possibilities as to the
verb from which ἠρωτήθη may be found to have come;
ἠρωτήθη may be found to have come from ἀρωτέω, ἀρωτάω,
ἐρωτέω, or ἐρωτάω. Trying each of these in the lexicon, we discover that the last is correct.

350. [323] καλέω is an exception to the rule just given. It
does not lengthen the final ε of the stem before the σ of the
future and aorist systems. The aorist passive, moreover, is
irregularly formed (ἐκλήθην).

---

1. This lengthening of the final vowel of the stem of these contracting
verbs has nothing to do with contraction. The contraction appears only
in the progressive system.

Accent Matters

351. [316.C] *Accent of Contracting Syllables*

In the contracting verbs, the accent is somewhat more important than in other verbs, because the accent is a clue to the presence of the contracted vowel. In most of the contracted forms, the accent ends up being a circumflex, and thus the presence of the circumflex on the ending is often, though not always, an indicator of contraction.

The specific rules for accenting contracting verbs are as follows:

1. If either of the contracted syllables had an accent, the resulting syllable receives an accent. If the resulting syllable is a penult or an antepenult, the general rules of accent (see §11) will always tell which kind of accent it has. If the resulting syllable is an ultima, it has a circumflex.

Examples: (1) φιλέομεν makes φιλουμεν, in accordance with contraction rule A5 (§342). Since one of the two syllables that united to make ου had an accent, ου must have an accent. The general rules of accent declare that if the ultima is short, a long penult, if accented at all, must have the circumflex. Hence φιλοῦμεν is correct. (2) τιμαόμεθα makes τιμωμεθα in accordance with rule A4. Since one of the two syllables that united to make ω had an accent, ω must have an accent. But in accordance with the general rules of accent, only an acute can stand on an antepenult. Therefore τιμώμεθα is correct. (3) δηλόεις makes δηλοις in accordance with rule B3. Since one of the two syllables that united to make οι had an accent, οι must have an accent. The general rules of accent will permit either an acute or a circumflex to stand on a long ultima. But the present rule gives special guidance. Therefore δηλοῖς is correct.

2. If neither of the contracted syllables had an accent, the resulting syllable receives none.

Example: ἐφίλεε makes ἐφιλει in accordance with rule A3. Since neither of the two syllables that unite to make ει is accented, ει receives no accent, and ἐφίλει is correct.

352. [324] Exercises

A. 1. οὐκ εὐλογήσει ὁ θεὸς τὸν μὴ περιπατοῦντα κατὰ τὰς ἐντολὰς τοῦ Ἰησοῦ. 2. οἱ ἀγαπώμενοι ὑπὸ τοῦ Ἰησοῦ ἀγαπῶσι τὸν ἀγαπῶντα αὐτούς. 3. λαλοῦντος τοῦ Ἰησοῦ τοῖς ἀκολουθοῦσιν ἤρξατο ὁ ἄρχων παρακαλεῖν αὐτὸν ἀπελθεῖν. 4. ἀκολουθήσαντες τῷ λαλήσαντι ταῦτα ζητήσωμεν τὸν οἶκον αὐτοῦ. 5. εἰ ἀγαπῶμεν τὸν θεόν, τηρῶμεν τὰς ἐντολὰς αὐτοῦ καὶ ποιῶμεν τὰ λαλούμενα ἡμῖν ὑπὸ τοῦ Ἰησοῦ. 6. τοῦτο ποιήσαντος τοῦ Ἰησοῦ ἐλάλει περὶ αὐτοῦ ὁ θεραπευθεὶς τῷ ἀκολουθοῦντι ὄχλῳ. 7. ἐθεώρουν οἱ ἀπόστολοι τὰ ἔργα τὰ ποιούμενα ὑπὸ Ἰησοῦ ἐν τῷ περιπατεῖν αὐτοὺς σὺν αὐτῷ. 8. μετὰ τὸ βληθῆναι εἰς φυλακὴν τὸν προφήτην οὐκέτι περιεπάτει ὁ Ἰησοῦς ἐν τῇ χώρᾳ ἐκείνῃ. 9. οἱ ἀγαπῶντες τὸν θεὸν ποιοῦσι τὰς ἐντολὰς αὐτοῦ. 10. ταῦτα ἐποίουν τῷ Ἰησοῦ καὶ οἱ θεραπευθέντες ὑπ᾽ αὐτοῦ. 11. ἐζήτουν αὐτὸν οἱ ὄχλοι, ἵνα θεωρῶσι τὰ ποιούμενα ὑπ᾽ αὐτοῦ. 12. οὐ φιλοῦσι τὸν Ἰησοῦν οἱ μὴ ποιοῦντες τὰς ἐντολὰς αὐτοῦ. 13. ἀγαπῶμεν τὸν θεὸν ἐν ταῖς καρδίαις ἡμῶν ἀγαπῶντες καὶ τοὺς ἀδελφούς. 14. ταῦτα ἐλάλησεν ὁ Ἰησοῦς τοῖς ἀκολουθοῦσιν αὐτῷ ἔτι περιπατῶν μετ᾽ αὐτῶν ἐν τῇ χώρᾳ τῶν Ἰουδαίων. 15. ἐὰν μὴ περιπατῶμεν κατὰ τὰς ἐντολὰς τοῦ Ἰησοῦ, οὐ θεωρήσομεν τὸ πρόσωπον αὐτοῦ. 16. μετὰ τὸ καλέσαι αὐτοὺς τὸν Ἰησοῦν οὐκέτι περιεπάτουν ἐν ταῖς ὁδοῖς τοῦ πονηροῦ οὐδὲ ἐποίουν τὰ πονηρά. 17. ταῦτα ἐποιεῖτε ἡμῖν διὰ τὸ ἀγαπᾶν ὑμᾶς τὸν καλέσαντα ὑμᾶς εἰς τὴν βασιλείαν αὐτοῦ. 18. τῷ Ἰησοῦ λαλήσαντι ταῦτα μετὰ τὸ ἐγερθῆναι ἐκ νεκρῶν προσεκύνησαν οἱ κληθέντες ὑπ᾽ αὐτοῦ. 19. ἐθεώρουν τὸν Ἰησοῦν σταυρούμενον ὑπὸ τῶν στρατιωτῶν αἱ ἀκολουθήσασαι αὐτῷ ἐκ τῆς Γαλιλαίας. 20. οὐ θεωρήσομεν αὐτὸν ἐὰν μὴ ἀκολουθῶμεν αὐτῷ περιπατοῦντι ἐν τῇ Γαλιλαίᾳ.

B. 1. Jesus spoke those things to those who were following him out of Galilee. 2. I was gazing at him who had loved me and died in behalf of me. 3. Let us worship the one who does these things and bless his holy name. 4. Those who were gazing at him as he was walking in Galilee were saying that they did not wish to follow him. 5. Having followed Jesus as he was walking in Galilee, they gazed at him also after he had been raised up from the dead. 6. Let us seek the one who has spoken to us words of hope. 7. Let us bless the name of the one who walked with us in the world and was crucified in behalf of us. 8. If you (s.) follow him who does these things, you will gaze at him in his glory. 9. If we do not love those who bless us, we will not love those who do evil things. 10. He loves us and makes clear to us his glory, in order that we may bless God for ever. 11. While the multitudes were following Jesus and were hearing the things that were being spoken by him, the rulers were saying that they did not love him. 12. I will show to those who have followed me the things that have been shown to me by Jesus. 13. These are those who love Jesus and gazed at his works and were called into his kingdom. 14. His brother exhorted him to follow Jesus in order that he might be with him for ever. 15. This parable we speak to those who love God and keep his commandments. 16. This is the child that blesses God and loves him.

Lesson 24

Future and First Aorist Active and Middle of Liquid
Verbs • Future Indicative of εἰμί • Reflexive
Pronouns • Double Accusative

353. [325] Vocabulary

ἀλλήλων, reciprocal pron., *of*
each other, of one another

ἀποθανοῦμαι, *I will die,* dep.
fut. of ἀποθνήσκω

ἀποκτενῶ, ἀπέκτεινα, fut. and
aor. of ἀποκτείνω, *I kill*

ἀποστελῶ, ἀπέστειλα, fut. and
aor. of ἀποστέλλω, *I send*

ἀρῶ, ἦρα, fut. and aor. of
αἴρω, *I take up, I take away*

βαλῶ, *I will throw, I will*
cast, fut. of βάλλω

ἑαυτοῦ, -ης, -ου, reflexive
pron., *of him-(her-, it-)self*

ἐγερῶ, ἤγειρα, fut. and aor.
of ἐγείρω, *I raise up*

ἐμαυτοῦ, reflexive pron., *of*
myself

ἐπί, prep. with gen., *over, on,*
at the time of; with dat.,
on, on the basis of, at; with
acc., *on, to, against* (ἐπί is
an exceedingly common,
but a rather difficult,
preposition. Its various
uses must be learned by
observation in reading.)

ἔσομαι, *I will be,* fut. of εἰμί

μενῶ, ἔμεινα, fut. and aor. of
μένω, *I remain*

μετανοέω, *I repent*

σεαυτοῦ, reflexive pron., *of*
yourself

σπείρω, σπερῶ, ἔσπειρα, —,
—, ἐσπάρην, *I sow*

φοβέομαι, dep. with passive
forms, *I am afraid, I fear,*
I am afraid of

354. [326] Liquid verbs are verbs whose stems end in λ, μ, ν, or ρ, these consonants being called *liquids*.

355. [327] The Future of Liquid Verbs

The Greek language hardly ever allows a liquid consonant next to a sibilant (*s* sound) within a word. When ordinary rules of word formation would result in such, some change occurs, usually a substitution of ε for the σ. Thus, the future active and middle of liquid verbs is formed, not by adding -σο/ε, as is the case with other verbs, but by adding -εο/ε, to the verb stem. The ε contracts with the following variable vowel, in accordance with the rules of contraction given in the preceding lesson. The future active and middle of liquid verbs is therefore conjugated exactly like the present of verbs in -εω.

356. [328] The future active indicative of κρίνω, *I judge*, is as follows:

	Sing.	Plur.
1.	κρινῶ	κρινοῦμεν
2.	κρινεῖς	κρινεῖτε
3.	κρινεῖ	κρινοῦσι(ν)

357. [329] Note that the only way in which the future active indicative in the three persons of the singular and in the third-person plural is distinguished (in appearance) from the present active indicative of κρίνω is by the accent. Therefore, to indicate the future tense of κρίνω the accent is mandatory.

358. [330] The future middle indicative of κρίνω is as follows:

	Sing.	Plur.
1.	κρινοῦμαι	κρινούμεθα
2.	κρινῇ	κρινεῖσθε
3.	κρινεῖται	κρινοῦνται

359. [331] Remember (see §164) that the verb stem is often disguised in the progressive (present) system. Thus the future of a liquid verb is often distinguished from the present by something more than the addition of the ε, just as the future of nonliquid verbs is often distinguished by something more than the addition of σ.

Example: The future of βάλλω is βαλῶ, βαλ- and not βαλλ- being the verb stem.

360. [332] Some verbs have liquid stems in the future but not in other tenses.

Example: The future of λέγω is ἐρῶ.[1]

The First Aorist of Liquid Verbs

361. [333] The first aorist active and middle of liquid verbs is formed not by adding -σα to the verb stem but by adding -α alone and making a change within the body of the word. This change usually consists in a lengthening of the vowel in the verb stem (ε lengthened not to η but to ει). The conjugation, in all the moods, is like the conjugation of other first aorists.

Examples: (1) The first aorist active of μένω, *I remain*, is ἔμεινα (indic.), μείνω (subj.), μεῖναι (infin.), and μείνας (part.). (2) The first aorist active of ἀποστέλλω, *I send*, is ἀπέστειλα (indic.), ἀποστείλω (subj.), ἀποστεῖλαι (infin.), and ἀποστείλας (part.).

362. [334] Of course, liquid verbs may have second aorists or irregular aorists. So the aorist of βάλλω is a second aorist, ἔβαλον. Some verbs, moreover, may have a progressive stem

---

1. Originally there were three separate words for "say." By the time of the New Testament, the λεγ- stem was used almost exclusively in the progressive system, the εἰπ- stem in the aorist, and the ἐρ- stem in the future, perfect, and aorist passive. The result is that these different stems can be regarded as simply different parts of one verb. Similar things have occurred in English. For example, the simple past tense of *go* is *went*, which was originally from the word *wend*.

ending in a liquid, and yet not be liquid verbs. Thus λαμβάνω is not a liquid verb, the verb stem being λαβ-. The student is reminded again that one cannot always predict what the various tense systems of a Greek verb will be. The lexicon must be consulted.

363. [335] Future Indicative of εἰμί

The future indicative of εἰμί, *I am,* is as follows:

	Sing.	Plur.
1.	ἔσομαι	ἐσόμεθα
2.	ἔσῃ	ἔσεσθε
3.	ἔσται	ἔσονται

Notice that the conjugation is just like that of the future middle of λύω, except that in the third-person singular the variable vowel is omitted, ἔσται standing instead of ἔσεται.

364. [336] The English Preparatory Use of *There*

The word *there* is sometimes put before the verb in an English sentence without any special force except as an indication that the subject is to follow the verb. This "preparatory" *there* is not translated at all in Greek.

Examples: (1) χαρὰ ἔσται ἐν οὐρανῷ, *there will be joy in heaven* (literally, *joy will be in heaven*). (2) ἦσαν μαθηταὶ ἐν τῷ οἴκῳ, *there were disciples in the house* (literally, *disciples were in the house*).

Declension of Reflexive Pronouns

365. [337] The declension of ἐμαυτοῦ, -ῆς, *of myself,* the reflexive pronoun of the first person, is as follows:

	Sing.		Plur.	
	Masc.	**Fem.**	**Masc.**	**Fem.**
Gen.	ἐμαυτοῦ	ἐμαυτῆς	ἑαυτῶν	ἑαυτῶν
Dat.	ἐμαυτῷ	ἐμαυτῇ	ἑαυτοῖς	ἑαυταῖς
Acc.	ἐμαυτόν	ἐμαυτήν	ἑαυτούς	ἑαυτάς

366. [338] The declension of σεαυτοῦ, -ῆς, *of yourself*, the reflexive pronoun of the second person, is as follows:

	Sing.		Plur.	
	Masc.	**Fem.**	**Masc.**	**Fem.**
Gen.	σεαυτοῦ	σεαυτῆς	ἑαυτῶν	ἑαυτῶν
Dat.	σεαυτῷ	σεαυτῇ	ἑαυτοῖς	ἑαυταῖς
Acc.	σεαυτόν	σεαυτήν	ἑαυτούς	ἑαυτάς

367. [339] The declension of ἑαυτοῦ, -ῆς, -οῦ, *of him-(her-, it-)self*, the reflexive pronoun of the third person, is as follows:

	Sing.			Plur.		
	Masc.	**Fem.**	**Neut.**	**Masc.**	**Fem.**	**Neut.**
Gen.	ἑαυτοῦ	ἑαυτῆς	ἑαυτοῦ	ἑαυτῶν	ἑαυτῶν	ἑαυτῶν
Dat.	ἑαυτῷ	ἑαυτῇ	ἑαυτῷ	ἑαυτοῖς	ἑαυταῖς	ἑαυτοῖς
Acc.	ἑαυτόν	ἑαυτήν	ἑαυτό	ἑαυτούς	ἑαυτάς	ἑαυτά

368. [340] Notice that the declension of the reflexive pronouns is like that of αὐτός, except that there is no nominative case, and in the reflexive pronouns of the first and second persons no neuter gender. Since a reflexive refers back to the subject, it cannot itself be the subject (hence, no nominative), and first and second persons, since they refer to people, must always be either masculine or feminine (hence, no neuter).

369. [341] In the plural, ἑαυτῶν, which originally belonged only to the pronoun ἑαυτοῦ of the third person, is made to do duty for all three persons. Thus ἑαυτῶν may mean *of ourselves* or *of yourselves* as well as *of themselves,* depending on the subject of the controlling verb.

370. [342] Use of Reflexive Pronouns

Reflexive pronouns are pronouns that refer back to the subject of the clause.

Examples: (1) οὐ λαλῶ περὶ ἐμαυτοῦ, *I do not speak concerning myself;* (2) οὐ δοξάζεις σεαυτόν, *you (s.) do not glorify yourself;* (3) οὐκ ἔχει ζωὴν ἐν ἑαυτῷ, *he has not life in himself;* (4) δοξάζετε ἑαυτούς, *you (p.) glorify yourselves.*

371. [343] Reciprocal Pronoun

The reciprocal pronoun is ἀλλήλων, *of one another, of each other.* It occurs in the New Testament only in the forms ἀλλήλων, *of one another,* ἀλλήλοις, *to or for one another,* and ἀλλήλους, *one another* (e.g., βλέπουσιν ἀλλήλους, *they see one another*).

372. Double Accusative

Certain verbs may sometimes have more than one accusative.

1. A double accusative of person and thing occurs where the person (one object) receives a thing (the other object) by the action of verbs involving teaching, clothing, anointing, and requesting.

Example: ἐδίδασκεν ἡμᾶς τὸν λόγον τοῦ θεοῦ, *he was teaching us the word of God.*

2. A double accusative of object and complement occurs where one accusative is the direct object and the other predicates something about it (one thing is said to be another).

Lesson 24

This occurs with verbs of calling (declaring), making (appointing), regarding, having, or taking. Examples: πατέρα αὐτοῦ ἔλεγεν τὸν θεόν, *he was calling God his father* (literally, *he was saying God [to be] his father*). ποιήσει τὸν υἱὸν αὐτοῦ τὸν ἄρχοντα τοῦ κόσμου, *he will make his son [to be] ruler of the world*. Other instances where more than one accusative may occur will be noted in later lessons.

373. [344] Exercises

A. 1. οὐ γὰρ ἑαυτοὺς κηρύσσομεν ἀλλὰ Χριστὸν Ἰησοῦν κύριον, ἑαυτοὺς δὲ δούλους ὑμῶν διὰ Ἰησοῦν. 2. ὁ ἐγείρας τὸν κύριον Ἰησοῦν ἐγερεῖ καὶ ἡμᾶς σὺν Ἰησοῦ. 3. εἶπεν ὁ μαθητὴς ὅτι ἀποθανεῖται ὑπὲρ τοῦ Ἰησοῦ. 4. οὐκ ἐγεροῦμεν αὐτοὶ ἑαυτούς, ὁ δὲ Ἰησοῦς ἐγερεῖ ἡμᾶς ἐν τῇ ἐσχάτῃ ἡμέρᾳ. 5. τὸν μὴ γινώσκοντα ἁμαρτίαν ὑπὲρ ἡμῶν ἁμαρτίαν ἐποίησεν. 6. ἐὰν ἀγαπᾶτε ἀλλήλους, ἔσεσθε μαθηταὶ τοῦ ἀποθανόντος ὑπὲρ ὑμῶν. 7. ἐὰν πιστεύσητε εἰς τὸν Ἰησοῦν, μετ᾽ αὐτοῦ μενεῖτε εἰς τὸν αἰῶνα. 8. ὁ ἀγαπῶν τὸν υἱὸν ἀγαπᾷ καὶ τὸν ἀποστείλαντα αὐτόν. 9. χαρὰ ἔσται ἐπὶ τῷ ἁμαρτωλῷ τῷ ἐπὶ τῷ ῥήματι τοῦ Ἰησοῦ μετανοήσαντι. 10. οἱ ἀποκτείναντες τὸν Ἰησοῦν καὶ διώξαντες τοὺς μαθητὰς αὐτοῦ ἐκβαλοῦσι καὶ ἡμᾶς. 11. ἐπιστρέψαντες οὗτοι ἐπὶ τὸν θεὸν ἔμειναν ἐν τῇ ἐκκλησίᾳ αὐτοῦ. 12. ἐγείραντος τοῦ θεοῦ τοὺς νεκροὺς ἐσόμεθα σὺν τῷ κυρίῳ εἰς τοὺς αἰῶνας τῶν αἰώνων. 13. οὐκ εἰς ἐμαυτὸν ἐπίστευσα, ἀλλ᾽ εἰς τὸν κύριον. 14. ἔξεστιν ἡμῖν λαβεῖν δῶρα ἀπ᾽ ἀλλήλων, ἀλλ᾽ οὐκ ἀποκτεῖναι οὐδὲ διῶξαι ἀλλήλους. 15. οὗτος μέν ἐστιν ὁ ἄρχων ὁ ἀποκτείνας τοὺς προφήτας, ἐκεῖνος δέ ἐστιν ὁ ἁμαρτωλὸς ὁ μετανοήσας ἐπὶ τῷ ῥήματι τοῦ Ἰησοῦ. 16. ἐὰν δὲ τοῦτο εἴπωμεν κατ᾽ αὐτοῦ, φοβούμεθα τοὺς ὄχλους, λέγουσι γὰρ εἶναι αὐτὸν προφήτην. 17. ἀποστελεῖ πρὸς αὐτοὺς διδασκάλους καὶ προφήτας, ἵνα μετανοήσωσιν καὶ φοβῶνται τὸν θεόν. 18. μακάριοί εἰσιν οὐχ οἱ ἑαυτοὺς δοξάζοντες ἀλλ᾽ οἱ δοξάζοντες τὸν ἀποστείλαντα τὸν υἱὸν αὐτοῦ εἰς τὸν κόσμον. 19. ὁ λαὸς εἶπεν· τὸ αἷμα αὐτοῦ ἐφ᾽ ἡμᾶς καὶ ἐπὶ τὰ τέκνα ἡμῶν. 20. ταῦτα ἐροῦμεν τοῖς ἀποσταλεῖσι πρὸς ἡμᾶς προφήταις. 21. λάβωμεν τοὺς λόγους αὐτοῦ τὴν ζωὴν ἀπὸ τῶν νεκρῶν.

B. 1. When Jesus has taken away our sins, we shall be holy for ever. 2. Let us not begin to say[1] in ourselves that we do not know him. 3. We will not fear the ruler who killed the prophets, for God will send his angels to us. 4. When the soldiers had killed Jesus our Lord, we were afraid and went away from him. 5. He said that it was not necessary for us to see each other. 6. If you (p.) persecute and kill those who are being sent to you, you will no longer be the people of God. 7. The multitudes went away, but those who remained said that he had the words of life. 8. When Jesus had spoken these things and had sent his disciples into the villages of Galilee, the Pharisees were afraid of the people. 9. Having killed Jesus, they will cast out of their synagogues those who have believed on him. 10. The apostle himself did not save himself, but God was the one who saved him. 11. When the Lord had spoken this parable, those rulers said that they would kill those who had been sent by him. 12. Unless Jesus himself sends us, we will not be disciples of him. 13. Unless you (p.) repent, you will remain in sin for ever. 14. He who said this word to the one who sent the apostles will say the same word also to those who have been sent by him. 15. Those good disciples, having loved those who were following Jesus, will love also those who follow his apostles. 16. Those who saw him as he was walking in Galilee will gaze at him in heaven for ever.

---

1. With ἄρχομαι, *I begin*, the progressive infinitive, not the aorist infinitive, should be used.

Lesson 25

More Nouns of the Third Declension
- *Adjectives of the Third Declension*

374. [345] Vocabulary

ἀληθής, -ές, adj., *true*

ἀνήρ, ἀνδρός, ὁ, *a man*
(ἀνήρ is usually a man as distinguished from women and children; ἄνθρωπος is a human being as distinguished from other beings.)

ἀρχιερεύς, ἀρχιερέως, ὁ, *a chief priest*

βασιλεύς, βασιλέως, ὁ, *a king*

γένος, γένους, τό, *a race, a kind*

γραμματεύς, γραμματέως, ὁ, *a scribe*

ἔθνος, ἔθνους, τό, *a nation;* plur., τὰ ἔθνη, *the nations, the Gentiles*

ἱερεύς, ἱερέως, ὁ, *a priest*

μήτηρ, μητρός, ἡ, *a mother*

ὀξύς, -εῖα, -ύ, adj., *sharp*

ὄρος, ὄρους, τό, *a mountain*

πατήρ, πατρός, ὁ, *a father*

πίστις, πίστεως, ἡ, *faith*

πλήρης, -ες, adj., *full*

πόλις, πόλεως, ἡ, *a city*

χάρις, χάριτος, ἡ, *grace*

375. [346] Before studying the present lesson, the student should review the paradigms in lesson 17.

208

376. [347] The declension of χάρις, χάριτος, ἡ, *grace,* is as follows:

	Sing.	**Plur.**
Nom.	χάρις	χάριτες
Gen.	χάριτος	χαρίτων
Dat.	χάριτι	χάρισι(ν)
Acc.	χάριν	χάριτας

377. [348] This noun differs from those in §220 in that the accusative singular ending is -ν instead of -α. The final τ of the stem (χαριτ-) drops out before the -ν. If χάρις were declined like ἐλπίς, the accusative singular would be χάριτα.

378. [349] The declension of πόλις, πόλεως (stem πολι-), ἡ, *a city,* is as follows:

	Sing.	**Plur.**
Nom.	πόλις	πόλεις
Gen.	πόλεως	πόλεων
Dat.	πόλει	πόλεσι(ν)
Acc.	πόλιν	πόλεις

379. [351] πόλις represents a large class of feminine third-declension nouns ending in -ις with genitives in -εως. Since it differs so greatly from other third-declension nouns, it is probably best to memorize this paradigm as though entirely new rather than to try to remember all the changes.[1]

---

1. [350] The final ι of the stem is changed to ε except in the nominative, accusative, and vocative singular. πόλει in the dative singular is contracted from πόλε-ι, and πόλεις in the nominative plural from πόλε-ες, in accordance with the rules of contraction given in lesson 23. The accusative plural has -εις, instead of -εας or (as the rules of contraction would require) -ηις. The accusative singular has instead of -α the ν-ending that appears in certain other third-declension nouns such as χάρις. The gen-

380. [352] The declension of γένος, γένους (stem γενεσ-), τό, *a race,* is as follows:

	Sing.	**Plur.**
Nom./Acc.	γένος	γένη
Gen.	γένους	γενῶν
Dat.	γένει	γένεσι(ν)

381. [353] The final σ of the stem (γενεσ-) is dropped except in the nominative singular. The ε that is then left at the end of the stem is contracted with the vowels of the regular third-declension endings, in accordance with the rules of contraction given in lesson 23 (§342).

382. [354] These third-declension nouns in -ος, -ους are declined alike and are all of neuter gender.

383. [355] The declension of βασιλεύς, βασιλέως (stem βασιλευ-), ὁ, *a king,* is as follows:

	Sing.	**Plur.**
Nom.	βασιλεύς	βασιλεῖς
Gen.	βασιλέως	βασιλέων
Dat.	βασιλεῖ	βασιλεῦσι(ν)
Acc.	βασιλέα	βασιλεῖς

384. [356] The final υ of the stem is dropped before those endings that begin with a vowel. Contraction takes place in the dative singular and nominative plural. The genitive singular has -ως instead of -ος (compare πόλις). But the accusative singular has the α-ending, not the ν-ending.

---

itive singular ending is -ως instead of -ος. The accent in the genitive singular and plural of this class of nouns is the only exception to the rule that if the ultima is long, the antepenult cannot be accented (see §11).

385. [357] These nouns in -ευς, -εως are masculine. They generally denote a person of a particular calling or profession.
386. [358] Observe the declension of πατήρ and of ἀνήρ in §606.
387. [359] The declension of other third-declension nouns will give little difficulty once the genitive singular and the gender are known. Only the dative plural is sometimes troublesome, but its forms can at least be easily recognized when they occur.
388. The declension of the adjective ὀξύς, -εῖα, -ύ, *sharp*, is as follows:

| | **Sing.** | | | **Plur.** | | |
	Masc.	**Fem.**	**Neut.**	**Masc.**	**Fem.**	**Neut.**
Nom.	ὀξύς	ὀξεῖα	ὀξύ	ὀξεῖς	ὀξεῖαι	ὀξέα
Gen.	ὀξέως	ὀξείας	ὀξέως	ὀξέων	ὀξειῶν	ὀξέων
Dat.	ὀξεῖ	ὀξείᾳ	ὀξεῖ	ὀξέσι(ν)	ὀξείαις	ὀξέσι(ν)
Acc.	ὀξύν	ὀξεῖαν	ὀξύ	ὀξεῖς	ὀξείας	ὀξέα

As with the noun βασιλεύς, the final υ of the stem is changed to an ε through much of the declension. Several New Testament adjectives whose stem ends in υ are declined like ὀξύς.
389. [360] The declension of ἀληθής, -ές (stem ἀληθεσ-), *true*, is as follows:

| | **Sing.** | | **Plur.** | |
	Masc./Fem.	**Neut.**	**Masc./Fem.**	**Neut.**
Nom.	ἀληθής	ἀληθές	ἀληθεῖς	ἀληθῆ
Gen.	ἀληθοῦς	ἀληθοῦς	ἀληθῶν	ἀληθῶν
Dat.	ἀληθεῖ	ἀληθεῖ	ἀληθέσι(ν)	ἀληθέσι(ν)
Acc.	ἀληθῆ	ἀληθές	ἀληθεῖς	ἀληθῆ

Lesson 25

390. [362] This is the first adjective studied thus far that is declined according to the third declension in the feminine as well as in the masculine and neuter. In this class of adjectives masculine and feminine forms are identical. **391.** [361] The final σ of the stem is dropped in most of the forms, and contraction then takes place. Compare πόλις, γένος, and βασιλεύς.

392. [363] Exercises

A. 1. ἀληθῆ ἐστι τὰ λαλούμενα ὑπὸ τοῦ ἱερέως τούτου. 2. συνελθόντων τῶν ἀρχιερέων καὶ γραμματέων ἵνα ἀποκτεί-νωσι τὸν ἄνδρα τοῦτον, προσηύξαντο οἱ μαθηταὶ ἐν τῷ ἱερῷ. 3. ὁ βασιλεὺς ὁ ἀγαθὸς εἶπεν ὅτι οὐ θέλει ἀποκτεῖναι τοῦτον. 4. χάριτι δὲ ἐσώθησαν ἐκεῖνοι οἱ ἁμαρτωλοὶ καὶ ἠγέρθησαν ἐν δόξῃ. 5. τῇ γὰρ χάριτι σῳζόμεθα διὰ πίστεως ἵνα δοξάζωμεν τὸν θεόν. 6. ἰδὼν τὸν πατέρα καὶ τὴν μητέρα αὐτοῦ ἐν τῇ πόλει ἔμεινεν σὺν αὐτοῖς. 7. εἰς τὰ ἔθνη ἀποστελεῖς τοὺς ἀποστόλους σου, ἵνα κηρύσσωσιν αὐτοῖς τὸ εὐαγγέλιον τῆς χάριτός σου. 8. ἀγαθὸς ἦν οὗτος ὁ ἀνὴρ καὶ πλήρης πνεύματος ἁγίου καὶ πίστεως. 9. ἰδόντες δὲ τὴν χάριν τοῦ θεοῦ παρεκάλεσαν τὰ ἔθνη μένειν ἐν τῇ χάριτι σὺν χαρᾷ καὶ ἐλπίδι. 10. καταβαινόντων δὲ αὐτῶν ἐκ τοῦ ὄρους ἐλάλει ταῦτα ὁ Ἰησοῦς. 11. ἀγαπήσωμεν τοὺς πατέρας καὶ τὰς μητέρας ἡμῶν, ἵνα τηρήσωμεν τὴν ἐντολὴν τοῦ θεοῦ. 12. τῶν ἀρχιερέων ἰδόντων τοὺς συνερχομένους εἰς τὸ ἀκούειν τοῦ ἀνδρὸς εἶπον πρὸς ἑαυτοὺς οἱ ἄρχοντες ὅτι δεῖ αὐτὸν ἀποθανεῖν. 13. οἱ βασιλεῖς οἱ πονηροὶ ἀπέκτειναν καὶ τοὺς ἄνδρας καὶ τὰ τέκνα. 14. ὁ δὲ θεὸς ἤγειρεν αὐτούς, ἵνα δο-ξάζωσιν αὐτὸν εἰς τὸν αἰῶνα. 15. ἐὰν μὴ χάριν ἔχωμεν καὶ πίστιν καὶ ἐλπίδα, οὐ μετανοήσουσι τὰ ἔθνη ἐπὶ τῷ λόγῳ ἡμῶν. 16. τοῖς ἀνδράσι τοῖς πεμφθεῖσιν ὑπὸ τοῦ βασιλέως προσηνέγκαμεν τὸν πατέρα καὶ τὴν μητέρα ἡμῶν. 17. ἐλθὼν πρὸς τὸν βασιλέα ταύτης τῆς χώρας παρεκάλεσας αὐτὸν μὴ ἀποκτεῖναι τὸν ἄνδρα τοῦ-τον. 18. εἰ ἀληθῆ ἐστι τὰ λεγόμενα ὑπὸ τῶν ἀκολουθησάντων

τῷ ἀνδρὶ ἐν τῇ Γαλιλαίᾳ ἀποκτενοῦσιν αὐτὸν οἱ ἀρχιερεῖς.
19. διὰ πίστεως σώσει τοὺς πιστεύοντας εἰς τὸ ὄνομα αὐτοῦ.
20. ἐδέξαντο δὲ καὶ τὰ ἔθνη τὸ ῥῆμα τοῦ Ἰησοῦ τὸ ἀληθές.
  B. 1. God's grace will be preached to every race and nation.
2. When the scribes had entered into that city, the disciples
went away to the mountains. 3. We saw that the word that
was being spoken by the man was true. 4. When the Lord had
said this to the chief priests, the ruler marveled. 5. The father
of him who killed the men will kill also the children. 6. God
will raise up from the dead those who have been saved by his
grace. 7. You (p.) will be saved by God through faith. 8. On
account of the faith of the fathers and of the mothers, the children will die in the evil city. 9. The city, being itself full of sin,
has also a wicked king. 10. If we enter into those cities having our hearts full of grace and faith and hope, those who
repent at our word will see the king in his glory. 11. Jesus said
to the scribes who were following that he was going into the
holy city. 12. If we love the brothers, we will bless also the one
who sent them into the nations. 13. The king said to my father
that the chief priests and Pharisees wished to kill those who
were following Jesus. 14. While Jesus was speaking these
things in that wicked city, the chief priests were gathering
together the soldiers in order that they might kill him.
15. Those who have not the grace of God in their hearts have
neither life nor hope. 16. If you (p.) go into those cities and
villages, you will see the king who killed your fathers and your
mothers.

Lesson 26

Declension of πᾶς, πολύς, μέγας, and Numerals
• Attributive and Substantive Uses of Prepositional
Phrases and of the Genitive • Accusative of Extent of
Time and Space

393. [364] Vocabulary

δύο, *two*

εἷς, μία, ἕν, *one*

ἕξ, indecl., *six*

ἔτος, ἔτους, τό, *a year*
(declined like γένος)

ἤ, conj., *or*

ἤθελον, imperfect indic. of
θέλω (with an apparently
irregular augment, but
the original form of the
verb was ἐθελέω, which
lost its final ε in the progressive system generally
and lost its initial ε in
the present indicative)

Ἰάκωβος, ὁ, *James*

καθαρός, -ά, -όν, adj., *clean,
pure*

μέγας, μεγάλη, μέγα, adj.,
great

μηδείς, μηδεμία, μηδέν, *no
one, nothing* (with moods
other than the indicative)

ὀλίγος, -η, -ον, adj., *little, few*

οὐδείς, οὐδεμία, οὐδέν, *no
one, nothing* (with the
indicative)

πᾶς, πᾶσα, πᾶν, adj., *all, every*

πεντακισχίλιοι, -αι, -α, *five
thousand*

πέντε, indecl., *five*

πλῆθος, πλήθους, τό, *a multitude* (declined like γένος)

πολύς, πολλή, πολύ, adj.,
much, many

πούς, ποδός, ὁ, *a foot* (the
dative plural is ποσί[v])
στάδιον, τό (plural τὰ στάδια, but also masc. οἱ στάδιοι), *a stadium, a furlong*

τέσσαρες, -α, *four*
τρεῖς, τρία, *three*
ὡς, adv., *as;* with numerals,
about

394. [365] The declension of πᾶς, πᾶσα, πᾶν, adj., *all, every,*
is as follows:

	Sing.			Plur.		
	Masc.	**Fem.**	**Neut.**	**Masc.**	**Fem.**	**Neut.**
Nom.	πᾶς	πᾶσα	πᾶν	πάντες	πᾶσαι	πάντα
Gen.	παντός	πάσης	παντός	πάντων	πασῶν	πάντων
Dat.	παντί	πάσῃ	παντί	πᾶσι(ν)	πάσαις	πᾶσι(ν)
Acc.	πάντα	πᾶσαν	πᾶν	πάντας	πάσας	πάντα

395. [366] The masculine and neuter stem is παντ-, and the
word is declined nearly like the first aorist active participle of
λύω. But the accent is slightly irregular in the masculine and
neuter, since it follows the rule for monosyllables of the third
declension (see §232) in the singular but not in the plural.

The Use of πᾶς

396. [367–69] πᾶς can modify a noun without an article, or
it can stand in either the predicate position or in the attributive position, or it can stand by itself as a substantive. The differences in meaning between these uses of πᾶς are not altogether obvious. Generally the following prevails:

1. When used with an anarthrous noun (i.e., a noun without the definite article), πᾶς in the singular means *every, each,
every kind of;* in the plural, *all.* Examples: πᾶσα πόλις, *every
city;* πᾶσαι πόλεις, *all cities.*

2. In the predicate position, πᾶς in the singular means *the
whole of,* i.e., all the individuals making up the substantive

215

modified. Examples: πᾶσα ἡ πόλις, *all the city* (i.e., *everyone in the city*); πᾶσα ἡ ἀλήθεια, *the whole truth;* πᾶν τὸ σῶμα, *the whole body.* In the plural it means *all, all members of a group.* Example: πάντες οἱ μαθηταί, *all the disciples* (i.e., all the people making up the group known as "the disciples").

πᾶς frequently stands in the predicate position with a participle. Examples: πᾶς ὁ πιστεύων, *everyone who believes;* πάντες οἱ πιστεύοντες, *all those who believe;* πάντα τὰ ὄντα ἐκεῖ, *all the things that are/were/will be there.*

3. In the attributive position, πᾶς in both singular and plural means *the whole,* the noun being regarded as a whole, in contrast to its individual parts. Examples: ὁ πᾶς νόμος, *the whole law;* οἱ σὺν ἐμοὶ πάντες ἀδελφοί, *the whole body of the brothers who are/were/will be with me.*

4. Like other adjectives, πᾶς can be used substantively. Examples: πάντες ἥμαρτον, *all (people) have sinned;* ἐκεῖνος ὑμᾶς διδάξει πάντα, *that person will teach you all things.*

397. [370] Declension of πολύς and of μέγας

Learn the declension of πολύς, πολλή, πολύ, *much, many, great,* and of μέγας, μεγάλη, μέγα, *great,* in §615 and §616. Except for the short forms in the nominative and accusative of the masculine and neuter singular, these two adjectives are declined like ordinary adjectives of the second and first declension.

Numerals

398. [371] The declension of εἷς, μία, ἕν, *one,* is as follows:

	Masc.	Fem.	Neut.
Nom.	εἷς	μία	ἕν
Gen.	ἑνός	μιᾶς	ἑνός
Dat.	ἑνί	μιᾷ	ἑνί
Acc.	ἕνα	μίαν	ἕν

The slight irregularities should be noticed. Also take careful note of the rough breathings and accents on εἷς and ἕν, distinguishing them from the prepositions εἰς and ἐν.

399. [372] The declension of οὐδείς, οὐδεμία, οὐδέν, *no one,* and μηδείς, μηδεμία, μηδέν, *no one,* is like that of εἷς except for the accent in the nominative masculine.

400. [373] δύο, *two,* is indeclinable (the same for all cases and genders) except that it has a dative form δυσί(ν).

401. [374] The declension of τρεῖς, τρία, *three,* and of τέσσαρες, τέσσαρα, *four,* may be found in §630.

402. [375] The other cardinal numerals up to διακόσιοι, *two hundred,* are indeclinable. For reference, a table of cardinal and ordinal numbers is given in §656 (chart 8), but it need not be memorized at this point.

Attributive and Substantive Uses of Prepositional Phrases and of the Genitive

403. [376] Prepositional phrases are frequently treated as attributive adjectives, being placed after the article.

Example: οἱ ἐν ἐκείνῃ τῇ πόλει μαθηταί, or οἱ μαθηταὶ οἱ ἐν ἐκείνῃ τῇ πόλει, *the in-that-city disciples,* or *(by a free translation) the disciples who are* [or, if the leading verb is past, *were*] *in that city.* Here the prepositional phrase takes the exact place of an attributive adjective. Remember that οἱ ἀγαθοὶ μαθηταί or οἱ μαθηταὶ οἱ ἀγαθοί means *the good disciples* (see §71). If in these two Greek phrases ἐν τῇ πόλει be substituted for the attributive adjective ἀγαθοί, we have the idiom now under discussion.

404. [377] Like other attributive adjectives, these prepositional phrases can be used substantively.

Example: As οἱ ἀγαθοί means *the good men,* so οἱ ἐν τῇ πόλει means *the in-the-city men,* or *the men who are* [or *were*] *in the city.*

217

405. [378] A noun in the genitive case can be used in this same way.

Examples: As οἱ ἀγαθοί means *the good men,* so οἱ τοῦ Ἰησοῦ means *the of-Jesus men, the belonging-to-Jesus men, the ones/the men/those who belong to Jesus.* Compare τὰ τοῦ πνεύματος, *the things of the Spirit.*

406. [379] The genitive in this usage may indicate various relationships. Sometimes it indicates sonship. Thus ὁ τοῦ Ζεβεδαίου may mean *the son of Zebedee.* The context must determine. All that is certainly implied in the Greek is that the person spoken of is connected in some way with Zebedee. The literal meaning of the phrase is *the of-Zebedee man.*

407. [380] Notice that *the disciples who are in the city* may be expressed by οἱ μαθηταὶ οἱ ὄντες ἐν τῇ πόλει, *the being-in-the-city disciples.* But the ὄντες is not needed. So also *those who are in the city* might be οἱ ὄντες ἐν τῇ πόλει, *the being-in-the-city people.* But again the ὄντες is not needed. The prepositional phrase can be used as an attributive adjective just as well as the participle (with its modifiers) can.

408. [381] All three of the idioms just discussed (οἱ ἐν τῇ πόλει μαθηταί, οἱ ἐν τῇ πόλει, and οἱ τοῦ Ἰησοῦ) are important. It should now be increasingly evident how much of Greek syntax is dependent on the distinction between the attributive and the predicate position (see §§69–75).

409. [382] Accusative of Extent of Space and Time

The accusative is used to express extent of space or time, answering the question *how far?* or *how long?*[1]

---

1. Here is another case where a sentence may have more than one accusative (see §372).

Examples: ἐπορεύθην μετ᾽ αὐτοῦ στάδιον ἕν, *I went with him one furlong;* ἔμεινα μίαν ἡμέραν, *I remained one day;* ἐδίδασκεν αὐτοὺς τρία ἔτη, *he taught them (for) three years.*

410. [383] Exercises

A. 1. μείνας σὺν αὐτῷ ἔτη δύο ἦλθεν εἰς ἐκείνην τὴν πόλιν. 2. ἰδὼν δὲ τοὺς ἐν τῇ μεγάλῃ πόλει ἔγραψε καὶ τοῖς ἐν τῇ μικρᾷ.[1] 3. πορευθέντες δὲ οἱ τοῦ Ἰακώβου σταδίους ὡς πέντε εἶδον τὸν Ἰησοῦν καὶ πάντας τοὺς μετ᾽ αὐτοῦ μαθητάς. 4. ἀκούσαντες δὲ ταῦτα πάντα οἱ ἐν τῇ συναγωγῇ εἶπον ὅτι θέλουσιν ἰδεῖν τὸν ταῦτα ποιοῦντα. 5. ἐθαύμασεν πᾶν τὸ πλῆθος ἐν τῷ βλέπειν αὐτοὺς τὰ ποιούμενα ὑπὸ τοῦ Ἰησοῦ. 6. οὐκ ἔμεινε μίαν ἡμέραν ὁ μετὰ δύο ἔτη ἰδὼν τὸν ἀπόστολον τὸν εὐαγγελισάμενον αὐτόν. 7. τῶν ἀρχιερέων ὄντων ἐν ἐκείνῃ τῇ μεγάλῃ πόλει ἔμεινεν ὁ Ἰησοῦς ἐν τῇ κώμῃ ἡμέρας ὡς πέντε ἢ ἕξ. 8. δεῖ τοὺς ἐν ταῖς πόλεσιν ἐξελθεῖν εἰς τὰ ὄρη. 9. θεραπευθέντος ὑπὸ τοῦ Ἰησοῦ τοῦ ὑπὸ τῶν τεσσάρων προσενεχθέντος αὐτῷ ἐδόξασαν πάντες οἱ ἐν τῇ οἰκίᾳ τὸν ποιήσαντα τὰ μεγάλα ταῦτα. 10. πρὸ δέ τοῦ ἐλθεῖν τοὺς ἐκ τῶν πόλεων ἦν ὁ Ἰησοῦς μετὰ τῶν μαθητῶν αὐτοῦ ἐν τῇ ἐρήμῳ. 11. ἐποιήθη μὲν δι᾽ αὐτοῦ ὁ κόσμος καὶ πάντα τὰ ἐν αὐτῷ, αὐτὸς δὲ ἐγένετο δι᾽ ἡμᾶς ὡς δοῦλος. 12. τοῦτο ἐποίησεν ἵνα σώσῃ πάντας τοὺς πιστεύοντας εἰς αὐτόν. 13. πᾶς ὁ ἀγαπῶν τὸν θεὸν ἀγαπᾷ καὶ τοὺς ἀδελφούς. 14. συνήχθησαν πάντες οἱ ἐν τῇ πόλει ἵνα ἀκούσωσι τὰ λεγόμενα ὑπὸ τῶν ἀποστόλων. 15. ταῦτα ἔλεγον οἱ ἐν τῷ οἴκῳ πᾶσι τοῖς ἀρχιερεῦσι καὶ γραμματεῦσι διὰ τὸ γινώσκειν αὐτοὺς πάντα τὰ περὶ τοῦ Ἰησοῦ. 16. ταῦτα ἐποίει ὁ βασιλεὺς τῶν Ἰουδαίων, ἤθελε γὰρ ἀποκτεῖναι τὰ ἐν τῇ κώμῃ παιδία. 17. οὐδεὶς γινώσκει πάντα τὰ ἐν τῷ κόσμῳ εἰ μὴ ὁ ποιήσας τὰ πάντα. 18. σωθήσεται οὐδεὶς ἐὰν μὴ διὰ πίστεως· ἐτήρησε γὰρ οὐδεὶς πάσας τὰς ἐντολὰς τοῦ θεοῦ. 19. προσευχώμεθα ὑπὲρ τῶν διωκόντων ἡμᾶς, ἵνα γενώμεθα υἱοὶ τοῦ πατρὸς ἡμῶν τοῦ ἐν

---

1. What noun is naturally to be supplied with τῇ μικρᾷ?

οὐρανοῖς. 20. μακάριοι οἱ καθαροί, αὐτοὶ γὰρ τὸν θεὸν ὄψονται. 21. εὐθὺς ἦρεν ὁ πονηρὸς τὸ παρὰ τὴν ὁδὸν σπαρέν.

B. 1. The chief priests saw that all the things that were being spoken by Jesus were true. 2. In that place there were about five thousand men with many gifts and many garments. 3. Many are those that go down into the evil way, but few are those who walk in the ways of life. 4. If you become disciples of me, I will show you all things. 5. By the grace of God we all have become disciples of Jesus. 6. Through faith we have become children of our Father who is in heaven, for Jesus has saved us. 7. Let us do all the things that are in the law, according to the things that are being said to us by the prophets. 8. In that great city we saw three disciples of the Lord praying to their Father in heaven.[1] 9. When Jesus had called one of the three men who were in the boat, he spoke to him all the things concerning the kingdom of God. 10. We were in the same city one year, but Jesus sent us into all the villages that are in Galilee. 11. When Jesus had done all these great things, the Pharisees said that a demon was in him. 12. When Jesus had spoken all these things to the multitudes who were in the cities and villages, he sent the disciples in order that they might preach in the other cities also. 13. All the churches will see the one who saved them through his grace and sent to them the apostles. 14. Many kings and priests will say that all the things that have been spoken by Jesus are true. 15. We saw no one in that great city except one disciple and a few children. 16. Those who belonged to Jesus died on account of their faith.

---

1. Does *in heaven* modify *praying* or *Father*? If it is taken as modifying *Father*, the prepositional phrase should be put in the attributive position.

Lesson 27

Interrogative and Indefinite Pronouns
• *Deliberative and Indirect Questions* • *The Relative
Pronoun* • *Conditional Relative Clauses*

411. [384] Vocabulary

αἰτέω, *I ask, I request*

εἰ, *whether* (in indirect questions); the common meaning, *if,* has already been given.

ἐπερωτάω, *I ask a question of, I question*

ἐρωτάω, *I ask a question, I ask a question of, I question, I ask* (Originally ἐρωτάω meant *to ask* in the sense of *to question,* and αἰτέω meant *to ask* in the sense of *to request,* but in New Testament Greek ἐρωτάω is frequently used in the latter sense as well as in the former.)

καρπός, ὁ, *a fruit*

κρίσις, κρίσεως, ἡ, *a judgment*

ὅπου, adv., *where* (relative)

ὅς, ἥ, ὅ, rel. pron., *who, which, that*

ὅταν for ὅτε ἄν, *whenever* (with subjunctive)

ὅτε, adv., *when* (relative)

οὖν, conj., *accordingly, therefore, then* (postpositive, like δέ and γάρ. See §94.)

ποῦ, adv., *where?* (interrogative)

πῶς, adv., *how?* (interrogative)

τίς, τί, interrogative pron., *who? which? what?*

τις, τι, indefinite pron., *someone, something, a certain one, a certain thing*

φάγομαι, fut. (very irregular), ἔφαγον, 2nd aor., of ἐσθίω, *I eat*

221

Interrogative and Indefinite Pronouns

412. [385] The declension of the interrogative pronoun, τίς, τί, *who? which? what?* is as follows:

| | **Sing.** | | **Plur.** | |
	Masc./Fem.	**Neut.**	**Masc./Fem.**	**Neut.**
Nom.	τίς	τί	τίνες	τίνα
Gen.	τίνος	τίνος	τίνων	τίνων
Dat.	τίνι	τίνι	τίσι(ν)	τίσι(ν)
Acc.	τίνα	τί	τίνας	τίνα

413. [386] The declension is according to the third declension in all three genders, the masculine and feminine being alike throughout, and the neuter differing from the masculine and feminine only in the nominative and accusative.

414. [387] The acute accent in the interrogative pronoun is never changed to the grave. Further, *its accent must always be written* to distinguish it from the indefinite pronoun, which, it will be seen, is identical in form but different in accent.

Example: τί λέγει; *what does he say?*

415. [388] The declension of the indefinite pronoun, τις, τι, *someone, something, a certain one, a certain thing,* is as follows:

| | **Sing.** | | **Plur.** | |
	Masc./Fem.	**Neut.**	**Masc./Fem.**	**Neut.**
Nom.	τις	τι	τινές	τινά
Gen.	τινός	τινός	τινῶν	τινῶν
Dat.	τινί	τινί	τισί(ν)	τισί(ν)
Acc.	τινά	τι	τινάς	τινά

416. [389] The indefinite pronoun is declined like the interrogative pronoun except that all the forms of the indefinite pronoun are enclitic and receive an accent only when the rules in §101 so prescribe. Thus to distinguish the interrogative from the indefinite pronoun it is crucial to note the accent. If the first syllable is accented, it is the interrogative; if not, the indefinite.

417. [390] Both the interrogative and the indefinite pronouns can be used either with a noun or separately.

Examples: (1) τίνα καρπὸν ἔχετε; *what fruit do you have?* (2) τί λέγεις; *what do you say?* (3) ἄνθρωπός τις, *a certain man;* (4) εἶπέν τις, *a certain person said.*

418. [391] The accusative singular neuter, τί, of the interrogative pronoun is often used adverbially to mean *why.*

Example: τί ποιεῖτε ταῦτα; *why do you do these things?*

419. [394] Deliberative Questions

In Greek, deliberative questions use the subjunctive mood. A deliberative question is a question that expects an answer in the imperative mood.

Examples: (1) ποιήσωμεν τοῦτο ἢ μὴ ποιήσωμεν; *should we do this or should we not do it?* The answer expected is in the imperative—*do it* or *do not do it.* (2) τί ποιήσωμεν; *what should we do?* The natural answer is *do this* or *do that,* or the like.

Indirect Questions

420. [392] Indirect questions, like the ordinary form of indirect discourse (see §332), retain the same mood and tense as those that would have been found in the direct discourse lying behind the indirect.

421. [393] The same interrogative words are commonly used in indirect questions as those that are used in direct questions.

Examples: (1) ἠρώτησεν αὐτὸν τίς ἐστιν, *he asked him who he was.* The direct question lying behind the indirect was τίς εἶ; *who are you?* (2) εἶπεν αὐτοῖς ποῦ μένει, *he told them where*

he was staying. The direct question that he was answering was
ποῦ μένεις; *where are you staying?* (3) υἱὸς τοῦ ἀνθρώπου οὐκ
ἔχει ποῦ τὴν κεφαλὴν κλίνῃ, *the Son of Man does not have anywhere to lay his head* (that is, *anywhere he may lay his head*).
Here a deliberative question was implied: *where may the Son
of Man lay his head?* so κλίνῃ is subjunctive.

The Relative Pronoun

422. [395] The declension of the relative pronoun, ὅς, ἥ, ὅ,
who, which, that, is as follows:

	Sing.			**Plur.**		
	Masc.	**Fem.**	**Neut.**	**Masc.**	**Fem.**	**Neut.**
Nom.	ὅς	ἥ	ὅ	οἵ	αἵ	ἅ
Gen.	οὗ	ἧς	οὗ	ὧν	ὧν	ὧν
Dat.	ᾧ	ᾗ	ᾧ	οἷς	αἷς	οἷς
Acc.	ὅν	ἥν	ὅ	οὕς	ἅς	ἅ

423. [396] Notice that except for ὅ instead of ὅν in the nominative and accusative singular neuter (compare αὐτός and
ἐκεῖνος), the declension of the relative pronoun is like that of
a regular adjective of the second and first declension. The
nominative singular feminine and the nominative plural masculine and feminine are like the corresponding forms of the
article except that the article in those forms has no accent.
Once again, the accent is crucial and *must* be used on the relative pronouns.

424. [397] Like other pronouns, the relative pronoun agrees
with its antecedent in gender and number, but its case is determined by its function in its own clause.

Examples: (1) ὁ ἀπόστολος ὃν εἶδες ἀπῆλθεν, *the apostle
whom you saw went away;* the relative pronoun is accusative
because it is the direct object of εἶδες; (2) ἀληθῆ ἦν πάντα ἃ

εἶπεν ὁ Ἰησοῦς, *all things that Jesus said were true;* (3) ὁ μαθητὴς ὃν ἠγάπησεν ὁ Ἰησοῦς ἦν ἐν τῷ οἴκῳ, *the disciple whom Jesus loved was in the house.*

425. [398] Where the antecedent of the relative pronoun is in the genitive or dative case and the relative pronoun itself would naturally be in the accusative case as the object of the verb in the relative clause, it is often *attracted* to the case of its antecedent.

Examples: πάντων δὲ θαυμαζόντων ἐπὶ πᾶσιν οἷς ἐποίει εἶπεν πρὸς τοὺς μαθητὰς αὐτοῦ . . . , *but when all were wondering at all the things that he was doing, he said to his disciples.* . . . Here οἷς would have been accusative if it had retained the case that it would have had in its own clause. But it is attracted to the case of πᾶσιν.

426. [399] The antecedent of the relative pronoun is frequently left unexpressed. Thus ὅς can mean *he who;* ἥ, *she who;* ὅ, *that which, what;* οἵ, *the men who,* or *they who;* αἵ, *the women who;* ἅ, *the things that.*

Examples: (1) οὐκ ἔξεστίν μοι ὃ θέλω ποιῆσαι, *it is not lawful for me to do that which I wish* (or *to do what I wish*). (2) ὃς γὰρ οὐκ ἔστιν καθ᾽ ὑμῶν ὑπὲρ ὑμῶν ἐστιν, *for he who is not against you is for you.* (3) ἔχω ὃ θέλω, *I have what I want.* Here the English word *what* is a short way of saying *the thing that* or *that which* and so correctly translates ὅ. Compare εἶπον αὐτῷ τί ἐποίησα, *I told him what I did.* Here the English word *what* corresponds to an interrogative "what?" in an implied question ("What did you do?"). For this construction Greek uses the actual interrogative τί.

Conditional Relative Clauses

427. [400] The indefinite relative clauses that in English are marked by the suffix *-ever* added to the relative word (e.g., *whoever, whichever, whatever, wherever, whenever*) ordinarily have in Greek the subjunctive with the particle ἄν or ἐάν. This is one of the commonest uses of the subjunctive.

Examples: (1) ὃς γὰρ ἐὰν θέλῃ τὴν ψυχὴν αὐτοῦ σῶσαι οὐ σώσει αὐτήν, *for whoever wishes to save his life will not save it;* (2) ὃς ἂν πιστεύσῃ σωθήσεται, *whoever believes [or will believe] will be saved;* (3) εἰς ἣν δ᾽ ἂν πόλιν εἰσέλθητε ὄψεσθε ἐν αὐτῇ μαθητάς, *and into whatever city you enter [or will enter] you will see disciples in it;* (4) ὅπου ἐὰν ᾖ ὁ διδάσκαλος ἐκεῖ ἔσονται καὶ οἱ διδασκόμενοι ὑπ᾽ αὐτοῦ, *wherever the teacher is, there will be also those who are being taught by him.*

428. [401] Notice that the verb in the English translation of these conditional relative clauses can be either future indicative or present indicative. It often makes little difference which is used. In such clauses the present indicative in English frequently refers to future time.

429. [402] Exercises

A. 1. ὃς ἐὰν μὴ δέξηται ὑμᾶς τοῦτον οὐ δέξεται ὁ βασιλεύς. 2. ἃ ἐὰν ποιήσωμεν ὑμῖν, ποιήσετε καὶ ὑμεῖς ἡμῖν. 3. ἐρωτήσαντός τινος αὐτοὺς τί φάγῃ ἀπεκρίθησαν αὐτῷ λέγοντες[1] ὅτι δεῖ αὐτὸν φαγεῖν τὸν ἄρτον τὸν ἐν τῷ οἴκῳ. 4. τίνος[2] ἔσται ταῦτα πάντα ἐν τῇ ἐσχάτῃ ἡμέρᾳ; 5. ὅταν ἔλθῃ ὁ υἱὸς τοῦ ἀνθρώπου τίνες ἔσονται οἱ πιστεύοντες; 6. ὃς ἂν λύσῃ μίαν τῶν ἐντολῶν ποιεῖ ὃ οὐκ ἔξεστιν ποιεῖν. 7. ἃ εἶπεν ὑμῖν ὁ προφήτης ἔτι ὢν μεθ᾽ ὑμῶν ταῦτα ἐροῦσι καὶ οἱ εὐαγγελισάμενοι ἡμᾶς. 8. ἐάν τις ἀπὸ νεκρῶν πορευθῇ πρὸς αὐτούς, μετανοήσουσιν. 9. ὃς ἐὰν μὴ

---

1. As previously noted, predicate participles may function in ways other than temporally. The progressive participle of λέγω should often be translated simply *saying,* not *while saying.*

2. A noun or pronoun in the genitive case may stand in the predicate with the verb εἰμί. Thus ἡ βασιλεία ἐστὶ τοῦ θεοῦ or θεοῦ ἐστιν ἡ βασιλεία means *the kingdom is God's* or *the kingdom belongs to God.*

ἀκούσῃ τῶν προφητῶν οὐδὲ μετανοήσει ἐάν τινα ἴδῃ τῶν νεκρῶν. 10. οἳ ἂν εἴπωσιν ἃ οὐκ ἔστιν ἀληθῆ οὐ λήμψονται καρπόν τινα τοῦ ἔργου αὐτῶν. 11. ἔλεγεν ὅτι ἐάν τις ἐγερθῇ ἐκ νεκρῶν μετανοήσουσιν. 12. ἠρώτησαν τὸν προφήτην οἱ ἐν τῇ Γαλιλαίᾳ εἰ οἱ νεκροὶ ἀκούσουσι τῆς φωνῆς τοῦ κυρίου. 13. εἶπεν οὖν αὐτοῖς ὅτι ἐν τῇ κρίσει ἀκούσουσιν πάντες τοῦ κυρίου. 14. ἐλθόντες οἱ Φαρισαῖοι εἴς τινα κώμην ἐπηρώτησαν τοὺς ἐν αὐτῇ λέγοντες· Ποῦ[1] εἰσιν οἱ τοῦ προφήτου; ἃ γὰρ λέγουσι περὶ αὐτῶν οἱ ἐν τῇ Γαλιλαίᾳ οὐκ ἔστιν ἀληθῆ. 15. ἔλεγε δὲ ὁ ἐπερωτηθείς· Τί ἐπερωτᾷς με; οὐ γὰρ θέλω ἀποκρίνεσθαί σοι οὐδέν.[2] 16. ἔλεγεν οὖν τῶν μαθητῶν τις τῷ ἀποστόλῳ· Τί ποιήσει οὗτος; ὁ δὲ ἀπόστολος εὐθὺς ἀπεκρίθη αὐτῷ λέγων· Ποιήσει ὁ θεὸς ἃ θέλει καὶ πάντα ἃ θέλει ἐστὶν ἀγαθά. 17. ἃ ἔβλεπε τὸν κύριον ποιοῦντα ταῦτα ἤθελε καὶ αὐτὸς ποιεῖν. 18. οὐ ποιεῖ ὁ υἱὸς ἀφ᾽ ἑαυτοῦ οὐδὲν ἐὰν μή τι βλέπῃ τὸν πατέρα ποιοῦντα.

B. 1. We did what those who were in the same city asked. 2. The priests whom we saw while they were still there asked us who those disciples were. 3. Whoever does not do what I say will not receive from me what he asks. 4. A certain scribe went into the city in order that he might take the books that the prophets had written. 5. Into whatever nation we go, let us seek the disciples who are in it. 6. What should we say concerning all these things? 7. They asked us what they should say concerning those in the city. 8. A certain man, having come to Jesus, said that he wished to be healed. 9. Whoever asks anything will receive what he asks. 10. They asked Jesus what the will of God was. 11. Whoever kills his brother will come into the judgment. 12. Why then do you eat what it is not law-

1. Modern printed editions of Greek texts mark the beginning of direct discourse by capitalizing the first word.

2. The Greek language frequently uses a double negative where it is not allowable in English. Thus οὐ λέγω οὐδέν means *I do not say anything,* or *I say nothing.*

ful to eat? 13. Whoever is not taught by the Lord will not know him. 14. When the chief priests had seen what Jesus was doing, they sent a certain messenger to the Pharisees. 15. Where should we abide? For the night is coming and no one has said to us what we should do.

Lesson 28

The Imperative Mood • The Vocative Case

430. [403] Vocabulary

ἁγιάζω, *I sanctify, I consecrate, I make/keep holy*

ἀγρός, ὁ, *a field*

γῆ, ἡ, *earth, land* (γῆ has the
circumflex accent
throughout because there
has been contraction.)

ἐγγύς, adv., *near*

ἐλεέω, *I have mercy on, I pity*

ὅσος, -η, -ον, rel. adj., *as great
as, as much as, as many as*

ὅστις, ἥτις, ὅ τι, (plur.
οἵτινες), indef. rel. pron.,
*whoever, whichever,
whatever*[1]

οὖς, ὠτός, τό, *an ear* (dat.
plur. ὠσί[ν])

ὀφθαλμός, ὁ, *an eye*

σκότος, σκότους, τό, *darkness* (declined like γένος)

ὕδωρ, ὕδατος, τό, *water*

φῶς, φωτός, τό, *light*

χείρ, χειρός, ἡ, *a hand*

431. [404] The imperative mood occurs in the New Testament in both the progressive and aorist tenses.

---

1. This indefinite relative pronoun is scarcely used except in the nominative case. It is sometimes used almost like the simple relative pronoun
ὅς and sometimes in a way synonymous with ὅς ἄν or ὅς ἐάν but with a
verb in the indicative rather than subjunctive mood.

Lesson 28

432. [405] The progressive imperative, active, middle, and passive, is formed on the progressive stem; the aorist imperative, active and middle, on the aorist stem; and the aorist passive imperative, on the aorist passive stem. There is, of course, no augment (see §264).

433. [406] The imperative mood has no first person, but only second and third.

434. [407] The progressive active imperative of λύω is as follows:

Sing.		Plur.	
2. λῦε	*loose*	λύετε	*loose*
3. λυέτω	*let him (her, it) loose*	λυέτωσαν	*let them loose*

435. [408] The progressive middle imperative of λύω is as follows:

Sing.		Plur.	
2. λύου	*loose for yourself*	λύεσθε	*loose for yourselves*
3. λυέσθω	*let him (her, it) loose for him-(her-, it-)self*	λυέσθωσαν	*let them loose for themselves*

436. [409] The progressive passive imperative of λύω is as follows:

Sing.		Plur.	
2. λύου	*be loosed*	λύεσθε	*be loosed*
3. λυέσθω	*let him (her, it) be loosed*	λυέσθωσαν	*let them be loosed*

230

437. [410] Notice that the progressive active and the progressive middle and passive imperative have the variable theme vowel o/ε.

438. [411] The aorist active imperative of λύω is as follows:

Sing.		**Plur.**	
2. λῦσον	*loose*	λύσατε	*loose*
3. λυσάτω	*let him (her, it) loose*	λυσάτωσαν	*let them loose*

439. [412] The aorist middle imperative of λύω is as follows:

Sing.		**Plur.**	
2. λῦσαι	*loose for yourself*	λύσασθε	*loose for yourselves*
3. λυσάσθω	*let him (her, it) loose for him- (her-, it-)self*	λυσάσθωσαν	*let them loose for themselves*

440. [413] Notice that the aorist active and the aorist middle imperative have the characteristic -σα of the aorist stem. This -σα is disguised only in λῦσον, the first aorist active imperative, second-person singular.

441. [414] The aorist passive imperative of λύω is as follows:

Sing.		**Plur.**	
2. λύθητι	*be loosed*	λύθητε	*be loosed*
3. λυθήτω	*let him (her, it) be loosed*	λυθήτωσαν	*let them be loosed*

442. [415] Notice that the aorist passive imperative has the characteristic -θε of the aorist passive stem. This -θε is lengthened to -θη.

443. [416] The second aorist active imperative of λείπω, *I leave,* is as follows:

	Sing.		**Plur.**	
2.	λίπε	*leave*	λίπετε	*leave*
3.	λιπέτω	*let him (her, it) leave*	λιπέτωσαν	*let them leave*

444. [417] The second aorist middle imperative of λείπω is as follows:

	Sing.		**Plur.**	
2.	λιποῦ	*leave for yourself*	λίπεσθε	*leave for yourselves*
3.	λιπέσθω	*let him (her, it) leave for him- (her-, it-)self*	λιπέσθωσαν	*let them leave for themselves*

445. [418] The second aorist active and the second aorist middle imperative are of course formed on the second aorist stem. They have the same endings as the progressive imperative.

446. Note that the second-person plural endings of all the above paradigms are identical to the second-person plural endings of the corresponding indicative verb. Further, substituting -ω for the final -ε of the second-person plural yields the third-person singular imperative, and substituting -ωσαν produces the third-person plural. Only the second-person singulars have unique forms that must be newly memorized. The imperatival endings are summarized, along with endings in other moods, in §650 (chart 2).

447. [420] **The Tenses in the Imperative Mood**

There is no distinction of time between the tenses in the imperative mood. The aorist imperative refers to the action without saying anything about its duration or repetition, while the progressive imperative views it as continuing or as being repeated. Thus λῦσον means simply *loose*, while λῦε means *continue loosing*, or the like. Ordinarily it is impossible to bring out the difference in an English translation (compare §306).

448. [421] The Use of the Imperative

The imperative mood is used in commands.

Examples: ἀκούσατε τοὺς λόγους μου, *hear my words;* ὁ ἔχων ὦτα ἀκουέτω, *let him who has ears hear.* The English language has, properly speaking, no imperative of the third person. Hence in translating the Greek imperative of the third person we have to use the helping verb *let,* so that the noun or pronoun that is the subject of the imperative in Greek becomes the object of the helping verb in English.

449. [422] Prohibition

Prohibition (the negative of a command) is expressed by the progressive imperative with μή or by the aorist subjunctive with μή.

Examples: (1) μὴ λῦε or μὴ λύσῃς, *do not loose* (μὴ λύῃς or μὴ λῦσον would be wrong); (2) μὴ λυέτω or μὴ λύσῃ, *let him not loose;* (3) μὴ λύετε or μὴ λύσητε, *do not loose;* (4) μὴ λυέτωσαν or μὴ λύσωσιν, *let them not loose.*

450. [423] Progressive Imperative of εἰμί

The progressive imperative of εἰμί, *I am,* is as follows:

Sing.		**Plur.**	
2. ἴσθι	*be*	ἔστε	*be*
3. ἔστω	*let him (her, it) be*	ἔστωσαν	*let them be*

233

The Vocative Case

451. In addition to the regular cases, Greek has a special case used only for direct address, when asking for someone's attention, as in διδάσκαλε, θέλομεν ἀπὸ σοῦ σημεῖον ἰδεῖν, *teacher, we want to see a sign from you.* However, the vocative form is usually the same as the nominative. In fact, all plural nouns, all neuter nouns, all first-declension *feminine* nouns, all monosyllabic nouns, and a few other third-declension nouns have identical forms for nominative and vocative. The instances where the vocative differs from the nominative can be summarized as follows:

1. First-declension *masculine* (but not feminine) singular nouns, instead of the nominative -ης, have -α. Thus προφῆτα, *O prophet*; μαθητά, *O disciple*, etc.

2. Second-declension masculine and feminine (but not neuter) nouns, and masculine singular adjectives of first/second declension, have -ε instead of -ος. Thus κύριε, ἐλέησον, *Lord, have mercy.*

3. Some third-declension masculine and feminine (but not neuter) nouns, and some third-declension adjectives, slightly alter the final syllable of the nominative (usually by shortening the vowel or the ending).

Examples: the vocative of πατήρ is πάτερ; that of πόλις, πόλι; that of ἀληθής, ἀληθές.

It should be noted that even nouns that have a distinct vocative form sometimes appear in nominative form when used as vocatives.

Vocative cases are included with the paradigms of nouns and adjectives in the back of the book.

Accent Matters

452. [419] The second aorist middle imperative second-person singular (e.g., λιποῦ) always has an irregular accent, instead of following the rule of recessive accent.

Lesson 28

Further, the forms εἰπέ, ἐλθέ, from λέγω and ἔρχομαι, have an irregular accent.

453. [424] Exercises

A. 1. ἐὰν δὲ μὴ ἀκούσῃ, παράλαβε μετὰ σοῦ ἔτι ἕνα ἢ δύο. 2. ὃ ἐὰν ἴδητε τὸν Χριστὸν ποιοῦντα, τοῦτο ποιήσατε καὶ ὑμεῖς. 3. κύριε, ἐλέησον ἡμᾶς, οὐ γὰρ ἐποιήσαμεν ἃ ἐκέλευσας. 4. μὴ εἰσέλθῃ εἰς τὴν πόλιν ὁ ἐν τῷ ὄρει. 5. οὕτως οὖν προσεύχεσθε ὑμεῖς, Πάτερ ἡμῶν ὁ ἐν τοῖς οὐρανοῖς· ἁγιασθήτω τὸ ὄνομά σου· ἐλθάτω[1] ἡ βασιλεία σου· γενηθήτω[2] τὸ θέλημά σου, ὡς ἐν οὐρανῷ καὶ ἐπὶ γῆς. 6. ἀπόλυσον οὖν, κύριε, τὰ πλήθη· ἤδη γὰρ ἔρχεται ἡ νύξ. 7. μηδεὶς ἐξέλθῃ εἰς τὰ ὄρη, προσευξάσθωσαν δὲ πάντες τῷ πατρὶ αὐτῶν τῷ ἐν τοῖς οὐρανοῖς. 8. λαβὼν αὐτὸν ἄγε πρὸς ἡμᾶς. 9. μηδενὶ εἴπητε ὃ εἴδετε. 10. ἐγέρθητε[3] καὶ μὴ φοβεῖσθε· ὁ γὰρ κύριος σώσει ὑμᾶς. 11. πάντα οὖν ὅσα ἐὰν εἴπωσιν ὑμῖν ποιήσατε καὶ τηρεῖτε, κατὰ δὲ τὰ ἔργα αὐτῶν μὴ ποιεῖτε· λέγουσιν γὰρ καὶ οὐ ποιοῦσιν. 12. ἔλεγεν αὐτῷ μαθητής τις Κύριε, κέλευσόν με ἐλθεῖν πρὸς σὲ ἐπὶ τὰ ὕδατα. ὁ δὲ Ἰησοῦς εἶπεν Ἐλθέ. 13. ὅσα ἐὰν ἀκούσητε τοῖς ὠσὶν ὑμῶν καὶ ἴδητε τοῖς ὀφθαλμοῖς ὑμῶν εἴπετε καὶ τοῖς ἔθνεσιν. 14. ἃ ἐὰν ἀκούσητε ἐν τῷ σκότει κηρύξατε ἐν τῷ φωτί. 15. μακάριος ὅστις φάγεται ἄρτον ἐν τῇ βασιλείᾳ τοῦ θεοῦ. 16. ἐν ἐκείνῃ τῇ πόλει εἰσὶν ἱερεῖς πονηροί, οἵτινες οὐ ποιοῦσι τὸ θέλημα τοῦ θεοῦ. 17. ἐξελθόντες εἴπετε πᾶσι τοῖς ἔθνεσι τοῖς ἐπὶ πάσης τῆς γῆς ἃ ἐποίησεν ὁ θεὸς τοῖς ἀγαπῶσιν αὐτόν. 18. ὅταν κληθῇς ὑπό τινος, πορεύθητι. 19. ὅταν ἴδητε ταῦτα γινόμενα, γνώσεσθε ὅτι ἐγγύς ἐστιν ἡ κρίσις.

1. A first aorist ending is here placed on a second aorist stem, as frequently occurs in New Testament Greek (see §194 footnote and §544).
2. The aorist passive of γίνομαι is the same in meaning as the aorist middle, the verb being deponent throughout. The meaning of the verb here is *to take place, to be done*.
3. The passive of ἐγείρω is frequently used as a deponent meaning *I arise, I rise*.

20. ἴδετε πάντες ὑμεῖς τὰς χεῖράς μου· οὐ γὰρ ἐποίησαν αὗται αἱ χεῖρες ὧν λέγουσιν ἐκεῖνοι οὐδέν.

B. 1. Speak (p.) to all the Gentiles the things that I have spoken to you. 2. Do not say in your (p.) heart that you do not wish to do the things that the king commands. 3. Let no one fear those evil priests, for whoever does the will of God will go out with joy. 4. Let him who has saved us through his blood have mercy on us in these evil days. 5. Whoever loves God will come to the light, but he who does not love him will walk in the darkness. 6. As many things as you (p.) do, do in the light, in order that the name of God may be kept holy. 7. Let these men be baptized, for Christ has saved them through his word. 8. Pray to your (s.) Father in heaven, for he will do whatever things you ask. 9. Let not the king say this, for we are all faithful men. 10. Let us not do the things that the evil men said to us. 11. Have mercy (p.) on all, for the Lord has had mercy on you. 12. As many things as are good, do (p.); but as many things as are evil, do not even speak concerning these. 13. The disciples asked the apostle what they should eat, and the apostle said to them, "Go into the villages and eat the bread that is in them." 14. Do not begin to say in yourselves that you do not know the truth. 15. Let those who are in the fields not return into their houses. 16. Lord, save me, for I have broken your commandments.

Lesson 29

The Perfect Tense • *The Pluperfect Tense*

454. [425] Vocabulary

ἀκήκοα, perf. act. indic. of ἀκούω, *I hear* (The final o of the perfect stem does not contract. See §341.)

βεβάπτισμαι, perf. pass. indic. of βαπτίζω, *I baptize*

γέγονα, perf. indic. of γίνο-μαι, *I become* (γίνεται, *it comes to pass, it happens*)

γέγραφα, γέγραμμαι, perf. act. and perf. pass. indic. of γράφω, *I write*

γεννάω, *I beget, I become the parent of*

ἐγγίζω, *I come near*

ἐγήγερται, perf. pass. indic., third-pers. sing., of ἐγείρω, *I raise up*

ἔγνωκα, perf. act. indic. of γινώσκω, *I know*

ἐλήλυθα, perf. indic. of ἔρχομαι, *I come, I go*

ἐρρέθην, aor. pass. indic. (aor. pass. part. ῥηθείς) of λέγω, *I say*

ἑώρακα, perf. act. indic. of βλέπω (ὁράω), *I see*

θνήσκω, *I die* (used only in the perfect, τέθνηκα, *I am*

237

dead. In other tenses ἀπο-   Πέτρος, ὁ, *Peter*
θνῄσκω is used.)   πληρόω, *I fulfill*
μαρτυρέω, *I bear witness*

455. [426] The perfect active indicative of λύω is as follows:

Sing.	**Plur.**
1. λέλυκα	λελύκαμεν
2. λέλυκας	λελύκατε
3. λέλυκε(ν)	λελύκασι (or λέλυκαν)

456. [427] The perfect active infinitive of λύω is λελυκέναι.

457. [428] The perfect active participle of λύω is λελυκώς, λελυκυῖα, λελυκός.

458. [429] The forms given above constitute the *perfect system*, which is formed from the fourth of the principal parts, λέλυκα.

459. [430] The perfect system is regularly formed by adding κ (in the indicative κα) to the basal stem (the uninflected core) of the verb, and by prefixing the *reduplication*. The reduplication consists of the first consonant of the verb stem followed by ε. Reduplication marks the perfect system—it does not indicate time.

460. [431] The perfect, being a primary tense, might be expected to have primary personal endings. But in the active indicative the endings are exactly like the (secondary) endings of the first aorist, except in the third-person plural, and even in the third-person plural λέλυκαν sometimes stands instead of λελύκασι(ν).

461. [432] The perfect subjunctive and perfect imperative are so rare that they need not be learned at this point.

462. [433] The declension of the perfect active participle of λύω is as follows:

238

Sing.

	Masc.	**Fem.**	**Neut.**
Nom.	λελυκώς	λελυκυῖα	λελυκός
Gen.	λελυκότος	λελυκυίας	λελυκότος
Dat.	λελυκότι	λελυκυίᾳ	λελυκότι
Acc.	λελυκότα	λελυκυῖαν	λελυκός

Plur.

	Masc.	**Fem.**	**Neut.**
Nom.	λελυκότες	λελυκυῖαι	λελυκότα
Gen.	λελυκότων	λελυκυιῶν	λελυκότων
Dat.	λελυκόσι(ν)	λελυκυίαις	λελυκόσι(ν)
Acc.	λελυκότας	λελυκυίας	λελυκότα

463. [434] Notice that the perfect active participle, like the other active participles and like the aorist passive participle, is declined according to the third declension in the masculine and neuter and according to the first declension in the feminine.

Formation of the Perfect Stem in Various Verbs

464. As with all the other tenses, so also with the perfect the endings within the system are constant and applicable to the perfect tense of any verb, but the actual perfect stem to which they are attached can be ascertained only by referring to the fourth (for active) and fifth (for middle and passive) principal parts. However, certain guidelines that apply to most verbs to a greater or lesser extent can help the student to recognize or guess forms before checking a lexicon.

1. As we have just seen, perfect active indicative is usually formed as: reduplication + basal stem + tense formant (κ) + connecting theme vowel (α) + appropriate ending (secondary A, except third-person plural). Thus: λε-λυ-

239

κ-α-μεν, *we have loosed*. In this case, as in most, the reduplication consists of a repetition of the first letter of the stem with the vowel ε.

2. [437] If, however, the verb's basal stem begins with a fricative (φ, θ, χ), the corresponding full stop (π, τ, κ) is the consonant used for the reduplication.[1]

    Examples: the perfect of φανερόω is πεφανέρωκα; that of θεραπεύω, τεθεράπευκα.

3. [436] If the basal stem begins with a compound sibilant (ψ, ζ, ξ), or with two consonants *where the second consonant is not a liquid*, the reduplication is simply ε.

    Examples: the perfect of ζητέω is ἐζήτηκα; that of ἀποστέλλω, ἀπέσταλκα (note that the reduplication, like the augment, comes after the prepositional prefix). But the perfect of πληρόω is πεπλήρωκα (second consonant of πλ- is liquid).

4. [435] If the verb stem begins with a vowel or diphthong, the reduplication consists in the lengthening of that vowel or diphthong. In this case the reduplication looks like the augment. Unlike the augment, however, reduplication is preserved in all moods, not just the indicative.

    Examples: The perfect active of ἐλπίζω is ἤλπικα, and of αἰτέω, ᾔτηκα. However, it is not always predictable. The perfect of ἀκούω is ἀκήκοα; that of ὁράω, ἑώρακα.

5. [438] If the verb stem ends with a vowel, that vowel is regularly lengthened before the κ of the perfect active, just as it is before the σ of the future and first aorist.

    Examples: ἠγάπηκα from ἀγαπάω, πεφίληκα from φιλέω.

6. [439] If the verb stem ends with τ, δ, or θ, that letter is dropped before the κ of the perfect.

    Example: ἤλπικα from ἐλπίζω (stem ἐλπίδ-).

---

1. For definitions of the linguistic terms used in this section, see chart 4 (§652) and the glossary in the back of the book.

7. [440] Some verbs do not have the customary κ in the perfect tense. These are, however, conjugated exactly the same, except that there is no κ.

Examples: γέγραφα from γράφω; ἀκήκοα from ἀκούω.

Perfect Middle and Passive

465. [442] The perfect middle and passive indicative of λύω is as follows:

	Sing.	**Plur.**
1.	λέλυμαι	λελύμεθα
2.	λέλυσαι	λέλυσθε
3.	λέλυται	λέλυνται

466. [443] The perfect middle and passive infinitive of λύω is λελύσθαι.

467. [444] The perfect middle and passive participle of λύω is λελυμένος, -η, -ον (declined like a regular adjective of the second and first declension).

468. [445] The forms given above constitute the *perfect middle system*, which is formed from the fifth of the principal parts, λέλυμαι.

469. [446] The reduplication is the same as in the perfect active.

470. [447] In the indicative, the primary middle endings (see §115) are added directly to the stem, without an intervening variable vowel. They are not modified at all. So in the infinitive and participle -σθαι and -μενος are added directly to the stem.

471. [448] If the verb stem ends with a vowel, that vowel is regularly lengthened before the endings in the perfect middle and passive, as before the tense suffixes in the future, first aorist, perfect active, and aorist passive.

Example: μεμαρτύρημαι from μαρτυρέω.

Lesson 29

472. [449] If the verb stem ends with a consonant, various changes occur when the endings of the perfect middle and passive are put on. These changes generally involve the final consonant of the stem accommodating itself for ease of pronunciation to the first consonant of the ending.

Example: the perfect passive indicative of γράφω is γέγραμμαι, γέγραψαι, γέγραπται, γεγράμμεθα, γέγραφθε, (γέγραται).[1]

These alterations are best learned by observation, but a chart of the various changes may be found in §653.

Use of the Perfect Tense

473. [451] There is no English tense that corresponds exactly to the Greek perfect. The translations *I have loosed* for λέλυκα, *I have loosed for myself* for λέλυμαι (middle), and *I have been loosed* for λέλυμαι (passive) may often serve in the exercises, but they are makeshifts at best. It has already been noted (see §177) that these same English expressions may often translate the aorist tense rather than the perfect.

474. [452.1–2, 4] The Greek perfect tense denotes the present state resultant upon a past action.

Examples:

1. If someone asks an official, "What is your relation to that prisoner?" and he replies, "I have released him," then the verb in this answer of the official would be λέλυκα. The perfect would express the present state of things resultant upon his past action of releasing. But if, on the other hand, someone asks an official, "What is the history of your dealings with that prisoner?" and he answers, "I have released the prisoner

---

1. As a substitute for the third-person plural of such verbs, εἰσί with a plural perfect passive participle is used. See §593 on periphrasis in lesson 34.

three times and imprisoned him again three times," then the first verb of this answer of the official would be ἔλυσα, not λέλυκα, because there is here no thought of the present state resultant upon the past action. Indeed, the act of releasing had no result continuing into the present. But even if it had a permanent result, the verb referring to it would be aorist, not perfect, unless the present result rather than merely the past action were specially in view. Thus even if, after the question, "What have you done?" the official said merely, "I have released the prisoner," and even if as a matter of fact the releasing had a permanent result, still the aorist tense ἔλυσα might very well be used; for the point under consideration might be the history of the official's dealings with the prisoner and not the present state of affairs. The distinction is often a fine one. But the perfect should not be used in the exercises unless there is some clear reason for deserting the aorist.

2. The perfect passive is often much easier to translate into English than the perfect active. Thus γέγραπται means *it is written* (in the Scriptures). Here the English *it is written* is not a present tense at all, but reproduces the Greek perfect very well; the meaning is *it stands written*, or, *it is in a state of having been written*. Both English and Greek here refer to a present state resultant upon an act of writing that took place long ago.

3. ἐλήλυθα, the perfect of ἔρχομαι, means *I am come*, and γέγονα means *I am become*. It so happens that because of the peculiar nature of the verbs *to come* and *to become* in English, we have a neat way of translating the Greek perfect of ἔρχομαι and γίνομαι.

Of course the student should not think that *I am come* has anything to do with the passive voice. It is not at all like *I am loosed*.

475. [452.3] Perfect Participles

Perfect participles may be used like simple adjectives. The perfect *passive* participle can often be translated neatly by the simple English passive participle used as an adjective. Thus λόγος γεγραμμένος means *a written word*, ὁ ἠγαπημένος μαθητής means *the beloved disciple*, οἱ δεδιωγμένοι means *the persecuted ones*, etc. But the Greek perfect *active* participle is very hard to translate. The student should carefully avoid thinking that *having loosed* is specially connected with the perfect. Indeed, the perfect active participle is as often as not best translated with an English present participle, not the English perfect. In the overwhelming majority of cases, the English *having loosed* corresponds best to the aorist—the participle *having* merely indicating that the action has taken place prior to the action of the main verb in the sentence. In general, take note that the Greek aorist is much more common than the perfect.

476. [450] Pluperfect Tense

The pluperfect tense is so rare that its forms need not be memorized at this point. It can, however, often be identified by the fact that it usually has *both* the augment *and* reduplication (the augment coming before the reduplication), although in the New Testament the augment is frequently missing. Further, the active voice of the pluperfect uses a very distinctive ει as the vowel connecting the perfect stem to the secondary A endings (thus, the first-person singular is ἐλελύκειν). The pluperfect middle and passive uses secondary B endings (thus, ἐλελύμην). The pluperfect is a secondary tense. Like the imperfect, it occurs only in the indicative mood.

The meaning of the pluperfect is exactly the same as the perfect, except that the abiding result in view is itself in the past. Thus, if σέσωσμαι means *I am presently in a state of having been saved*, ἐσεσώσμην means *I was (at some point in the past) in a state of having been saved*.

477. [453] The conjugation of λύω has now been completed. The student should review it thoroughly as a whole, using the paradigm given in §631. The verb should be learned in columns, strictly in the order given. Thus "progressive-active" should form one idea in the student's mind, and under it should be subsumed the various moods. Notice particularly how the various parts of the verb are connected with the several principal parts.

Accent Matters

478. As indicated by the paradigm of the perfect active participle (§462), the accent of the nominative singular masculine and neuter falls on the ultima, that of the feminine, on the penult. The accentuation of the other forms of the participle conforms to the noun rule throughout, the feminine genitive plural following the special rule for first-declension nouns (see §56).

In perfect middle and passive participles, the accent stays on the penult throughout (λελυμένος, -μένη, -μένον, etc.). The perfect active and the middle and passive infinitives are also accented on the penult (λελυκέναι; λελύσθαι).

479. [454] Exercises

A. 1. οὐδείς ἐστιν δίκαιος κατὰ τὸν νόμον εἰ μὴ ὁ ποιήσας πάντα τὰ γεγραμμένα ἐν τῷ βιβλίῳ τοῦ νόμου. 2. εὐηγγελίσατο πάντα τὸν λαὸν λέγων ὅτι ἤγγικεν ἡ βασιλεία τῶν οὐρανῶν. 3. ὃ ἑωράκαμεν καὶ ἀκηκόαμεν λέγομεν καὶ ὑμῖν, ἵνα καὶ ὑμεῖς πιστεύσητε εἰς τὸν Χριστόν. 4. καὶ ἐν τούτῳ γινώσκομεν ὅτι ἐγνώκαμεν αὐτόν, ἐὰν τὰς ἐντολὰς αὐτοῦ τηρῶμεν. 5. ὁ ἀγαπῶν τὸν γεννήσαντα ἀγαπᾷ τὸν γεγεννημένον ἐξ αὐτοῦ. 6. πᾶς ὁ γεγεννημένος ἐκ τοῦ θεοῦ οὐχ ἁμαρτάνει, ἀλλ᾽ ὁ γεννηθεὶς ἐκ τοῦ θεοῦ τηρεῖ αὐτόν. 7. τοῦτο γέγονεν,[1] ὅτι οὕτως γέγραπται διὰ τοῦ προφήτου. 8. τὸ γεγεννημένον ἐκ τῆς σαρκὸς σάρξ ἐστιν, καὶ τὸ γεγεννημένον ἐκ τοῦ πνεύματος πνεῦμά ἐστιν. 9. αὕτη δέ ἐστιν ἡ κρίσις, ὅτι τὸ φῶς ἐλήλυθεν εἰς τὸν κόσμον καὶ ἠγάπησαν οἱ ἄνθρωποι τὸ σκότος. 10. ἔλεγον οὖν οἱ Ἰουδαῖοι τῷ τεθεραπευμένῳ· Οὐκ ἔξεστιν ποιῆσαι τοῦτο. 11. ἐγὼ ἐλήλυθα ἐν τῷ ὀνόματι τοῦ πατρός μου καὶ οὐ δέχεσθέ με. 12. ἀλλ᾽ εἶπον ὑμῖν ὅτι καὶ ἑωράκατέ με καὶ οὐ πιστεύετε. 13. ἐὰν μὴ φάγητε τὴν σάρκα τοῦ υἱοῦ τοῦ ἀνθρώπου καὶ πίητε αὐτοῦ τὸ αἷμα, οὐκ ἔχετε ζωὴν ἐν ἑαυτοῖς. 14. τὰ ῥήματα ἃ ἐγὼ λελάληκα ὑμῖν πνεῦμά ἐστιν καὶ ζωή ἐστιν. 15. ἀπεκρίθη αὐτῷ Πέτρος· Κύριε, πρὸς τίνα ἀπελευσόμεθα; ῥήματα ζωῆς ἔχεις, καὶ ἡμεῖς πεπιστεύκαμεν καὶ ἐγνώκαμεν ὅτι σὺ εἶ ὁ ἅγιος τοῦ θεοῦ. 16. ταῦτα αὐτοῦ λαλοῦντος πολλοὶ ἐπίστευσαν εἰς αὐτόν. 17. γέγραπται ὅτι δύο ἀνθρώπων ἡ μαρτυρία ἀληθής ἐστιν. 18. ταῦτα εἶπεν πρὸς τοὺς πεπιστευκότας εἰς αὐτὸν Ἰουδαίους. 19. νῦν δὲ ζητεῖτέ με ἀποκτεῖναι, ἄνθρωπον ὃς τὴν ἀλήθειαν ὑμῖν λελάληκα,[2] ἣν ἤκουσα παρὰ τοῦ θεοῦ. 20. εὐλογημένος ὁ ἐρχόμενος ἐν ὀνόματι κυρίου.

B. 1. Where is the priest? He is already come. 2. All the baptized disciples are in the small city. 3. The priests having been baptized came together into the same house. 4. Where is the multitude? It has already come near. 5. What is in your (s.) heart? I have believed on the Lord. 6. Are you (s.) faithful? I have kept the faith. 7. It is written through the prophet that the Messiah is coming in these days, and we know that his kingdom is come near. 8. Children beloved by your Father, enter into the joy kept in heaven for those who have believed on Christ. 9. Who is this man? He is a child begotten by God.

1. γίνομαι here means *to take place, to come to pass, to happen*.
2. The relative pronoun agrees with its antecedent in person as well as in gender and number. In this sentence, the antecedent of ὅς is ἄνθρωπον, which is first person because it is in apposition to the personal pronoun με.

10. Having been crucified by the soldiers, the Lord died, but now he is risen. 11. Brothers beloved by all the disciples, why do you not pity the little ones? 12. Those who are come out of the darkness into the light know that God will do all the things written in the Law and the Prophets. 13. All the things written or spoken through this prophet are true. 14. This is come to pass in order that that which was said by the Lord through the prophet might be fulfilled. 15. If you (s.) are already loosed, give thanks to him who loosed you. 16. Where is the prophet whom the soldiers persecuted? He is become king of many cities.

Lesson 30

Comparison of Adjectives • Declension of μείζων
• Genitive of Comparison and Use of ἤ • Adverb
Formation • Adverbs Used as Prepositions • Genitive
of the Articular Infinitive Expressing Purpose
• Dative of Respect • Accusative of Reference
• Cases Expressing Time • Possessive Adjectives
• μή Used as a Conjunction • ἵνα with
the Subjunctive in Various Uses • μή with
the Indicative in Questions Expecting a Negative
Answer • Future as Imperative

480. [455] Vocabulary

ἐλάσσων, -ον, *less,* comparative of μικρός

ἐμός, -ή, -όν, poss. adj., *belonging to me, my*

ἔμπροσθεν, adv., *in front, in the presence of* (with gen.)

ἐνώπιον, adv., *before, in the sight of, in the presence of* (with gen.)

ἔξω, adv., *outside, outside of* (with gen.)

ἐχθρός, ὁ, *an enemy*

ἤ, conj., *than* (The meaning *or* has already been given.)

ἡμέτερος, -α, -ον, poss. adj., *belonging to us, our*

ἴδιος, -α, -ον, *private, belonging to one's self, one's own* ἱκανός, -ή, -όν, *sufficient, worthy, considerable*

ἰσχυρότερος, -α, -ον, *stronger,* comparative of ἰσχυρός, -ά, -όν, *strong*

καλῶς, adv., *well*

κρείσσων, -ον, *better,* comparative of ἀγαθός (occasionally spelled κρείττων, -ον)

μᾶλλον, adv., *more, rather*

μείζων, -ον, *greater,* comparative of μέγας

μή, conj., *lest, in order that not* (The adverbial use of μή = *not* has already been given.)

μήποτε, *lest, lest perhaps*

ὅπως, *in order that* (takes the subjunctive; used very much as ἵνα is used)

πάλιν, adv., *again*

πλείων, -ον, *more,* comparative of πολύς

σάββατον, τό, *sabbath* (The plural τὰ σάββατα, with irregular dative τοῖς σάββασι[ν]), is often used in the singular sense.)

σός, -ή, -όν, poss. adj., *belonging to you* (s.), *your*

ὑμέτερος, -α, -ον, poss. adj., *belonging to you* (p.), *your*

Comparison of Adjectives

481. [456] The comparative degree of many (but by no means all) adjectives is formed by adding the suffix -τερος, -τέρα, -τερον (declined like a regular adjective of the second and first declension).

Example: μικρός, *small;* μικρότερος, *smaller.*

482. [457] The superlative degree ends in -τατος, -τάτη, -τατον, or -ιστος, -ίστη, -ιστον, but in the New Testament the superlative is rather rare.

483. [458] A number of adjectives have irregular comparative and superlative forms. These can be learned from the lexicon as they occur.

Example: μικρός, *little;* ἐλάσσων, *less;* ἐλάχιστος, *least.*

484. [459] The declension of μείζων, -ον, *greater*, the comparative of μέγας, is as follows:

	Sing.		**Plur.**	
	Masc./Fem.	**Neut.**	**Masc./Fem.**	**Neut.**
Nom.	μείζων	μεῖζον	μείζονες	μείζονα
Gen.	μείζονος	μείζονος	μειζόνων	μειζόνων
Dat.	μείζονι	μείζονι	μείζοσι(ν)	μείζοσι(ν)
Acc.	μείζονα	μεῖζον	μείζονας	μείζονα

485. [461] The shortened form, μείζω, can stand in the accusative singular masculine and feminine and in the neuter plural nominative and accusative; and the shortened form, μείζους, can stand in the nominative and accusative plural masculine and feminine.

486. [460] The comparative adjectives ἐλάσσων, *less*, πλείων, *more*, and κρείσσων, *better*, are declined in the same way.

487. [462] Genitive of Comparison and Use of ἤ, *than*

Comparison in English uses comparative adjectives with the word *than*. In the sentence *wisdom is better than gold*, the word *better* is the comparative adjective applying to the primary noun in the comparison, *wisdom*, and *gold* is preceded by the word *than* to indicate that it is the secondary noun, the thing to which the primary noun is being compared. In Greek, the function of *than* is accomplished either by (1) putting the secondary noun in the genitive case (a genitive of comparison) or by (2) using the word ἤ followed by the secondary noun in the same case as the primary noun.

Examples: (1) μείζονα τούτων ποιήσει, *greater things than these will he do.* (2) ἠγάπησαν οἱ ἄνθρωποι μᾶλλον τὸ σκότος ἢ τὸ φῶς, *people loved darkness more than light.* Here φῶς is accusative. The meaning is *people loved darkness more than they loved light.*

Adverb Formation

488. [463] Many adverbs are formed from adjectives by substituting ς for ν at the end of the genitive plural masculine and neuter.

Example: καλός, *good;* genitive plural, καλῶν; adverb, καλῶς, *well.*

489. [464] The comparative degree of adverbs is like the accusative singular neuter of the comparative degree of the corresponding adjective; and the superlative degree of the adverb is like the accusative plural neuter of the superlative degree of the corresponding adjective.

490. [465] Many adverbs, however, are of diverse forms that must be learned by observation.

491. [466] Adverbs Used as Prepositions

Certain adverbs, especially adverbs of place, can function as prepositions with the genitive case.

Example: ἔξω, *outside;* ἔξω τῆς πόλεως, *outside of the city;* ἐγγὺς τῆς πόλεως, *near the city.*

See §655 for a list of some common "improper" prepositions.

492. [468] Genitive of the Articular Infinitive Expressing Purpose

The genitive of the articular infinitive, without any preposition, is sometimes used to express purpose.

Example: ἦλθεν πρὸς τὸν προφήτην τοῦ βαπτισθῆναι ὑπ' αὐτοῦ, *he came to the prophet in order to be baptized by him.* Recall that for the most part the articular infinitive is used in the same constructions as those in which an ordinary noun with the article can be used (see §§325–27). This use of the genitive to express purpose, however, would not be possible for an ordinary noun.

493. [469] Dative of Respect

The dative is used to indicate the respect in which anything exists or is true.

Example: γινωσκόμενος τῷ προσώπῳ, *being known by face* (i.e., *being known so far as the face is concerned*); καθαρὸς τῇ καρδίᾳ, *pure in heart* (i.e., *pure so far as the heart is concerned*); ἀνὴρ ὀνόματι Ἰάκωβος, *a man by name James* (i.e., *a man who is James so far as the name is concerned*).

494. [470] Accusative of Reference

The accusative of reference is very much the same in meaning as the dative of respect but is less frequently used.

Example: τὸν ἀριθμὸν ὡς πεντακισχίλιοι, *about five thousand in number*.

Cases Expressing Time

495. In addition to the accusative of time, which denotes extent of time (§409), the genitive and dative cases are also used with expressions of time, with different functions.

496. [467] The genitive of time is used to express *time within which*. This denotes the *kind* of time during which the action occurred.

Example: παρέλαβε τὸ παιδίον καὶ τὴν μητέρα αὐτοῦ νυκτός, *he took the young child and his mother by night*.

497. [471–72] The dative of time is used to express *time when*. It often occurs with the preposition ἐν.

Examples: (1) ἐθεράπευσε τῷ σαββάτῳ, *he healed on the sab-bath.* (2) ἐγήγερται ἐν τρίτῃ ἡμέρᾳ, *he was raised on the third day.*

498. To help distinguish the functions of the various cases indicating time, the following summary may be helpful:

Genitive of time: (time during which) answers the question, *what kind of time?*

Dative of time: (time at which, or on which) answers the question, *when?*

Accusative of time: (the extent of time) answers the question, *how long?*

Possessive Adjectives

499. [473] The possessive adjectives ἐμός, *my,* σός, *your* (s.), ἡμέτερος, *our,* ὑμέτερος, *your* (p.), are sometimes used instead of the genitive case of the personal pronouns when emphasis is desired. These possessive adjectives are declined like regular adjectives of the second and first declension. They can stand in the attributive position with the article.

Examples: ὁ ἐμὸς λόγος, *the belonging-to-me word* (i.e., *my word*); ἡ χαρὰ ἡ ἐμή, *my joy;* τὸ θέλημα τὸ ἐμόν, *my will;* τὰ ἐμὰ πάντα σά ἐστιν, *all the belonging-to-me things are yours* (i.e., *all my things are yours*); ὁ ἡμέτερος λόγος, *our word;* ὁ ὑμέτερος λόγος, *your word.*

500. [474] This usage is comparatively infrequent. The common way of saying *my word* is not ὁ ἐμὸς λόγος or ὁ λόγος ὁ ἐμός, but ὁ λόγος μου (*the word of me*).

501. ἴδιος is a special type of adjective that indicates that the noun modified is specially and uniquely related to a particular person or thing. As a simple adjective, it sometimes means *private,* but it often functions as a kind of general-purpose possessive adjective: *my own, his own, our own, their own,* etc. The phrase κατ' ἰδίαν means *privately.*

μή Used as a Conjunction

502. [475] Words denoting fear are followed by μή, *lest*, with the subjunctive. μή is here not an adverb, as is the case when it means *not*, but a conjunction.

Example: φοβοῦμαι μὴ ἔλθῃ means *I fear lest he come* (i.e., *I fear the possibility that he will come*, not *I fear he might not come*).

503. [476] Negative clauses of purpose may also be introduced by the simple μή instead of by ἵνα μή.

Example: τοῦτο ποιεῖτε μὴ εἰσέλθητε εἰς κρίσιν, *do this lest you come into judgment*.

504. [477] ἵνα with the Subjunctive in Various Uses

ἵνα with the subjunctive overlaps with the infinitive in expressing purpose. In the Greek of the New Testament, this overlapping has expanded to the point where most other uses of the infinitive can also be represented by ἵνα with the subjunctive. In particular, it is very frequently used after words of exhorting, wishing, and striving in the same way an infinitive might be used.

Examples: (1) εἰπὲ τῷ λίθῳ τούτῳ ἵνα γένηται ἄρτος, *say to this stone that it become bread*. (2) αὕτη ἐστὶν ἡ ἐντολὴ ἡ ἐμὴ ἵνα ἀγαπᾶτε ἀλλήλους, *this is my commandment, that you should love one another*.

μή with the Indicative in Questions Expecting a Negative Answer

505. [478] Questions expecting a negative answer are expressed by μή with the indicative.

506. [479] This rule constitutes an important exception to the general rule for the use of οὐ and μή (see §244). Questions expecting a *positive* answer have οὐ with the indicative. Example: μὴ ἰσχυρότεροι αὐτοῦ ἐσμεν; *are we stronger than he?* The answer expected is, "No, of course not." Compare οὐκ ἰσχυρότεροί ἐσμεν αὐτοῦ; *are we not stronger than he?* Here the answer expected is, "Yes, certainly we are."

507. Future as Imperative

A verb in the future tense sometimes has the force of an imperative, especially in quotations from the Old Testament. This usage is virtually identical with English usage.

Example: ἀγαπήσεις τὸν κύριον τὸν θεόν σου, *you shall love the Lord your God.*

508. [480] Exercises

A. 1. παρακαλῶ δὲ ὑμᾶς ἵνα τὸ αὐτὸ λέγητε πάντες. 2. ὅσα ἐὰν θέλητε ἵνα ποιῶσιν ὑμῖν οἱ ἄνθρωποι, οὕτως καὶ ὑμεῖς ποιεῖτε· οὗτος γάρ ἐστιν ὁ νόμος καὶ οἱ προφῆται. 3. κέλευσον οὖν τηρηθῆναι τὸ σῶμα ὑπὸ τῶν στρατιωτῶν, μήποτε ἐλθόντες οἱ μαθηταὶ λάβωσιν αὐτὸ καὶ εἴπωσιν τῷ λαῷ ὅτι ἠγέρθη ἐκ τῶν νεκρῶν. 4. οὐκ ἔστι δοῦλος μείζων τοῦ πέμψαντος αὐτόν. 5. μείζονα ταύτης ἀγάπην οὐδεὶς ἔχει, ἵνα τις ἀποθάνῃ ὑπὲρ τῶν ἄλλων. 6. πάλιν ἀπέστειλεν ἄλλους δούλους πλείονας τῶν πρώτων. 7. εἰ δίκαιόν ἐστιν ἐνώπιον τοῦ θεοῦ ὑμῶν ἀκούειν μᾶλλον ἢ τοῦ θεοῦ, κρίνατε. 8. ἐγὼ δὲ λέγω ὑμῖν· Ἀγαπᾶτε τοὺς ἐχθροὺς ὑμῶν καὶ προσεύχεσθε ὑπὲρ τῶν διωκόντων ὑμᾶς, ὅπως γένησθε υἱοὶ τοῦ πατρὸς ὑμῶν τοῦ ἐν οὐρανοῖς. 9. εἶπεν αὐτοῖς ὁ Ἰησοῦς ὅτι ἔξεστι τοῖς σάββασι καλῶς ποιεῖν. 10. ἔμεινεν δὲ ὁ Ἰησοῦς ἐκεῖ διὰ τὸ εἶναι τὸν τόπον ἐγγὺς τῆς πόλεως. 11. τότε συναχθήσονται ἔμπροσθεν αὐτοῦ πάντα τὰ ἔθνη. 12. μὴ ποίει τοῦτο· οὐ γὰρ ἱκανός εἰμι ἵνα εἰς τὴν οἰκίαν μου εἰσέλθῃς.

13. ἐλθόντες οἱ στρατιῶται νυκτὸς ἔλαβον τὸν ἄνδρα καὶ ἀγαγόντες αὐτὸν ἔξω ἀπέκτειναν. 14. τῇ μὲν σαρκὶ οὐκ ἐστε μεθ᾽ ἡμῶν, τῇ δὲ καρδίᾳ ἐστὲ ἐγγύς. 15. μὴ περιπατοῦμεν κατὰ σάρκα; οὐκ ἔχομεν τὸ πνεῦμα τοῦ θεοῦ; 16. εἰσῆλθεν εἰς τὴν οἰκίαν τοῦ ἀρχιερέως τοῦ εἶναι ἐγγὺς τοῦ τόπου ὅπου ἦν ὁ Ἰησοῦς. 17. εἰς τὰ ἴδια ἦλθεν καὶ οἱ ἴδιοι αὐτὸν οὐ παρέλαβον. 18. ἐγὼ ἐλήλυθα ἐν τῷ ὀνόματι τοῦ πατρός μου, καὶ οὐ λαμβάνετέ με· ἐὰν ἄλλος ἔλθῃ ἐν τῷ ὀνόματι τῷ ἰδίῳ, ἐκεῖνον λήμψεσθε. 19. μὴ ἐποίησα τὸ ἴδιον θέλημα; οὐ μᾶλλον ἐποίησα τὸ σόν; 20. εἰ ἐμὲ ἐδίωξαν, καὶ ὑμᾶς διώξουσιν· εἰ τὸν λόγον μου ἐτήρησαν, καὶ τὸν ὑμέτερον τηρήσουσιν. 21. καὶ ἀπολύσας τοὺς ὄχλους ἀνέβη εἰς τὸ ὄρος κατ᾽ ἰδίαν προσεύξασθαι. 22. Ἀγαπήσεις τὸν πλησίον[1] σου ὡς σεαυτόν. 23. μείζων τούτων ἄλλη ἐντολὴ οὐκ ἔστιν.

B. 1. Those who have done one work well will also do greater things. 2. He who rules his own house well does a greater thing than he who takes many cities. 3. Why do you do these things? Are you kings and priests? Are you not servants? 4. Those who were in the darkness urged us that we should pity them and not cast them out. 5. Those who belong to me are in the city, and those who belong to you (s.) are outside of it, but we will all be in the presence of God. 6. Are you (s.) stronger than the one who made the earth and the sea and all the things that are in them? 7. Do not fear (p.) him who kills the body, but fear rather him who has made all things. 8. When you (p.) have seen your own brothers, you shall go also to the Gentiles. 9. We have more servants than you (p.), but ours are not sufficient to evangelize[2] all the Gentiles. 10. Those who worship the Lord by day and by night will be stronger than those who persecute them. 11. More are those

1. πλησίον, ὁ, (indeclinable), *neighbor.*

2. What construction has been used after ἱκανός to express the idea *sufficient that they should . . . ?*

who are with us than those who are with them. 12. Being with you (p.) in heart, not in countenance, we exhorted you that you should do well all the things that we had commanded you. 13. The priests went out of the city, lest perhaps the scribes see them doing that which it is not lawful to do. 14. If anyone stronger than we comes against us, we will not remain in our city. 15. Since Jesus had healed a certain man on the sabbath, the scribes were afraid lest the people should make him a king. 16. It is better to die in behalf of the brothers than to do what the apostles exhorted us that we should not do.

Lesson 31

Conjugation of δίδωμι • *Second Aorist of* γινώσκω
• *First Aorist Endings on Second Aorist Stems*
• *Historical Present*

509. [481] Vocabulary

αἰώνιος, -ον, adj. of two ter-
minations, the feminine
being like the masculine
throughout, *eternal*

ἀντί, prep. with gen., *instead
of, for, in exchange for*

ἀποδίδωμι, *I give back, I give
what is owed or promised,
I render, I pay*

γυνή, γυναικός, ἡ (with an
irregular accent in some
forms, see §607), *a woman*

δίδωμι, *I give*

ἔγνων, 2nd aor. (of μι form)
of γινώσκω, *I know*

ἐξουσία, ἡ, *authority* (followed by a genitive,
authority over)

ἔσχον, 2nd aor. of ἔχω, *I have*

ζάω, *I live* (has η instead of
α in the progressive sys-
tem; e.g., ζῇς, ζῇ instead
of ζᾷς, ζᾷ)

ἰδού, demonstrative particle,
look! behold!

μόνος, -η, -ον, adj., *alone, only*

ὁράω, *I see*[1]

---

1. The progressive system of this verb is much less common than
the progressive system of βλέπω. The common verb *to see* in the New

258

παραδίδωμι, *I deliver over*   ποῖος, -α, -ον, interrogative
πειράζω, *I tempt*   pron., *what sort of?*
                           Σίμων, Σίμωνος, ὁ, *Simon*

510. [482] The verbs that have been studied so far, with the exception of the irregular verb εἰμί, all belong to the same conjugation. They have various ways of forming their principal parts, but the endings that are appended to the principal parts all belong to the same type. There is in Greek one other conjugation. It is called the μι conjugation (to distinguish it from the ω conjugation that has been studied thus far), because its first-person singular present active indicative ends in μι.

511. The stems of all μι verbs end in a vowel, either α, ε, ο, or υ. In many of their forms the final stem vowel is lengthened, α and ε to η, and ο to ω.

512. [483] Verbs in μι differ from verbs in ω only in the progressive and second aorist systems.

513. [484–85] The stem of the μι verb, δίδωμι, *I give*, is δο-. Its principal parts are as follows:

δίδωμι, δώσω, ἔδωκα, δέδωκα, δέδομαι, ἐδόθην.

514. [486] The future δώσω is entirely regular, the final ο of the stem being lengthened before the σ of the future exactly as in the case, for example, of δηλόω. From δώσω all of the future active and middle is formed, in exactly the same way as the corresponding forms of λύω.

515. [487] The first aorist ἔδωκα is quite regular except that κ stands instead of σ.

516. [488] The perfect active δέδωκα is entirely regular. From δέδωκα all of the perfect active is quite regularly formed.

Testament is βλέπω, ὄψομαι, εἶδον, ἑώρακα, (ὦμμαι), ὤφθην. Yet since βλέπω also has a future βλέψω and a first aorist ἔβλεψα, it will perhaps be more convenient to give ὄψομαι etc. as the principal parts of ὁράω rather than of βλέπω.

517. [489] The perfect middle δέδομαι is regular except that the final vowel of the stem is not lengthened before the personal endings (see §471). From δέδομαι all of the perfect middle and passive is quite regularly formed.

518. [490] The aorist passive ἐδόθην is regular except that the final vowel of the stem is not lengthened before the tense suffix -θε. From ἐδόθην all of the aorist passive and future passive is quite regularly formed.

The Progressive System of δίδωμι

519. [491] Recall that the sign of the perfect system is a reduplication of the initial consonant with the vowel ε. The μι verbs have reduplication not only in the perfect but also in the progressive system, but with an ι instead of ε. Thus the progressive stem of the δο- root is διδο-. The reduplication with ι rather than ε is the sign of the progressive system for all μι verbs.

520. [492] The present active indicative of δίδωμι is as follows:

Sing.		**Plur.**	
1. δίδωμι	*I give*	δίδομεν	*we give*
2. δίδως	*you* (s.) *give*	δίδοτε	*you* (p.) *give*
3. δίδωσι(ν)	*he (she, it) gives*	διδόασι(ν)	*they give*

521. [493] The final vowel of the stem (the stem with the reduplication being διδο-) is lengthened in the singular number, but not in the plural.

522. [494] The personal endings are added directly to the stem, without any variable theme vowel.[1]

523. [495] These endings are -μι, -ς, -σι, -μεν, -τε, -ασι.

---

1. For this reason μι verbs are sometimes called "athematic," or non-thematic, verbs.

524. [503] The imperfect active indicative of δίδωμι is as follows:

Sing.		**Plur.**	
1. ἐδίδουν	*I was giving*	ἐδίδομεν	*we were giving*
2. ἐδίδους	*you (s.) were giving*	ἐδίδοτε	*you (p.) were giving*
3. ἐδίδου	*he (she, it) was giving*	ἐδίδοσαν	*they were giving*

525. [504] The characteristic reduplication found in the present, δι-, appears here since the imperfect, like the present, is part of the progressive system. The augment is regular. The final vowel of the stem is lengthened in the singular, as in the present, but in the imperfect it is lengthened to ου instead of to ω. The same secondary endings appear as in the ω conjugation except that the alternative ending -σαν appears instead of -ν in the third-person plural (see §134).

526. [505] The present and imperfect middle and passive of δίδωμι simply add directly to the stem the primary B endings (δίδομαι, etc.) and the secondary B endings (ἐδιδόμην, etc.) but without the second-person singular contraction. The complete paradigm of the progressive system may be found in §638. Only a few of these forms occur in the New Testament. They can easily be recognized as they occur.

527. [496] The progressive active subjunctive of δίδωμι is as follows:

	Sing.	**Plur.**
1.	διδῶ	διδῶμεν
2.	διδῷς	διδῶτε
3.	διδῷ	διδῶσι(ν)

Lesson 31

528. [497] There has been contraction here, as is shown by the accent. The personal endings are the same as in ω verbs.

529. [498] The progressive active imperative of δίδωμι is as follows:

Sing.		**Plur.**	
2. δίδου	give	δίδοτε	give
3. διδότω	let him (her, it) give	διδότωσαν	let them give

530. [499] The progressive active infinitive is διδόναι, *to give.*

531. [500–501] The present active participle is διδούς, διδοῦσα, διδόν, *giving.* The genitive singular is διδόντος, διδούσης, διδόντος. The masculine and neuter are declined regularly according to the third declension, and the feminine regularly according to the first declension. The dative plural masculine and neuter is διδοῦσι(ν).

Aorist Active and Middle of δίδωμι

532. [506] The aorist active of δίδωμι is peculiar in that it is first aorist in the indicative and second aorist in the other moods.

533. [507] The aorist active indicative of δίδωμι is as follows:

Sing.		**Plur.**	
1. ἔδωκα	I gave	ἐδώκαμεν	we gave
2. ἔδωκας	you (s.) gave	ἐδώκατε	you (p.) gave
3. ἔδωκε(ν)	he (she, it) gave	ἔδωκαν	they gave

534. [508] Notice that the conjugation is exactly like that of ἔλυσα, the first aorist active of λύω. But the tense suffix is κ instead of σ (see §§179–85).

535. [509] The aorist active subjunctive of δίδωμι is as follows:

	Sing.	Plur.
1.	δῶ	δῶμεν
2.	δῷς	δῶτε
3.	δῷ	δῶσι(ν)

536. [510] The conjugation is exactly like the progressive active subjunctive. But the second aorist has the mere verb stem, whereas the progressive prefixes the reduplication δι-.

537. [511] The aorist active imperative of δίδωμι is as follows:

	Sing.		Plur.	
2.	δός	*give*	δότε	*give*
3.	δότω	*let him (her, it) give*	δότωσαν	*let them give*

538. [512] These forms are like the progressive imperatives (without the reduplication), except for δός in the second-person singular.

539. [513] The aorist active infinitive is δοῦναι, *to give.*

540. [514] The aorist active participle is δούς, δοῦσα, δόν, *having given.* It is declined like the progressive participle διδούς.

541. [515] The aorist middle of δίδωμι occurs only a very few times in the New Testament. The forms can easily be understood with the aid of a lexicon.

The Second Aorist of γινώσκω

542. [516] γινώσκω, *I know,* is an ω verb. But it has a second aorist active of the μι form. The stem is γνο-, which is nearly everywhere lengthened to γνω-.

543. [517] Learn the conjugation of the aorist of γινώσκω in §643. Pay special attention to the second aorist active imperative second singular (γνῶθι). The participle (γνούς, γνοῦσα, γνόν) is declined like the aorist participle of δίδωμι (δούς, δοῦσα, δόν).

544. [521] First Aorist Endings on Second Aorist Stems

Frequently in the New Testament, first aorist endings instead of second aorist endings are used on second aorist stems.

Examples: εἶπαν instead of εἶπον (third-person plural), εἰπόν instead of εἰπέ (imperative). This usage is much more common in some parts of the aorist than in others. εἶπον in the indicative has almost exclusively first aorist forms (see §194 footnote).

545. Historical Present

In narrative prose in the New Testament, the present tense is sometimes used to narrate a past action. This occurs only in narrative, and is most often used with the verb λέγει, which in this case should be translated *he said*. The context makes it clear that a past, not a present, action is in view.

Accent Matters

546. [502] In μι verbs, the accent of all active participles, both progressive and aorist, falls on the last syllable of the basal stem, which in the nominative singular masculine and neuter is the ultima, and in the feminine, the penult (prog. act. part.: διδούς, διδοῦσα, διδόν). The only exception to this pattern is the feminine genitive plural (prog. act. part.: διδουσῶν), which follows the special rule for first-declension nouns (see §56).[1] The active infinitives, both progressive and aorist, are also accented on the last syllable of the

---

1. No feminine genitive plural participial form of a μι verb appears in the New Testament, so this point need not be memorized.

basal stem (prog. act. infin.: διδόναι; aor. act. infin.: δοῦναι).
The participles and infinitives of the progressive middle and
passive and the aorist middle are recessively accented (prog.
mid./pass. part.: διδόμενος, διδομένη, διδόμενον, etc.; prog.
mid./pass. infin.: δίδοσθαι).

547. [522] Exercises

A. 1. παρέδωκα γὰρ ὑμῖν ἐν πρώτοις ὃ καὶ παρέλαβον, ὅτι
Χριστὸς ἀπέθανεν ὑπὲρ τῶν ἁμαρτιῶν ἡμῶν κατὰ τὰς γραφάς.
2. μὴ ἔχοντος δὲ αὐτοῦ ἀποδοῦναι ἀπέλυσεν αὐτὸν ὁ κύριος αὐτοῦ. 3. δίδοτε, καὶ δοθήσεται ὑμῖν. 4. θέλω δὲ τούτῳ τῷ ἐσχάτῳ
δοῦναι ὡς καὶ σοί. 5. ἐσθιόντων δὲ αὐτῶν λαβὼν ὁ Ἰησοῦς ἄρτον
καὶ εὐλογήσας ἔκλασεν[1] καὶ δοὺς τοῖς μαθηταῖς εἶπεν· Λάβετε
φάγετε, τοῦτό ἐστιν τὸ σῶμά μου. καὶ λαβὼν ποτήριον[2] καὶ εὐ-
χαριστήσας ἔδωκεν αὐτοῖς λέγων· Πίετε ἐξ αὐτοῦ πάντες. 6. καὶ
εἶπαν πρὸς αὐτόν· Εἰπὸν ἡμῖν ἐν ποίᾳ ἐξουσίᾳ ταῦτα ποιεῖς, ἢ
τίς ἐστιν ὁ δούς σοι τὴν ἐξουσίαν ταύτην. 7. ὁ γὰρ ἄρτος τοῦ
θεοῦ ἐστιν ὁ καταβαίνων ἐκ τοῦ οὐρανοῦ καὶ ζωὴν διδοὺς τῷ
κόσμῳ. 8. οὐ βλέπεις εἰς πρόσωπον[3] ἀνθρώπων, ἀλλ᾽ ἐπ᾽ ἀληθείας
τὴν ὁδὸν τοῦ θεοῦ διδάσκεις· ἔξεστιν δοῦναι κῆνσον[4] Καίσαρι[5]
ἢ οὔ; δῶμεν ἢ μὴ δῶμεν; 9. λέγει αὐτῷ ὁ Ἰησοῦς· Πορεύου, ὁ υἱός
σου ζῇ. ἐπίστευσεν ὁ ἄνθρωπος τῷ λόγῳ ὃν εἶπεν αὐτῷ ὁ Ἰησοῦς
καὶ ἐπορεύετο. 10. ὁρᾶτε μή τις κακὸν ἀντὶ κακοῦ τινι ἀποδῷ.
11. ἦλθεν ἡ ὥρα, ἰδοὺ παραδίδοται ὁ υἱὸς τοῦ ἀνθρώπου εἰς τὰς
χεῖρας τῶν ἁμαρτωλῶν. ἐγείρεσθε, ἄγωμεν·[6] ἰδοὺ ὁ παραδιδούς
με ἤγγικεν. 12. Ὑμῖν δέδοται γνῶναι τὰ μυστήρια τῆς βασιλείας
τῶν οὐρανῶν, ἐκείνοις δὲ οὐ δέδοται. 13. καὶ ὅταν ἄγωσιν ὑμᾶς

1. Aorist active indicative of κλάω, *I break.*
2. ποτήριον, τό, *a cup.*
3. "To see into someone's face" is an idiom for "to be influenced by
that person's opinions."
4. κῆνσος, ὁ, *tax.* (This word can violate the rule noted in §355 because
it is a transliteration of the Latin word *census.*)
5. Καίσαρ, ὁ, *Caesar.*
6. ἄγω is sometimes used in the intransitive sense, *I go.*

παραδιδόντες, μὴ προμεριμνᾶτε[1] τί λαλήσητε, ἀλλ᾽ ὃ ἐὰν δοθῇ ὑμῖν ἐν ἐκείνῃ τῇ ὥρᾳ τοῦτο λαλεῖτε· οὐ γάρ ἐστε ὑμεῖς οἱ λαλοῦντες ἀλλὰ τὸ πνεῦμα τὸ ἅγιον. 14. καὶ ταχὺ[2] πορευθεῖσαι εἴπατε τοῖς μαθηταῖς αὐτοῦ ὅτι ἠγέρθη ἀπὸ τῶν νεκρῶν. 15. εἶπεν αὐτοῖς· Δότε αὐτοῖς ὑμεῖς φαγεῖν. 16. ἐξήρχετο δὲ καὶ δαιμόνια ἀπὸ πολλῶν κράζοντα καὶ λέγοντα ὅτι[3] Σὺ εἶ ὁ υἱὸς τοῦ θεοῦ.

B. 1. The woman urged the apostle that he might give her something. 2. Those who had killed the women said that they had known the king. But he said that he was not willing to give them what they asked. 3. If we believe on him who loved us and gave himself in behalf of us, we will have eternal life instead of death. 4. While the apostle was giving to the children the things that they had asked, the women were giving gifts to us. 5. The Lord delivered over the gospel to the apostles, and they delivered it over to the Gentiles. 6. What should we give back to him who gave himself in behalf of us? 7. Look, he gives us eternal life. Let us therefore do his will. 8. What should anyone give instead of his life? 9. Whatever we give to him will not be enough. 10. Whatever you (s.) wish that people should give to you, give also to them. 11. Let them give thanks to those who delivered over to them the gospel. 12. They asked the Lord what they should give to him. And he said to them that to do the will of God is greater than all the gifts. 13. Those women are giving back to the children the things that they have taken from them, lest the king cast them out of the city. 14. When the priests had said these things to those who were in the city, the apostle departed. 15. What is this? Will he give us his flesh? 16. Whatever he asks I will give. But he gave to me eternal life.

---

1. προμεριμνάω, I worry ahead of time.

2. ταχύς, -εῖα, -ύ, adj., quick (declined like ὀξύς). The neuter singular, ταχύ, often functions adverbially to mean quickly, as in the above sentence.

3. ὅτι frequently introduces direct (instead of indirect) discourse. When it introduces direct discourse, it must be left untranslated. In such cases, it takes the place of our quotation marks.

Lesson 32

Conjugation of τίθημι and ἀφίημι • *Accusative and Infinitive after ὥστε in Result Clauses* • *The Article before μέν and δέ*

548. [523] Vocabulary

ἀνοίγω, *I open* (For the principal parts of this verb and the other verbs, see the general vocabulary.)

ἀρχή, ἡ, *a beginning, a first thing, a principle*

ἀφίημι, *I let go, I permit, I leave, I forgive* (When it means *forgive*, ἀφίημι takes the acc. of the thing forgiven and the dat. of the person to whom it is forgiven.)

ἐπιτίθημι, *I lay upon* (with acc. of the thing laid and dat. of the person or thing upon which it is laid)

εὑρίσκω, *I find*

καθώς, adv., *just as*

καιρός, ὁ, *a time, a fixed time, an appointed time, an appropriate season*

κωλύω, *I hinder, I prevent*

μνημεῖον, τό, *a tomb*

μόνον, adv., *only*

οὔτε, *and not, nor* (οὔτε ... οὔτε, *neither . . . nor*)

πῦρ, πυρός, τό, *a fire*

στόμα, στόματος, τό, *a mouth*

τίθημι, *I place, I put;* τίθημι τὴν ψυχήν, *I lay down my life*

τοιοῦτος, τοιαύτη, τοιοῦτο, adj., *such* (often used with the article)

ὑπάγω, *I go away*

Lesson 32

χαίρω, *I rejoice* (ἐχάρην, 2nd
    aor. pass., *I rejoiced*)
χρόνος, ὁ, *time* (especially *a
    period* or *duration of time,
    *as distinguished from

καιρός, *a definite* or
    appointed time)
ὧδε, adv., *hither, here*
ὥσπερ, adv., *just as*
ὥστε, conj., *so that*

549. [524] The principal parts of the μι verb τίθημι, *I place,
I put,* are as follows:

τίθημι, θήσω, ἔθηκα, τέθεικα, τέθειμαι, ἐτέθην.

550. [525] The stem is θε-. The progressive system is reduplicated after the same manner as δίδωμι. The future is regular. The first aorist is regular except that (like δίδωμι) it has κ
instead of σ. The perfect active and the perfect middle are regular except that θε- is lengthened to θει- instead of to θη-. The
aorist passive is regular except that (1) the final vowel of the
stem is not lengthened, and (2) the stem θε- is changed to τε-
to avoid having two thetas come in successive syllables.

551. [526] Learn the active voice of the progressive system
of τίθημι in §640.

552. [527] The treatment of the stem and of the endings in
the progressive system is very much the same as in the case
of δίδωμι. The declension of the participle τιθείς is like that of
λυθείς, the aorist passive participle of λύω.

553. [528] Learn the active voice of the aorist system of
τίθημι in §641.

554. [529] Like δίδωμι, τίθημι has a first aorist active in the
indicative and a second aorist active in the other moods. The
second aorist participle θείς is declined like the progressive
participle τιθείς.

555. [530] The present middle and aorist middle forms of
τίθημι can easily be recognized when they occur, if it be remembered that the second aorist has the mere verb stem θε-, whereas
the progressive has the stem τιθε-. Thus if a form ἀνεθέμην be
encountered, the student should see that ἀν- is plainly the

preposition ἀνα, -ε- is the augment, -θε- is the stem of τίθημι, and -μην is the secondary ending in the first-person singular middle. Therefore, the form is second aorist middle indicative, first-person singular. On the other hand, ἐτίθεντο belongs to the progressive system because it has the τι-, which is the sign of the progressive system; it is imperfect, not present, because it has the augment and a secondary ending. It is evidently imperfect middle or passive indicative, third-person plural.

The Conjugation of ἀφίημι

556. [531] ἀφίημι, *I let go, I permit, I leave, I forgive*, is a compound verb composed of the preposition ἀπό (ἀφ' before the rough breathing) and the μι verb ἵημι. The stem of ἵημι is ἑ-.

557. The principal parts of ἀφίημι are as follows:
ἀφίημι, ἀφήσω, ἀφῆκα, —, ἀφέωμαι, ἀφέθην.

558. [532] ἀφίημι has a number of forms that look unusual, but they can ordinarily be recognized if it be remembered that the ῐ- before the stem ἑ- is the sign of the progressive system, and that the short forms with ἑ- alone are second aorist. Thus the aorist subjunctive is ἀφῶ, just as that of τίθημι is θῶ, and the aorist participle is ἀφείς, just as that of τίθημι is θείς.

Two forms are especially unusual. The perfect middle and passive is ἀφέωμαι. The imperfect, ἤφιον, is irregularly augmented on the prepositional prefix.

559. [534] Accusative and Infinitive after ὥστε in Result Clauses

ὥστε commonly occurs with the accusative and infinitive to express result. It is translated *so that*, meaning *with the result that*.[1]

---

1. [535] The accent of ὥστε appears to violate the general rules of accent, but originally the τε was an enclitic separate from ὥς. The same is true of ὥσπερ, *just as*, and οὔτε, *neither*.

Example: ἐθεράπευσεν αὐτούς· ὥστε τὸν ὄχλον θαυμάσαι, *he healed them, with the result that the crowd marveled.*

This is very close in meaning to ἵνα with the subjunctive, but whereas the latter expresses purpose or *intended* result (whether actual or not), ὥστε with the infinitive generally expresses *actual* result (whether intended or not). This subtle distinction was being blurred by the time the New Testament was written, but mostly it still holds true.

The Article before μέν and δέ

560. [518] Before μέν or δέ the article is often used as a pronoun meaning *he, she, it, they.* Examples: (1) τοῦτο ἠρώτησαν αὐτόν. ὁ δὲ ἀπεκρίθη αὐτοῖς, *this they asked him. And he answered them.* (2) ἦλθον πρὸς αὐτοὺς αἰτῶν τι παρ᾽ αὐτῶν· οἱ δὲ ἐποίησαν οὐδέν, *I came to them asking something from them. But they did nothing.*

561. [519] Notice carefully that this is virtually the *only* situation where the article standing alone may function as a pronoun.[1] This usage is quite different from all the uses of the article that have been studied up till now.

Accent Matters

562. The participles and active infinitives of τίθημι and ἀφίημι are accented according to the same rule as those of δίδωμι (see §546). Thus the progressive active participle of τίθημι is τιθείς, τιθεῖσα, τιθέν, and the active infinitives are similarly accented (prog. act. infin.: τιθέναι; aor. act. infin.: θεῖναι). Again like δίδωμι, the participles and infinitives of the progressive middle and passive and the aorist middle are recessively accented (prog. mid./pass. part.: τιθέμενος, τιθεμένη, τιθέμενον, etc.; prog. mid./pass. infin.: τίθεσθαι).

---

1. The quotation of Aratus by Paul in Acts 17:28 is the only exception in the New Testament.

563. [537] Exercises

A. 1, διὰ τοῦτό με ὁ πατὴρ ἀγαπᾷ ὅτι ἐγὼ τίθημι τὴν ψυχήν μου, ἵνα πάλιν λάβω αὐτήν. οὐδεὶς ἦρεν αὐτὴν ἀπ᾽ ἐμοῦ, ἀλλ᾽ ἐγὼ τίθημι αὐτὴν ἀπ᾽ ἐμαυτοῦ. ἐξουσίαν ἔχω θεῖναι αὐτήν, καὶ ἐξουσίαν ἔχω πάλιν λαβεῖν αὐτήν. ταύτην τὴν ἐντολὴν ἔλαβον παρὰ τοῦ πατρός μου. 2. αὕτη ἐστὶν ἡ ἐντολὴ ἡ ἐμή, ἵνα ἀγαπᾶτε ἀλλήλους καθὼς ἠγάπησα ὑμᾶς. μείζονα ταύτης ἀγάπην οὐδεὶς ἔχει, ἵνα τις τὴν ψυχὴν αὐτοῦ θῇ ὑπὲρ τῶν φίλων[1] αὐτοῦ. 3. οἱ δὲ εὐθέως ἀφέντες τὸ πλοῖον καὶ τὸν πατέρα αὐτῶν ἠκολούθησαν αὐτῷ. 4. ὁ δὲ Ἰησοῦς εἶπεν· Ἄφετε τὰ παιδία καὶ μὴ κωλύετε αὐτὰ ἐλθεῖν πρός με· τῶν γὰρ τοιούτων ἐστὶν ἡ βασιλεία τῶν οὐρανῶν. καὶ ἐπιθεὶς τὰς χεῖρας αὐτοῖς ἐπορεύθη ἐκεῖθεν.[2] 5. καὶ προσευξάμενοι ἐπέθηκαν αὐτοῖς τὰς χεῖρας. 6. τότε ἐπετίθεσαν τὰς χεῖρας ἐπ᾽ αὐτούς, καὶ ἐλάμβανον πνεῦμα ἅγιον. 7. ἀκούσαντες δὲ ἐβαπτίσθησαν εἰς τὸ ὄνομα τοῦ κυρίου Ἰησοῦ· καὶ ἐπιθέντος αὐτοῖς τοῦ Παύλου[3] χεῖρας ἦλθε τὸ πνεῦμα τὸ ἅγιον ἐπ᾽ αὐτούς. 8. ζωοποιεῖ[4] ὁ υἱὸς τοῦ θεοῦ ὃν θέλει. 9. ὑμεῖς ὃ ἠκούσατε ἀπ᾽ ἀρχῆς,[5] ἐν ὑμῖν μενέτω. ἐὰν ἐν ὑμῖν μείνῃ ὃ ἀπ᾽ ἀρχῆς ἠκούσατε, καὶ ὑμεῖς ἐν τῷ υἱῷ καὶ ἐν τῷ πατρὶ μενεῖτε. 10. καὶ ἐγένετο ὡσεὶ[6] νεκρός, ὥστε τοὺς πολλοὺς λέγειν ὅτι ἀπέθανεν. 11. καὶ ἰδοὺ εἷς προσελθὼν αὐτῷ εἶπεν· Διδάσκαλε, τί ἀγαθὸν ποιήσω ἵνα σχῶ ζωὴν αἰώνιον; ὁ δὲ εἶπεν αὐτῷ Τί με ἐρωτᾷς περὶ τοῦ ἀγαθοῦ; εἷς ἐστιν ὁ ἀγαθός. εἰ δὲ θέλεις εἰς τὴν ζωὴν εἰσελθεῖν τήρει τὰς ἐντολάς. 12. καὶ ἀνοίξας τὸ βιβλίον εὗρεν τὸν τόπον. 13. τὰ δὲ ἐκπορευόμενα ἐκ τοῦ στόματος ἐκ τῆς

1. φίλος, ὁ, *a friend.*
2. ἐκεῖθεν, adv., *thence, from there.*
3. Παῦλος, ὁ, *Paul.*
4. ζωοποιέω, *I make alive, I give life to.*
5. In many such phrases the article is omitted in Greek where it is used in English.
6. ὡσεί is a strengthened form of ὡς.

καρδίας ἐξέρχεται. 14. οὐ περὶ τούτων δὲ ἐρωτῶ μόνον, ἀλλὰ καὶ περὶ τῶν πιστευόντων διὰ τοῦ λόγου αὐτῶν εἰς ἐμέ, ἵνα πάντες ἓν ὦσιν, καθὼς σύ, πατήρ, ἐν ἐμοὶ κἀγὼ ἐν σοί, ἵνα καὶ αὐτοὶ ἐν ἡμῖν ὦσιν, ἵνα ὁ κόσμος πιστεύῃ ὅτι σύ με ἀπέστειλας. 15. εἶπεν οὖν ὁ Ἰησοῦς· Ἔτι χρόνον μικρὸν μεθ' ὑμῶν εἰμι καὶ ὑπάγω πρὸς τὸν πέμψαντά με. 16. αὐτὸς δὲ σωθήσεται, οὕτως δὲ ὡς διὰ πυρός. 17. καὶ ἐὰν ἑπτάκις[1] τῆς ἡμέρας ἁμαρτήσῃ εἰς σὲ καὶ ἑπτάκις ἐπιστρέψῃ πρὸς σὲ λέγων· Μετανοῶ, ἀφήσεις αὐτῷ. 18. καὶ ὃς ἐὰν εἴπῃ λόγον κατὰ τοῦ υἱοῦ τοῦ ἀνθρώπου, αφεθήσεται αὐτῷ· ὃς δ' ἂν εἴπῃ κατὰ τοῦ πνεύματος τοῦ ἁγίου, οὐκ ἀφεθήσεται αὐτῷ οὔτε ἐν τούτῳ τῷ αἰῶνι οὔτε ἐν τῷ μέλλοντι.

B. 1. This commandment he laid upon them, that they should lay down their lives in behalf of their brothers. 2. If you (p.) forgive those who persecute you, I also will forgive you. 3. When the men had found him who had done this thing, they left him and went away. 4. Having put the body into the tomb, he went away. 5. We saw those who were laying down their lives in behalf of the children. 6. The women saw where the body was placed. 7. We ought to give thanks to him who has forgiven us our sins. 8. We did not know him, but he knew us. 9. Give me the body in order that I may place it in a tomb. 10. He has shown all things to you, in order that you might place them in your hearts. 11. The apostle said to those who were questioning him that he would not put these gifts into the temple. 12. After we had seen the sign that Jesus had said he would do, we believed on him. 13. Lord, open our eyes, that we might find good things in your law. 14. Tongues of fire were placed over their heads, and they rejoiced greatly.

---

1. ἑπτάκις, adj., *seven times*.

Lesson 33

*Conjugation of ἵστημι • Verbal Adjectives
• Conditions Contrary to Fact • Uses of γίνομαι*

564. [538] Vocabulary

ἀνίστημι, transitive, *I cause to rise,* in the pres., fut., and 1st aor. act.; intransitive, *I stand up, I arise,* in the 2nd aor. and perf. act., and in the middle

δοκέω, *I seem, I think*

δύναμαι, dep., *I am able* (the progressive system conjugated like the middle of ἵστημι)

δύναμις, δυνάμεως, ἡ, *power, a miracle*

ἔβην, 2nd aor. (of the μι form) of βαίνω (conjugated like the 2nd aor. of ἵστημι)

ἕτερος, -α, -ον, *another* (sometimes, but not always, implies difference of kind, whereas ἄλλος often denotes mere numerical distinction)

ἵστημι, transitive, *I cause to stand,* in the pres., fut., and 1st aor. act.; intransitive, *I stand,* in the perf. (which has the sense of a present = *I stand*) and in the 2nd aor.

κάθημαι, dep. of the μι form, *I sit* (prog. part. καθή-μενος, *sitting*)

ὅλος, -η, -ον, adj., *whole, all*

273

ὅμοιος, -α, -ον, adj., *like, sim-*
ilar (with the dative of
that to which something
is similar)

παραγίνομαι, *I become*
near, I arrive, I come
(παραγίνομαι εἰς τὴν
πόλιν, *I arrive in the*
city.)

φανερόω, *I make known, I*
reveal

φημί, *I say* (μι verb with
stem φα-; much less com-
mon than λέγω)

ὡς, adv. and conj., *as,*
when (Some of its other
uses have already been
studied.)

565. [539] The principal parts of the μι verb ἵστημι, *I cause*
to stand, are as follows:

ἵστημι, στήσω, ἔστησα, ἔστηκα, ἔσταμαι, ἐστάθην, 2nd aor.
act. ἔστην.

566. [540] The stem is στα-. The progressive system is reduplicated by the prefixing of ἱ-. The future and first aorist systems are perfectly regular, the στα- of the stem being lengthened to στη- before the σ of the tense suffixes. The perfect active
is regular (note that the ε- of the reduplication has the rough
breathing). The perfect middle and passive retains the στα- of
the stem unchanged instead of lengthening its vowel. The aorist
passive also retains the στα-, but otherwise is regular.

567. [541] Learn the active voice of the progressive system
of ἵστημι in §642.

568. [542] The treatment of the stem and of the endings in
the progressive system is very much the same as in the case
of δίδωμι and τίθημι. The declension of the participle ἱστάς is
like that of λύσας, the aorist active participle of λύω, except
for the accent.

569. [543] Learn the middle and passive forms of the progressive system of ἵστημι in §642. Notice that the endings are
joined directly to the reduplicated stem ἱστα-, except in the
subjunctive mood.

570. [544a] ἵστημι differs from δίδωμι and τίθημι in that it has a complete first aorist active as well as a complete second aorist active.

571. [545] Learn the second aorist active of ἵστημι in §643.

572. [546] Notice that the conjugation is very much like that of the aorist passive of λύω. The participle στάς is declined like the progressive participle ἱστάς.

573. [547] A second aorist middle of ἵστημι does not occur.

574. [544b] ἵστημι can be either intransitive *(I stand)* or transitive-causative *(I cause something to stand)*. When memorizing the vocabulary, the student should take special care to remember that in the progressive system, the future, and the first aorist system, ἵστημι and its compounds are causal and may take direct objects; in the perfect and second aorist systems, and in the middle voice, they are intransitive. Further, it should be noted that the perfect is translated as an English present. Thus, ἑστήκαμεν means *we stand* (not *we have stood* or *we have caused to stand*).

575. [548] In addition to the first perfect active participle, ἑστηκώς, ἵστημι has a second perfect participle ἑστώς, ἑστῶσα, ἑστός, genitive ἑστῶτος, etc. Both ἑστηκώς and ἑστώς mean *standing*.

576. Verbal Adjectives

All contracting verbs, and several other verbs as well, can form what is called a verbal adjective by removing the -σω of the future and adding -τός to the resultant stem. The meaning of the verbal adjective is like the past participle in English, but it can only be used as a simple adjective. Thus λυτός means *loosed;* ἀγαπητός means *beloved*. It can, like other simple adjectives, be used substantively.

Verbal adjectives are declined like ἀγαθός, and they are always accented on the ultima.

577. [551] Conditions Contrary to Fact

Conditions contrary to fact are expressed by the secondary tenses of the indicative in both protasis and apodosis. The protasis is introduced by εἰ, and the apodosis has the particle ἄν, which, however, is sometimes omitted.

Example: κύριε, εἰ ἦς ὧδε, οὐκ ἂν ἀπέθανεν ὁ ἀδελφός μου, *Lord, if you had been here, my brother would not have died.*

Uses of γίνομαι

578. [552] Thus far, in the exercises, it has usually been possible to translate γίνομαι by the English word *become.* But very often, in the New Testament, such a translation is impossible. The English word *become* requires a predicate nominative, but in many cases γίνομαι has no predicate nominative. In such cases it means *happen, come into being, come to pass, appear, arise, be made.* Sometimes it can be translated by the words *come* or *be.*

Examples: (1) ἐν ἐκείναις ταῖς ἡμέραις ἐγένετο ἱερεύς τις, *in those days there was (appeared in history) a certain priest.* (2) πάντα δι᾽ αὐτοῦ ἐγένετο, *all things came into being* (or *were made*) *through him.* (3) εἶδεν τὰ γενόμενα, *he saw the things that had happened.* (4) φωνὴ ἐγένετο ἐκ τῶν οὐρανῶν, *a voice came out of the heavens.* But it must not be supposed that γίνομαι is a verb of motion.

579. [553] In the New Testament, καὶ ἐγένετο (or ἐγένετο δέ) reflects a Hebrew idiom that does little more than carry forward a narrative. It is sometimes translated *and it came to pass,* or *and it happened that,* though frequently it may be best simply to leave it untranslated. There are three forms of this usage, which may be illustrated as follows:[1]

---

1. This method of illustration is taken, in essentials, from J. H. Moulton, *Grammar of New Testament Greek,* vol. 1, *Prolegomena,* 2nd ed. (Edinburgh: Clark, 1906), 16.

1. καὶ ἐγένετο αὐτὸν ἐλθεῖν, *and it came to pass that he came*, literally *and him coming happened*. Here the accusative and infinitive are the subject of ἐγένετο in a way that is at least after the analogy of ordinary Greek usage, though it is awkward.

2. καὶ ἐγένετο καὶ ἦλθεν, *and it came to pass and he came.* The literal English translation is intolerable here, and the Greek also is not in accordance with the ordinary usage of the Greek language.

3. καὶ ἐγένετο ἦλθεν, *and it came to pass he came.* This also is not an ordinary Greek usage, two finite verbs being juxtaposed without a conjunction. Both 2 and 3, as well as 1, may be translated freely *and it came to pass that he came*, or simply *then he came.*

Accent Matters

580. The participles and infinitives of ἵστημι are accented according to the same rules as the other μι verbs (see §546).

581. [554] Exercises

A. 1. διὰ τοῦτο ὁ κόσμος οὐ γινώσκει ἡμᾶς ὅτι οὐκ ἔγνω αὐτόν. Ἀγαπητοί, νῦν τέκνα θεοῦ ἐσμεν, καὶ οὔπω ἐφανερώθη τί ἐσόμεθα. οἴδαμεν ὅτι ἐὰν φανερωθῇ ὅμοιοι αὐτῷ ἐσόμεθα, ὅτι ὀψόμεθα αὐτὸν καθώς ἐστιν. 2. ζητήσετέ με καὶ οὐχ εὑρήσετε, καὶ ὅπου εἰμὶ ἐγὼ ὑμεῖς οὐ δύνασθε ἐλθεῖν. 3. καὶ συνέρχεται πάλιν ὁ ὄχλος, ὥστε μὴ δύνασθαι αὐτοὺς μηδὲ ἄρτον φαγεῖν. 4. ἠκούσατε ὅτι ἐγὼ εἶπον ὑμῖν· Ὑπάγω καὶ ἔρχομαι πρὸς ὑμᾶς. εἰ ἠγαπᾶτέ με, ἐχάρητε ἂν ὅτι πορεύομαι πρὸς τὸν πατέρα, ὅτι ὁ πατὴρ μείζων μού ἐστιν. 5. εὗρεν ἄλλους ἑστῶτας καὶ λέγει αὐτοῖς· Τί ὧδε ἑστήκατε ὅλην τὴν ἡμέραν; 6. προφήτην ὑμῖν ἀναστήσει κύριος ὁ θεὸς ἐκ τῶν ἀδελφῶν ὑμῶν ὡς ἐμέ· αὐτοῦ ἀκούσεσθε[1] κατὰ πάντα ὅσα ἂν λαλήσῃ ὑμῖν. 7. καὶ ἀναστὰς ὁ ἀρχιερεὺς εἶπεν αὐτῷ· Οὐδὲν ἀποκρίνῃ; 8. ἔδωκεν αὐτοῖς δύναμιν καὶ ἐξουσίαν ἐπὶ πάντα τὰ δαιμόνια. 9. ἐγένετο δὲ ἐν τῷ βαπτισθῆναι ἅπαντα[2] τὸν λαὸν καὶ Ἰησοῦ βαπτισθέντος καὶ προσευχομένου ἀνεῳχθῆναι τὸν οὐρανόν, καὶ καταβῆναι τὸ πνεῦμα τὸ ἅγιον. 10. ἐγένετο δὲ ἐν ταῖς ἡμέραις ἐκείναις ἐξελθεῖν αὐτὸν εἰς τὰ ὄρη προσεύξασθαι. 11. ἐξῆλθον δὲ ἰδεῖν τὸ γεγονός, καὶ ἦλθον πρὸς τὸν Ἰησοῦν, καὶ εὗρον καθήμενον τὸν ἄνθρωπον ἀφ᾽ οὗ τὰ δαιμόνια ἐξῆλθον. 12. καὶ ἐγένετο ἐν τῷ εἶναι αὐτὸν ἐν τόπῳ τινὶ προσευχόμενον, ὡς ἐπαύσατο,[3] εἶπέν τις τῶν μαθητῶν αὐτοῦ πρὸς αὐτόν· Κύριε δίδαξον ἡμᾶς προσεύχεσθαι, καθὼς καὶ Ἰωάννης[4] ἐδίδαξεν τοὺς μαθητὰς αὐτοῦ. 13. ὁ δὲ ἔφη αὐτῷ· Ἀγαπήσεις κύριον τὸν θεόν σου ἐν ὅλῃ τῇ καρδίᾳ σου. 14. δοκεῖτε ὅτι εἰρήνην παρεγενόμην δοῦναι ἐν τῇ γῇ; 15. περὶ τίνος ὁ προφήτης λέγει τοῦτο; περὶ ἑαυτοῦ ἢ περὶ ἑτέρου τινός; 16. αὐτὸς ὑμᾶς βαπτίσει ἐν πνεύματι ἁγίῳ καὶ πυρί. 17. βλέπετε οὖν πῶς ἀκούετε· ὃς ἂν γὰρ ἔχῃ, δοθήσεται αὐτῷ, καὶ ὃς ἂν μὴ ἔχῃ, καὶ ὃ δοκεῖ ἔχειν ἀρθήσεται ἀπ᾽ αὐτοῦ. 18. εἶπεν δὲ αὐτῷ· Εἰ Μωϋσέως[5] καὶ τῶν προφητῶν οὐκ ἀκούουσιν, οὐδ᾽ ἐάν τις ἐκ νεκρῶν ἀναστῇ πεισθήσονται.

B. 1. He forgave those who had risen up against their king. 2. We know that those who are sitting in the house will not go out until they see the apostle. 3. When Jesus had gone down from the mountain, the disciples saw the man sitting in the house. 4. We saw the apostles standing in the presence of the chief priests. 5. When the women had arrived in the city, they saw Jesus doing many miracles. 6. In those days there rose up a certain king who did not know us. 7. You (s.) have revealed

1. The future of ἀκούω is here deponent.

2. ἅπας, ἅπασα, ἅπαν, all (a strengthened form of πᾶς).

3. παύομαι (middle), I cease.

4. Ἰωάννης, -ου, ὁ, John.

5. Μωϋσῆς, -έως, ὁ, Moses.

yourself to those who are sitting in darkness. 8. When he had seen these things, he did not know what he was saying. 9. We are not able to know all these things unless the Lord reveals them to us. 10. We have found the one who is able to take away our sins. 11. We know that no one is able to do what the king does.

Lesson 34

Conjugation of δείκνυμι, ἀπόλλυμι, and οἶδα
• *Aorist Participle Denoting Identical or Coordinate*
Action • *Use of ἕως, ἄχρι, and μέχρι* • *Optative Mood*
• *Periphrasis* • *οὐ μή with Aorist Subjunctive or*
Future Indicative

582. Vocabulary

ἄρα, *then, therefore*

ἀπόλλυμι (or ἀπολλύω), *I destroy;* mid., *I perish*

ἄχρι, with gen., *up to, as far as, until;* as a conjunction, *until, while*

δείκνυμι (or δεικνύω), *I show, I demonstrate*

διό, *therefore, for this reason*

ἐπιθυμία, ἡ, *a strong desire, lust*

ἐργάζομαι, dep., *I work*

ἕως, conj., *until, while;* as a preposition with gen., *up to, as far as, unto*

θλῖψις, -εως, ἡ, *tribulation*

θρόνος, ὁ, *a throne*

μέσος, -η, -ον, *middle, in the midst*

μέχρι, with gen., *until, as far as, to the degree that;* as a conj., *until*

οἶδα, 2nd perf. used as pres., *I know*

τε, enclitic conj., *and, furthermore, also;* τε . . . τε, *not only . . . but also* (τε is somewhat closer to *and*, while δέ is somewhat closer to *but*.)

τελέω, fut. τελέσω, aor.
ἐτέλεσα, *I finish, I complete, I bring to an end*
τύπος, ὁ, *a type, a pattern*

φαίνω, *I shine;* mid., *I
appear, I become visible*
φεύγω, *I flee*
χρεία, ἡ, *a need*

583. [533] The verbs δείκνυμι and ἀπόλλυμι in the New Testament sometimes take μι endings in the present (progressive) indicative. Elsewhere, and sometimes even in the progressive system, they are conjugated like λύω. The principal parts of δείκνυμι and ἀπόλλυμι may be found in the vocabularies.

Note that the ἀπ- of ἀπόλλυμι is a prepositional prefix; thus the ο, not the initial α, is augmented in the aorist and imperfect indicative.

584. [549] οἶδα, *I know,* exists only in the perfect system. The perfect indicative is translated as though it were a present. The perfect of οἶδα is conjugated like other perfects, though the reduplication is irregular, and there is no κ.

585. The subjunctive of οἶδα is εἰδῶ. It is conjugated regularly.

586. The imperative stem of οἶδα is unexpected, but its conjugation is regular except for the second singular:

	Sing.	**Plur.**
2.	ἴσθι	ἴστε
3.	ἴστω	ἴστωσαν

Note that the second-person singular is identical to the second singular imperative of εἰμί. Context will determine which verb is intended.

587. The (perfect) infinitive of οἶδα is εἰδέναι, and the participle is εἰδώς, εἰδυῖα, εἰδός (declined like λελυκώς).

588. οἶδα is the one word in the New Testament that commonly appears in the pluperfect. Since the perfect of οἶδα has a present meaning, the pluperfect serves as an imperfect. The pluperfect active indicative of οἶδα is ᾔδειν, ᾔδεις, ᾔδει, ᾔδειμεν, ᾔδειτε, ᾔδεισαν.

589. The entire conjugation of οἶδα is found in §645.

590. [520] Aorist Participle Denoting Identical or Coordinate Action

In §§242, 274 it was said that the progressive participle views the action as in progress, as ongoing at the time of the leading verb, whereas the aorist participle views the action simply. Ordinarily this means that the aorist participle will refer to something that occurred prior to the action of the leading verb. But since the tenses in the participle do not have to do with time, there are certain cases where the aorist participle represents action not prior to but identical to or coordinate with the action of the leading verb. That is, the aorist participle may denote the same act as the leading verb (identical action), or an act so closely coordinated with the leading verb that the leading verb and participial actions are regarded as a unit (coordinate action). This is especially common with verbs of speaking and verbs of coming and going.

Take note, however, that in such cases the aorist participle is still to be regarded as a simple action, not as an action in progress at the time of the leading verb. The closest English equivalent is simply to join the two words with "and," a grammatical device called *parataxis*.

Examples:

1. ἀποκριθεὶς εἶπεν ὁ Ἰησοῦς, *Jesus answered and said.* Here the "answering" and the "saying" represent the same act, and the participle simply defines more closely the action denoted by εἶπεν. The participle is not progressive, and thus does not mean *while he was answering he said.* That would rather be ἀποκρινόμενος εἶπεν. Nor does it mean *after he answered he*

said; that would imply that the answering and saying were separate acts. It is recommended that the free paratactic translation *he answered and said* be adopted invariably for this kind of construction, which is quite common in the Gospels. And it is exceedingly important that this idiom not be allowed to obscure the fact that in the majority of cases the simple action of the aorist participle is prior to the time of the leading verb. The student should carefully avoid any confusion between the progressive and aorist participle.

2. ὁ δὲ ἀποκριθεὶς εἶπεν, *and he answered and said* (with a slight emphasis on *he*). Of course ἀποκριθείς might here be taken as the substantive participle with ὁ, and the sentence might mean *and the one who had answered said.* But in a great many places where these words occur in the Gospels, the article is to be taken as a pronoun, and the ἀποκριθείς is joined only loosely to it in the manner indicated in the translation above.

3. ἐλθὼν ἐθεράπευσεν αὐτήν, *he came and healed her.* Here the "coming" could be understood as an act prior to the "healing," but in fact it would ordinarily indicate simply that the coming and the healing are regarded as two coordinate elements of one act. Again, the best way to translate this idiom is by parataxis.

591. [536] Use of ἕως, ἄχρι, and μέχρι

The conjunction ἕως, *until,* if it refers to a future time, is used with the subjunctive mood and usually is accompanied by the particle ἄν. If it refers to a time in the past or present, it occurs with the indicative. Rarely, with the present indicative, it means *while.*

Examples: (1) μείνατε ἕως ἂν ἔλθω, *remain until I come.* (2) εἰσήρχοντο ἕως ὁ οἶκος ἐπλήσθη, *they kept coming in until the house was filled.* (3) ἐργαζώμεθα ἕως ἔτι ἡμέρα ἐστίν, *let us work while it is still day.*

The word ἕως can also serve as an "improper" preposition with the genitive case, meaning *up to, to, unto, as far as.* The phrase ἕως οὗ, in which ἕως is a preposition and οὗ the genitive singular neuter of the relative pronoun, has the same meaning and is used the same way as ἕως (conjunction) alone. Examples: (1) ἠργάζετο ἕως τῆς νυκτός, *he was working until nighttime.* (2) ἔμεινεν ἕως οὗ ἦλθον, *he remained until I came.* (3) εἶπον ὅτι οὐ φάγονται ἕως οὗ πάντες οἱ ἐχθροὶ αὐτῶν ἀποθάνωσιν, *they said they would not eat until all their enemies had died.*

The prepositions ἄχρι and μέχρι are used in the same ways as ἕως, but are less commonly used as conjunctions. ἄχρι and μέχρι sometimes appear with a final ς (as ἄχρις or μέχρις) when the word following begins with a vowel.

592. [550] Optative Mood

In the classical period, Greek had another mood, the optative, in addition to those we have already studied. In New Testament Greek, however, most of the classical uses of the optative have almost entirely disappeared. The optative is sometimes retained to express a wish. For example, the frequent expression of Paul, μὴ γένοιτο (γένοιτο being the third-person singular, second aorist optative of γίνομαι), means *may it not happen!* or in more idiomatic English *God forbid!* or *perish the thought!* The other few optatives in the New Testament can be noted when they occur. For reference, the conjugation of the optative of λύω is given in §646 of the paradigm section, but it need not be memorized. The student may wish to note the distinctive addition of an ι to the theme vowel, and the use of secondary endings in all tenses.

593. Periphrasis

Greek participles can be used with various forms of the verb εἰμί to form the equivalent of certain moods and tenses. This idiom, called *periphrasis*, is quite similar to English idiom. It is especially common to find εἰμί with a perfect passive participle standing for the indicative perfect passive.

Examples: ἀποθνήσκοντες ἦμεν, *we were dying* (periphrastic imperfect active indicative); ἐστὲ σεσωσμένοι, *you are saved* (periphrastic perfect passive indicative); ἵνα λελυμένος ᾖ, *in order that he might be loosed* (periphrastic perfect passive subjunctive).

The following table summarizes the periphrastic tenses:

Tense of Participle	Tense of εἰμί	Periphrastic Tense
progressive	+ present	= present
progressive	+ imperfect	= imperfect
progressive	+ future	= future
perfect	+ present	= perfect
perfect	+ imperfect	= pluperfect
perfect	+ future	= future perfect

594. οὐ μή with Aorist Subjunctive or Future Indicative

The compound negative οὐ μή is used with either aorist subjunctive or future indicative to denote an emphatic negation of the future.

Example: ὃς ἂν μὴ δέξηται τὴν βασιλείαν τοῦ θεοῦ ὡς παιδίον, οὐ μὴ εἰσέλθῃ εἰς αὐτήν, *whoever does not receive the kingdom of God like a child will certainly not enter it.*

595. Exercises

A. 1. λέγει αὐτοῖς· Ὑμεῖς δὲ τίνα με λέγετε εἶναι; ἀποκριθεὶς δὲ Σίμων Πέτρος εἶπεν· Σὺ εἶ ὁ Χριστὸς ὁ υἱὸς τοῦ θεοῦ τοῦ ζῶντος.¹ 2. καὶ προσελθὼν ὁ πειράζων εἶπεν αὐτῷ· Εἰ υἱὸς εἶ τοῦ θεοῦ, εἰπὲ ἵνα οἱ λίθοι οὗτοι ἄρτοι γένωνται. ὁ δὲ ἀποκριθεὶς εἶπεν· Γέγραπται· οὐκ ἐπ᾽ ἄρτῳ μόνῳ ζήσεται ὁ ἄνθρωπος. 3. εἶπεν αὐτοῖς· Δότε αὐτοῖς ὑμεῖς φαγεῖν. 4. ἀλλὰ ἐλθὼν ἐπίθες τὴν χεῖρά σου ἐπ᾽ αὐτὴν καὶ ζήσεται. 5. κύριε, σῶσον, ἀπολλύμεθα. 6. ἔλεγον οὖν αὐτῷ· Ποῦ ἐστιν ὁ πατήρ σου; ἀπεκρίθη Ἰησοῦς· Οὔτε ἐμὲ οἴδατε οὔτε τὸν πατέρα μου· εἰ ἐμὲ ᾔδειτε, καὶ τὸν πατέρα μου ἂν ᾔδειτε. 7. τότε οὖν εἰσῆλθεν καὶ ὁ ἄλλος μαθητὴς ὁ ἐλθὼν πρῶτος εἰς τὸ μνημεῖον, καὶ εἶδεν καὶ ἐπίστευσεν· οὐδέπω² γὰρ ᾔδεισαν τὴν γραφήν, ὅτι δεῖ αὐτὸν ἐκ νεκρῶν ἀναστῆναι. 8. εἰ ἐν Σοδόμοις³ ἐγενήθησαν αἱ δυνάμεις αἱ γενόμεναι ἐν σοί, ἔμεινεν ἂν μέχρι τῆς σήμερον.⁴ 9. ὁ γὰρ πατὴρ φιλεῖ τὸν υἱὸν καὶ πάντα δείκνυσιν αὐτῷ ἃ αὐτὸς ποιεῖ, καὶ μείζονα τούτων δείξει αὐτῷ ἔργα, ἵνα ὑμεῖς θαυμάζητε. 10. ἰδοὺ ἄγγελος κυρίου φαίνεται κατ᾽ ὄναρ τῷ Ἰωσὴφ⁵ λέγων· Ἐγερθεὶς παράλαβε τὸ παιδίον καὶ τὴν μητέρα αὐτοῦ καὶ φεῦγε εἰς Αἴγυπτον⁶ καὶ ἴσθι ἐκεῖ ἕως ἂν εἴπω σοι· μέλλει γὰρ Ἡρῴδης⁷ ζητεῖν τὸ παιδίον τοῦ ἀπολέσαι αὐτό. 11. ὁ δὲ Ἰησοῦς οὐκέτι οὐδὲν ἀπεκρίθη, ὥστε θαυμάζειν τὸν Πιλᾶτον.⁸ 12. καὶ μὴ φοβεῖσθε

1. Two adjacent nouns in the same case without any connecting conjunction, preposition, or linking verb may be in *apposition*, meaning that the second noun is simply another way of referring to the same entity as the first.

2. οὐδέπω, *not yet.*

3. Σόδομα, -ων, τά, plural in singular sense, *Sodom.*

4. σήμερον, adv., *today;* ἡ σήμερον (supply ἡμέρα), *today.*

5. ὄναρ, τό, *dream;* Ἰωσήφ, ὁ, *Joseph* (both nouns indeclinable).

6. Αἴγυπτος, -ου, ἡ, *Egypt.*

7. Ἡρῴδης, -ου, ὁ, *Herod.*

8. Πιλᾶτος, -ου, ὁ, *Pilate.*

ἀπὸ τῶν ἀποκτεννόντων τὸ σῶμα, τὴν δὲ ψυχὴν μὴ δυναμένων ἀποκτεῖναι· φοβεῖσθε δὲ μᾶλλον τὸν δυνάμενον καὶ ψυχὴν καὶ σῶμα ἀπολέσαι ἐν γεέννῃ.¹ 13. ὅταν δὲ διώκωσιν ὑμᾶς ἐν τῇ πόλει ταύτῃ, φεύγετε εἰς τὴν ἑτέραν· ἀμὴν γὰρ λέγω ὑμῖν, οὐ μὴ τελέσητε τὰς πόλεις τοῦ Ἰσραὴλ ἕως ἂν ἔλθῃ ὁ υἱὸς τοῦ ἀνθρώπου.² 14. καὶ ὑμεῖς μιμηταὶ³ ἡμῶν ἐγενήθητε καὶ τοῦ κυρίου, δεξάμενοι τὸν λόγον ἐν θλίψει πολλῇ μετὰ χαρᾶς πνεύματος ἁγίου, ὥστε γενέσθαι ὑμᾶς τύπον πᾶσιν τοῖς πιστεύουσιν. 15. ἀπεκρίθη Ἰωάννης καὶ εἶπεν· Οὐ δύναται ἄνθρωπος λαμβάνειν οὐδὲ ἓν ἐὰν μὴ ᾖ δεδομένον αὐτῷ ἐκ τοῦ οὐρανοῦ. 16. ἀπεκρίθη Ἰησοῦς καὶ εἶπεν αὐτῇ· Εἰ ᾔδεις τὴν δωρεὰν⁴ τοῦ θεοῦ καὶ τίς ἐστιν ὁ λέγων σοι, Δός μοι πεῖν, σὺ ἂν ᾔτησας αὐτὸν καὶ ἔδωκεν ἄν σοι ὕδωρ ζῶν. 17. Τί οὖν ἐροῦμεν; ὁ νόμος ἁμαρτία; μὴ γένοιτο· ἀλλὰ τὴν ἁμαρτίαν οὐκ ἔγνων εἰ μὴ διὰ νόμου· τήν τε γὰρ ἐπιθυμίαν οὐκ ᾔδειν εἰ μὴ ὁ νόμος ἔλεγεν· Οὐκ ἐπιθυμήσεις.⁵

B. 1. Until the Lord comes, there will be sin upon the earth. 2. If someone seems to be wise in his own eyes, let him watch out, lest he fall. 3. He died for us, with the result that we have now become his children. 4. If you (s.) remain in him until he comes, you will certainly not perish. 5. And it happened that, after having risen from the dead, Jesus appeared to his disciples and said, "All authority is given to me." 6. If you (s.) had preached in the midst of this people, they would have repented, so that they would not have been destroyed. 7. There will be much tribulation on the earth until the Son of Man appears, seated on his throne.

1. γέεννα, ἡ, *Gehenna, hell.*
2. ἀμήν, particle, *amen, truly, indeed;* Ἰσραήλ, ὁ, *Israel* (indeclinable).
3. μιμητής, ὁ, *an imitator.*
4. δωρεά, ἡ, *a gift.*
5. ἐπιθυμέω, *I covet, I desire strongly, I lust.*

Paradigms

First Declension

596. [555] The declension of ὥρα, ἡ, stem ὡρα-, *an hour;* ἀλήθεια, ἡ, stem ἀληθεια-, *truth;* δόξα, ἡ, stem δοξα-, *glory;* and γραθή, ἡ, stem γραφα-, *a writing, a Scripture,* is as follows:

	Sing.			
Nom./Voc.	ὥρα	ἀλήθεια	δόξα	γραφή
Gen.	ὥρας	ἀληθείας	δόξης	γραφῆς
Dat.	ὥρᾳ	ἀληθείᾳ	δόξῃ	γραφῇ
Acc.	ὥραν	ἀλήθειαν	δόξαν	γραφήν
	Plur.			
Nom./Voc.	ὥραι	ἀλήθειαι	δόξαι	γραφαί
Gen.	ὡρῶν	ἀληθειῶν	δοξῶν	γραφῶν
Dat.	ὥραις	ἀληθείαις	δόξαις	γραφαῖς
Acc.	ὥρας	ἀληθείας	δόξας	γραφάς

597. [556] The declension of προφήτης, ὁ, stem προφητα-, *a prophet;* and μαθητής, ὁ, stem μαθητα-, *a disciple,* is as follows:

288

	Sing.	
Nom.	προφήτης	μαθητής
Gen.	προφήτου	μαθητοῦ
Dat.	προφήτῃ	μαθητῇ
Acc.	προφήτην	μαθητήν
Voc.	προφῆτα	μαθητά
	Plur.	
Nom./Voc.	προφῆται	μαθηταί
Gen.	προφητῶν	μαθητῶν
Dat.	προφήταις	μαθηταῖς
Acc.	προφήτας	μαθητάς

Second Declension

598. [557] The declension of λόγος, ὁ, stem λογο-, *a word;*
ἄνθρωπος, ὁ, stem ἀνθρωπο-, *a man;* υἱός, ὁ, stem υἱο-, *a son;*
and δοῦλος, ὁ, stem δουλο-, *a slave,* is as follows:

	Sing.			
Nom.	λόγος	ἄνθρωπος	υἱός	δοῦλος
Gen.	λόγου	ἀνθρώπου	υἱοῦ	δούλου
Dat.	λόγῳ	ἀνθρώπῳ	υἱῷ	δούλῳ
Acc.	λόγον	ἄνθρωπον	υἱόν	δοῦλον
Voc.	λόγε	ἄνθρωπε	υἱέ	δοῦλε
	Plur.			
Nom./Voc.	λόγοι	ἄνθρωποι	υἱοί	δοῦλοι
Gen.	λόγων	ἀνθρώπων	υἱῶν	δούλων
Dat.	λόγοις	ἀνθρώποις	υἱοῖς	δούλοις
Acc.	λόγους	ἀνθρώπους	υἱούς	δούλους

599. [558] The declension of δῶρον, τό, stem δωρο-, *a gift,*
is as follows:

	Sing.	**Plur.**
Nom./Acc./Voc.	δῶρον	δῶρα
Gen.	δώρου	δώρων
Dat.	δώρῳ	δώροις

Third Declension

600. [559] The declension of νύξ, ἡ, stem νυκτ-, *a night;* σάρξ, ἡ, stem σαρκ-, *flesh;* ἄρχων, ὁ, stem ἀρχοντ-, *a ruler,* is as follows:

	Sing.		
Nom./Voc.	νύξ	σάρξ	ἄρχων
Gen.	νυκτός	σαρκός	ἄρχοντος
Dat.	νυκτί	σαρκί	ἄρχοντι
Acc.	νύκτα	σάρκα	ἄρχοντα
	Plur.		
Nom./Voc.	νύκτες	σάρκες	ἄρχοντες
Gen.	νυκτῶν	σαρκῶν	ἀρχόντων
Dat.	νυξί(ν)	σαρξί(ν)	ἄρχουσι(ν)
Acc.	νύκτας	σάρκας	ἄρχοντας

601. [560] The declension of ἐλπίς, ἡ, stem ἐλπιδ-, *hope,* and χάρις, ἡ, stem χαριτ-, *grace,* is as follows:

	Sing.	
Nom.	ἐλπίς	χάρις
Gen.	ἐλπίδος	χάριτος
Dat.	ἐλπίδι	χάριτι
Acc.	ἐλπίδα	χάριν
Voc.	ἐλπί	χάρις

	Plur.	
Nom./Voc.	ἐλπίδες	χάριτες
Gen.	ἐλπίδων	χαρίτων
Dat.	ἐλπίσι(ν)	χάρισι(ν)
Acc.	ἐλπίδας	χάριτας

602. [561] The declension of ὄνομα, τό, stem ὀνοματ-, *a name,* is as follows:

	Sing.	**Plur.**
Nom./Acc./Voc.	ὄνομα	ὀνόματα
Gen.	ὀνόματος	ὀνομάτων
Dat.	ὀνόματι	ὀνόμασι(ν)

603. [562] The declension of γένος, τό, stem γενεσ-, *a race,* is as follows:

	Sing.	**Plur.**
Nom./Acc./Voc.	γένος	γένη
Gen.	γένους	γενῶν
Dat.	γένει	γένεσι(ν)

604. [563] The declension of πόλις, ἡ, stem πολι-, *a city,* is as follows:

	Sing.	**Plur.**
Nom.	πόλις	πόλεις
Gen.	πόλεως	πόλεων
Dat.	πόλει	πόλεσι(ν)
Acc.	πόλιν	πόλεις
Voc.	πόλι	πόλεις

605. [564] The declension of βασιλεύς, ὁ, stem βασιλευ-, *a king*, is as follows:

	Sing.	**Plur.**
Nom.	βασιλεύς	βασιλεῖς
Gen.	βασιλέως	βασιλέων
Dat.	βασιλεῖ	βασιλεῦσι(ν)
Acc.	βασιλέα	βασιλεῖς
Voc.	βασιλεῦ	βασιλεῖς

606. [565] The declension of πατήρ, ὁ, stem πατερ-, *a father;* and ἀνήρ, ὁ, stem ἀνερ-, *a man,* is as follows:

	Sing.	
Nom.	πατήρ	ἀνήρ
Gen.	πατρός	ἀνδρός
Dat.	πατρί	ἀνδρί
Acc.	πατέρα	ἄνδρα
Voc.	πάτερ	ἄνερ
	Plur.	
Nom./Voc.	πατέρες	ἄνδρες
Gen.	πατέρων	ἀνδρῶν
Dat.	πατράσι(ν)	ἀνδράσι(ν)
Acc.	πατέρας	ἄνδρας

μήτηρ, μητρός, ἡ, *a mother,* is declined like πατήρ.

607. [566] The declension of χείρ, ἡ, stem χειρ-, *a hand;* and γυνή, ἡ, stem γυναικ-, *a woman,* is as follows:

	Sing.	
Nom.	χείρ	γυνή
Gen.	χειρός	γυναικός
Dat.	χειρί	γυναικί
Acc.	χεῖρα	γυναῖκα
Voc.	χείρ	γύναι

	Plur.	
Nom./Voc.	χεῖρες	γυναῖκες
Gen.	χειρῶν	γυναικῶν
Dat.	χερσί(ν)	γυναιξί(ν)
Acc.	χεῖρας	γυναῖκας

608. [567] The Article

The declension of the article, ὁ, ἡ, τό, *the,* is as follows:

	Sing.			**Plur.**		
	Masc.	**Fem.**	**Neut.**	**Masc.**	**Fem.**	**Neut.**
Nom.	ὁ	ἡ	τό	οἱ	αἱ	τά
Gen.	τοῦ	τῆς	τοῦ	τῶν	τῶν	τῶν
Dat.	τῷ	τῇ	τῷ	τοῖς	ταῖς	τοῖς
Acc.	τόν	τήν	τό	τούς	τάς	τά

Adjectives

609. [568] The declension of ἀγαθός, -ή, -όν, *good,* is as follows:

	Sing.			**Plur.**		
	Masc.	**Fem.**	**Neut.**	**Masc.**	**Fem.**	**Neut.**
Nom.	ἀγαθός	ἀγαθή	ἀγαθόν	ἀγαθοί	ἀγαθαί	ἀγαθά
Gen.	ἀγαθοῦ	ἀγαθῆς	ἀγαθοῦ	ἀγαθῶν	ἀγαθῶν	ἀγαθῶν
Dat.	ἀγαθῷ	ἀγαθῇ	ἀγαθῷ	ἀγαθοῖς	ἀγαθαῖς	ἀγαθοῖς
Acc.	ἀγαθόν	ἀγαθήν	ἀγαθόν	ἀγαθούς	ἀγαθάς	ἀγαθά
Voc.	ἀγαθέ	ἀγαθή	ἀγαθόν	ἀγαθοί	ἀγαθαί	ἀγαθά

610. [569] The declension of μικρός, -ά, -όν, *small,* is as follows:

	Sing.			Plur.		
	Masc.	**Fem.**	**Neut.**	**Masc.**	**Fem.**	**Neut.**
Nom.	μικρός	μικρά	μικρόν	μικροί	μικραί	μικρά
Gen.	μικροῦ	μικρᾶς	μικροῦ	μικρῶν	μικρῶν	μικρῶν
Dat.	μικρῷ	μικρᾷ	μικρῷ	μικροῖς	μικραῖς	μικροῖς
Acc.	μικρόν	μικράν	μικρόν	μικρούς	μικράς	μικρά
Voc.	μικρέ	μικρά	μικρόν	μικροί	μικραί	μικρά

611. [570] The declension of δίκαιος, -α, -ον, *righteous,* is as follows:

	Sing.			Plur.		
	Masc.	**Fem.**	**Neut.**	**Masc.**	**Fem.**	**Neut.**
Nom.	δίκαιος	δικαία	δίκαιον	δίκαιοι	δίκαιαι	δίκαια
Gen.	δικαίου	δικαίας	δικαίου	δικαίων	δικαίων	δικαίων
Dat.	δικαίῳ	δικαίᾳ	δικαίῳ	δικαίοις	δικαίαις	δικαίοις
Acc.	δίκαιον	δικαίαν	δίκαιον	δικαίους	δικαίας	δίκαια
Voc.	δίκαιε	δικαία	δίκαιον	δίκαιοι	δίκαιαι	δίκαια

612. [571] The declension of μείζων, μεῖζον, *greater,* is as follows:

	Sing.		Plur.	
	Masc./		**Masc./**	
	Fem.	**Neut.**	**Fem.**	**Neut.**
Nom.	μείζων	μεῖζον	μείζονες (μείζους)	μείζονα (μείζω)
Gen.	μείζονος	μείζονος	μειζόνων	μειζόνων
Dat.	μείζονι	μείζονι	μείζοσι(ν)	μείζοσι(ν)
Acc.	μείζονα (μείζω)	μεῖζον	μείζονας (μείζους)	μείζονα (μείζω)

613. [572] The declension of ἀληθής, -ές, *true,* is as follows:

	Sing.		Plur.	
	Masc./Fem.	**Neut.**	**Masc./Fem.**	**Neut.**
Nom.	ἀληθής	ἀληθές	ἀληθεῖς	ἀληθῆ
Gen.	ἀληθοῦς	ἀληθοῦς	ἀληθῶν	ἀληθῶν
Dat.	ἀληθεῖ	ἀληθεῖ	ἀληθέσι(ν)	ἀληθέσι(ν)
Acc.	ἀληθῆ	ἀληθές	ἀληθεῖς	ἀληθῆ
Voc.	ἀληθές	ἀληθές	ἀληθεῖς	ἀληθῆ

614. [573] The declension of πᾶς, πᾶσα, πᾶν, *all,* is as follows:

	Sing.			Plur.		
	Masc.	**Fem.**	**Neut.**	**Masc.**	**Fem.**	**Neut.**
Nom.	πᾶς	πᾶσα	πᾶν	πάντες	πᾶσαι	πάντα
Gen.	παντός	πάσης	παντός	πάντων	πασῶν	πάντων
Dat.	παντί	πάσῃ	παντί	πᾶσι(ν)	πάσαις	πᾶσι(ν)
Acc.	πάντα	πᾶσαν	πᾶν	πάντας	πάσας	πάντα

615. [574] The declension of πολύς, πολλή, πολύ, *much,* is as follows:

	Sing.			Plur.		
	Masc.	**Fem.**	**Neut.**	**Masc.**	**Fem.**	**Neut.**
Nom.	πολύς	πολλή	πολύ	πολλοί	πολλαί	πολλά
Gen.	πολλοῦ	πολλῆς	πολλοῦ	πολλῶν	πολλῶν	πολλῶν
Dat.	πολλῷ	πολλῇ	πολλῷ	πολλοῖς	πολλαῖς	πολλοῖς
Acc.	πολύν	πολλήν	πολύ	πολλούς	πολλάς	πολλά

616. [575] The declension of μέγας, μεγάλη, μέγα, *great,* is as follows:

	Sing.			**Plur.**		
	Masc.	**Fem.**	**Neut.**	**Masc.**	**Fem.**	**Neut.**
Nom.	μέγας	μεγάλη	μέγα	μεγάλοι	μεγάλαι	μεγάλα
Gen.	μεγάλου	μεγάλης	μεγάλου	μεγάλων	μεγάλων	μεγάλων
Dat.	μεγάλῳ	μεγάλῃ	μεγάλῳ	μεγάλοις	μεγάλαις	μεγάλοις
Acc.	μέγαν	μεγάλην	μέγα	μεγάλους	μεγάλας	μεγάλα
Voc.	μεγάλε	μεγάλη	μέγα	μεγάλοι	μεγάλαι	μεγάλα

617. The declension of ὀξύς, -εῖα, -ύ, *sharp,* is as follows:

	Sing.			**Plur.**		
	Masc.	**Fem.**	**Neut.**	**Masc.**	**Fem.**	**Neut.**
Nom.	ὀξύς	ὀξεῖα	ὀξύ	ὀξεῖς	ὀξεῖαι	ὀξέα
Gen.	ὀξέως	ὀξείας	ὀξέως	ὀξέων	ὀξειῶν	ὀξέων
Dat.	ὀξεῖ	ὀξείᾳ	ὀξεῖ	ὀξέσι(ν)	ὀξείαις	ὀξέσι(ν)
Acc.	ὀξύν	ὀξεῖαν	ὀξύ	ὀξεῖς	ὀξείας	ὀξέα

Participles

618. [576] The declension of λύων, λύουσα, λῦον, *loosing,* the progressive active participle of λύω, is as follows:

	Sing.			**Plur.**		
	Masc.	**Fem.**	**Neut.**	**Masc.**	**Fem.**	**Neut.**
Nom.	λύων	λύουσα	λῦον	λύοντες	λύουσαι	λύοντα
Gen.	λύοντος	λυούσης	λύοντος	λυόντων	λυουσῶν	λυόντων
Dat.	λύοντι	λυούσῃ	λύοντι	λύουσι(ν)	λυούσαις	λύουσι(ν)
Acc.	λύοντα	λύουσαν	λῦον	λύοντας	λυούσας	λύοντα

619. [577] The declension of λύσας, λύσασα, λῦσαν, *having loosed,* the aorist active participle of λύω, is as follows:

	Sing.		
	Masc.	**Fem.**	**Neut.**
Nom.	λύσας	λύσασα	λῦσαν
Gen.	λύσαντος	λυσάσης	λύσαντος
Dat.	λύσαντι	λυσάσῃ	λύσαντι
Acc.	λύσαντα	λύσασαν	λῦσαν
	Plur.		
	Masc.	**Fem.**	**Neut.**
Nom.	λύσαντες	λύσασαι	λύσαντα
Gen.	λυσάντων	λυσασῶν	λυσάντων
Dat.	λύσασι(ν)	λυσάσαις	λύσασι(ν)
Acc.	λύσαντας	λυσάσας	λύσαντα

620. [578] The declension of λελυκώς, λελυκυῖα, λελυκός, the perfect active participle of λύω, is as follows:

	Sing.		
	Masc.	**Fem.**	**Neut.**
Nom.	λελυκώς	λελυκυῖα	λελυκός
Gen.	λελυκότος	λελυκυίας	λελυκότος
Dat.	λελυκότι	λελυκυίᾳ	λελυκότι
Acc.	λελυκότα	λελυκυῖαν	λελυκός
	Plur.		
	Masc.	**Fem.**	**Neut.**
Nom.	λελυκότες	λελυκυῖαι	λελυκότα
Gen.	λελυκότων	λελυκυιῶν	λελυκότων
Dat.	λελυκόσι(ν)	λελυκυίαις	λελυκόσι(ν)
Acc.	λελυκότας	λελυκυίας	λελυκότα

621. [579] The declension of λυθείς, λυθεῖσα, λυθέν, *having been loosed,* the aorist passive participle of λύω, is as follows:

	Sing.		
	Masc.	**Fem.**	**Neut.**
Nom.	λυθείς	λυθεῖσα	λυθέν
Gen.	λυθέντος	λυθείσης	λυθέντος
Dat.	λυθέντι	λυθείσῃ	λυθέντι
Acc.	λυθέντα	λυθεῖσαν	λυθέν

	Plur.		
	Masc.	**Fem.**	**Neut.**
Nom.	λυθέντες	λυθεῖσαι	λυθέντα
Gen.	λυθέντων	λυθεισῶν	λυθέντων
Dat.	λυθεῖσι(ν)	λυθείσαις	λυθεῖσι(ν)
Acc.	λυθέντας	λυθείσας	λυθέντα

622. [580] The declension of ὤν, οὖσα, ὄν, *being,* the participle of εἰμί, is as follows:

	Sing.			**Plur.**		
	Masc.	**Fem.**	**Neut.**	**Masc.**	**Fem.**	**Neut.**
Nom.	ὤν	οὖσα	ὄν	ὄντες	οὖσαι	ὄντα
Gen.	ὄντος	οὔσης	ὄντος	ὄντων	οὐσῶν	ὄντων
Dat.	ὄντι	οὔσῃ	ὄντι	οὖσι(ν)	οὔσαις	οὖσι(ν)
Acc.	ὄντα	οὖσαν	ὄν	ὄντας	οὔσας	ὄντα

Pronouns

623. [581] The declensions of the personal pronouns, ἐγώ, *I;* σύ, *you* (s.); and αὐτός, -ή, -ό, *he, she, it,* are as follows:

Sing.		Masc.	Fem.	Neut.
Nom.	ἐγώ	σύ	αὐτός	αὐτή	αὐτό
Gen.	ἐμοῦ (μου)	σοῦ	αὐτοῦ	αὐτῆς	αὐτοῦ
Dat.	ἐμοί (μοι)	σοί	αὐτῷ	αὐτῇ	αὐτῷ
Acc.	ἐμέ (με)	σέ	αὐτόν	αὐτήν	αὐτό

Plur.			Masc.	Fem.	Neut.
Nom.	ἡμεῖς	ὑμεῖς	αὐτοί	αὐταί	αὐτά
Gen.	ἡμῶν	ὑμῶν	αὐτῶν	αὐτῶν	αὐτῶν
Dat.	ἡμῖν	ὑμῖν	αὐτοῖς	αὐταῖς	αὐτοῖς
Acc.	ἡμᾶς	ὑμᾶς	αὐτούς	αὐτάς	αὐτά

624. [582] The declension of οὗτος, αὕτη, τοῦτο, *this,* is as follows:

	Sing.			Plur.		
	Masc.	Fem.	Neut.	Masc.	Fem.	Neut.
Nom.	οὗτος	αὕτη	τοῦτο	οὗτοι	αὗται	ταῦτα
Gen.	τούτου	ταύτης	τούτου	τούτων	τούτων	τούτων
Dat.	τούτῳ	ταύτῃ	τούτῳ	τούτοις	ταύταις	τούτοις
Acc.	τοῦτον	ταύτην	τοῦτο	τούτους	ταύτας	ταῦτα

ἐκεῖνος, -η, -ο, *that,* has the same endings as αὐτός.

625. [583] The declension of the relative pronoun, ὅς, ἥ, ὅ, *who, which, what,* is as follows:

	Sing.			Plur.		
	Masc.	Fem.	Neut.	Masc.	Fem.	Neut.
Nom.	ὅς	ἥ	ὅ	οἵ	αἵ	ἅ
Gen.	οὗ	ἧς	οὗ	ὧν	ὧν	ὧν
Dat.	ᾧ	ᾗ	ᾧ	οἷς	αἷς	οἷς
Acc.	ὅν	ἥν	ὅ	οὕς	ἅς	ἅ

626. [584] The declension of the interrogative pronoun, τίς, τί, *who? which? what?* and the indefinite pronoun, τις, τι, *someone, something,* is as follows:

	Sing.		Plur.	
	Masc./Fem.	**Neut.**	**Masc./Fem.**	**Neut.**
Nom.	τίς	τί	τίνες	τίνα
Gen.	τίνος	τίνος	τίνων	τίνων
Dat.	τίνι	τίνι	τίσι(ν)	τίσι(ν)
Acc.	τίνα	τί	τίνας	τίνα

	Sing.		Plur.	
	Masc./Fem.	**Neut.**	**Masc./Fem.**	**Neut.**
Nom.	τις	τι	τινές	τινά
Gen.	τινός	τινός	τινῶν	τινῶν
Dat.	τινί	τινί	τισί(ν)	τισί(ν)
Acc.	τινά	τι	τινάς	τινά

627. [585] The declension of the reflexive pronouns, ἐμαυτοῦ, -ῆς, *of myself;* and σεαυτοῦ, -ῆς, *of yourself,* is as follows:

	Sing.		Plur.	
	Masc.	**Fem.**	**Masc.**	**Fem.**
Gen.	ἐμαυτοῦ	ἐμαυτῆς	ἑαυτῶν	ἑαυτῶν
Dat.	ἐμαυτῷ	ἐμαυτῇ	ἑαυτοῖς	ἑαυταῖς
Acc.	ἐμαυτόν	ἐμαυτήν	ἑαυτούς	ἑαυτάς

	Sing.		Plur.	
	Masc.	**Fem.**	**Masc.**	**Fem.**
Gen.	σεαυτοῦ	σεαυτῆς	ἑαυτῶν	ἑαυτῶν
Dat.	σεαυτῷ	σεαυτῇ	ἑαυτοῖς	ἑαυταῖς
Acc.	σεαυτόν	σεαυτήν	ἑαυτούς	ἑαυτάς

628. [586] The declension of the reflexive pronoun, ἑαυτοῦ, -ῆς, -οῦ, *of himself, of herself, of itself,* is as follows:

	Sing.			**Plur.**		
	Masc.	**Fem.**	**Neut.**	**Masc.**	**Fem.**	**Neut.**
Gen.	ἑαυτοῦ	ἑαυτῆς	ἑαυτοῦ	ἑαυτῶν	ἑαυτῶν	ἑαυτῶν
Dat.	ἑαυτῷ	ἑαυτῇ	ἑαυτῷ	ἑαυτοῖς	ἑαυταῖς	ἑαυτοῖς
Acc.	ἑαυτόν	ἑαυτήν	ἑαυτό	ἑαυτούς	ἑαυτάς	ἑαυτά

Numerals

629. [587] The declension of εἷς, μία, ἕν, *one,* is as follows:

	Masc.	**Fem.**	**Neut.**
Nom.	εἷς	μία	ἕν
Gen.	ἑνός	μιᾶς	ἑνός
Dat.	ἑνί	μιᾷ	ἑνί
Acc.	ἕνα	μίαν	ἕν

630. [588] The declension of τρεῖς, τρία, *three,* is as follows:

	Masc./Fem.	**Neut.**
Nom.	τρεῖς	τρία
Gen.	τριῶν	τριῶν
Dat.	τρισί(ν)	τρισί(ν)
Acc.	τρεῖς	τρία

The declension of τέσσαρες, τέσσαρα, *four,* is as follows:

	Masc./Fem.	**Neut.**
Nom.	τέσσαρες	τέσσαρα
Gen.	τεσσάρων	τεσσάρων
Dat.	τέσσαρσι(ν)	τέσσαρσι(ν)
Acc.	τέσσαρας	τέσσαρα

301

631. [589] The Regular Verb

The conjugation of λύω, *I loose,* stem λυ-, is as follows:

Principal Part	First				Second		Third		Fourth		Fifth	Sixth	
	Pres. (Prog.) Act.	Imp. Act.	Pres. (Prog.) M/P.	Imp. M/P.	Fut. Act.	Fut. Mid.	Aor. Act.	Aor. Mid.	Perf. Act.	Plup. Act.	Perf. M/P.	Aor. Pass.	Fut. Pass.
Indic. Sg. 1.	λύω	ἔλυον	λύομαι	ἐλυόμην	λύσω	λύσομαι	ἔλυσα	ἐλυσάμην	λέλυκα	(ἐ)λελύκειν	λέλυμαι	ἐλύθην	λυθήσομαι
2.	λύεις	ἔλυες	λύῃ	ἐλύου	λύσεις	λύσῃ	ἔλυσας	ἐλύσω	λέλυκας	(ἐ)λελύκεις	λέλυσαι	ἐλύθης	λυθήσῃ
3.	λύει	ἔλυε(ν)	λύεται	ἐλύετο	λύει	λύσεται	ἔλυσε(ν)	ἐλύσατο	λέλυκε(ν)	(ἐ)λελύκει	λέλυται	ἐλύθη	λυθήσεται
Pl. 1.	λύομεν	ἐλύομεν	λυόμεθα	ἐλυόμεθα	λύσομεν	λυσόμεθα	ἐλύσαμεν	ἐλυσάμεθα	λελύκαμεν	(ἐ)λελύκειμεν	λελύμεθα	ἐλύθημεν	λυθησόμεθα
2.	λύετε	ἐλύετε	λύεσθε	ἐλύεσθε	λύσετε	λύσεσθε	ἐλύσατε	ἐλύσασθε	λελύκατε	(ἐ)λελύκειτε	λέλυσθε	ἐλύθητε	λυθήσεσθε
3.	λύουσι(ν)	ἔλυον	λύονται	ἐλύοντο	λύσουσι(ν)	λύσονται	ἔλυσαν	ἐλύσαντο	λελύκασι(ν) or λέλυκαν	(ἐ)λελύκεισαν	λέλυνται	ἐλύθησαν	λυθήσονται
Subj. Sg. 1.	λύω		λύωμαι				λύσω	λύσωμαι				λυθῶ	
2.	λύῃς		λύῃ				λύσῃς	λύσῃ				λυθῇς	
3.	λύῃ		λύηται				λύσῃ	λύσηται				λυθῇ	
Pl. 1.	λύωμεν		λυώμεθα				λύσωμεν	λυσώμεθα				λυθῶμεν	
2.	λύητε		λύησθε				λύσητε	λύσησθε				λυθῆτε	
3.	λύωσι(ν)		λύωνται				λύσωσι(ν)	λύσωνται				λυθῶσι(ν)	
Impv. Sg. 2.	λῦε		λύου				λῦσον	λῦσαι				λυθήτι	
3.	λυέτω		λυέσθω				λυσάτω	λυσάσθω				λυθήτω	
Pl. 2.	λύετε		λύεσθε				λύσατε	λύσασθε				λύθητε	
3.	λυέτωσαν		λυέσθωσαν				λυσάτωσαν	λυσάσθωσαν				λυθήτωσαν	
Infin.	λύειν		λύεσθαι		λύσειν[1]	λύσεσθαι	λῦσαι	λύσασθαι	λελυκέναι		λελύσθαι	λυθῆναι	
Part.	λύων		λυόμενος		λύσων[2]	λυσόμενος	λύσας	λυσάμενος	λελυκώς		λελυμένος	λυθείς	
	λύουσα		λυομένη		λύσουσα	λυσομένη	λύσασα	λυσαμένη	λελυκυῖα		λελυμένη	λυθεῖσα	
	λῦον		λυόμενον		λῦσον	λυσόμενον	λῦσαν	λυσάμενον	λελυκός		λελυμένον	λυθέν	

1. Future infinitives are very rare in the New Testament.
2. Future participles are very rare in the New Testament.

Contracting Verbs

632. [590] The progressive system of τιμάω, *I honor*, is as follows:

		Pres. (Prog.) Act.	Imperf. Act.	Pres. (Prog.) Mid./Pass.	Imperf. Mid./Pass.
Indic. Sg.	1.	(τιμάω) τιμῶ	(ἐτίμαον) ἐτίμων	(τιμάομαι) τιμῶμαι	(ἐτιμαόμην) ἐτιμώμην
	2.	(τιμάεις) τιμᾷς	(ἐτίμαες) ἐτίμας	(τιμάῃ) τιμᾷ	(ἐτιμάου) ἐτιμῶ
	3.	(τιμάει) τιμᾷ	(ἐτίμαε) ἐτίμα	(τιμάεται) τιμᾶται	(ἐτιμάετο) ἐτιμᾶτο
Pl.	1.	(τιμάομεν) τιμῶμεν	(ἐτιμάομεν) ἐτιμῶμεν	(τιμαόμεθα) τιμώμεθα	(ἐτιμαόμεθα) ἐτιμώμεθα
	2.	(τιμάετε) τιμᾶτε	(ἐτιμάετε) ἐτιμᾶτε	(τιμάεσθε) τιμᾶσθε	(ἐτιμάεσθε) ἐτιμᾶσθε
	3.	(τιμάουσι[ν]) τιμῶσι(ν)	(ἐτίμαον) ἐτίμων	(τιμάονται) τιμῶνται	(ἐτιμάοντο) ἐτιμῶντο
Subj. Sg.	1.	(τιμάω) τιμῶ		(τιμάωμαι) τιμῶμαι	
	2.	(τιμάῃς) τιμᾷς		(τιμάῃ) τιμᾷ	
	3.	(τιμάῃ) τιμᾷ		(τιμάηται) τιμᾶται	
Pl.	1.	(τιμάωμεν) τιμῶμεν		(τιμαώμεθα) τιμώμεθα	
	2.	(τιμάητε) τιμᾶτε		(τιμάησθε) τιμᾶσθε	
	3.	(τιμάωσι[ν]) τιμῶσι(ν)		(τιμάωνται) τιμῶνται	
Impv. Sg.	2.	(τίμαε) τίμα		(τιμάου) τιμῶ	
	3.	(τιμαέτω) τιμάτω		(τιμαέσθω) τιμάσθω	
Pl.	2.	(τιμάετε) τιμᾶτε		(τιμάεσθε) τιμᾶσθε	
	3.	(τιμαέτωσαν) τιμάτωσαν		(τιμαέσθωσαν) τιμάσθωσαν	
Infin.		(τιμάειν) τιμᾶν		(τιμάεσθαι) τιμᾶσθαι	
Part.		(τιμάων) τιμῶν		(τιμαόμενα) τιμώμενα	
		(τιμάουσα) τιμῶσα		(τιμαομένη) τιμωμένη	
		(τιμάον) τιμῶν		(τιμαόμενον) τιμώμενον	

633. [591] The progressive system of φιλέω, *I love*, is as follows:

		Pres. (Prog.) Act.	Imperf. Act.	Pres. (Prog.) Mid./Pass.	Imperf. Mid./Pass.
Indic. Sg.	**1.**	(φιλέω) φιλῶ	(ἐφίλεον) ἐφίλουν	(φιλέομαι) φιλοῦμαι	(ἐφιλεόμην) ἐφιλούμην
	2.	(φιλέεις) φιλεῖς	(ἐφίλεες) ἐφίλεις	(φιλέῃ) φιλῇ	(ἐφιλέου) ἐφιλοῦ
	3.	(φιλέει) φιλεῖ	(ἐφίλεε) ἐφίλει	(φιλέεται) φιλεῖται	(ἐφιλέετο) ἐφιλεῖτο
Pl.	**1.**	(φιλέομεν) φιλοῦμεν	(ἐφιλέομεν) ἐφιλοῦμεν	(φιλεόμεθα) φιλούμεθα	(ἐφιλεόμεθα) ἐφιλούμεθα
	2.	(φιλέετε) φιλεῖτε	(ἐφιλέετε) ἐφιλεῖτε	(φιλέεσθε) φιλεῖσθε	(ἐφιλέεσθε) ἐφιλεῖσθε
	3.	(φιλέουσι[ν]) φιλοῦσι(ν)	(ἐφίλεον) ἐφίλουν	(φιλέονται) φιλοῦνται	(ἐφιλέοντο) ἐφιλοῦντο
Subj. Sg.	**1.**	(φιλέω) φιλῶ		(φιλέωμαι) φιλῶμαι	
	2.	(φιλέῃς) φιλῇς		(φιλέῃ) φιλῇ	
	3.	(φιλέῃ) φιλῇ		(φιλέηται) φιλῆται	
Pl.	**1.**	(φιλέωμεν) φιλῶμεν		(φιλεώμεθα) φιλώμεθα	
	2.	(φιλέητε) φιλῆτε		(φιλέησθε) φιλῆσθε	
	3.	(φιλέωσι[ν]) φιλῶσι(ν)		(φιλέωνται) φιλῶνται	
Impv. Sg.	**2.**	(φιλεε) φίλει		(φιλέου) φιλοῦ	
	3.	(φιλεέτω) φιλείτω		(φιλεέσθω) φιλείσθω	
Pl.	**2.**	(φιλέετε) φιλεῖτε		(φιλέεσθε) φιλεῖσθε	
	3.	(φιλεέτωσαν) φιλείτωσαν		(φιλεέσθωσαν) φιλείσθωσαν	
Infin.		(φιλέειν) φιλεῖν		(φιλέεσθαι) φιλεῖσθαι	
Part.		(φιλέων) φιλῶν		(φιλεόμενος) φιλούμενος	
		(φιλέουσα) φιλοῦσα		(φιλεομένη) φιλουμένη	
		(φιλέον) φιλοῦν		(φιλεόμενον) φιλούμενον	

634. [592] The progressive system of δηλόω, *I make clear*, is as follows:

	Pres. (Prog.) Act.	Imperf. Act.	Pres. (Prog.) Mid./Pass.	Imperf. Mid./Pass.
Indic. Sg. 1.	(δηλόω) δηλῶ	(ἐδήλοον) ἐδήλουν	(δηλόομαι) δηλοῦμαι	(ἐδηλοόμην) ἐδηλούμην
2.	(δηλόεις) δηλοῖς	(ἐδήλοες) ἐδήλους	(δηλόῃ) δηλοῖ	(ἐδηλόου) ἐδηλοῦ
3.	(δηλόει) δηλοῖ	(ἐδήλοε) ἐδήλου	(δηλόεται) δηλοῦται	(ἐδηλόετο) ἐδηλοῦτο
Pl. 1.	(δηλόομεν) δηλοῦμεν	(ἐδηλόομεν) ἐδηλοῦμεν	(δηλοόμεθα) δηλούμεθα	(ἐδηλοόμεθα) ἐδηλούμεθα
2.	(δηλόετε) δηλοῦτε	(ἐδηλόετε) ἐδηλοῦτε	(δηλόεσθε) δηλοῦσθε	(ἐδηλόεσθε) ἐδηλοῦσθε
3.	(δηλόουσι(ν)) δηλοῦσι(ν)	(ἐδήλοον) ἐδήλουν	(δηλόονται) δηλοῦνται	(ἐδηλόοντο) ἐδηλοῦντο
Subj. Sg. 1.	(δηλόω) δηλῶ		(δηλόωμαι) δηλῶμαι	
2.	(δηλόῃς) δηλοῖς		(δηλόῃ) δηλοῖ	
3.	(δηλόῃ) δηλοῖ		(δηλόηται) δηλῶται	
Pl. 1.	(δηλόωμεν) δηλῶμεν		(δηλοώμεθα) δηλώμεθα	
2.	(δηλόητε) δηλῶτε		(δηλόησθε) δηλῶσθε	
3.	(δηλόωσι(ν)) δηλῶσι(ν)		(δηλόωνται) δηλῶνται	
Impv. Sg. 2.	(δήλοε) δήλου		(δηλόου) δηλοῦ	
3.	(δηλοέτω) δηλούτω		(δηλοέσθω) δηλούσθω	
Pl. 2.	(δηλόετε) δηλοῦτε		(δηλόεσθε) δηλοῦσθε	
3.	(δηλοέτωσαν) δηλούτωσαν		(δηλοέσθωσαν) δηλούσθωσαν	
Infin.	(δηλόειν) δηλοῦν		(δηλόεσθαι) δηλοῦσθαι	
Part.	(δηλόων) δηλῶν		(δηλοόμενος) δηλούμενος	
	(δηλόουσα) δηλοῦσα		(δηλοομένη) δηλουμένη	
	(δηλόον) δηλοῦν		(δηλοόμενον) δηλούμενον	

635. [593] Second Aorist Active and Middle

The second aorist active and middle of λείπω, *I leave,* is as follows:

			2nd Aor. Act.	2nd Aor. Mid.
Indic. Sg.	**1.**		ἔλιπον	ἐλιπόμην
	2.		ἔλιπες	ἐλίπου
	3.		ἔλιπε(ν)	ἐλίπετο
Pl.	**1.**		ἐλίπομεν	ἐλιπόμεθα
	2.		ἐλίπετε	ἐλίπεσθε
	3.		ἔλιπον	ἐλίποντο
Subj. Sg.	**1.**		λίπω	λίπωμαι
	2.		λίπῃς	λίπῃ
	3.		λίπῃ	λίπηται
Pl.	**1.**		λίπωμεν	λιπώμεθα
	2.		λίπητε	λίπησθε
	3.		λίπωσι(ν)	λίπωνται
Impv. Sg.	**2.**		λίπε	λιποῦ
	3.		λιπέτω	λιπέσθω
Pl.	**2.**		λίπετε	λίπεσθε
	3.		λιπέτωσαν	λιπέσθωσαν
Infin.			λιπεῖν	λιπέσθαι
Part.			λιπών	λιπόμενος
			λιποῦσα	λιπομένη
			λιπόν	λιπόμενον

Future and Aorist of Liquid Verbs

636. [594] The future active and middle of κρίνω, *I judge,* is as follows:

		Fut. Act. Indic.	Fut. Mid. Indic.
Sing.	**1.**	κρινῶ	κρινοῦμαι
	2.	κρινεῖς	κρινῇ
	3.	κρινεῖ	κρινεῖται
Plur.	**1.**	κρινοῦμεν	κρινούμεθα
	2.	κρινεῖτε	κρινεῖσθε
	3.	κρινοῦσι(ν)	κρινοῦνται

637. [595] The first aorist active and middle of κρίνω, *I judge,* is as follows:

		1st Aor. Act.	1st Aor. Mid.
Indic. Sg.	**1.**	ἔκρινα	ἐκρινάμην
	2.	ἔκρινας	ἐκρίνω
	3.	ἔκρινε(ν)	ἐκρίνατο
Pl.	**1.**	ἐκρίναμεν	ἐκρινάμεθα
	2.	ἐκρίνατε	ἐκρίνασθε
	3.	ἔκριναν	ἐκρίναντο
Subj. Sg.	**1.**	κρίνω	κρίνωμαι
	2.	κρίνῃς	κρίνῃ
	3.	κρίνῃ	κρίνηται
Pl.	**1.**	κρίνωμεν	κρινώμεθα
	2.	κρίνητε	κρίνησθε
	3.	κρίνωσι(ν)	κρίνωνται
Impv. Sg.	**2.**	κρῖνον	κρῖναι
	3.	κρινάτω	κρινάσθω
Pl.	**2.**	κρίνατε	κρίνασθε
	3.	κρινάτωσαν	κρινάσθωσαν
Infin.		κρῖναι	κρίνασθαι
Part.		κρίνας	κρινάμενος
		κρίνασα	κριναμένη
		κρῖναν	κρινάμενον

Verbs in μι

638. [596] The progressive system of δίδωμι, stem δο-, *I give,*
is as follows:

			Pres. (Prog.) Act.	Imperf. Act.	Pres. (Prog.) M./P.	Imperf. M./P.
Indic. Sg.	1.		δίδωμι	ἐδίδουν	δίδομαι	ἐδιδόμην
	2.		δίδως	ἐδίδους	δίδοσαι	ἐδίδοσο
	3.		δίδωσι(ν)	ἐδίδου	δίδοται	ἐδίδοτο
Pl.	1.		δίδομεν	ἐδίδομεν	διδόμεθα	ἐδιδόμεθα
	2.		δίδοτε	ἐδίδοτε	δίδοσθε	ἐδίδοσθε
	3.		διδόασι(ν)	ἐδίδοσαν	δίδονται	ἐδίδοντο
Subj. Sg.	1.		διδῶ		διδῶμαι	
	2.		διδῷς		διδῷ	
	3.		διδῷ		διδῶται	
Pl.	1.		διδῶμεν		διδώμεθα	
	2.		διδῶτε		διδῶσθε	
	3.		διδῶσι(ν)		διδῶνται	
Impv. Sg.	2.		δίδου		δίδοσο	
	3.		διδότω		διδόσθω	
Pl.	2.		δίδοτε		δίδοσθε	
	3.		διδότωσαν		διδόσθωσαν	
Infin.			διδόναι		δίδοσθαι	
Part.			διδούς		διδόμενος	
			διδοῦσα		διδομένη	
			διδόν		διδόμενον	

639. [597] The aorist active and middle of δίδωμι, *I give*, is as follows:

			Aor. Act.	Aor. Mid.
Indic. Sg.	**1.**		ἔδωκα	ἐδόμην
	2.		ἔδωκας	ἔδου
	3.		ἔδωκε(ν)	ἔδοτο
Pl.	**1.**		ἐδώκαμεν	ἐδόμεθα
	2.		ἐδώκατε	ἔδοσθε
	3.		ἔδωκαν	ἔδοντο
Subj. Sg.	**1.**		δῶ	δῶμαι
	2.		δῷς	δῷ
	3.		δῷ	δῶται
Pl.	**1.**		δῶμεν	δώμεθα
	2.		δῶτε	δῶσθε
	3.		δῶσι(ν)	δῶνται
Impv. Sg.	**2.**		δός	δοῦ
	3.		δότω	δόσθω
Pl.	**2.**		δότε	δόσθε
	3.		δότωσαν	δόσθωσαν
Infin.			δοῦναι	δόσθαι
Part.			δούς	δόμενος
			δοῦσα	δομένη
			δόν	δόμενον

640. [598] The progressive system of τίθημι, stem θε-, *I place*, is as follows:

		Pres. (Prog.) Act.	Imperf. Act.	Pres. (Prog.) M./P.	Imperf. M./P.
Indic. Sg.	1.	τίθημι	ἐτίθην	τίθεμαι	ἐτιθέμην
	2.	τίθης	ἐτίθεις	τίθεσαι	ἐτίθεσο
	3.	τίθησι(ν)	ἐτίθει	τίθεται	ἐτίθετο
Pl.	1.	τίθεμεν	ἐτίθεμεν	τιθέμεθα	ἐτιθέμεθα
	2.	τίθετε	ἐτίθετε	τίθεσθε	ἐτίθεσθε
	3.	τιθέασι(ν)	ἐτίθεσαν	τίθενται	ἐτίθεντο
Subj. Sg.	1.	τιθῶ		τιθῶμαι	
	2.	τιθῇς		τιθῇ	
	3.	τιθῇ		τιθῆται	
Pl.	1.	τιθῶμεν		τιθώμεθα	
	2.	τιθῆτε		τιθῆσθε	
	3.	τιθῶσι(ν)		τιθῶνται	
Impv. Sg.	2.	τίθει		τίθεσο	
	3.	τιθέτω		τιθέσθω	
Pl.	2.	τίθετε		τίθεσθε	
	3.	τιθέτωσαν		τιθέσθωσαν	
Infin.		τιθέναι		τίθεσθαι	
Part.		τιθείς τιθεῖσα τιθέν		τιθέμενος τιθεμένη τιθέμενον	

311

641. [599] The aorist active and middle of τίθημι, *I place,* is as follows:

			Aor. Act.	Aor. Mid.
Indic. Sg.	**1.**	ἔθηκα	ἐθέμην
	2.	ἔθηκας	ἔθου
	3.	ἔθηκε(ν)	ἔθετο
Pl.	**1.**	ἐθήκαμεν	ἐθέμεθα
	2.	ἐθήκατε	ἔθεσθε
	3.	ἔθηκαν	ἔθεντο
Subj. Sg.	**1.**	θῶ	θῶμαι
	2.	θῆς	θῇ
	3.	θῇ	θῆται
Pl.	**1.**	θῶμεν	θώμεθα
	2.	θῆτε	θῆσθε
	3.	θῶσι(ν)	θῶνται
Impv. Sg.	**2.**	θές	θοῦ
	3.	θέτω	θέσθω
Pl.	**2.**	θέτε	θέσθε
	3.	θέτωσαν	θέσθωσαν
Infin.		θεῖναι	θέσθαι
Part.		θείς	θέμενος
		θεῖσα	θεμένη
		θέν	θέμενον

642. [600] The progressive system of ἵστημι, stem στα-, *I cause to stand,* is as follows:

		Pres. (Prog.) Act.	Imperf. Act.	Pres. (Prog.) M./P.	Imperf. M./P.
Indic. Sg.	**1.**	ἵστημι	ἵστην	ἵσταμαι	ἱστάμην
	2.	ἵστης	ἵστης	ἵστασαι	ἵστασο
	3.	ἵστησι(ν)	ἵστη	ἵσταται	ἵστατο
Pl.	**1.**	ἵσταμεν	ἵσταμεν	ἱστάμεθα	ἱστάμεθα
	2.	ἵστατε	ἵστατε	ἵστασθε	ἵστασθε
	3.	ἱστᾶσι(ν)	ἵστασαν	ἵστανται	ἵσταντο
Subj. Sg.	**1.**	ἱστῶ		ἱστῶμαι	
	2.	ἱστῇς		ἱστῇ	
	3.	ἱστῇ		ἱστῆται	
Pl.	**1.**	ἱστῶμεν		ἱστώμεθα	
	2.	ἱστῆτε		ἱστῆσθε	
	3.	ἱστῶσι(ν)		ἱστῶνται	
Impv. Sg.	**2.**	ἵστη		ἵστασο	
	3.	ἱστάτω		ἱστάσθω	
Pl.	**2.**	ἵστατε		ἵστασθε	
	3.	ἱστάτωσαν		ἱστάσθωσαν	
Infin.		ἱστάναι		ἵστασθαι	
Part.		ἱστάς		ἱστάμενος	
		ἱστᾶσα		ἱσταμένη	
		ἱστάν		ἱστάμενον	

313

643. [601] The second aorist active of ἵστημι, *I stand* (intransitive in second aorist); and of γινώσκω, stem γνο-, *I know,* is as follows:

		2nd Aor. Act.	2nd Aor. Act.
Indic. Sg.	**1.**	ἔστην	ἔγνων
	2.	ἔστης	ἔγνως
	3.	ἔστη	ἔγνω
Pl.	**1.**	ἔστημεν	ἔγνωμεν
	2.	ἔστητε	ἔγνωτε
	3.	ἔστησαν	ἔγνωσαν
Subj. Sg.	**1.**	στῶ	γνῶ
	2.	στῇς	γνῷς
	3.	στῇ	γνῷ (γνοῖ)
Pl.	**1.**	στῶμεν	γνῶμεν
	2.	στῆτε	γνῶτε
	3.	στῶσι(ν)	γνῶσι(ν)
Impv. Sg.	**2.**	στῆθι	γνῶθι
	3.	στήτω	γνώτω
Pl.	**2.**	στῆτε	γνῶτε
	3.	στήτωσαν	γνώτωσαν
Infin.		στῆναι	γνῶναι
Part.		στάς	γνούς
		στᾶσα	γνοῦσα
		στάν	γνόν

644. [602] The conjugation of εἰμί, *I am,* is as follows:

		Present (Prog.)	**Imperf.**	**Future**
Indic. Sg.	**1.**	εἰμί	ἤμην	ἔσομαι
	2.	εἶ	ἦς	ἔσῃ
	3.	ἐστί(ν)	ἦν	ἔσται
Pl.	**1.**	ἐσμέν	ἦμεν	ἐσόμεθα
	2.	ἐστέ	ἦτε	ἔσεσθε
	3.	εἰσί(ν)	ἦσαν	ἔσονται
Subj. Sg.	**1.**	ὦ		
	2.	ᾖς		
	3.	ᾖ		
Pl.	**1.**	ὦμεν		
	2.	ἦτε		
	3.	ὦσι(ν)		
Impv. Sg.	**2.**	ἴσθι		
	3.	ἔστω		
Pl.	**2.**	ἔστε		
	3.	ἔστωσαν		
Infin.		εἶναι		
Part.		ὤν		
		οὖσα		
		ὄν		

Conjugation of οἶδα

645. [603] The conjugation of οἶδα, *I know*, is as follows:

			Perf.	**Plup.**
Indic. Sg.	**1.**		οἶδα	ᾔδειν
	2.		οἶδας	ᾔδεις
	3.		οἶδε(ν)	ᾔδει
Pl.	**1.**		οἴδαμεν	ᾔδειμεν
	2.		οἴδατε	ᾔδειτε
	3.		οἴδασι(ν)	ᾔδεισαν
Subj. Sg.	**1.**		εἰδῶ	
	2.		εἰδῇς	
	3.		εἰδῇ	
Pl.	**1.**		εἰδῶμεν	
	2.		εἰδῆτε	
	3.		εἰδῶσι(ν)	
Impv. Sg.	**2.**		ἴσθι	
	3.		ἴστω	
Pl.	**2.**		ἴστε	
	3.		ἴστωσαν	
Infin.			εἰδέναι	
Part.			εἰδώς	
			εἰδυῖα	
			εἰδός	

Optative Mood

646. The optative of λύω is conjugated as follows:

		Progressive		**Aorist**		
		Act.	**Mid./Pass.**	**Act.**	**Mid.**	**Pass.**
Sg.	**1.**	λύοιμι	λυοίμην	λύσαιμι	λυσαίμην	λυθείην
	2.	λύοις	λύοιο	λύσαις	λύσαιο	λυθείης
	3.	λύοι	λύοιτο	λύσαι	λύσαιτο	λυθείη
Pl.	**1.**	λύοιμεν	λυοίμεθα	λύσαιμεν	λυσαίμεθα	λυθείημεν
	2.	λύοιτε	λύοισθε	λύσαιτε	λύσαισθε	λύθείητε
	3.	λύοιεν	λύοιντο	λύσαιεν	λύσαιντο	λυθείησαν

647. The second aorist optative is like the progressive optative, except that it is formed on the second aorist stem: λίποιμι (act. 1st pers. sg.), λιποίμην (mid./pass. 1st pers. sg.), etc.

648. The only optative form of εἰμί in the New Testament is the third-person singular: εἴη.

Charts

649. Chart 1: Verb Formation

All finite verbs are formed by adding various components to a verbal stem. The chart below illustrates how verbs are commonly composed.

Tense	Augm.	Redupl.	Stem	Tense Formant	Theme Vowel	Ending	Principal Part Used
Indicative Mood							
Pres. Act.	—	—	λυ	—	o/ε	Primary A	1st
Pres. Mid./Pass.	—	—	λυ	—	o/ε	Primary B	"
Impf. Act.	ε	—	λυ	—	o/ε	Secondary A	"
Impf. Mid./Pass.	ε	—	λυ	—	o/ε	Secondary B	"
Fut. Act.	—	—	λυ	σ	o/ε	Primary A	2nd
Fut. Mid.	—	—	λυ	σ	o/ε	Primary B	"
Fut. Pass.	—	—	λυ	θησ	o/ε	Primary B	6th
1st Aor. Act.	ε	—	λυ	σ	α	Secondary A	3rd
1st Aor. Mid.	ε	—	λυ	σ	α	Secondary B	"
2nd Aor. Act.	ε	—	different stem		o/ε	Secondary A	"
2nd Aor. Mid.	ε	—	different stem		o/ε	Secondary B	"

Tense	Augm.	Redupl.	Stem	Tense Formant	Theme Vowel	Ending	Principal Part Used
Indicative Mood							
Aor. Pass.	ε	—	λυ	θ	η	Secondary A	6th
Perf. Act.	—	λε	λυ	κ	α	Secondary A	4th
Perf. Mid./Pass.	—	λε	λυ	—	—	Primary B	5th
Plup. Act	ε	λε	λυ	κ	ει	Secondary A	4th
Plup. Mid./Pass.	ε	λε	λυ	—	—	Secondary B	5th
Subjunctive Mood							
Prog. Act.		—	λυ	—	ω/η	Primary A	1st
Prog. Mid./Pass.		—	λυ	—	ω/η	Primary B	"
1st Aor. Act.		—	λυ	σ	ω/η	Primary A	3rd
1st Aor. Mid.		—	λυ	σ	ω/η	Primary B	"
2nd Aor. Act.		—	different stem	—	ω/η	Primary A	"
2nd Aor. Mid.		—	different stem	—	ω/η	Primary B	"
Aor. Pass.		—	λυ	θ	ω/η	Primary A	6th
Imperative Mood							
Prog. Act.		—	λυ	—	ε	Imperatival A	1st
Prog. Mid./Pass.		—	λυ	—	ε	Imperatival B	"
1st Aor. Act.		—	λυ	σ	α*	Imperatival A	3rd
1st Aor. Mid.		—	λυ	σ	α	Imperatival B	"
2nd Aor. Act.		—	different stem	—	ε*	Imperatival A	"
2nd Aor. Mid.		—	different stem	—	ε	Imperatival B	"
Aor. Pass.		—	λυ	θ	η	Imperatival A	6th

* The theme vowel is often dropped or obscured in the second-person singular imperatives.

650. Chart 2: Verb Endings

Person & Number	Primary A	Primary B	Secondary A	Secondary B	Imperatival A	Imperatival B
1st sing.	ω	μαι	ν	μην		
2nd sing.	ις	σαι (contracts)	ς	σο (contracts)	–, ν, θι (τι), ς (varies)	σο (contracts)
3rd sing.	ι	ται	—	το	τω	σθω
1st plur.	μεν	μεθα	μεν	μεθα		
2nd plur.	τε	σθε	τε	σθε	τε	σθε
3rd plur.	ουσι	νται	ν or σαν	ντο	τωσαν	σθωσαν

651. Chart 3: Vowel Contractions

Final vowels of the contracting verbs combine with the theme vowel of the ending according to the following:

Final Vowel of Stem \\ First Vowel of Ending	α	ε	η	ει	η	ο	ου	ω
α	α	α	α	ᾳ	ᾳ	ω	ω	ω
ε	η	ει	η	ει	η	ου	ου	ω
ο	ω	ου	ω	οι	οι	ου	ου	ω

Exceptions: (1) the progressive active infinitive of verbs in -αω is contracted from -άειν to -ᾶν instead of -ᾷν; (2) the progressive active infinitive of verbs ending in -οω is contracted from -όειν to -οῦν instead of -οῖν.

These are not real exceptions, however, because the -ειν ending of infinitives is itself a contraction of ε-εν.

652. Chart 4: Greek Consonant Classification

There are basically three areas of the mouth used in forming Greek consonants: (1) the lips (labials), (2) the tip of the tongue touching the front of the mouth or back of the teeth (dentals), and (3) the back of the tongue touching the back of the mouth (velars).[1] There are four ways of producing the consonants: (1) by completely stopping the air flow (stops), (2) by letting some air scrape through (fricatives), (3) by letting the sound go around the tongue (laterals) or through the nose (nasals), and (4) by combining a stop with the *s* sound (compound sibilants). Each of these combinations may be either voiced (using the vocal cords) or unvoiced, though not all combinations are used in Greek. The following chart classifies the Greek consonants according to their qualities.

1. This analysis is greatly simplified. A more precise description can be found in David Alan Black, *Linguistics for Students of New Testament*

	Place of Articulation	Lips (Labials)	Teeth (Dentals)	Back of Mouth (Velars)
Method of Sound Production				
Stop	unvoiced	π	τ	κ
	voiced	β	δ	γ
Fricative	unvoiced	φ	θ	χ
Liquid	laterals– voiced	(F)*	λ	—
	nasals– voiced	μ	ν	(γ)**
Compound sibilant	unvoiced	ψ	—	ξ
	voiced	—	ζ	—

*The digamma (F), pronounced like the English w, was obsolete long before New Testament times but was still used as a numeral.

**The γ before another velar consonant is pronounced like ng in English.

There are two more consonants in Greek that do not fit this schema: the simple unvoiced sibilant σ and the retroflex liquid ρ. Also, occasionally ι and υ are used as consonants in Greek when transliterating names from other languages. They function like the English y and w respectively.

653. Chart 5: Perfect Middle and Passive Endings

In the perfect middle and passive, the ending is attached directly to the stem. If the stem ends in a consonant, the final consonant of a stem and the initial consonant of the ending will combine as indicated in the following chart:

Greek: A Survey of Basic Concepts and Applications, 2nd ed. (Grand Rapids: Baker, 1995), 25–35.

Final Consonant of Stem \ Initial Consonant of Ending	μ	σ	τ	σθ
Labials π, β, φ, (ψ)	μμ	ψ	πτ	φθ
Velars κ, γ, χ, (ξ)	γμ	ξ	κτ	χθ
Dentals τ, δ, θ, (ζ)	σμ	σ	στ	σθ
λ	λμ	λσ	λτ	λθ
ρ	ρμ	ρσ	ρτ	ρθ
ν	μμ	νσ	ντ	νθ

The perfect middle and passive third-person plural of verbs with consonantal endings use a periphrastic perfect consisting of the perfect middle and passive participle + εἰσί.

Examples: σεσωσμένοι εἰσι, *they are saved;* τὰ ὀνόματα αὐτῶν γεγράμμενά εἰσιν, *their names are written.*

The periphrastic perfect also occurs with other persons and numbers.

654. Chart 6: New Testament Proper Prepositions

There are only seventeen "proper" prepositions (which can be used as prefixes to verbs), but several of these can occur with more than one case (and different meanings), making a total of twenty-nine functional prepositions.[1]

---

1. Statistics for charts 6 and 7 are based on search results from the *Analytical Greek New Testament,* 2nd ed., by Barbara and Timothy Friberg (based on *The Greek New Testament,* 4th rev. ed. [Stuttgart: Deutsche Bibelgesellschaft, 1993]), using *Bible Windows 5.0* (Cedar Hill, Tex.: Silver Mountain Software, 1997).

Preposition	Case	Meanings (most common meaning is italicized)	Number of Occurrences
ἀνά	acc.	In NT only in certain phrases: ἀνὰ μέσον = in the midst of; ἀνὰ μέρος = in turn; and distributively = each, apiece. Also used as prep. prefix with meaning "up" or "again."	13
ἀντί	gen.	*instead of*, in place of, as, for, in exchange for, in behalf of (orig., opposite)	22
ἀπό	gen.	*from*, away from, out from (occasionally = because, with the help of)	646
διά	gen.	*through*, during, by means of, by, with	387
	acc.	*on account of*, because of, for the sake of	280
εἰς	acc.	*into*, toward, to, up to, for, on, with respect to, in (with infin. = in order to, so as to)	1767
ἐκ, ἐξ	gen.	*from, out of*, away from, by, by reason of	914
ἐν	dat.	*in*, on, near, among, in the presence of, with, by, within, by means of	2752
ἐπί	gen.	*on, upon, at*, near, before, over, on the basis of, about, in the time of	220
	dat.	*on*, in, above, upon, on the basis of, against, at, near, to, in addition to, for, in the time of	187
	acc.	*across, over, upon, to*, up to, toward, against, at	483
κατά	gen.	*down from, against*, deep into, throughout	74
	acc.	*according to*, along, over, toward, by, at, for, corresponding to	399
μετά	gen.	*with*, among	365
	acc.	*after*, behind	105

Preposition	Case	Meanings (most common meaning is italicized)	Number of Occurrences
παρά	gen.	*from,* from the side of	82
	dat.	*by* (the side of), *beside,* at, near, with, among, for	53
	acc.	along, *near,* beside, at the edge of (in comparisons = more than, beyond; the phrase παρὰ μικρόν = almost)	59
περί	gen.	*about, concerning,* on account of, for	294
	acc.	*around,* near, with, with regard to	39
πρό	gen.	*before,* in front of, for	47
πρός	gen.	to the advantage of	1
	dat.	*near,* by, at, in addition to	7
	acc.	*to, toward,* for (πρός μικρόν = for a little while), for the purpose of, with, with reference to, in accordance with	692
σύν	dat.	*with,* together with	128
ὑπέρ	gen.	*in behalf of,* for, for the sake of, about, concerning	130
	acc.	*above, over,* over and above (beyond), more than	19
ὑπό	gen.	*by* (expressing agency)	169
	acc.	*under,* below	51

655. Chart 7: New Testament Improper Prepositions

In addition to the proper prepositions there are a number of adverbs that effectively serve as prepositions and are referred to as "improper" prepositions. They do *not* occur as prepositional prefixes on verbs. With very rare exceptions, these improper prepositions occur with the genitive case only. Listed here are all the improper prepositions that occur ten or more times in the New Testament.[1]

Preposition	Case	Meaning	Number of Occurrences
ἄχρι(ς)	gen.	until	49
ἐγγύς	gen. or dat.	near, at hand	31
ἔμπροσθεν	gen.	in front of	48
ἕνεκεν/ἕνεκα	gen.	because of, on account of	26
ἐνώπιον	gen.	before, in the presence of	94
ἔξω	gen.	outside	63
ἔξωθεν	gen.	from outside	13
ἐπάνω	gen.	above, upon	19
ἕως	gen.	until, as far as	108
μέχρι	gen.	until	16
πέραν	gen.	beyond, on the other side of	23
πλήν	gen.	except	31
πλησίον	gen.	near	17
πρίν	gen.	before	13
χωρίς	gen.	apart from, without, away from, except for (occasionally occurs *after* the word it governs)	41

1. Improper prepositions are also used as *adverbs,* of course, and the number of occurrences listed may not reflect the frequency of use as *prepositions.*

656. Chart 8: Greek Numbers

In the following chart, the forms in **bold** occur in the New Testament (but this list is not exhaustive). The remaining forms have been either patterned after numbers that occur in the New Testament or drawn from the Septuagint. Classical Attic forms have been used to complete the chart of ordinals above 600; it is uncertain whether these forms were still used in the Koiné, or Hellenistic, period.

By New Testament times, the letters of the Greek alphabet also served as numerals. Often a mark was written above or beside the letter to indicate that it was to be read as a numeral. In addition to the familiar twenty-four letters of the Greek alphabet, three obsolete letters were used: stigma (ς = 6; replacing the ancient digamma [Ϝ]), koppa (ϙ = 90), and sampi (ϡ = 900). Of these twenty-seven letters, the first nine represent 1–9 (ones), the second nine 10–90 (tens), and the third nine 100–900 (hundreds). The sequence begins again at 1000. As an aid to the student, the modern Arabic equivalents appear next to the letter sign.

		Cardinal	Ordinal
1	α̅	εἷς, μία, ἕν	πρῶτος, -η, -ον
2	β̅	δύο	δεύτερος, -α, -ον
3	γ̅	τρεῖς, τρία	τρίτος, -η, -ον
4	δ̅	τέσσαρες, -α	τέταρτος, -η, -ον
5	ε̅	πέντε	πέμπτος, -η, -ον
6	ς̅	ἕξ	ἕκτος, -η, -ον
7	ζ̅	ἑπτά	ἕβδομος, -η, -ον
8	η̅	ὀκτώ	ὄγδοος, -η, -ον
9	θ̅	ἐννέα	ἔνατος, -η, -ον
10	ι̅	δέκα	δέκατος, -η, -ον
11	ι̅α̅	ἕνδεκα	ἑνδέκατος, -η, -ον
12	ι̅β̅	δώδεκα	δωδέκατος, -η, -ον

Charts

		Cardinal	**Ordinal**
13	ιγ̅	δεκατρεῖς	τρισκαιδέκατος, -η, -ον
14	ιδ̅	δεκατέσσαρες	τεσσαρεσκαιδέκατος, -η, -ον
15	ιε̅	δεκαπέντε	πεντεκαιδέκατος, -η, -ον
16	ι ϛ̅	δεκαέξ	ἑκκαιδέκατος, -η, -ον
17	ιζ̅	δεκαεπτά	ἑπτακαιδέκατος, -η, -ον
18	ιη̅	δεκαοκτώ	ὀκτωκαιδέκατος, -η, -ον
		(or δέκα καὶ ὀκτώ)	
19	ιθ̅	δεκαεννέα	ἐννεακαιδέκατος, -η, -ον
20	κ̅	εἴκοσι(ν)	εἰκοστός, -ή, -όν
23	κγ̅	εἴκοσι τρεῖς	τρίτος (-ή, -όν) καὶ εἰκοστός (-ή, -όν)
24	κδ̅	εἴκοσι τέσσαρες	τέταρτος (-ή, -όν) καὶ εἰκοστός (-ή, -όν)
25	κε̅	εἴκοσι πέντε	πέντε καὶ εἰκοστός (-ή, -όν)
30	λ̅	τριάκοντα	τριακοστός, -ή, -όν
40	μ̅	τεσσεράκοντα	τεσσερακοστός, -ή, -όν
50	ν̅	πεντήκοντα	πεντηκοστός, -ή, -όν
60	ξ̅	ἑξήκοντα	ἑξηκοστός, -ή, -όν
70	ο̅	ἑβδομήκοντα	ἑβδομηκοστός, -ή, -όν
80	π̅	ὀγδοήκοντα	ὀγδοηκοστός, -ή, -όν
90	ϙ̅	ἐνενήκοντα	ἐνενηκοστός, -ή, -όν
100	ρ̅	ἑκατόν	ἑκατοστός, -ή, -όν
200	σ̅	διακόσιοι, -αι, -α	διακοσιοστός, -ή, -όν
300	τ̅	τριακόσιοι, -αι, -α	τριακοσιοστός, -ή, -όν
400	υ̅	τετρακόσιοι, -αι, -α	τετρακοσιοστός, -ή, -όν
500	φ̅	πεντακόσιοι, -αι, -α	πεντακοσιοστός, -ή, -όν
600	χ̅	ἑξακόσιοι, -αι, -α	ἑξακοσιοστός, -ή, -όν
700	ψ̅	ἑπτακόσιοι, -αι, -α	ἑπτακοσιοστός, -ή, -όν
800	ω̅	ὀκτακόσιοι, -αι, -α	ὀκτακοσιοστός, -ή, -όν
900	ϡ̅	ἐνακόσιοι, -αι, -α	ἐνακοσιοστός, -ή, -όν
1,000	͵α	χίλιοι, -αι, -α	χιλιοστός, -ή, -όν
2,000	͵β	δισχίλιοι, -αι, -α	δισχιλιοστός, -ή, -όν

328

		Cardinal	Ordinal
3,000	͵γ	τρισχίλιοι, -αι, -α	τρισχιλιοστός, -ή, -όν
4,000	͵δ	τετρακισχίλιοι, -αι, -α	τετραχιλιοστός, -ή, -όν
5,000	͵ε	πεντακισχίλιοι, -αι, -α (or χιλιάδες πέντε)	πενταχιλιοστός, -ή, -όν
7,000	͵ζ	ἑπτακισχίλιοι, -αι, -α (or χιλιάδες ἑπτά)	ἑπταχιλιοστός, -ή, -όν
10,000	͵ι or M̄^α*	μύριοι, -αι, -α (or δέκα χιλιάδες)	μυριοστός, -ή, -όν
20,000	͵κ or M̄^β*	εἴκοσι χιλιάδες (or δισμυριάδες)	δισμυριοστός, -ή, -όν
50,000	͵ν or M̄^ε*	μυριάδες πέντε	πεντακισμυριοστός, -ή, -όν
100,000	͵ρ or M̄^ι*	μυριάδες δέκα	δεκακισμυριοστός, -ή, -όν

*For multiples of ten thousand, M (sometimes written ΜΥ) stands not as the numeral 40 but as the abbreviation of μύριοι.

Glossary

accusative—the case of direct object, direction or destination, and specification. See also *case*.

active—see *voice*.

adjective—a word that modifies a noun or other substantive. That is, it either provides more description of the noun in question (a descriptive adjective) or narrows the field of entities represented by that noun (a limiting adjective). Thus *the red book* is more specific than just *the book*, and it provides more information about the book. The adjective *red* has modified the word *book*.

Adjectives function in sentences either as *attributive* adjectives, which in English precede the noun they modify, or as *predicate* adjectives, which in English follow a linking verb, usually a form of *is* or *becomes*. See also *predicate*.

- *Interrogative adjectives* ask the question *which?* In Greek the role of interrogative adjective is covered by the interrogative pronoun.
- *Possessive adjectives* indicate that the noun modified is owned by the person or thing represented by that adjective. They function like possessive pronouns in English, but they must agree in gender, number, and case with the noun that they modify.

- *Comparative adjectives* are the "more" adjectives. The comparative adjective of *fast* is *faster* (i.e., *more fast*).
- *Superlative adjectives* are the "most" adjectives. The superlative adjective of *fast* is *fastest* (i.e., *most fast*).

adverb—adverbs modify verbs, adjectives, other adverbs, or whole clauses. They indicate some circumstance regarding the word they modify, such as manner (he has been acting *strangely*), time (she has not made progress *lately*), location (it was cold *outside*), or intensity (they were *very* upset). Most English adverbs are formed from adjectives by adding *-ly* to the end. Many Greek adverbs end with -ως.

- Interrogative adverbs ask the questions *when? where? how?* or *why?*

agreement—grammatical concurrence that indicates that certain elements of a sentence are related. Adjectives in Greek must agree in gender, number, and case with the nouns they modify, and the subject and verb of a clause must agree in number and person. A pronoun agrees in gender and number with the word it stands for, but its case is determined by its function in a clause. Agreement does *not* mean that the endings look the same—it means that the gender, case, number, or person represented by the ending of one word concurs with the gender, case, number, or person represented by the ending of the other.

anarthrous—having no article.

antecedent—the noun (or other substantive) to which a pronoun refers. See also *light antecedent*.

antepenult—the third from the last syllable.

aorist—the tense that "indicates nothing" about the *aspect* or viewpoint of the action of a verb. In the indicative mood, the aorist tense is used for simple past actions.

apodosis—the clause in a conditional sentence that expresses that which results if the condition is true. It is the *then* clause of an *if . . . then* sentence. See also *protasis.*

article—a word attached to a noun or other substantive indicating generality (indefinite article) or specificity (definite article). Greek has only a definite article, roughly equivalent to the English word *the.*

aspect—the property of a verb that indicates the speaker or author's viewpoint on that verb's kind of action: progressive, perfective, or neither of these. See also *tense.*

attraction—the tendency of a relative pronoun to adopt the case of its antecedent particularly if the antecedent is genitive or dative.

attributive—an adjective or adjectival clause that is so closely attached to the substantive it modifies as to share in the substantive's function in the sentence.

attributive position—the position that denotes an attributive function of an adjective, either (1) between an article and its noun or (2) following its noun but preceded by its own article.

augment—a verbal prefix used in the indicative mood to indicate past action.

basal stem—see *stem.*

breathing—a mark placed over an initial vowel, diphthong, or ρ that indicates whether or not an *h* sound introduces its voicing.
- *Rough breathing,* indicated by ( ) over the vowel, results in an *h* sound preceding the vowel.
- *Smooth breathing,* indicated by ( ) over the vowel, is not pronounced.

case—the property of a substantive that indicates its function in a sentence. The four major cases in Greek are the *nom-*

inative (serving as subject or predicate), the *genitive* (denoting possession, source, separation, and certain other functions), *dative* (for indirect object, means, location, and certain other functions), and *accusative* (for direct objects, destination, specification, quantity, and certain other functions). There is also a *vocative* case, usually like the nominative in form, used to address people or objects.

clause—a unit within a sentence that contains at least a subject and a verb. Independent clauses can exist as complete sentences, since they express complete thoughts in and of themselves. Dependent, or subordinate, clauses do not express complete thoughts, and are introduced by subordinating conjunctions or relative pronouns.

comparative—see under *adjective*.

compound sibilant—see *sibilant*.

compound verb—a verb with a prepositional prefix.

conjugation—(1) the laying out of the various forms (the morphology) of a verb. The conjugation of a particular tense, voice, and mood of a particular verb means the spelling out of the first, second, and third persons, both singulars and plurals, of that tense, voice, and mood of the verb in question. The complete conjugation spells out every possible form in every tense, voice, and mood. A complete conjugation of λύω is presented in §631; (2) a class of verbs that share a common morphology. Greek has two conjugations: the nonthematic (μι) verbs, and the thematic (like λύω).

conjunction—a joining word that connects words, phrases, or clauses.

- *Coordinating conjunctions* (*and, but, or*) join two words or phrases of the same type.
- *Subordinating conjunctions* attach a clause that cannot stand by itself to the main (independent) clause

of a sentence. Though Greek, like English, has several subordinating conjunctions, they are not used quite as often, because English clauses with subordinating conjunctions (*while, when, after, since, because, as*) are often represented in Greek by participial phrases.

consonant—a letter that is not a vowel. Consonants mark the boundaries of syllables, whereas vowels (or diphthongs) constitute their centers.

contraction—the combining of two letters or diphthongs into one.

copula—a word that equates or directly connects two elements of a sentence. Verbal copulas include *is* and *becomes;* adverbial copulas include *as* and *even.* Sometimes conjunctions are called copulas.

dative—the case of indirect object, location, and instrumentality (means). See also *case.*

declension—(1) the laying out of the various forms (the morphology) of a noun or adjective; (2) a classification of a set of nouns and adjectives according to their morphological patterns. Greek has three declensions: the first or "a" declension (for nouns and adjectives that have α or η endings), the second or "o" declension (for nouns that have ο or ω endings), and the third declension, which includes everything else.

definite—in grammar, refers to a word that indicates the specificity of a noun. The *definite article* is the word that marks out a noun or other substantive as being specific—a particular instance of the noun is in view. Since proper nouns (names of people and places) are definite, they often have a definite article in Greek (as opposed to English).

deliberative—asking a question that expects a command as an answer.

demonstrative—a pointing pronoun (*this, that, these, those*). See also *pronoun*.

dental—a consonant formed with the tongue touching the back or bottom of the upper teeth. The dental consonants in Greek are τ, δ, θ, ν, and the compound sibilant ζ.

dependent—see *clause*.

deponent—a type of verb in Greek that occurs not in the active voice but only in the middle or passive, with an essentially active meaning.

diphthong—a combination of vowels that is pronounced as a single vowel sound, and constitutes the center of a single syllable.

direct object—the noun or substantive that is acted on or accomplished by the action of an active voice transitive verb.

discourse—narration of another person's speech. *Direct discourse* is quotation, where the actual words purported to be spoken by the person are recorded; *indirect discourse* simply relates the content of the reported speech.

elision—the omission of a final or initial sound in pronunciation. Its most common occurrence in New Testament Greek is the dropping of the final vowel of a preposition when the following word begins with a vowel.

enclitic—a word without its own accent, closely linked to the preceding word and affecting its accentuation. Compare *proclitic*.

finite verb—any verb describing a particular action, as opposed to action considered in the abstract (an infinitive).

fricative—a consonant whose sound is made by forcing air through a partially closed passage. The fricatives in Greek are φ, θ, and χ.

full stop—(1) a consonant that entirely closes off the passage of air. The voiced full stops in Greek are β, γ, and δ; the unvoiced full stops are κ, π, and τ; (2) a punctuation mark that concludes a sentence: a period, question mark, or exclamation point.

gender—a characteristic of nouns and adjectives. Nouns have a set gender; adjectives (including participles) agree in gender (as well as case and number) with the nouns they modify. There are three genders in Greek: masculine, feminine, and neuter. The gender of a noun has almost nothing to do with sex. Though men, and the jobs done mostly by men, are masculine gender, and women and their jobs are feminine, the gender of most nouns is fairly unpredictable. Material objects are often masculine or feminine, and occasionally nouns referring to people are neuter.

genitive—the case of possession, source, separation, and other relationships. See also *case*.

idiom—a way of saying something that is characteristic of or unique to the language in which it is said.

imperative—the mood of commanded action. See also *mood*.

imperfect—the past progressive tense of the indicative mood.

indefinite—see *pronoun*.

indicative—the mood of reality or certainty. See also *mood*.

indirect object—the indirect recipient or beneficiary of an action. This only occurs with certain verbs, such as those of giving, sending, and saying (I sent *him* a gift).

infinitive—a verb that has been turned into a substantive (noun). That is, the action of the verb is taken as a thing, an abstraction. English infinitives are preceded by *to*, as *to see, to go.* As a noun, an infinitive can have adjective modifiers, and it may function the way a noun does; but as a verb, it can itself take a direct object and have adverbial modifiers and subordinate clauses. In Greek an infinitive can also be the object of a preposition. Greek infinitives may have a "subject" of the infinitive's action, though this is not a true subject, and is in the accusative, not the nominative case (see §§328, 330, 559).

inflection—the addition of prefixes and/or suffixes to a word stem to indicate grammatical features such as tense, voice, mood, person, gender, number, or case.

- *Uninflected forms* are word stems without grammatically defining prefixes and suffixes.

interjection—a word unrelated to other elements of the sentence, used for emotive effect.

interrogative—asking a question. Interrogative pronouns ask *who? what? whose?* or *which?* Interrogative adverbs ask *where? when? why?* or *how?* See also under *adjective.*

intransitive—not capable of taking a direct object.

labial—a consonant formed with the lips. The labial consonants in Greek are π, β, φ, μ, and the compound sibilant ψ.

leading verb—the verb or verbal form upon which a participle depends.

lexical form—The form of a word found at the head of an entry in a lexicon (dictionary). In English the lexical form is the infinitive; in Greek it is the first-person singular of the present active (or middle or passive in case of deponents) indicative.

light antecedent—an indefinite word that simply marks the slot in a sentence to be occupied by an infinitive, relative, participial, or other clause used substantively. In

English, the words *one, there, it, those, that, he, she,* and *they* may serve as light antecedents. In the sentence *it is important to remember that there are those who have not eaten,* the word *it* is the light antecedent for the infinitive *to remember* (the subject of *is important*), the word *there* is a light antecedent for *those who have not eaten* (the subject of *are*), and the word *those* is a light antecedent for *who* (the subject of *have not eaten*). Greek does not use light antecedents, but when translating into English they are often stylistically necessary.

linking verb—an equative verb such as *is* or *becomes* that connects a predicate to a subject.

liquid—refers to consonants that are voiced (vocal cords vibrating) but not stopped. In Greek the liquids are λ, μ, ν, and ρ. *Liquid verbs* are verbs whose stem ends in a liquid consonant.

middle—see *voice.*

modifier—a word that describes or limits another word. Modifiers include *adjectives* and *adverbs.*

monosyllabic—consisting of only one syllable.

mood—the characteristic of a verb that indicates the relation of the verb to reality. *Indicative* mood indicates reality or certainty, *subjunctive* mood indicates probability or potentiality, *imperative* mood indicates commanded action, and the rare *optative* mood expresses improbability or wish. Sometimes *participle* and *infinitive* are also regarded as moods.

morphology—a description of the way words change or are formed in different contexts or for different functions.

nominative—the case of the subject of the sentence, the predicate, or of a noun without a sentence function. See also *case.*

noun—a word that refers to a person, place, thing, or idea. *Proper* nouns are capitalized in Greek as well as English and refer to names of people, places, institutions, titles, etc. that are unique identifiers.

number—a characteristic of all substantives and verbs that indicates whether the word involves one thing or person or more than one. Though older Greek had traces of a *dual* number, in New Testament Greek, as in English, there are only *singular* and *plural*.

object—the noun or other substantive that is acted upon. The *direct object* is the person or thing affected or accomplished by the action of an active-voice transitive verb. The *object of a preposition* is the receiving noun of the relationship expressed by the preposition (comes after the preposition). The *indirect object* is the personal recipient or beneficiary or indirect target of the action of certain transitive verbs, such as those of giving, sending, saying, and showing.

paradigm—the laying out of the morphology of a word as an example of the morphology of all words of the same class.

parsing—the complete identification of a verb or verbal form. Finite verbs are identified according to their tense, voice, mood, person, number, and lexical form. A participle is identified by tense, voice, the fact that it is a participle, gender, number, case, and lexical form. Infinitives, of course, have no person, and are always neuter singular, so they are parsed simply by identifying tense, voice, the fact that they are infinitives, and the lexical form.

participle—a verb that has been turned into an adjective. That is, it is a verb form that describes or limits some other word in the sentence. As an adjective, a participle may modify a substantive (noun), in which case it must agree in gender, number, and case with the word it modifies, and is termed an *attributive* participle. Or it can stand on its own as a substantive adjective, usually with an article in front of it. Participles can also serve adverbially, modifying a verb or adjective, adverb, infinitive, or another participle. In this case they are in *predicate* position and are called *circumstantial participles*.

passive—see *voice*.

penult—the next to the last syllable.

perfect—the verbal aspect indicating a state of affairs resultant upon a completed action.

periphrastic tense—a construction using an auxiliary verb and a participle in place of a finite verb. In Greek the auxiliary verb is always a form of εἰμί.

person—the property of a verb that denotes whether the speaker or speakers (first person), the person or persons spoken to (second person), or some other person(s) or thing(s) (third person) is the subject of that verb.

phrase—a group of words functioning as a unit within a sentence but lacking either a subject or a predicate or both.

pluperfect—the past tense of the perfect system.

possessive—see under *adjective* and under *pronoun*.

predicate—generally, the verbal element of a sentence that includes the verb, its objects, and the phrases governed by the verb. It is also used in the more narrow sense of a noun or adjective that is stated to be a characteristic or an equivalent of the subject by the use of a linking verb such as *is* or *becomes*. That is, it describes the subject of the sentence, where that description is all that the sentence accomplishes (the grass is *green*). *Predicate posi-*

tion refers to the position of an adjective that implies a predication (the verb *is*), or the position of a participle or phrase that implies an adverbial function (as opposed to adjectival).

prefix—a letter or letters attached to the front of a word.

preposition—a word that indicates a relationship between nouns, pronouns, or other substantives. *Proper* prepositions are very few in number, and may be prefixed to verbs; *improper* prepositions are really adverbs serving as prepositions.

prepositional prefix—a preposition attached to the beginning of a verb that narrows the direction or focus of the verb.

present tense—the simple form of the progressive tense in the indicative mood, used to indicate action presently occurring or customary action.

primary tenses—all the tenses that are not past in time. Primary tenses are characterized by primary endings.

proclitic—a word so closely linked to the word following it that it does not have its own accent.

progressive—the aspect of a verb that denotes continuing, repeated, or customary action. In the indicative mood, the simple progressive form usually indicates present time action. The past progressive is the imperfect tense. See also *aspect* and *tense*.

pronoun—a word that stands in place of a noun or other substantive.

- *Demonstrative pronouns* are pointers (*this, that, these, those*).
- *Indefinite pronouns* stand for people or things but without specifying which ones (*anyone, someone, some, a certain person, some things*).

- *Intensive pronouns* are third-person personal pronouns used to intensify whatever nouns or pronouns or understood pronouns they agree with (*I myself, you yourself, she herself, we ourselves,* etc.).
- *Interrogative pronouns* introduce questions (*who? what?*). See also *interrogative*.
- *Personal pronouns* refer to specific people or things (*we, her, them, you, it,* etc.).
- *Possessive pronouns* in English (*my, your, his, her, its,* etc.) are represented in Greek either by the genitive case of the personal pronouns or by the possessive adjectives.
- *Reciprocal pronouns* are similar to reflexive pronouns, but a reciprocal pronoun represents not the subject itself, but the constituent individuals of the subject (*one another, each other, for each other, of each other*). Like reflexive pronouns, they do not occur in the nominative (or vocative) case.
- *Reflexive pronouns* are pronouns that are not themselves the subject of a clause but that refer back to the subject (*myself, yourself, herself, ourselves,* etc.). Thus they do not occur in the nominative (or vocative) case. These should be distinguished from the intensive pronouns, although they are translated similarly.
- *Relative pronouns* introduce relative clauses that are usually adjectival (*who, which, that*). They subordinate one clause to another, connecting it to a substantive or understood substantive in the main clause as a modifier of that substantive.

protasis—the clause in a conditional sentence that sets forth the condition. It is the *if* clause in an *if-then* sentence. See also *apodosis*.

reduplication—the repeating of an initial consonant or lengthening of an initial vowel that characterizes the perfect system, and in the case of -μι verbs, the progressive system.

reflexive—referring back to the subject. See also under *pronoun*.

relative clause—a subordinate clause, introduced by a relative pronoun, adjective, or adverb, which modifies a word, phrase, or another clause.

secondary tenses—all the tenses of the indicative mood that are past in time. They are characterized by (1) an augment and (2) secondary endings.

semantic—having to do with meaning.

sentence—a group of words expressing a complete thought. At a minimum, a sentence must have a subject and a verb, though one of these might be understood, as in the case of the imperative "Stop!" which means "You must stop."

sibilant—a consonant producing a hissing sound. Greek has one pure sibilant, the letter σ, and three compound sibilants, ζ, ξ, and ψ.

stem—the part of a verb within a particular tense or system that remains the same throughout that system and to which are added the prefixes and suffixes that specify time (in the indicative mood), person, number, voice, and mood. The *basal stem* is the entirely uninflected core of a verb (e.g., λυ-).

stop—see *full stop*.

subject—the main noun or substantive of a sentence or clause, which performs the action of the verb (or is acted upon, if the verb is passive).

subjunctive—the mood of probability or potentiality. See also *mood*.

substantive—any word or group of words that functions as a noun. All nouns and infinitives are substantives; but in Greek, adjectives, adjective clauses, prepositional phrases, adverbs, and even whole sentences can be treated as substantives, usually by putting the definite article in front of the word or phrase.

suffix—a letter or group of letters attached to the end of a word.

superlative—see under *adjective.*

syllable—a pronunciation unit of a word, with a vowel or diphthong at its center.

system—the set of all forms of a verb that are formed from the same stem or principal part. For example, the present and imperfect indicative of a verb, with its progressive participles, infinitives, subjunctives, imperatives, and optatives in all voices, make up that verb's progressive system.

tense—the property of a verb that indicates *aspect* (way of viewing the action) and, in the indicative mood, *time* of the action. In Greek, tense primarily reflects a perspective on the action that the speaker or writer wishes to convey. The three tense systems in Greek are the *progressive* (denoting the aspect of continuing, customary, or repeated action), *perfect* (denoting a state of affairs that results from a completed action), and *aorist* (which does not reflect any particular view of the action). In the indicative mood (but not in other moods) tense refers to time of action as well as aspect. The indicative mood therefore has two subtenses in the progressive system, the *present* and the *imperfect,* and two subtenses in the perfect system, the *perfect* and the *pluperfect.* There is also a *future* tense (mostly in the indicative mood).

tense formant—the letter affixed to certain verb stems that characterizes a particular tense.

thematic—refers to verbs that have a theme vowel connecting the stem of a verb to the personal, participial, or infinitival ending. The μι verbs are nonthematic verbs; all others are thematic, although the perfect middle and passive of all verbs are nonthematic.

transitive—capable of taking a direct object.

ultima—the final syllable of a word.

uninflected forms—see under *inflection*.

velar—a consonant made by touching the middle or back of the roof of the mouth (the velum) with the middle or back of the tongue. The velar consonants in Greek are κ, γ, χ, and the compound sibilant ξ. (The original edition of Machen referred to these as *palatal* consonants.)

verb—a word that indicates action or state. Every sentence must have a verb, although sometimes the verb can be implied, or understood.

- *Intransitive verbs* cannot have a direct object.
- *Transitive verbs* take direct objects when in the active voice. Only transitive verbs can form the passive in addition to the active voice. Since English verbs in the passive voice cannot take objects, all English passive verbs are intransitive. In Greek, however, certain passive forms that are deponent may rarely take an object.

vocative—the case used for direct address. See also *case*.

voice—the characteristic of a verb that indicates whether the subject is doing the action (*active* voice), being acted upon (*passive* voice), or, in Greek, doing an action that somehow results in the subject also being acted upon (*middle* voice).

voiced consonant—a consonant pronounced by vibrating the vocal cords while producing the consonant. In Greek the voiced consonants are the full stops β, γ, δ, the compound sibilant ζ, and the liquids λ, μ, ν, and ρ.

vowel—a letter pronounced with the mouth open and the vocal cords vibrating.

- *Closed vowels* are pronounced with the mouth mostly closed: ι, υ.
- *Open vowels* are pronounced with the mouth mostly open: α, ε, ο, η, ω.

Greek-English Vocabulary

The enclosing of a verb form in parentheses indicates that no part of the tense system indicated by that form occurs in the New Testament. The numerals refer to sections.

ἀγαθός, -ή, -όν, adj., 62, 609, *good*
ἀγαπάω, ἀγαπήσω, ἠγάπησα, ἠγάπηκα, ἠγάπημαι, ἠγαπήθην, 339, *I love*
ἀγάπη, ἡ, *love*
ἀγαπητός, -ή, -όν, adj., *beloved*
ἄγγελος, ὁ, *a messenger, an angel*
ἁγιάζω, (ἁγιάσω), ἡγίασα, (ἡγίακα), ἡγίασμαι, ἡγιάσθην, *I sanctify, I consecrate, I make/keep holy*
ἅγιος, -α, -ον, adj., *holy*
ἀγρός, ὁ, *a field*
ἄγω, ἄξω, ἤγαγον, (ἦχα), ἦγμαι, ἤχθην, *I lead*
ἀδελφός, ὁ, *a brother*
αἷμα, αἵματος, τό, *blood*
αἴρω, ἀρῶ, ἦρα, ἦρκα, ἦρμαι, ἤρθην, *I take up, I take away*
αἰτέω, αἰτήσω, ᾔτησα, ᾔτηκα, (ᾔτημαι), ᾐτήθην, *I ask* (in the sense of request), *I ask for*
αἰών, αἰῶνος, ὁ, *an age*
αἰώνιος, -ον, adj., 509, *eternal*
ἀκήκοα, 2nd perf. of ἀκούω

ἀκολουθέω, ἀκολουθήσω, ἠκολούθησα, ἠκολούθηκα, *I follow* (takes the dative)

ἀκούω, ἀκούσω, ἤκουσα, ἀκήκοα, (ἤκουσμαι), ἠκούσθην, *I hear* (takes the genitive or the accusative)

ἀλήθεια, ἡ, 58, 596, *truth*

ἀληθής, -ές, adj., 389–91, 613, *true*

ἀλλά, conj., *but* (a stronger adversative than δέ)

ἀλλήλων, -οις, -ους, reciprocal pron., 371, *of each other, of one another*

ἄλλος, -η, -ο, *other, another*

ἁμαρτάνω, ἁμαρτήσω, ἡμάρτησα or ἥμαρτον, ἡμάρτηκα, (ἡμάρτημαι), (ἡμαρτήθην), *I sin*

ἁμαρτία, ἡ, *a sin, sin*

ἁμαρτωλός, ὁ, *a sinner*

ἄν, a particle that cannot be translated separately into English, 427, 577, 591

ἀναβαίνω, *I go up.* See βαίνω for principal parts.

ἀναβλέπω, *I look up, I receive my sight.* See βλέπω for principal parts.

ἀναλαμβάνω, *I take up.* See λαμβάνω for principal parts.

ἀνεῳχθῆναι, aor. pass. infin. of ἀνοίγω

ἀνήρ, ἀνδρός, ὁ, 606, *a man* (as distinguished from women and children)

ἄνθρωπος, ὁ, 598, *a man* (as distinguished from other beings), *a human being*

ἀνίστημι, *I cause to rise;* in the intransitive tenses and in the middle, *I stand up, I arise.* See ἵστημι for explanation and for principal parts.

ἀνοίγω, ἀνοίξω, ἀνέῳξα or ἤνοιξα or ἠνέῳξα, ἀνέῳγα, ἀνέῳγμαι or ἠνέῳγμαι or ἤνοιγμαι, ἀνεῴχθην or ἠνοίχθην or ἠνεῴχθην, *I open*

ἀντί, prep. with gen., *instead of, for, in exchange for*

ἀπέθανον, 2nd aor. of ἀποθνήσκω

ἀπέρχομαι, *I go away, I depart*. See ἔρχομαι for principal parts.

ἀπέστειλα, aor. of ἀποστέλλω

ἀπό, prep. with gen., *from*

ἀποδίδωμι, *I give back, I give what is owed* or *promised, I pay*. See δίδωμι for principal parts.

ἀποθνήσκω, ἀποθανοῦμαι, ἀπέθανον, *I die*

ἀποκρίνομαι, (ἀποκρινοῦμαι), ἀπεκρινάμην, (ἀποκέκριμαι), ἀπεκρίθην, dep. with passive forms and rarely with middle forms, *I answer* (takes the dative)

ἀποκτείνω, ἀποκτενῶ, ἀπέκτεινα, aor. pass. ἀπεκτάνθην, *I kill*

ἀπόλλυμι or ἀπολλύω, ἀπολέσω or ἀπολῶ, ἀπώλεσα, ἀπόλωλα, 2nd aor. mid. ἀπωλόμην, 583, *I destroy;* middle, *I perish*

ἀπολύω, *I release, I dismiss*. See λύω for principal parts.

ἀποστέλλω, ἀποστελῶ, ἀπέστειλα, ἀπέσταλκα, ἀπέσταλμαι, ἀπεστάλην, *I send* (with a commission)

ἀπόστολος, ὁ, *an apostle*

ἄρα, *then, therefore*

ἄρτος, ὁ, *a piece of bread, a loaf, bread*

ἀρχή, ἡ, *a beginning*

ἀρχιερεύς, ἀρχιερέως, ὁ, *a chief priest, a high priest*

ἄρχω, ἄρξω, ἦρξα, *I rule* (takes the genitive); middle, 373 (footnote), *I begin*

ἄρχων, ἄρχοντος, ὁ, 220, 600, *a ruler*

ἀρῶ, fut. of αἴρω

ἀσπάζομαι, *I greet, I salute*

αὐτός, -ή, -ό, 97, 109, 623, pron., *himself, herself, itself, same;* personal pron., *he, she, it*

ἀφίημι, ἀφήσω, ἀφῆκα, ——, ἀφέωμαι, ἀφέθην, 556–58, *I let go, I leave, I permit; I forgive* (with the accusative of the sin or debt forgiven and the dative of the person forgiven)

ἄχρι(ς), prep. with gen., 591, *up to, as far as, until*. As a conj., *until*

βαίνω, βήσομαι, ἔβην, βέβηκα, 168, 564, *I go* (occurs in the New Testament only in composition)

βάλλω, βαλῶ, ἔβαλον, βέβληκα, βέβλημαι, ἐβλήθην, *I throw, I cast, I put*

βαπτίζω, βαπτίσω, ἐβάπτισα, (βεβάπτικα), βεβάπτισμαι, ἐβαπτίσθην, *I baptize*

βασιλεία, ἡ, *a kingdom*

βασιλεύς, βασιλέως, ὁ, 383–85, 605, *a king*

βήσομαι, fut. of βαίνω

βιβλίον, τό, *a book*

βλέπω, βλέψω, ἔβλεψα, *I see.* (βλέπω is the common word for *I see* in the present and imperfect. In the other tenses the principal parts given under ὁράω are commonly used.)

Γαλιλαία, ἡ, *Galilee*

γάρ, conj., postpositive, *for*

γέγονα, 2nd perf. of γίνομαι

γενήσομαι, fut. of γίνομαι

γεννάω, γεννήσω, ἐγέννησα, γεγέννηκα, γεγέννημαι, ἐγεννήθην, *I beget, I become the parent of;* also of the mother, *I bear*

γένος, γένους, τό, 380–82, 603, *a race, a kind*

γῆ, ἡ, 430, *earth, a land*

γίνομαι, γενήσομαι, ἐγενόμην, γέγονα, γεγένημαι, ἐγενήθην, 453 (footnote), 578–79, 592, *I become, I come into being, I appear in history, I am;* γίνεται, *it comes to pass, it happens*

γινώσκω, γνώσομαι, ἔγνων, ἔγνωκα, ἔγνωσμαι, ἐγνώσθην, 542–43, 643, *I know*

γλῶσσα, ἡ, *tongue, language*

γνώσομαι, fut. of γινώσκω

γράμμα, γράμματος, τό, *a letter*

γραμματεύς, γραμματέως, ὁ, *a scribe*

γραφή, ἡ, 54–55, 59, 596, *a writing, a Scripture;* αἱ γραφαί, *the Scriptures*

γράφω, γράψω, ἔγραψα, γέγραφα, γέγραμμαι, ἐγράφην, 215, 279,
I write
γυνή, γυναικός, ἡ, 607, a woman

δαιμόνιον, τό, a demon
δέ, conj., postpositive, 93–94, and, but
δεῖ, impersonal verb, 316, it is necessary
δείκνυμι or δεικνύω, δείξω, ἔδειξα, (δέδειχα), δέδειγμαι, ἐδεί-
χθην, 583, I show
δέχομαι, δέξομαι, ἐδεξάμην, δέδεγμαι, ἐδέχθην, I receive
δηλόω, δηλώσω, ἐδήλωσα, (δεδήλωκα), (δεδήλωμαι), ἐδηλώθην,
344–49, 634, I make clear, I show
διά, prep. with gen., through; with acc., on account of
διδάσκαλος, ὁ, a teacher
διδάσκω, διδάξω, ἐδίδαξα, (δεδίδαχα), (δεδίδαγμαι), ἐδιδάχθην,
I teach
δίδωμι, δώσω, ἔδωκα, δέδωκα, δέδομαι, ἐδόθην, 510–41, 638–39,
I give
διέρχομαι, I go through. See ἔρχομαι for principal parts.
δίκαιος, -α, -ον, adj., 611, righteous
δικαιοσύνη, ἡ, righteousness
διό, therefore, for this reason
διώκω, διώξω, ἐδίωξα, δεδίωκα, δεδίωγμαι, ἐδιώχθην, I pursue,
I persecute
δοκέω, (δόξω), ἔδοξα, I think, I seem
δόξα, ἡ, 52–53, 596, glory
δοξάζω, δοξάσω, ἐδόξασα, (δεδόξακα), δεδόξασμαι, ἐδοξάσθην,
I glorify
δοῦλος, ὁ, 42, 598, a slave, a servant
δύναμαι, δυνήσομαι, (δεδύνημαι), ἠδυνήθην or ἠδυνάσθην,
imperfect ἐδυνάμην or ἠδυνάμην, 564, I am able
δύναμις, δυνάμεως, ἡ, power
δύο, 400, dat. δυσί(ν), two
δῶρον, τό, 37–38, 599, a gift

ἐάν, conditional particle, with subj., 311, *if;* ἐὰν μή, 314, *unless, except*

ἐάν, particle, sometimes used with the subj. in the same way as ἄν

ἑαυτοῦ, -ῆς, -οῦ, reflexive pron., 367–69, 628, *of himself, of herself, of itself*

ἔβαλον, 2nd aor. of βάλλω

ἐβλήθην, aor. pass. of βάλλω

ἐγγίζω, ἐγγιῶ or ἐγγίσω, ἤγγισα, ἤγγικα, *I come near*

ἐγγύς, adv., *near*

ἐγείρω, ἐγερῶ, ἤγειρα, ———, ἐγήγερμαι, ἠγέρθην, *I raise up;* in passive sometimes as deponent, *I rise*

ἐγενήθην, aor. pass. (in form) of γίνομαι

ἐγενόμην, 2nd aor. of γίνομαι

ἔγνωκα, perf. of γινώσκω

ἔγνων, 2nd aor. of γινώσκω

ἐγνώσθην, aor. pass. of γινώσκω

ἐγώ, ἐμοῦ or μου, pron., 95, 623, *I*

ἐδιδάχθην, aor. pass. of διδάσκω

ἔθνος, ἔθνους, τό, *a nation;* plur., *nations, Gentiles*

εἰ, particle, 311–13, *if, whether;* εἰ μή, 314, *unless, except*

εἶδον, 2nd aor. of ὁράω (or βλέπω)

εἰμί, ἔσομαι, 622, 644, *I am*

εἶπον, 2nd aor. of λέγω (sometimes regarded as second aorist of φημί)

εἰρήνη, ἡ, *peace*

εἰς, prep. with acc., *into*

εἷς, μία, ἕν, numeral, 398, 629, *one*

εἰσέρχομαι, *I go in, I enter.* See ἔρχομαι for principal parts.

ἐκ (before vowels ἐξ), prep. with gen., *out of*

ἕκαστος, -η, -ον, *each*

ἐκβάλλω, *I throw out, I cast out*

ἐκεῖ, adv., *there*

ἐκεῖνος, -η, -ο, pron., 107–8, *that*
ἐκηρύχθην, aor. pass. of κηρύσσω
ἐκκλησία, ἡ, *a church*
ἐκπορεύομαι, *I go out*
ἔλαβον, 2nd aor. of λαμβάνω
ἐλεέω, ἐλεήσω, ἠλέησα, (ἠλέηκα), ἠλέημαι, ἠλεήθην, *I pity, I have mercy on*
ἐλεύσομαι, fut. of ἔρχομαι
ἐλήλυθα, 2nd perf. of ἔρχομαι
ἐλήμφθην, aor. pass. of λαμβάνω
ἐλπίζω, ἐλπιῶ, ἤλπισα, ἤλπικα, *I hope*
ἐλπίς, ἐλπίδος, ἡ, 220, 601, *a hope*
ἐμαυτοῦ, -ῆς, refl. pron., 365, 627, *of myself*
ἔμεινα, aor. of μένω
ἐμός, -ή, -όν, possessive adj., 499–500, *my, belonging to me*
ἔμπροσθεν, adv., *in front, before, in the presence of*
ἐν, prep. with dat., *in*
ἐντολή, ἡ, *a commandment*
ἐνώπιον, adv., *in front of, in the presence of, before*
ἐξ, form of ἐκ used before vowels
ἕξ, indeclinable, numeral, *six*
ἐξέρχομαι, *I go out, I come out.* See ἔρχομαι for principal parts.
ἔξεστι(ν), impersonal verb, 316, *it is lawful*
ἐξουσία, ἡ, *authority*
ἔξω, adv., *outside*
ἕξω, fut. of ἔχω
ἑόρακα or ἑώρακα, perf. of ὁράω
ἐπαγγελία, ἡ, *a promise*
ἔπεσον, 2nd aor. of πίπτω
ἐπερωτάω, *I ask a question of, I question, I interrogate*
ἐπί, prep. with gen., *over, on, at the time of;* with dat., *on the basis of, at;* with acc., *on, to, against*
ἐπιθυμία, ἡ, *a strong desire, lust*

353

ἐπιστρέφω, ἐπιστρέψω, ἐπέστρεψα, (ἐπέστροφα), ἐπέστραμμαι, ἐπεστράφην, *I turn to, I turn, I return*

ἐπιτίθημι, *I place upon, I put upon, I lay upon* (with acc. of the thing placed and dat. of the person or thing upon which it is placed)

ἐπλήσθην, aor. pass. of πίμπλημι

ἐργάζομαι, *I work*

ἔργον, τό, *a work*

ἔρημος, ἡ, *a desert*

ἐρρέθην or ἐρρήθην, aor. pass. of λέγω (or φημί)

ἔρχομαι, ἐλεύσομαι, ἦλθον, ἐλήλυθα, *I come, I go*

ἐρῶ, fut. of λέγω (sometimes regarded as future of φημί)

ἐρωτάω, ἐρωτήσω, ἠρώτησα, (ἠρώτηκα), (ἠρώτημαι), ἠρωτήθην, *I ask* (originally of asking a question, but in the New Testament also of asking in the sense of requesting)

ἐσθίω, φάγομαι, ἔφαγον, *I eat*

ἔσομαι, fut. of εἰμί

ἔσχατος, -η, -ον, adj., *last*

ἔσχον, 2nd aor. of ἔχω

ἕτερος, -α, -ον, 564, *other, another, different*

ἔτι, adv., *still, yet*

ἑτοιμάζω, ἑτοιμάσω, ἡτοίμασα, ἡτοίμακα, ἡτοίμασμαι, ἡτοιμάσθην, *I prepare*

ἔτος, ἔτους, τό, *a year*

ευ- Verbs beginning thus are sometimes augmented to ηυ- and sometimes not.

εὐαγγελίζω, (εὐαγγελίσω), εὐηγγέλισα, (εὐηγγέλικα), εὐηγγέλι-σμαι, εὐηγγελίσθην, in middle often deponent, *I preach the gospel, I evangelize* (with acc. of the message preached and acc. or dat. of the person to whom it is preached)

εὐαγγέλιον, τό, *a gospel*

εὐθέως, adv., *immediately, right away*

εὐθύς, adv., *immediately, right away*

εὐλογέω, εὐλογήσω, εὐλόγησα, εὐλόγηκα, εὐλόγημαι,
εὐλογήθην, *I bless*
εὑρίσκω, εὑρήσω, εὗρον, εὕρηκα, (εὕρημαι), εὑρέθην, *I find*
εὐχαριστέω, εὐχαριστήσω, εὐχαρίστησα, (εὐχαρίστηκα), (εὐ-
χαρίστημαι), εὐχαριστήθην, *I give thanks*
ἔφαγον, 2nd aor. of ἐσθίω
ἔφη, imperf. act. indic. 3rd pers. sing. of φημί
ἐχθρός, ὁ, *an enemy*
ἔχω, ἕξω, ἔσχον, ἔσχηκα, imperf. εἶχον, *I have*
ἑώρακα or ἑόρακα, perf. of ὁράω
ἕως, adv. with gen., *up to, until;* conj., 591, *while, until*

ζάω, ζήσω or ζήσομαι, ἔζησα, *I live*
ζητέω, ζητήσω, ἐζήτησα, *I seek*
ζωή, ἡ, *life*

ἤ, conj., 487, *than, or*
ἤγαγον, 2nd aor. of ἄγω
ἠγέρθην, aor. pass. of ἐγείρω
ἤδη, adv., *already*
ἤθελον, imperf. of θέλω
ἦλθον, 2nd aor. of ἔρχομαι
ἡμέρα, ἡ, *a day*
ἡμέτερος, -α, -ον, poss. adj., 499, *our, belonging to us*
ἤνεγκα or ἤνεγκον, aor. of φέρω
ἠνέχθην, aor. pass. of φέρω
ἦρα, aor. of αἴρω

θάλασσα, ἡ, *a lake, a sea*
θάνατος, ὁ, *death*
θαυμάζω, θαυμάσομαι, ἐθαύμασα, (τεθαύμακα), aor. pass.
ἐθαυμάσθην, *I wonder, I marvel, I wonder at*
θέλημα, θελήματος, τό, *a will*
θέλω, θελήσω, ἠθέλησα, imperf. ἤθελον, 393, *I wish, I am willing*

355

Greek-English Vocabulary

θεός, ὁ, *God*
θεραπεύω, θεραπεύσω, ἐθεράπευσα, (τεθεράπευκα), τεθεράπευ-
μαι, ἐθεραπεύθην, *I heal*
θεωρέω, θεωρήσω, ἐθεώρησα, *I gaze at, I stare intently at*
θλῖψις, -εως, ἡ, *tribulation*
θνήσκω, used only in perf. τέθνηκα, *I am dead,* and in pluperfect
θρόνος, ὁ, *a throne*

Ἰάκωβος, ὁ, *James*
ἴδιος, -α, -ον, adj., 501, *one's own*
ἰδού, particle, *look! behold!*
ἰδών, ἰδοῦσα, ἰδόν, 2nd aor. part. of ὁράω
ἱερεύς, ἱερέως, ὁ, *a priest*
ἱερόν, τό, *a temple* (compare ναός)
Ἰησοῦς, -οῦ, ὁ, 334, *Jesus*
ἱκανός, -ή, -όν, *sufficient, able, considerable, worthy*
ἱμάτιον, τό, *a garment*
ἵνα, conj., 309–10, 504, *in order that* (with subj.)
Ἰουδαῖος, ὁ, *a Jew*
ἵστημι, στήσω, ἔστησα, 2nd aor. ἔστην, ἔστηκα, (ἔσταμαι),
ἐστάθην, 565–75, 642–43, *I cause to stand* (in pres., imperf.,
fut., 1st aor., and in passive); *I stand* (in 2nd aor. and in perf.)
ἰσχυρότερος, -α, -ον, adj., *stronger* (comparative degree of
ἰσχυρός, -ά, -όν, *strong*)

κἀγώ = καὶ ἐγώ
καθαρός, -ά, -όν, adj., *pure, clean*
κάθημαι, dep., *I sit*
καθώς, adv., *just as*
καί, 152, *and, even, also;* καί ... καί, 154, *both ... and*
καιρός, ὁ, *a time, an appointed time*
κακός, -ή, -όν, adj., *bad, evil*
καλέω, καλέσω, ἐκάλεσα, κέκληκα, κέκλημαι, ἐκλήθην, 350, *I call*

356

καλός, -ή, -όν, adj., *good, beautiful*
καλῶς, adv., *well*
καρδία, ἡ, *a heart*
καρπός, ὁ, *a fruit*
κατά, prep. with gen., *down from, against;* with acc., *according to, throughout, during*
καταβαίνω, *I go down*
κατέρχομαι, *I come down, I go down*
κελεύω, (κελεύσω), ἐκέλευσα, *I command*
κεφαλή, ἡ, *a head*
κηρύσσω, κηρύξω, ἐκήρυξα, (κεκήρυχα), (κεκήρυγμαι), ἐκηρύχθην, *I proclaim, I preach*
κόσμος, ὁ, *a world, the world*
κράζω, *I cry out*
κρείσσων, -ον, adj., *better* (used as comparative degree of ἀγαθός)
κρίνω, κρινῶ, ἔκρινα, κέκρικα, κέκριμαι, ἐκρίθην, 356–59, 636–37, *I judge*
κρίσις, κρίσεως, ἡ, *a judgment*
κύριος, ὁ, *a lord, the Lord*
κωλύω, (κωλύσω), ἐκώλυσα, (κεκώλυκα), (κεκώλυμαι), ἐκωλύθην, *I hinder, I prevent*
κώμη, ἡ, *a village*

λαλέω, λαλήσω, ἐλάλησα, λελάληκα, λελάλημαι, ἐλαλήθην, *I speak*
λαμβάνω, λήμψομαι, ἔλαβον, εἴληφα, εἴλημμαι, ἐλήμφθην, *I take, I receive*
λαός, ὁ, *a people*
λέγω, ἐρῶ, εἶπον, εἴρηκα, εἴρημαι, ἐρρέθην or ἐρρήθην, *I say*
λείπω, λείψω, ἔλιπον, (λέλοιπα), λέλειμμαι, ἐλείφθην, 198–202, 320, 635, *I leave*
λήμψομαι, fut. of λαμβάνω

357

λίθος, ὁ, *a stone*
λόγος, ὁ, 31–32, 598, *a word*
λοιπός, -ή, -όν, adj., *remaining;* οἱ λοιποί, *the rest*
λύω, λύσω, ἔλυσα, λέλυκα, λέλυμαι, ἐλύθην, 631, 646, *I loose,
I destroy, I break*

μαθητής, ὁ, 597, *a disciple*
μακάριος, -α, -ον, adj., *blessed*
μᾶλλον, adv., *more, rather*
μαρτυρέω, μαρτυρήσω, ἐμαρτύρησα, μεμαρτύρηκα, μεμαρτύρημαι, ἐμαρτυρήθην, *I bear witness, I witness*
μαρτυρία, ἡ, *a witnessing, a witness*
μέγας, μεγάλη, μέγα, adj., 397, 616, *great*
μείζων, -ον, adj., 484–85, 612, *greater* (comparative degree of
μέγας)
μέλλω, μελλήσω, imperfect ἤμελλον or ἔμελλον, *I am about* (to
do something), *I am going* (to do something)
μέν . . . δέ, *on the one hand . . . on the other* (used in contrasts.
Often it is better to leave the μέν untranslated and translate the δέ by *but.*)
μένω, μενῶ, ἔμεινα, μεμένηκα, *I remain, I abide*
μέσος, -η, -ον, adj., *middle, in the midst*
μετά, prep. with gen., *with;* with acc., *after*
μετανοέω, μετανοήσω, μετενόησα, *I repent*
μέχρι(ς), adv., 591, *until*
μή, negative adverb, 244, 505–6, *not* (used with moods other
than the indicative)
μή, conj., 502–3, *lest, in order that not* (with the subj.)
μηδέ, *and not, nor, not even;* μηδέ . . . μηδέ, *neither . . . nor*
μηδείς, μηδεμία, μηδέν, 399, *no one, nothing*
μηκέτι, adv., *no longer*
μήποτε, *lest perhaps* (with the subj.)
μήτηρ, μητρός, ἡ, 606, *a mother*

μικρός, -ά, -όν, adj., 63, 610, *little, small*
μνημεῖον, τό, *a tomb*
μόνον, adv., *only*
μόνος, -η, -ον, adj., *alone, only*
μυστήριον, τό, *a mystery*

ναός, ὁ, *a temple* (the temple building itself, as distinguished from ἱερόν, the whole sacred precinct)
νεκρός, -ά, -όν, adj., *dead*
νόμος, ὁ, *a law, the Law*
νῦν, adv., *now*
νύξ, νυκτός, ἡ, 220, 600, *a night*

ὁ, ἡ, τό, definite article, 64–68, 608, *the*
ὁδός, ἡ, *a way, a road*
οἶδα, 2nd perf. used as present, 584–89, 645, *I know*
οἰκία, ἡ, *a house*
οἶκος, ὁ, *a house*
οἶνος, ὁ, *wine*
ὀλίγος, -η, -ον, adj., *few, little*
ὅλος, -η, -ον, adj., *whole, all*
ὅμοιος, -α, -ον, adj., *like, similar*
ὄνομα, ὀνόματος, τό, 229, 602, *a name*
ὀξύς, -εῖα, -ύ, adj., 388, 617, *sharp*
ὅπου, adv., *where* (relative)
ὅπως, conj., *in order that* (with subj.)
ὁράω, ὄψομαι, εἶδον, ἑώρακα or ἑόρακα, (ὦμμαι), ὤφθην, 2nd aor. part. ἰδών, 194 (footnote), 268–69, 271, *I see*. (In the present ὁράω is less common than βλέπω.)
ὄρος, ὄρους, τό, *a mountain*
ὅς, ἥ, ὅ, rel. pron., 422–26, 625, *who, which*
ὅσος, ὅση, ὅσον, rel. adj., *as great as, as much as, as many as*
ὅστις, ἥτις, ὅτι, indef. rel. pron., *whoever, whichever, whatever*

359

ὅταν, *whenever* (with subj.)

ὅτε, adv., *when*

ὅτι, conj., 331–32, 547 (footnote), *that, because*

οὐ (οὐκ before vowels, οὐχ before the rough breathing), adv., 125, 244, *not*

οὐδέ, conj., 153, *and not, nor, not even;* οὐδέ . . . οὐδέ, 154, *neither . . . nor*

οὐδείς, οὐδεμία, οὐδέν, 399, *no one, nothing*

οὐκ, form of οὐ used before vowels and diphthongs that have smooth breathing

οὐκέτι, adv., *no longer*

οὖν, conj., postpositive, *accordingly, therefore*

οὔπω, adv., *not yet*

οὐρανός, ὁ, *heaven*

οὖς, ὠτός, τό, *an ear*

οὔτε, conj., 559 (footnote), *and not;* οὔτε . . . οὔτε, *neither . . . nor*

οὗτος, αὕτη, τοῦτο, demonstrative pron., 106, 108, 624, *this*

οὕτως, adv., *thus, so*

οὐχ, form of οὐ used before vowels and diphthongs that have rough breathing

ὀφείλω, *I owe, I ought*

ὀφθαλμός, ὁ, *an eye*

ὄχλος, ὁ, *a crowd, a multitude*

ὄψομαι, fut. of ὁράω

παιδίον, τό, *a little child*

πάλιν, adv., *again*

παρά, prep. with gen., *from;* with dat., *beside, in the presence of;* with acc., *alongside of*

παραβολή, ἡ, *a parable*

παραγίνομαι, *I become present, I arrive, I come.* See γίνομαι for principal parts.

παραδίδωμι, *I deliver over, I hand over.* See δίδωμι for principal parts.

παρακαλέω, *I exhort, I encourage, I urge, I comfort.* See καλέω for principal parts.

παραλαμβάνω, *I receive, I take along.* See λαμβάνω for principal parts.

πᾶς, πᾶσα, πᾶν, adj., 394–96, 614, *all, every*

πάσχω, (πείσομαι), ἔπαθον, πέπονθα, *I suffer, I experience*

πατήρ, πατρός, ὁ, 606, *a father*

πείθω, πείσω, ἔπεισα, πέποιθα, πέπεισμαι, ἐπείσθην, *I persuade*

πειράζω, (πειράσω), ἐπείρασα, (πεπείρακα), πεπείρασμαι, ἐπειράσθην, *I tempt, I attempt*

πέμπω, πέμψω, ἔπεμψα, (πέπομφα), (πέπεμμαι), ἐπέμφθην, *I send*

πεντακισχίλιοι, -αι, -α, *five thousand*

πέντε, indeclinable, *five*

περί, prep. with gen., *concerning, about;* with acc., *around*

περιπατέω, περιπατήσω, περιεπάτησα, περιπεπάτηκα, *I walk*

Πέτρος, ὁ, *Peter*

πίμπλημι, (πλήσω), ἔπλησα, ———, (πέπλησμαι), ἐπλήσθην, *I fill, I fulfill*

πίνω, πίομαι, ἔπιον, πέπωκα, (πέπομαι), ἐπόθην, *I drink*

πίπτω, πεσοῦμαι, ἔπεσον or ἔπεσα, πέπτωκα, *I fall*

πιστεύω, πιστεύσω, ἐπίστευσα, πεπίστευκα, πεπίστευμαι, ἐπιστεύθην, 192, *I believe* (takes the dat.); πιστεύω εἰς with acc., *I believe in* or *on*

πίστις, πίστεως, ἡ, *faith*

πιστός, -ή, -όν, adj., *faithful*

πλείων, -ον, adj., *more* (comparative degree of πολύς)

πλῆθος, πλήθους, τό, *a multitude*

πλήρης, -ες (sometimes indeclinable), adj., *full*

πληρόω, πληρώσω, ἐπλήρωσα, πεπλήρωκα, πεπλήρωμαι, ἐπληρώθην, *I fill, I fulfill*

πλοῖον, τό, *a boat*

πνεῦμα, πνεύματος, τό, *a spirit, the Spirit*

ποιέω, ποιήσω, ἐποίησα, πεποίηκα, πεποίημαι, (ἐποιήθην), *I do, I make*

ποῖος, -α, -ον, *what sort of?*

πόλις, πόλεως, ἡ, 378–79, 604, *a city*

πολύς, πολλή, πολύ, adj., 397, 615, *much, great;* in plur., *many*

πονηρός, -ά, -όν, adj., *evil*

πορεύομαι, πορεύσομαι, ἐπορευσάμην, πεπόρευμαι, ἐπορεύθην, dep., usually with passive forms, *I go*

πότε, interrog. adv., *when?*

ποτέ, particle, enclitic, *at some time;* μήποτε, *lest perhaps*

ποῦ, interrog. adv., *where?*

πούς, ποδός, ὁ, *a foot*

πρεσβύτερος, ὁ, *an old man, an elder*

πρό, prep. with gen., *before*

πρός, prep. with acc., *to*

προσέρχομαι, *I come to, I go to* (with dat.). See ἔρχομαι for principal parts.

προσεύχομαι, προσεύξομαι, προσηυξάμην, *I pray*

προσκυνέω, προσκυνήσω, προσεκύνησα, *I worship* (usually with dat., sometimes with acc.)

προσφέρω, *I bring to* (with acc. of the thing brought and dat. of the person to whom it is brought). See φέρω for principal parts.

πρόσωπον, τό, *a face, a countenance*

προφήτης, -ου, ὁ, 81, 597, *a prophet*

πρῶτος, -η, -ον, adj., *first*

πῦρ, πυρός, τό, *a fire*

πῶς, interrog. adv., *how?*

ῥηθείς, ῥηθεῖσα, ῥηθέν, aor. pass. part. of λέγω (φημί)

ῥῆμα, ῥήματος, τό, *a word*

σάββατον, τό, (plural σάββατα, σαββάτων, σάββασι[ν], sometimes with singular meaning), *a sabbath*

σάρξ, σαρκός, ἡ, 227, 232, 600, *flesh*

σεαυτοῦ, -ῆς, reflexive pron., 366, 627, *of yourself*

σημεῖον, τό, *a sign, a miracle*

Σίμων, Σίμωνος, ὁ, *Simon*

σκότος, σκότους, τό, *darkness*

σός, -ή, -όν, possessive adj., 499, *your* (s.), *belonging to you* (s.)

σοφία, ἡ, *wisdom*

σπείρω, (σπερῶ), ἔσπειρα, (ἔσπαρκα), ἔσπαρμαι, ἐσπάρην, *I sow*

στάδιον, τό; plur., τὰ στάδια or οἱ στάδιοι, *a stadium, a furlong*

σταυρόω, σταυρώσω, ἐσταύρωσα, (ἐσταύρωκα), ἐσταύρωμαι, ἐσταυρώθην, *I crucify*

στόμα, στόματος, τό, *a mouth*

στρατιώτης, -ου, ὁ, *a soldier*

σύ, σοῦ, pron., 96, 623, *you* (s.)

σύν, prep. with dat., *with*

συνάγω, *I gather together.* See ἄγω for principal parts.

συναγωγή, ἡ, *a synagogue*

συνέρχομαι, *I come together, I go together.* See ἔρχομαι for principal parts.

σχῶ, 2nd aor. subj. of ἔχω

σώζω, σώσω, ἔσωσα, σέσωκα, σέσω(σ)μαι, ἐσώθην, *I save*

σῶμα, σώματος, τό, *a body*

σωτηρία, ἡ, *salvation*

τε, conj., *and, further;* τε . . . τε, *not only . . . but also*

τέθηνκα, perf. of θνήσκω

τέκνον, τό, *a child*

τελέω, τελέσω, ἐτέλεσα, τετέλεκα, τετέλεσμαι, ἐτελέσθην, *I finish, I complete*

τέσσαρες, τέσσαρα, 630, *four*

τηρέω, τηρήσω, ἐτήρησα, τετήρηκα, τετήρημαι, ἐτηρήθην, *I keep* τίθημι, θήσω, ἔθηκα, τέθεικα, τέθειμαι, ἐτέθην, 549–55, 640–41, *I place, I put*

τιμάω, τιμήσω, ἐτίμησα, (τετίμηκα), τετίμημαι, (ἐτιμήθην), 344–48, 632, *I value, I honor*

τίς, τί, interrog. pron., 412–14, 417–18, 626, *who? which? what?*

τις, τι, indef. pron., 415–17, 626, *someone, something, a certain one, a certain thing, anyone, anything*

τοιοῦτος, τοιαύτη, τοιοῦτο, adj., *such*

τόπος, ὁ, *a place*

τότε, adv., *then*

τρεῖς, τρία, 630, *three*

τύπος, ὁ, *a pattern, a type*

τυφλός, ὁ, *a blind man*

ὕδωρ, ὕδατος, τό, *water*

υἱός, ὁ, 43–44, 598, *a son*

ὑμέτερος, -α, -ον, possessive adj., 499, *your* (p.), *belonging to you* (p.)

ὑπάγω, *I go away, I depart*

ὑπέρ, prep. with gen., *in behalf of;* with acc., *above*

ὑπό, prep. with gen., *by* (of the agent); with acc., *under*

ὑποστρέφω, ὑποστρέψω, ὑπέστρεψα, *I return*

φαίνω, (φανῶ), ἔφανα, (πέφηνα), (πέφαμαι), ἐφάνην, *I shine;* mid., *I appear, I become visible*

φανερόω, φανερώσω, ἐφανέρωσα, (πεφανέρωκα), πεφανέρωμαι, ἐφανερώθην, *I make known, I reveal*

Φαρισαῖος, ὁ, *a Pharisee*

φέρω, οἴσω, ἤνεγκα or ἤνεγκον, ἐνήνοχα, (ἐνήνεγμαι), ἠνέχθην, *I bear, I carry, I bring*

φεύγω, φεύξομαι, ἔφυγον, *I flee*

φημί, ἐρῶ, εἶπον, εἴρηκα, εἴρημαι, ἐρρέθην or ἐρρήθην, *I say*. (The principal parts may also be regarded as belonging to λέγω, which is far more common in the present than is φημί.)

φιλέω, (φιλήσω), ἐφίλησα, πεφίληκα, (πεφίλημαι), (ἐφιλήθην), 344–48, 633, *I love*

φοβέομαι, aor. ἐφοβήθην, dep. with pass. forms, *I fear*

φυλακή, ἡ, *a guard, a prison*

φωνή, ἡ, *a voice, a sound*

φῶς, φωτός, τό, *a light*

χαίρω, χαρήσομαι, 2nd aor. pass. ἐχάρην, *I rejoice*

χαρά, ἡ, *joy*

χάρις, χάριτος, ἡ, 376–77, 601, *grace*

χείρ, χειρός, ἡ, 607, *a hand*

χρεία, ἡ, *a need*

Χριστός, ὁ, *Messiah, Christ*

χρόνος, ὁ, *a period of time, time*

χώρα, ἡ, *a country, a region*

χωρίς, adv. with gen., *apart from*

ψυχή, ἡ, *a life, a soul*

ὧδε, adv., *hither, here*

ὤν, οὖσα, ὄν, pres. part. of εἰμί

ὥρα, ἡ, 49–51, 56–57, 596, *an hour*

ὡς, adv. and conj., *as* (with numerals, *about*)

ὥσπερ, 559 (footnote), *just as*

ὥστε, 559, *so that* (often followed by acc. and infin.)

ὤφθην, aor. pass. of ὁράω

English-Greek Vocabulary

For clarity and ease of use, this vocabulary gives the Greek words in their simplest form. Principal parts, gender, declension, and related information are provided in the Greek-English vocabulary.

a certain one, τις; a certain thing, neuter of τις
abide, μένω
able, ἱκανός
able, am, δύναμαι
about, περί with gen.
about (with numerals), ὡς
above, ὑπέρ with acc.
according to, κατά with acc.
accordingly, οὖν
after, μετά with acc.
again, πάλιν
against, ἐπί with acc., κατά with gen.
age, αἰών
all, πᾶς, ὅλος
alongside of, παρά with acc.
already, ἤδη
also, καί

am, εἰμί, γίνομαι
am able, δύναμαι
am about (to do something), μέλλω
am going (to do something), μέλλω
am willing, θέλω
and, καί, δέ, τε
and not, οὐδέ, οὔτε, μηδέ
angel, ἄγγελος
another, ἄλλος, ἕτερος
answer (verb), ἀποκρίνομαι
anyone, τις
anything, neut. of τις
apart from, χωρίς
apostle, ἀπόστολος
appear, middle of φαίνω
appear in history, γίνομαι
around, περί with acc.

arrive, παραγίνομαι
as, ὡς
as far as, ἄχρι(ς) with gen.
as great as, as much as, as
    many as, ὅσος
ask (a question), ἐρωτάω
ask (request), αἰτέω, ἐρωτάω
ask a question of, ἐπερωτάω
at, ἐπί with dat.
at some time, ποτέ
at the time of, ἐπί with gen.
authority, ἐξουσία

bad, κακός
baptize, βαπτίζω
be, εἰμί
bear (verb), φέρω; of a
    mother, γεννάω
bear witness, μαρτυρέω
beautiful, καλός
because, ὅτι
become, γίνομαι
become present, παραγίνομαι
become the parent of, γεν-
    νάω
become visible, middle of
    φαίνω
before, πρό with gen.
beget, γεννάω
begin, middle of ἄρχω
beginning, ἀρχή
behold! (particle), ἰδού
believe, πιστεύω

beloved, ἀγαπητός
beside, παρά with dat.
better, κρείσσων/κρείττων
bless, εὐλογέω
blessed, μακάριος
blind man, τυφλός
blood, αἷμα
boat, πλοῖον
body, σῶμα
book, βιβλίον
both . . . and, καί . . . καί
bread, ἄρτος
break, λύω
bring, φέρω
bring to, προσφέρω
brother, ἀδελφός
but, ἀλλά, δέ
by (of the agent), ὑπό with
    gen.
by means of, expressed by
    the simple dat.
by the side of, παρά with dat.

call, καλέω
carry, φέρω
cast, βάλλω
cast out, ἐκβάλλω
cause to rise, ἀνίστημι (in
    the transitive tenses)
cause to stand, ἵστημι (in
    the transitive tenses)
chief priest, ἀρχιερεύς

child, τέκνον; little child,
παιδίον
Christ, Χριστός
church, ἐκκλησία
city, πόλις
clean, καθαρός
clear, make, δηλόω
come, ἔρχομαι
come down, κατέρχομαι
come into being, γίνομαι
come near, ἐγγίζω
come out, ἐξέρχομαι
come to, προσέρχομαι
come to pass, γίνομαι
come together, συνέρχομαι
comfort (verb), παρακαλέω
command, κελεύω
commandment, ἐντολή
complete (verb), τελέω
concerning, περί with gen.
consecrate, ἁγιάζω
considerable, ἱκανός
countenance, πρόσωπον
country, χώρα
crowd, ὄχλος
crucify, σταυρόω
cry out, κράζω

darkness, σκότος
day, ἡμέρα
dead, νεκρός
dead, am, perfect of θνήσκω
death, θάνατος

deliver over, παραδίδωμι
demon, δαιμόνιον
depart, ὑπάγω, ἀπέρχομαι
desert, ἔρημος
destroy, ἀπόλλυμι, λύω
die, ἀποθνήσκω
disciple, μαθητής
dismiss, ἀπολύω
do, ποιέω
down from, κατά with gen.
drink, πίνω
during, use gen. alone or
κατά with acc.

each, ἕκαστος
each other, ἀλλήλων
ear, οὖς
earth, γῆ
eat, ἐσθίω
elder (noun), πρεσβύτερος
encourage, παρακαλέω
enemy, ἐχθρός
enter, εἰσέρχομαι
eternal, αἰώνιος
evangelize, εὐαγγελίζω
even, καί
evil, πονηρός, κακός
except, εἰ μή, ἐὰν μή
exhort, παρακαλέω
experience (verb), πάσχω
eye, ὀφθαλμός

face (noun), πρόσωπον
faith, πίστις

faithful, πιστός
fall, πίπτω
father, πατήρ
fear (verb), φοβέομαι
few, plural of ὀλίγος
field, ἀγρός
fill, πληρόω, πίμπλημι
find, εὑρίσκω
finish, τελέω
fire, πῦρ
first, πρῶτος
five, πέντε
five thousand, πεν-
    τακισχίλιοι
flee, φεύγω
flesh, σάρξ
follow, ἀκολουθέω
foot, πούς
for (prep.), use dat.
for (conj.), γάρ
for ever, εἰς τὸν αἰῶνα
for this reason, διό
forgive, ἀφίημι
four, τέσσαρες
from, ἀπό with gen., παρά
    with gen.
fulfill, πληρόω, πίμπλημι
full, πλήρης
furlong, στάδιον

Galilee, Γαλιλαία
garment, ἱμάτιον
gather together, συνάγω

gaze at, θεωρέω
Gentiles, plur. of ἔθνος
gift, δῶρον
give, δίδωμι
give thanks, εὐχαριστέω
give what is owed or prom-
    ised, ἀποδίδωμι
glorify, δοξάζω
glory, δόξα
go, πορεύομαι, ἔρχομαι,
    βαίνω
go away, ὑπάγω, ἀπέρχομαι
go down, καταβαίνω, κατέρ-
    χομαι
go in, εἰσέρχομαι
go out, ἐκπορεύομαι, ἐξέρχο-
    μαι
go through, διέρχομαι
go to, προσέρχομαι
go together, συνέρχομαι
go up, ἀναβαίνω
God, θεός
good, ἀγαθός, καλός
gospel, εὐαγγέλιον; preach
    the gospel, εὐαγγελίζω
grace, χάρις
great, μέγας, πολύς
greater, μείζων
greet, ἀσπάζομαι
guard (noun), φυλακή

hand, χείρ
hand over, παραδίδωμι

369

have, ἔχω
have mercy upon, ἐλεέω
he, αὐτός
head, κεφαλή
heal, θεραπεύω
hear, ἀκούω
heart, καρδία
heaven, οὐρανός
herself (intensive), feminine
of αὐτός
herself (reflexive), feminine
of ἑαυτοῦ
high priest, ἀρχιερεύς
himself (intensive), αὐτός
himself (reflexive), ἑαυτοῦ
hinder, κωλύω
holy, ἅγιος
holy, make/keep, ἁγιάζω
honor (noun), τιμή
honor (verb), τιμάω
hope (noun), ἐλπίς
hope (verb), ἐλπίζω
hour, ὥρα
house, οἶκος, οἰκία
how?, πῶς
human being, ἄνθρωπος

I, ἐγώ
if, εἰ, ἐάν
immediately, εὐθέως, εὐθύς
in, ἐν with dat.
in behalf of, ὑπέρ with gen.

in exchange for, ἀντί with
gen.
in front of, ἐνώπιον
in order that, ἵνα, ὅπως
in order that not, ἵνα μή, μή
in the midst, μέσος
in the presence of, παρά
with dat., ἐνώπιον,
ἔμπροσθεν
instead of, ἀντί with gen.
interrogate, ἐπερωτάω
into, εἰς with acc.
it, neuter of αὐτός (also
often other genders)
it is lawful, ἔξεστι(ν)
itself (intensive), neuter of
αὐτός (also often other
genders)
itself (reflexive), neuter of
ἑαυτοῦ (also often other
genders)

James, Ἰάκωβος
Jesus, Ἰησοῦς
Jew, Ἰουδαῖος
joy, χαρά
judge (verb), κρίνω
judgment, κρίσις
just as, καθώς, ὥσπερ

keep, τηρέω
keep holy, ἁγιάζω
kill, ἀποκτείνω

kind (noun), γένος
king, βασιλεύς
kingdom, βασιλεία
know, γινώσκω, οἶδα
known, make, φανερόω

lake, θάλασσα
land, γῆ
language, γλῶσσα
last, ἔσχατος
law, νόμος
lawful, it is, ἔξεστι(ν)
lay down (one's life), τίθημι
lay upon, ἐπιτίθημι
lead, ἄγω
leave, ἀφίημι, λείπω
lest, μή
lest perhaps, μήποτε
let go, ἀφίημι
letter, γράμμα
life, ζωή, ψυχή
light, φῶς
like (adj.), ὅμοιος
little, μικρός, ὀλίγος
little child, παιδίον
live, ζάω
loaf, ἄρτος
look! (particle), ἰδού
look up, ἀναβλέπω
loose (verb), λύω
lord, κύριος
love (noun), ἀγάπη
love (verb), ἀγαπάω, φιλέω
lust (noun), ἐπιθυμία

make, ποιέω
make clear, δηλόω
make/keep holy, ἁγιάζω
make known, φανερόω
man, ἄνθρωπος, ἀνήρ
many, πολύς (in plural)
marvel (verb), θαυμάζω
mercy, have . . . upon, ἐλεέω
messenger, ἄγγελος
Messiah, Χριστός
middle, μέσος
miracle, δύναμις, σημεῖον
more (adj.), πλείων
more (adv.), μᾶλλον
mother, μήτηρ
mountain, ὄρος
mouth, στόμα
much, πολύς
multitude, πλῆθος, ὄχλος
my, ἐμός
myself (reflexive), ἐμαυτοῦ
mystery, μυστήριον

name (noun), ὄνομα
nation, ἔθνος
near (adv.), ἐγγύς
near, come, ἐγγίζω
necessary, it is, δεῖ
need (noun), χρεία
neither . . . nor, οὐδέ . . .
   οὐδέ, μηδέ . . . μηδέ, οὔτε
   . . . οὔτε
night, νύξ
no longer, οὐκέτι, μηκέτι

371

no one, nothing, οὐδείς,
  μηδείς
not, οὐ, μή
not even, οὐδέ, μηδέ
not only . . . but also, τε . . .
  τε
not yet, οὔπω
now, νῦν

old man, πρεσβύτερος
on, ἐπί with gen.
on account of, διά with acc.
on the basis of, ἐπί with dat.
on the one hand . . . on the
  other, μέν . . . δέ
one, εἷς
one another, ἀλλήλων
one's own, ἴδιος
only (adj.), μόνος
only (adv.), μόνον
open, ἀνοίγω
or, ἤ
other, ἄλλος, ἕτερος
ought, ὀφείλω
our, ἡμέτερος
out of, ἐκ with gen.
outside, ἔξω
over, ἐπί with gen.
owe, ὀφείλω
own, one's, ἴδιος

parable, παραβολή
pattern, τύπος

pay (verb), ἀποδίδωμι
peace, εἰρήνη
people, λαός
perish, middle of ἀπόλλυμι
permit, ἀφίημι
persecute, διώκω
persuade, πείθω
Pharisee, Φαρισαῖος
piece of bread, ἄρτος
pity, ἐλεέω
place (noun), τόπος
place (verb), τίθημι
power, δύναμις
pray, προσεύχομαι
preach, κηρύσσω; preach
  the gospel, εὐαγγελίζω
prepare, ἑτοιμάζω
prevent, κωλύω
priest, ἱερεύς
prison, φυλακή
proclaim, κηρύσσω
promise (noun), ἐπαγγελία
prophet, προφήτης
pure, καθαρός
pursue, διώκω
put, τίθημι, βάλλω
put upon, ἐπιτίθημι

question (verb), ἐπερωτάω

race, γένος
raise up, ἐγείρω
rather, μᾶλλον

receive, δέχομαι, παραλαμβάνω, λαμβάνω
receive one's sight, ἀνα-
βλέπω
region, χώρα
rejoice, χαίρω
release, ἀπολύω
remain, μένω
remaining, λοιπός
repent, μετανοέω
rest, the, *see under* λοιπός
return, ὑποστρέφω
reveal, φανερόω
right away, εὐθέως, εὐθύς
righteous, δίκαιος
righteousness, δικαιοσύνη
rise, ἀνίστημι (in the intransitive tenses and in the
middle), passive of ἐγείρω
road, ὁδός
rule, ἄρχω
ruler, ἄρχων

sabbath, σάββατον
saint, ἅγιος
salute, ἀσπάζομαι
salvation, σωτηρία
same, αὐτός
sanctify, ἁγιάζω
save, σώζω
say, λέγω, φημί
scribe, γραμματεύς
Scripture, γραφή

sea, θάλασσα
secret, μυστήριον
see, βλέπω, ὁράω
seek, ζητέω
seem, δοκέω
send, πέμπω, ἀποστέλλω
servant, δοῦλος
sharp, ὀξύς
she, feminine of αὐτός
shine, φαίνω
show, δείκνυμι, δηλόω
sign, σημεῖον
similar, ὅμοιος
Simon, Σίμων
sin (noun), ἁμαρτία
sin (verb), ἁμαρτάνω
sinner, ἁμαρτωλός
sit, κάθημαι
slave, δοῦλος
small, μικρός
so, οὕτως
so that, ὥστε
soldier, στρατιώτης
someone, τις
something, neuter of τις
son, υἱός
soul, ψυχή
sow, σπείρω
speak, λαλέω
spirit, πνεῦμα
stadium, στάδιον
stand, ἵστημι (in the intransitive tenses)

373

stare intently at, θεωρέω
still, ἔτι
stone (noun), λίθος
strong desire, ἐπιθυμία
stronger, ἰσχυρότερος
such, τοιοῦτος
suffer, πάσχω
sufficient, ἱκανός
synagogue, συναγωγή

take, λαμβάνω
take along, παραλαμβάνω
take away, αἴρω
take up, αἴρω, ἀναλαμβάνω
teach, διδάσκω
teacher, διδάσκαλος
temple, ἱερόν (the whole
   sacred precinct), ναός (the
   temple building itself)
tempt, πειράζω
than, ἤ
thanks, give, εὐχαριστέω
that (conj.), ὅτι
that (demonstrative),
   ἐκεῖνος
the, ὁ
then, τότε, ἄρα
there, ἐκεῖ
therefore, οὖν, ἄρα, διό
think, δοκέω
this, οὗτος
three, τρεῖς
throne, θρόνος

through, διά with gen.
throughout, κατά with acc.
throw, βάλλω
throw out, ἐκβάλλω
thus, οὕτως
time, καιρός (appointed
   time), χρόνος (period of
   time)
to, πρός with acc., ἐπί with
   acc.; indirect object, dat.
   without prep.
together, gather, συνάγω
tomb, μνημεῖον
tongue, γλῶσσα
tribulation, θλῖψις
true, ἀληθής
truth, ἀλήθεια
turn to, turn, ἐπιστρέφω
two, δύο
type, τύπος

under, ὑπό with acc.
unless, εἰ μή, ἐὰν μή
until, ἕως, ἄχρι(ς), μέχρι(ς)
unto, πρός with acc.
up to, ἕως with gen., ἄχρι(ς)
   with the gen.
urge (verb), παρακαλέω

value (verb), τιμάω
value (noun), τιμή
village, κώμη
voice, φωνή

walk, περιπατέω
water, ὕδωρ
way, ὁδός
well (adv.), καλῶς
what?, neuter of τίς
what sort of?, ποῖος
whatever, neuter of ὅστις
when (relative), ὅτε
when?, πότε
whenever, ὅταν
where (relative), ὅπου
where?, ποῦ
which (relative), ὅς
which?, τίς
whichever, ὅστις
while, ἕως
who (relative), ὅς
who?, τίς
whoever, ὅστις
whole, ὅλος
why?, τί
wicked, πονηρός
will, θέλημα
willing, am, θέλω

wine, οἶνος
wisdom, σοφία
wish (verb), θέλω
with, μετά with gen., σύν
  with dat.
witness (verb), μαρτυρέω
witness (noun), μαρτυρία
woman, γυνή
wonder, wonder at, θαυμάζω
word, λόγος, ῥῆμα
work (verb), ἐργάζομαι
work (noun), ἔργον
world, κόσμος
worship (verb), προσκυνέω
worthy, ἱκανός
write, γράφω
writing, γραφή

year, ἔτος
yet, ἔτι
you, σύ (s.), ὑμεῖς (p.)
your, σός (s.), ὑμέτερος (p.)
yourself (reflexive), σεαυτοῦ

Frequency List

Prepared by Bruce M. Metzger

The following list of Greek words has been assembled in order to supplement J. Gresham Machen's *New Testament Greek for Beginners*. The 375 words in the vocabulary of the original edition of his grammar occur about 50 or more times in the New Testament. The present vocabulary adds 250 other words, most of which occur more than 25 times in the New Testament. The number of words in each grammatical category is as follows:

Verbs	60
Nouns	54
Adjectives	57
Adverbs, conjunctions, and particles	64
Numerals	15
Total	250

For further information beyond the primary meanings of the words cited below, the student is referred to any standard lexicon of the Greek Testament.

Verbs Occurring 50–100 Times

ἀσπάζομαι	I greet, salute
κράζω	I cry out

Verbs Occurring 25–50 Times

ἀγοράζω	I buy
ἀδικέω	I wrong, do wrong
ἀναγινώσκω	I read
ἀπαγγέλλω	I announce, report
ἀποκαλύπτω	I reveal
ἅπτομαι	I touch
ἀρνέομαι	I deny
ἀσθενέω	I am weak
βαστάζω	I bear, carry
βλασφημέω	I revile, blaspheme
γαμέω	I marry
δέω	I bind
διακονέω	I minister
δικαιόω	I justify, pronounce righteous
δουλεύω	I serve
ἐνδύω	I put on, clothe
ἐπιγινώσκω	I know well
ἐπικαλέομαι	I surname, invoke
ἐπιτιμάω	I rebuke, charge
ἐργάζομαι	I work
ἡγέομαι	I am chief; I think, regard
ἥκω	I am come
ἰάομαι	I heal
ἰσχύω	I am strong
καθαρίζω	I cleanse
καθίζω	I seat, sit
καταλείπω	I leave
καταργέω	I make void
κατοικέω	I dwell
καυχάομαι	I boast
κεῖμαι	I recline

377

κλαίω	I weep
κρατέω	I grasp, seize
λογίζομαι	I account, reckon
λυπέω	I grieve
μισέω	I hate
νικάω	I conquer
οἰκοδομέω	I build up
ὄμνυμι, ὀμνύω	I swear
παραγγέλλω	I command, charge
παρέρχομαι	I pass away, perish
παρίστημι	I am present, stand by
περισσεύω	I abound
πλανάω	I lead astray
πράσσω	I do, practice
προσκαλέομαι	I summon
προφητεύω	I prophesy
σκανδαλίζω	I cause to stumble
συνίημι	I understand
σφραγίζω	I seal
τελέω	I finish, fulfill
ὑπάρχω	I am, exist
ὑποτάσσω	I subject
φαίνω	I shine, appear
φεύγω	I flee
φρονέω	I think
φυλάσσω	I guard
φωνέω	I call

Nouns Occurring 50–100 Times

γλῶσσα	tongue
θρόνος	throne
κεφαλή	head
πρεσβύτερος	elder, presbyter

Nouns Occurring 25–50 Times

ἀδικία	unrighteousness
ἀνάστασις	resurrection
ἄνεμος	wind
ἀρνίον	lamb
γενεά	generation
γνῶσις	knowledge
δένδρον	tree
διάβολος	devil
διαθήκη	covenant
διακονία	ministry
διάκονος	minister
διδαχή	teaching
ἔλεος	mercy
ἑορτή	feast
ἐπιθυμία	desire, passion
ἥλιος	sun
θηρίον	beast
θλῖψις	tribulation
θυγάτηρ	daughter
θύρα	door
θυσία	sacrifice
κρίμα	judgment
μάρτυς	witness
μάχαιρα	sword
μέλος	member
μέρος	part
μισθός	wages
νεφέλη	cloud
οἶνος	wine
ὀργή	anger
παράκλησις	exhortation

379

παρουσία	presence, coming (esp. Christ's exalted advent in glory)
παρρησία	boldness (of speech)
πάσχα	passover
περιτομή	circumcision
πορνεία	fornication
ποτήριον	cup
πρόβατον	sheep
προσευχή	prayer
πτωχός	poor (man)
σπέρμα	seed
σταυρός	cross
συνείδησις	conscience
τιμή	honor
ὑπομονή	patient endurance
φίλος	friend
φόβος	fear
φυλή	tribe
χήρα	widow
χρεία	need

Adjectives Occurring 50–100 Times

ἀγαπητός	beloved
δεξιός	right (opp. left)
ἕκαστος	each
μέσος	middle
τοιοῦτος	such

Adjectives Occurring 10–50 Times

ἄδικος	unrighteous
ἀδύνατος	impossible
ἀκάθαρτος	unclean

ἀληθινός	true
ἀλλότριος	another's, strange
ἀμφότερος	both
ἄνομος	lawless
ἄξιος	worthy
ἅπας	all
ἄπιστος	unbelieving, faithless
ἀρχαῖος	old, ancient
ἀσθενής	weak, ill
ἄφρων	senseless
γνωστός	known
γυμνός	naked
δυνατός	possible, able
ἐκλεκτός	elect, chosen
ἐλάχιστος	least
ἐλεύθερος	free
ἔνοχος	liable, guilty
ἐπουράνιος	heavenly
ἕτοιμος	ready, prepared
εὐώνυμος	left (opp. right)
καινός	new
κενός	empty, vain
κλητός	called
κοινός	common, unclean
κρυπτός	hidden
κωφός	dumb, deaf
λευκός	white
μακρός	long
μωρός	foolish
νέος	young, new
παλαιός	old
περισσός	superabundant
πλούσιος	rich

πνευματικός	spiritual
ποικίλος	varied, manifold
πόσος	how great? how much? how many?
σαρκικός	carnal, fleshly
σοφός	wise
τέλειος	perfect, mature
τίμιος	precious, honorable
τοσοῦτος	so great, so much, so many
ὑγιής	whole, healthy
ὑμέτερος	your
ὑψηλός	high
ὕψιστος	highest
φανερός	manifest
φρόνιμος	prudent
χρύσεος	golden
χωλός	lame

Conjunctions Occurring 10–1000 Times

ἄρα	therefore, then
διό	wherefore
διότι	because
ἐπεί	when, since
ἐπειδή	since, because
καθάπερ	even as, as
μήπως	lest perchance
οὗ	where

Adverbs, Used Also as Prepositions or Conjunctions, Occurring 10–500 Times

ἅμα	together with, with
ἄχρι, ἄχρις	until, up to
ἕνεκα	on account of

ἔξωθεν	from without, without
ἐπάνω	above, over
μέχρι, μέχρις	until, unto
ὀπίσω	back, behind, after
πέραν	beyond, across
πλήν	except, nevertheless
πρίν	before

Other Adverbs and Particles Occurring 10–500 Times

ἀληθῶς	truly
ἀμήν	verily, amen
ἄνωθεν	from above, again
ἅπαξ	once, once for all
ἄρτι	now, just now
αὔριον	tomorrow
γέ	indeed, at least, really, even (etc.)
δεῦτε	come (you, pl.)
διατί	why?
εἶτα	then
ἐκεῖθεν	thence
ἐντεῦθεν	hence
ἐπαύριον	on the morrow
ἔπειτα	then
ἔσωθεν	from within, within
κακῶς	badly, ill
κάτω	down, below
λίαν	greatly
μακρόθεν	from afar, afar
μάλιστα	especially
μήτι	(negative interrogative; cf. §505)
ναί	yea, truly, yes

νυνί	now
ὅθεν	whence, wherefore
ὁμοθυμαδόν	with one accord
ὁμοίως	likewise
ὄντως	really
οὐαί	woe
οὐδέποτε	never
οὐχί	by no means, not so, nay
πάντοτε	always
παραχρῆμα	immediately
περισσοτέρως	more abundantly
πόθεν	whence
πολλάκις	often
πρότερον	before
πρωΐ	in the morning, early
πώς	perchance
σήμερον	today
σφόδρα	exceedingly
ταχέως	quickly
ταχύ	quickly
ὕστερον	afterwards
ὦ	O (interjection)
ὡσαύτως	likewise
ὡσεί	as, like, about

Numerals Occurring 10–200 Times

δέκα	ten
δεύτερος	second
δώδεκα	twelve
ἑπτά	seven
εἴκοσι	twenty
ἑκατόν	hundred
ἕκτος	sixth

ἔνατος	ninth
τεσσαράκοντα	forty
τέταρτος	fourth
τριάκοντα	thirty
τρίς	thrice
τρίτος	third
χιλιάς	thousand
χίλιοι	thousand

Section Number Correlations

As an aid to instructors who have built their courses around the original Machen grammar, the following table shows the section number correlations between the original (old) and revised (new) editons. A dash next to a number indicates that the section does not appear in the revised edition.

Old	New	Old	New	Old	New
1	1	18	16	34b	34
2	2	19	17	35	35
3	3	20	18	36	36
4	4	21	19	37	30 n.
5	5	22	20	38	42
6	6	23	23	39	43
7	7	24	24	40	44
8	8	25	25	41	37
9	9	26	26	42	38
10	10	27	27	43	39
11	11	28	28	44	40
12	12	29	29	45	45
13	22	30	30	46	46
14	41	31	31	47	47
15	13	32	—	48	49
16	14	33	32	49	50
17	15	34a	33	50	57

Old	New	Old	New	Old	New
51	56	81b	84	109d	120
52	—	81c	85	110	119
53	58	82	86	111	115
54	52	83	86	112	114
55	53	84	91	113	116
56	54	85	87	114	122
57	55	86	88	115	123
58	59	87	89	116	121
59	60	88	90	117	124
60	61	89	92	118	125
61	62	90	93	119	126
62a	63	91	94	120	127
62b	77	92	101	121	128
63	64	93	102	122	129
64	65	94	95	123	130
65	66	95	96	124	131
66	67	96	97	125	132
67	68	97	98	126	133
68	69	98	99	127	134
69	70	99	100	128	135
70	71	100	103	129	137
71	72	101	104	130	136
72	73	102	106	131	138
73	74	103	107	132	141
74	75	104	108	133	139
75	76	105	109	134	140
76	78	106	110	135	142
77	79	107	111	136	143
78	80	108	112	137	144
79	81	109a	113	138	145
80	82	109b	117	139	146
81a	83	109c	118	140	147

Section Number Correlations

Old	New	Old	New	Old	New
141	146	173	181	205	214
142	148	174	182	206	215
143	149	175	183	207	216
144	150	176	184	208	217
145	151	177	185	209	218
146	152	178	186	210	219
147	153	179	187	211	220
148	154	180	188	212	221
149	156	181	189	213	222
150	157	182	190	214a	231
151	158	183	191	214b	223
152	159	184	192	215	224
153	162	185	193	216	—
154	160	186	194	217	225
155	161	187	195	218	226
156	163	188	196	219	227
157	164	189	197	220	228
158	165	190	198	221	232
159	166	191	199	222	229
160	167	192	200	223	230
161	169	193	201	224	233
162	170	194	202	225	234
163	171	195	203	226	235
164	168	196	204	227	236
165	172	197	205	228a	237
166	173	198	206	228b	247
167	174	199	207	229	248
168	175	200	209	230	239
169	177	201	208	231	240
170	178	202	211	232	241
171	179	203	212	233	242
172	180	204	213	234	251

Old	New	Old	New	Old	New
235	254	266	286	298	322
236	255	267	290	299	323
237	256	268	291	300	324
238	257	269	292	301	325
239	245	270	293	302	326
240	259	271	294	303	327
241	260	272	295	304	328
242	261	273	296	305	329
243	262	274	297	306	330
244	263	275	298	307	331
245	264	276	299	308	332
246	265	277	300	309	333
247	266	278	301	310	334
248	267	279	302	311	335
249	268	280	303	312	338
250a	269	281	304	313	339
250b	277	282	305	314	340
251	271	283	306	315	341
252	272	284	314	316.A	342
253	273	285	308	316.B	342
254	274	286	309	316.C	351
255	275	287	310	317	345
256	244	288	311	318	344
257	278	289	312	319	346
258	279	290	313	320	347
259	280	291	315	321	348
260	281	292	316	322	349
261	282	293	317	323	350
262	283	294	319	324	352
263	289	295	337	325	353
264	284	296	320	326	354
265	285	297	321	327	355

Section Number Correlations

Old	New	Old	New	Old	New
328	356	360	389	392	420
329	357	361	391	393	421
330	358	362	390	394	419
331	359	363	392	395	422
332	360	364	393	396	423
333	361	365	394	397	424
334	362	366	395	398	425
335	363	367	396	399	426
336	364	368	396	400	427
337	365	369	396	401	428
338	366	370	397	402	429
339	367	371	398	403	430
340	368	372	399	404	431
341	369	373	400	405	432
342	370	374	401	406	433
343	371	375	402	407	434
344	373	376	403	408	435
345	374	377	404	409	436
346	375	378	405	410	437
347	376	379	406	411	438
348	377	380	407	412	439
349	378	381	408	413	440
350	379 n.	382	409	414	441
351	379	383	410	415	442
352	380	384	411	416	443
353	381	385	412	417	444
354	382	386	413	418	445
355	383	387	414	419	452
356	384	388	415	420	447
357	385	389	416	421	448
358	386	390	417	422	449
359	387	391	418	423	450

Old	New	Old	New	Old	New
424	453	453	477	485	513
425	454	454	479	486	514
426	455	455	480	487	515
427	456	456	481	488	516
428	457	457	482	489	517
429	458	458	483	490	518
430	459	459	484	491	519
431	460	460	486	492	520
432	461	461	485	493	521
433	462	462	487	494	522
434	463	463	488	495	523
435	464.4	464	489	496	527
436	464.3	465	490	497	528
437	464.2	466	491	498	529
438	464.5	467	496	499	530
439	464.6	468	492	500	531
440	464.7	469	493	501	531
441	—	470	494	502	546
442	465	471	497	503	524
443	466	472	497	504	525
444	467	473	499	505	526
445	468	474	500	506	532
446	469	475	502	507	533
447	470	476	503	508	534
448	471	477	504	509	535
449	472	478	505	510	536
450	476	479	506	511	537
451	473	480	508	512	538
452.1	474	481	509	513	539
452.2	474	482	510	514	540
452.3	475	483	512	515	541
452.4	474	484	513	516	542

Section Number Correlations

Old	New	Old	New	Old	New
517	543	546	572	576	618
518	560	547	573	577	619
519	561	548	575	578	620
520	590	549	584	579	621
521	544	550	592	580	622
522	547	551	577	581	623
523	548	552	578	582	624
524	549	553	579	583	625
525	550	554	581	584	626
526	551	555	596	585	627
527	552	556	597	586	628
528	553	557	598	587	629
529	554	558	599	588	630
530	555	559	600	589	631
531	556	560	601	590	632
532	558	561	602	591	633
533	583	562	603	592	634
534	559	563	604	593	635
535	559 n.	564	605	594	636
536	591	565	606	595	637
537	563	566	607	596	638
538	564	567	608	597	639
539	565	568	609	598	640
540	566	569	610	599	641
541	567	570	611	600	642
542	568	571	612	601	643
543	569	572	613	602	644
544a	570	573	614	603	645
544b	574	574	615		
545	571	575	616		

Index

Numerals refer to sections, except where preceded by p. or pp.

Index

Index

398